# AMERICA DANCING

# AMERICA DANCING

## FROM THE CAKEWALK TO THE MOONWALK

**MEGAN PUGH**

Yale UNIVERSITY PRESS

NEW HAVEN & LONDON

Excerpt from "Dances Before the Wall," from *The Collected Poems of Frank O'Hara,* by Frank O'Hara, copyright © 1971 by Maureen Granville-Smith, Administratrix of the Estate of Frank O'Hara, copyright renewed 1999 by Maureen O'Hara Granville-Smith and Donald Allen. Used by permission of Alfred A. Knopf, an imprint of the Knopf Doubleday Publishing Group, a division of Penguin Random House LLC. All rights reserved.

Yale University Press books may be purchased in quantity for educational, business, or promotional use. For information, please e-mail sales.press@yale.edu (U.S. office) or sales@yaleup.co.uk (U.K. office).

Set in Meridien and Futura types by Westchester Publishing Services. Printed in the United States of America.

Library of Congress Control Number: 2015939313

ISBN 978-0-300-20131-4 (cloth : alk. paper)

A catalogue record for this book is available from the British Library.

This paper meets the requirements of ANSI/NISO Z39.48–1992 (Permanence of Paper).

10  9  8  7  6  5  4  3  2  1

for my mother

# CONTENTS

# ACKNOWLEDGMENTS

One of the perks of writing this book was that watching dance counted as work. If I felt stuck, I could pull up a YouTube video, slide a DVD into my laptop, or head to a concert hall and watch other people move. In the pages that follow, I refer primarily to recorded dances, but live performances by the Paul Taylor Dance Company, San Francisco Ballet, American Ballet Theatre, and New York City Ballet—including productions of many of the pieces I discuss—also kindled my thoughts and excitement.

When I was still in college, Elizabeth Dillon made me want to understand the complexities of American performance, and Fred Strebeigh made me want to write better prose. Since then, many other teachers have helped me keep those goals in mind. Bryan Wagner has been deepening my thinking about this book since before I knew what I was thinking about. He has consistently encouraged me to keep the big picture in mind, on the page and off. Scott Saul provided advice, encouragement, and a model for what scholarship could look like; this book and I are better for it. Greil Marcus has given generously of his time and his knowledge for years. Thank you, Greil, for making so much seem possible, in writing and in life.

Linda Williams enriched this project with both comments on drafts and guidance through the history of musical films.

Eric Lott has influenced my ideas through his own work and his feedback on mine. I've also benefitted from conversations and correspondence with Julia Foulkes, Laura Horak, Deborah Jowitt, W. T. Lhamon, John Rockwell, and Laura Shapiro. Larry Billman, Paul Janusz, Julie Malnig, Teasel Muir-Harmony, Lewis Segal, and Michael Veal graciously answered my questions on topics ranging from outer space to reggae dancing.

Julie MacDonald, Vincent Paterson, and Paul Taylor took the time to grant me interviews that were both fascinating and enjoyable. Thanks as well to Lisa Labrado at Paul Taylor's American Modern Dance, and to company archivist Tom Patrick, who helped me access research materials from the opposite side of the country with ease and good cheer. I'm grateful to the staff at the New York Public Library for the Performing Arts, the University of California, Berkeley, Library, the San Francisco Public Library, and the Lewis and Clark College library. Thank you to Dr. Jonathan Prude for permission to quote from Agnes de Mille's papers; to Maureen Granville-Smith, for permission to quote from Frank O'Hara's "Dances Before the Wall"; to Paul B. Goode, for his photographs of the Paul Taylor Dance Company; to Edward Burns at the Carl Van Vechten Trust, for permission to reprint Van Vechten's photograph of Paul Taylor; and to Karen Langford and John Branka at Ziffren Law. I am also grateful to the Berkeley English Department, the Mabelle McLeod Lewis Memorial Foundation, and the Berkeley Center for Race and Gender Studies, all of which provided financial support as I researched and wrote parts of this book.

I worked out some of my ideas about Agnes de Mille, Fred Astaire, and Ginger Rogers in two pieces for *Boston Review;* readers of those essays will note some overlap with these chapters.

My editors there, Deb Chasman and Simon Waxman, provided stellar feedback. I'm also grateful to Jim Gaines, formerly of *FLYP*, which published some of my earliest thoughts about Michael Jackson back in 2009; some portions of that article persist in this book. That article also morphed into a presentation for the Berkeley conference *Michael Jackson: A Critical Reflection on a Life and a Phenomenon*, where I benefited from talks by and with my fellow presenters. I thank my fellow participants in Eric Lott's seminar at Dartmouth's Futures of American Studies Institute, Berkeley's Transatlantic American Studies Group, and a 2013 working group that Bryan Wagner put together at Berkeley, for their engagement with various parts of this book. I am grateful to Shad A. Small and Jonathan Shelley for their help polishing the manuscript. And I thank my students at Berkeley and at Lewis and Clark, in whose company I've felt lucky to think through so many of the ideas that follow.

Thanks to my agent, Paul Bresnick, for believing in this project and helping it come to fruition. At Yale University Press, my editor, Steve Wasserman, ushered this book into being with savvy and kindness. Eva Skewes has responded to my every query with a thoroughness that makes her speed all the more remarkable. Thanks to Susan Laity for her phenomenally attentive manuscript editing, and to my anonymous outside reader for his or her sharp eyes and smart suggestions.

In the years that I have been working on this book, many friends have served as advisers, editors, and co-conspirators. Lyn Hejinian has been a model of intellectual and personal generosity, practiced with rigor and with love. Monique Walton's perceptive powers always make me want to sharpen my own. Ben Schrom's enthusiasm for silent film and so much else has been helpfully infectious. Brian Pettit offered wisdom about tap dancing and brass bands. Chris Fan, my first friend in graduate school, offered comments on drafts and helped me access research materials. Monica Huerta's insights on these chapters have given them an enormous boost, and I feel lucky to call her a friend. Kate Marshall offered advice on publishing and made my baby laugh. On behalf of that baby and myself, I thank Adam Boardman, Ashlee Renfrow, and Laura Steele, whose care for Theo made it possible for me to steal away and work. Andy Horowitz has shared his friendship and writerly prowess with me for well over a decade; in many ways, this book is a product of our mutual enthusiasms, as well as his editorial hand. I miss the long talks and walks Gillian Osborne and I had when we both lived in San Francisco, but even at a distance, she continues to enliven my thinking and my writing. RJ Leland has now been a support and sounding board for well over half my life; only my sister, Elise Lauterbach, has filled those roles for longer. Her husband, Preston, had my love many years before he helped me navigate the publishing world; now he has my gratitude for that, too.

Thanks to my father, Robert Pugh, for teaching me that everyone's story matters, and to my mother, Dorothy Gunther Pugh, for teaching me—and so many others—to value dance. I also thank my in-laws, Becky Yeats and Steve Rose, for making me feel at home in a new city, raising my favorite person, and showering our son with love. My husband, Eliot Rose, has been an unwavering support, taking care of our household so I could hole up and write and then pulling me back into the world for adventures big and small. Eliot and Theo, you throw my favorite dance parties.

# AMERICA DANCING

# INTRODUCTION

## An American Style

Late on a spring evening in 1939, Bill "Bojangles" Robinson stood in Times Square and looked up. He was admiring an advertisement for his latest Broadway show, *The Hot Mikado:* a neon sign of himself tap-dancing. Robinson had been raised by his grandmother, a former slave, in Richmond, Virginia, the capital of the former Confederacy. Now, at age sixty-one, he was the most famous black performer in America and playing an emperor. He had worked his way up through vaudeville to star in his own revues, act opposite Shirley Temple in some of the most successful movies of the decade, and inspire a generation of performers. Scores of dancers attempted to replicate his signature routine, the stair dance. Hollywood's most famous tappers, Fred Astaire and Eleanor Powell, both paid him homage on film. Up at the Hoofers Club in Harlem, even his most talented peers struggled to understand how he hammered out such perfectly balanced, clean, and intricate rhythms. Both black and white critics heaped him with praise, and he influenced the way highbrow tastemakers conceived of a distinctively American style of dance. Bill Robinson wasn't just a crossover success. He was a pioneer.

If Robinson reminisced about his achievements that night in Times Square, he didn't do so for long. A white policeman,

William Christian, ordered him to get moving. When Robinson refused, Christian arrested him for disorderly conduct.[1] To eyes trained on that sign up above, Robinson represented a dream of black achievement. But while his steps traveled to artists on both sides of the color line, his own movements were restricted. On the ground, he was just another black man, subject to Jim Crow.

That tension, between the freedom of performance and the realities of everyday life, is central to the history of American dance and to what makes it American. Americans like to tell themselves stories about what happens on high, beneath shining lights, for applauding crowds. Down below, other forces are afoot, and they aren't always easy to acknowledge.

This is a book about American dancers who have been celebrated for embodying the country in movement. First come the thousands of amateurs and professionals who at the turn of the twentieth century threw their bodies into the high steps and ragtime rhythms of America's first nationwide dance craze: the cakewalk. The cakewalk was spirited, silly, and—to the dismay of some observers—historically black. It ushered in debates about race, class, dance, and nationhood that would continue in various forms for the next hundred years.

Then come a series of individual artists, beloved by masses of Americans and ambitious enough to try to address them: Bill Robinson, silver screen idols Fred Astaire and Ginger Rogers, ballet and Broadway choreographer Agnes de Mille, postmodern dance maker Paul Taylor, and pop icon Michael Jackson. Between them, these artists performed in just about every possible public venue for dance in the twentieth century: vaudeville palaces,

Broadway theaters, cabarets, nightclubs, opera houses, black movies, white movies, integrated movies, World's Fairs, stadium shows, television specials, music videos, street corners, and parades. Each dancer drew on a distinctive mix of sources and training, and each danced in a style different from the rest. Yet they all imagined an audience composed of the entire nation, and they spoke to that audience, reflected it, and seemed, in some elusive way, of it.

What makes a dance American? People have been asking that question for at least a hundred years. Their answers betray a longing for wholeness, as if the country and its art could be distilled to some core set of values. American dance, critics have maintained, should embody freedom, democracy, individualism, and community. It should be welcoming, strong, beautiful, and free. It should spring from the soil, reflect history, give form to present-day feelings, and prophesy a collective future. None of those descriptions deals with the question of how dancers might hold their heads, move their hips, or educate their feet. Instead, they offer impressionistic attitudes, attempts to make a coherent whole out of the national experience. But national experience is too varied, and too vexed, to pin down. America keeps shifting beneath Americans' feet.[2]

Still, the effort to define the nation by means of its art has had perpetual appeal. For the author and educator Constance Rourke, who took up the challenge in 1931, performance was at the heart of the process. Here's Rourke in *American Humor,* her pivotal study of the national identity, on the Yankee peddler, who swapped his way through stories and almanacs to the center of the popular stage: "The American stepped full-length into the public glare, and steadily heightened the early yellow light. He gazed at himself in the Yankee plays as in a bright mirror, and developed the habit of self-scrutiny, which may have its dangers for the infant or youth, whether the creature be national or human."[3] Rourke's pronouns are as shifty as the Yankee peddler's salesmanship. In her first sentence, the American is an actor, ushering in a new dawn. One period later, the American is a member of the audience, looking up at himself. In a feat of syntactical wizardry, Rourke gets at the give-and-take between what is performed and what is absorbed, the way art both shapes the world and is shaped by it.

Today, the assertion at the heart of Rourke's book—that there is such a thing as a "Americanness" waiting to be discovered—might sound dated. National archetypes seem like the stuff of smug exceptionalism, the belief that the country is elevated, and separate, from the rest of the world. They can also seem oppressively essentialist, erasing the differences among diverse populations. Performance both skirts and takes up those problems. Performing the country means turning it into an imaginative creation. In the hands of artists, or the bodies of dancers, America becomes an idea, something to bring citizens together as they test out who they are, and who they'd like to become.[4]

Americanness may be an impossible conceit, but as the stories in this book make clear, people keep trying to define it. It's a way for Americans to make sense of their home. It's a mantle American artists have been eager to claim for themselves, and a quality that American audiences have been eager to find in dance, where they seek to discover—or perhaps invent—truths that emerge, bare and essential, from bodies in motion. How we move, the thinking goes, should show us who we are.

Some of the dancers whose stories follow took pains to present their creations as quintessentially American. At the height of World War II, Agnes de Mille set her ballet *Rodeo* in the Old West, site of so many of the nation's fundamental myths. When Bill Robinson and Shirley Temple dance together in *The Littlest Rebel* and *The Little Colonel,* which take place during and after the Civil War, they charm both Yankees and Confederates, symbolically unifying a nation torn asunder. Paul Taylor, who has choreographed over a dozen dances set in various American pasts, says he prefers modern dance to ballet, in part, because it's homegrown.

But a sense of what makes the country itself often reverberates on lower frequencies, in the movements. Fred Astaire syncopates his way into ballet's entrechat-trois, a series of humming-bird-like beats of the leg, and inflects European tradition with the rhythms of black America. The dancers in Paul Taylor's *Company B* combine modern movements with Lindy Hop lifts and military marches, the angst of war bubbling up through the pep of popular culture. When Michael Jackson moonwalks, he follows in the steps of both 1970s California street dancers and nineteenth-century blackface minstrels. Histories that run so deep may not be consciously tapped into, or even recognizable. But they remind us that dance is not always as spontaneous as it might appear. Whether intentionally or not, dancers pick up, pass down, and repurpose other people's movements.

Dance is a notoriously slippery art. Unlike books, paintings, and recorded music, which can all be apprehended as discrete objects, dances don't exist without bodies to do them. Move a certain way, and the movement becomes you. But the movement is never yours—at least, not in the sense that a poem or a piece of Tupperware might be yours—because someone else can come along and imitate your steps. That slipperiness is one of the reasons dance can help us think about national identity: Americans have discovered themselves, in part, by pretending to be other people. What can we make of these imitations? They tell us that the history of American dance is composed not just of self-invention, but of love, mockery, and a longing for a mobility that can come from assuming someone else's character, imaginatively inhabiting that person's body, and making another's steps your own.[5]

Sometimes the borrowing is explicit. Fred Astaire and his co-choreographer Hermes Pan talked frankly about learning from black dancers, including both Bill Robinson and Pan's family's chauffeur. In the video for "Smooth Criminal," Michael Jackson pays open homage to Fred Astaire, wearing the same outfit as his idol in *The Bandwagon*'s "Girl Hunt" routine. When Agnes de Mille used square dancing in *Rodeo* to call up an old form of community, she plopped it smack in the middle of the piece. You can't miss it.

But at other times, histories are submerged. Watching *Rodeo*, you might not guess that de Mille imagined the leading cowboy's most climactic solo—as her choreographic notes make clear—as both jazzy and black, or that in the same scene he was supposed to take cues from the Italian-American comic Jimmy Durante. Yet those influences are part of why audiences and critics described *Rodeo* as a quintessentially American ballet, imbuing it with what Ralph Ellison calls "the homeness of home."[6]

Blending, masking, and mockery have been central to much of the art that has made Americans feel at home. "Everyone played the appropriation game," Ellison writes, and that "everyone" implicates the entire nation from its beginnings: Boston Tea Partiers donning feathered headdresses and caking their faces with war paint; white southerners adopting black speech patterns; Duke Ellington quoting from Chopin's funeral march; Elvis Presley singing like Arthur Crudup; Shirley Temple learning to tap from Bill Robinson; Fred Astaire and Ginger Rogers yoking vaudeville gags with ballet; Paul Taylor swiping steps from his employer Martha Graham and from strangers he watched on the street. Whether consciously or not, we are forever recombining vernacular forms, creating—as Ellison puts it—"a consciousness of who and what we have come to be." The vernacular can thus be a "gesture toward perfection," as the many coalesce into the one, *e pluribus unum.* But that ideal unified one is impossible to reach. Culture both coalesces and falls apart.[7]

Hybridity is not unique to the United States. That is how culture works. In the sixteenth century, enslaved African Americans in the Spanish colonies created the sensuous, percussive zarabanda, a dance that sailed across the Atlantic and eventually found its way into the French courts as the slower, statelier sarabande. In nineteenth-century Denmark, August Bournonville injected classical ballet with national folk dances, while Marius Petipa did the same in Russia. And in nineteenth-century Rio, Afro-Brazilians combined the polka with local lundu dancing to create the maxixe, which became an international ballroom sensation. Yet just as these histories depend upon particular places and times in which particular people forge new steps and styles, the histories of American dance reflect a country, and its people, on the move. Place matters.[8]

The artists who are the subjects of this book all combined dance forms and styles to conjure up the spirit of a nation, a spirit that their audiences recognized as the homeness of home. But digging up the sources of homeness can change that home. This is because of another dynamic, to which Ralph Ellison is equally attuned: histories do not simply become detached; they are repressed. "By pushing significant details of our experience into the underground of unwritten history, we not only overlook much which is positive, but we blur our conceptions of where and who we are," he writes. "It is as though we dread to acknowledge the complex, pluralistic nature of our society, and as a result we find ourselves stumbling upon our true national identity under circumstances in which we least expect to do so." This book is an attempt to make readers stumble.[9]

These days, when concert dance can seem to be the most elite of all art forms, and when social dancing appears to be more visible on reality-TV competitions than in everyday life, it can be hard to remember that dance has been central not just to American art but to American life, as artists shaped national identity in public movement. That identity was first embodied in the cakewalk, when in the same decade that "separate but equal" became law Americans from all walks of life rejoiced in a step that antebellum slaves had invented to mock their masters. It later took shape in the virtuosic tapping of Bill Robinson, who danced debonairly up the stairs to play an emperor and whom Hollywood forced to play second fiddle to a white toddler. It found a form in the blending of tap, ballet, ballroom, and social dance that Fred Astaire and Ginger Rogers presented as a homegrown vernacular, the many forming a one, even as, outside the movie houses, an economically depressed nation struggled with class and racial conflicts. It rested in the square dances that Henry Ford hoped would teach a mixed-race America to revere purer, whiter times, and that Agnes de Mille wished could restore hope to the nervous youth of the Atomic Age. It burst forth from the acrobatics of the Lindy Hop and made its way onto the country's toniest stages, as Agnes de Mille, George Balanchine, Jerome Robbins, Lew Christensen, and a host of other choreographers loosened the mores of ballet. It emerged in the damning commentary and pedestrian grace of Paul Taylor's choreography, and spread across the globe when Michael Jackson turned the moonwalk into a sign of technological domination and human ingenuity.

All these artists danced as part of a broader, public conversation about what America was and what it might become. For all of them, the country was haunted by histories, both acknowledged and unacknowledged, excised from their dances or buried somewhere deep inside them. The tapping of a foot can be the rapping of a séance table, Morse code from a forgotten past. These are stories of national creation, and of national haunting.

# 1 THE CAKEWALK, AMERICA'S FIRST NATIONAL DANCE

In the winter of 1884, a group of Philadelphians panicked: America had no national dance, and they needed one. They were planning a fundraiser for the Pennsylvania Museum and School of Industrial Art, to culminate in a March of the Nations, featuring a French minuet, a Dutch chain dance, girls in Spanish mantillas clacking castanets, and ladies in sensuous Gypsy dresses rattling tambourines. But when it came to performing their own traditional dance, these do-gooders were stumped. America was just over a hundred years old, and everyone who lived there—save for Native Americans, whose traditions the government was busily snuffing out—had come from somewhere else.[1]

One anonymous wag, responding to the Philadelphia dilemma for the *New York Times,* suggested turning to a value at the core of the nation's identity: financial greed. The male dancer could play a plumber, the female a housekeeper driven mad by his large bill. She would die of agony, and he'd sell her corpse to a medical school for extra cash. The writer didn't go into much detail about how to translate this scenario into dance steps, but he did offer an alternative: a male shop clerk would sell a female customer a coat, and they'd "fall into each other's arms and execute a wild *pas de deux* expressive of complete satisfaction and happiness."[2]

Neither proposal sparked a nationwide craze. Nor did the rosier offerings of America's dignified dance professors. Over the next decade and a half, the professors trotted out a series of new American dances at their annual conventions, including the Harvard Caprice, the Columbia, and the Esprit d'Amerique. In the wake of the Spanish American War, they debuted the Volunteer Skirmish, the Cadet Lancers, and Our Flag. They hoped that these dances, designed to promote nobility, grace, and what one newspaperman called the "the conventionalities of the drawing-room," would trickle down from proposal to practice. Their decrees had little clout.[3]

Outside America's swankiest ballrooms, though, a new dance was gaining ground, and it toppled drawing-room conventionalities. It fused African American and European-American movements. It traveled from the barnyards of southern plantations to the stages and dance halls of the industrial North. Set to the new, syncopated rhythms of ragtime, it became a sensation with both rich and poor, on both sides of the color line, and eventually, on both sides of the Atlantic. It started as a joke, and it became a contest of terpsichorean greatness: the cakewalk.

The cakewalk's basic steps are simple. You kick your legs forward in a high, exaggerated march, and promenade, usually in a circle, sometimes in a line. The dance invites individual embellishment, which can be virtuosic, comic, or both. In one of the earliest filmed cakewalks, shot at Coney Island, a crowd of beach bums in wool Victorian bathing suits do flips and play leapfrog as they trot across the sand. Watching, you can't help but wonder whether there is a musical accompaniment going on off-screen. Is someone singing the latest ragtime hit, voice raised above the crashing of the ocean? Or are the dancers snaking through the crowd propelled only on nerve, delighted at their own goofy ingenuity?[4]

To the American Society of Professors of Dancing, the cakewalk was a "deep-rooted evil." At their annual convention in 1900, they declared a ban on the dance and on the ragtime music that accompanied it. The prohibition was more gesture than law: it would only apply to the schools that dancing masters ran, and could not influence the revelers at Coney Island or anywhere else. But the professors insisted on telling anyone who'd listen that the cakewalk was a form of undignified romping, not a real dance. It was too silly, too easy, and—though they didn't say it outright—too black.[5]

But those qualities were all part of the cakewalk's appeal, and the dancing masters were powerless to stop it. In 1908, when the first International Conference of Dancing Masters hosted their own March of the Nations–style performance in Berlin, they chose the cakewalk, mixed with a two-step, to represent America. Some of the dance professors who had traveled across the ocean for the historic occasion protested, but the evidence was clear. America had found its national dance.[6]

You may know the cakewalk from the vaudevillian alien in *Space Balls* (1987) who comes tearing out of a human's stomach and cakewalks across an intergalactic diner counter, complete with cane and boater, or from the movie *Oklahoma!* (1955), where choreographer Agnes de Mille has cowboy Will Parker cakewalk atop a train after singing about the metropolitan wonders of Kansas City, or from Judy Garland and Margaret O'Brien's cakewalk finale to "Under the Bamboo Tree" in their living room in *Meet Me in St. Louis* (1944), or from Bill Robinson's awkward cakewalk with Lena Horne in *Stormy Weather* (1943), backed by a chorus whose dancing girls turn around to reveal bizarre, blackface daisies on the backs of their hats. These performances are all tinged with nostalgia for the heyday of the cakewalk, the turn of the twentieth century, a time when the dance was considered anything but quaint.

Footage from this era, when motion picture technology was just getting on its feet, is scarce. We're lucky that two short films, each just under thirty seconds, have survived: *Cakewalk* and *Comedy Cakewalk*. We don't know much about them—only that the American Mutoscope and Biograph Company made them on May 11, 1903, probably on the rooftop of its New York studio— and the names of the five black dancers, two couples and a male soloist, have been lost. But they are fine performers, portraying radically different characters in each film.[7]

In *Cakewalk*, the dancers face the camera in a line, as if preparing for military inspection, and march in place. The men wear tuxes, the women modest gowns that cover them from wrist to wrist and neck to feet. The soloist raises his hat and leaps forward, twirling his cane like a baton. Abandoning his erect posture for just a moment, he swings one leg out to the side, pivots around it in what ballet dancers would call a fouetté, and returns to his place in line. Another man tap-dances for a few seconds and does a quick turn, and then the whole group is off in an orderly parade

Cake-Walk

250 - I                             A. N. - PARIS

French postcard, "Cake-Walk," ca. 1900 (Courtesy of the Photographs and Prints Division, Schomburg Center for Research in Black Culture, The New York Public Library, Astor, Lenox and Tilden Foundations) that ends up right where it started. One woman waves a small American flag.

The dancers follow the same pattern in *Comedy Cakewalk,* but with a flamboyance that borders on the garish. The men have swapped their tuxes for suits, and one wears a flashy, ankle-length coat. The women's skirts are shorter, their matronly hair-dos covered by rakish, wide-brimmed hats. The soloist steals a few extra seconds of attention, crouching low to the ground to fan his rubber legs in and out, in and out, in the kind of flapping wingstep that would eventually give birth to the Charleston. When it's time to parade, the couples keep their own time and add their own flourishes. One man raises his hat for the length of the promenade, as if stuck in a perpetual greeting. His partner leans down, lifts her skirts, and scratches her ankle. The other woman tosses her handkerchief to the ground so that her part-ner must stop his frenetic baton twirling, pick up the handker-chief, and return it to her with exaggerated decorum. The whole performance is rather crass—these dancers seem like rubes, play-ing at respectability. Or are they respectable folk playing at being rubes?

That uncertainty cuts to the cakewalk's slippery core: it could be performed with grace or comedy, as a sign of social aspiration, a parody of those aspirations, or a wholesale rejection of aspiration in favor of rude, freewheeling, seemingly untamed motion. And there's another wrinkle in *Comedy Cakewalk:* the lighter-skinned dancers have darkened their faces. They're black, and they're wearing blackface.

The implications of black blackface are hard to pin down, in part because different audiences might interpret it in radically different ways. White audiences might accept what they saw as an accurate reflection of blackness, confirming and perpetuating stereotypes. But for black audiences, black blackface could be a mockery of white blackface, a means of puncturing stereotypes from behind the mask. Whatever audiences took away from *Comedy Cakewalk,* it points at a truth that was reenacted every time someone did the dance: race, and jokes about race, were central to the cakewalk's meaning. At whose expense wasn't always clear.

Everyone knew that black folks had invented the cakewalk, but the details were hazy. Some argued that the cakewalk was a direct holdover from "Darkest Africa," "an old savage custom," the *Boston Globe* reported, "that ended in fanatic frenzy and all-night orgies."[8] To many white Americans, black cakewalkers were pretentious dandies who—like the stock minstrel-show character Zip Coon, and the ankle-scratching lady in *Comedy Cakewalk*—aped high society and got it all wrong. Their supposed failure soothed white Americans who worried that, after the passage of the Thirteenth and Fifteenth Amendments, their national dominance might wane. Never fear, the garish clothes and grotesque moves of comic cakewalkers seemed to imply; these people are too ridiculous to be a threat.

That spirit is preserved in one origin story, printed in a 1903 Arizona newspaper: "At a dinner given by a wealthy plantation owner a rich negro and his wife were guests. The black pair were so inflated with pride at being there, and walked with so much studied 'air' that they attracted much attention. When the black couple had retired the host offered a prize of a cake to the man and woman giving the best imitation of the black pair's walk. Everybody wanted to win the prize. Men and women did their best to produce the pose and step of the high nosed negroes, and that was the first cakewalk."[9]

In fact, the reverse was true. Decades before the cakewalk became a nationwide craze, African American slaves had invented it to ridicule their white masters. Slave dancers would puff up their chests, point their noses in the air, and prance about with mincing steps, pillorying the pretensions of a society based on brutal exploitation. "The dance," explained the champion cakewalker Proctor Knott in 1902, "was a cross between a shamble and a strut, but it was original with the negro and exceedingly funny. Once a while one of the darkies would try to emulate the white dandy by walking across the floor, with head erect and chest expanded." Knott, speaking to a newspaper reporter, avoided overt racial animosity, but a former slave, talking to a younger black friend in 1901, was more frank. "Us slaves watched white folks' parties where the guests danced a minuet and then paraded in a grand march, with the ladies and gentlemen going different ways and then meeting again, arm in arm, and marching down the center together. Then we'd do it, too, *but we used to mock 'em,* every step. Sometimes the white folks noticed it, but they seemed to like it; I guess they thought we couldn't dance any better."[10]

The cakewalk was a form of parody but also of solidarity, and even rivalry, among dancers. At some plantation celebrations, the most talented dancers won prize cakes, made of stored-up provisions like cornmeal, baked in ashes. Cakewalkers performed alone or in couples, and blended their impressions of white performances with dance forms that were carried over from Africa, like the ring shout, percussive steps done in a circle. Sometimes the cakewalk included incredible stunts, such as a percussive, proto-tap breakdown, or balancing a jug of water on a hand while dancing. The latter feat seems emblematic of the care oppressed people must take with regulations weighing heavily upon them, and of the ways they can manage to improvise and excel even in confinement.

By the 1870s, newly emancipated blacks were doing some of those stunts up north—especially black waiters, whose jobs demanded an incredible sense of balance. One of the best, Tony Brown, was famous for carrying twenty cups of coffee at once. When a rival waxed the floor for a cakewalking contest, Brown slipped, sent a dozen water glasses flying, and was so humiliated he never showed his face in New York City again. A host of better-known black cakewalkers soon took his place, bringing the cakewalk from restaurants, barns, and recreational halls to the popular stage.[11]

White minstrels had set the precedent with the walkaround, the minstrel show's grand finale, in which the whole cast would sing and dance in a circular parade. By the 1890s, when African Americans began to star in, write, and sometimes even produce their own shows, the walkaround had been a constant on American stages for a good half-century. But the new generation of black actors changed things, in more ways than one. They broke from the ritualized structure of the minstrel show in favor of performances whose songs and dances were embedded in plots. Some black actors shed the burnt-cork mask altogether; others donned it to conform to public expectation or to parody the stereotypes they were up against. The most famous performers of this generation—actors like Ernest Hogan, Bert Williams, George

Walker, and Aida Overton Walker—made the cakewalk a centerpiece of their performances. A full third of the wildly successful 1898 all-black musical *Clorindy, or The Origins of the Cakewalk* was devoted to its titular dance.[12]

The cakewalk resembled the walkaround in some ways—a large cast, a circular procession—but its syncopated music, strutting steps, and improvised solos made it distinctly modern. Its varied forms offered an opportunity to join a group or to break from it and assert individual powers. All these aspects were on display in the performances of the Williams and Walker Company, which showcased some of the most advanced cakewalking

African Americans in formal dress at a cakewalk, ca. 1897 (Library of Congress)

of its day. Bert Williams, a comic genius, did a shuffling cake-walk, tottering forward with his weight on his heels, while George and Aida Overton Walker were debonair, festooning their elegant marching with flourishes that were the envy of amateur cakewalkers.[13]

Aida Overton Walker became a sought-after instructor for white high-society ladies, who marveled at her abilities. In her lessons, she emphasized the cakewalk's "grace and suppleness," and she disdained the "extravagant features" of comedy cake-walkers, such as women brandishing handkerchiefs or men pre-tending to tie their partners' shoes—moves, it's worth noting, that the public adored. In Aida Overton Walker's telling, these steps were from an "earlier period." In other words, the cakewalk was evolving.[14]

Walker did her best to uplift both the dance and her race, but when her white students did the cakewalk, they probably were not striving for respectability. Instead, they were venturing into the hazy terrain where respectability seemed to end, as white became black, and high became low. Some amateur white cake-walkers even donned blackface—a sign that wearing the mask, whether literal or figurative, was central to white dancers' enjoyment. Digging into black culture was a way for white cake-walkers to mount their own tittering rebellions. They brought their bodies into imagined, admiring sympathy with the same black Americans they ridiculed.[15]

Thumb through the theatrical and society pages of the 1890s, and you'll find stories about the cakewalk proliferating in a diz-zying whirl. Those stodgy dancing professors hadn't a prayer of squelching the national fervor. Across the country hundreds of black churches and social clubs organized cakewalks as fundraisers. Whites cakewalked at parties and hired black cakewalkers to perform at the festivities. Giant cakewalking competitions took place annually at Madison Square Garden, and a touring production of the cakewalk in San Francisco sold over ten thousand tickets in just two nights. After the white millionaire William K. Vanderbilt won a cakewalk competition at a friend's house, Bert Williams and George Walker took out an advertisement in the paper betting fifty dollars that they could beat him in a competition. Walter Gray, an African American cakewalk champion from Kansas, went for even higher stakes: a group of businessmen agreed to back "their saddle-colored champion" against Vanderbilt to the tune of five thousand dollars. Vanderbilt didn't take the bait, but the message was clear: these were challenges of black against white, working men against the elite, originators against imitators. And everyone knew who would have come out ahead. When two white couples competed against black cakewalkers in Hartford, Connecticut, the *Courant* reported that "as was to be expected, they had no chance for the prize." Black superiority was a foregone conclusion.[16]

English society was soon abuzz with news of the foreign fad. In 1901, when Mrs. George Keppel traveled to the States with her brother Lord Albemarle—both were friends of King Edward VII—she knew their trip would not be complete unless they witnessed America's national dance. A rich New York pal obligingly threw her a cakewalk party at "Uncle Billy" Miller's famous grillroom. After the guests had feasted on thirty-seven beefsteaks, with plenty of ale and sherry to chase it all down, they tromped upstairs to a private room, festooned with a huge American flag and, for good measure, a smaller British one. Pair by pair, six black couples cakewalked around the room. The enthusiastic on-lookers joined in from the sidelines. The men stood on the seats of their chairs, kept time by waving their top hats, and sang along with ragtime choruses in exaggerated black dialect. Their female companions, only slightly more demure, clapped so hard that they broke the seams of their fine kid gloves.[17]

By 1903, Europeans could see first-rate cakewalking on their own soil, when the Williams and Walker company took their musical *In Dahomey* to England, where it ran for seven months. Immediately after watching it, a wealthy white American expa-triate, Mrs. Frank Avery, hired some of the cast members to give a cakewalk at one A.M. at a party in her house in Grosvenor Square. Two princesses got wind of the surprise ahead of time and donned disguises so they could watch the American import without impropriety. Other members of the royal family were less concerned with appearances: the cast of *In Dahomey* gave a com-mand performance in the garden at Buckingham Palace. Some audience members were so taken with the cakewalk that they staged one of their own on the lawn. Soon what had begun as a titillating diversion among London society became a veritable craze. By July, King Edward had attended at least six parties with cakewalking, and was asking every American woman he met if she knew how to do the dance.[18]

The cakewalk kept spreading. The same year that Williams and Walker went to England, the French cinema wizard George Méliès filmed *Le cake-walk infernal* (The Infernal Cakewalk). The movie took place in hell and featured a pair of uncredited black dancers. At one point, Méliès used visual trickery to separate a dancer's arms and legs from his torso, literalizing the common-place descriptions of black dancers' body parts taking on lives of their own. Eventually, the frenzy is too much for even Satan to handle, and he banishes the dancers in a burst of smoke. The scene at a real-life party for Paris's Académie Julian wasn't so different. France's most acclaimed artists and fifty of their models, fueled by champagne and rhythm, cakewalked through the night and into the dawn. Some of them dressed as "Apaches" in war paint and feathers—a costume that suggests a jumbled conception of American primitivism, salaciousness, and power.[19]

In the eighteenth century, a popular figure for America abroad had been a white woman in an Indian headdress, symbolizing a blend of colonial and Native American culture, feminized and fecund. By the turn of the twentieth century, that figure was changing into the black cakewalker, sign of a wild motion that pointed, whether social dancers knew it or not, back to the days of slavery. From noble savage to high-stepping dancers: American identity had undergone a dramatic shift.[20]

It is worth pausing for a moment to parse what was going on in these performances. Amateur white European cakewalkers were imitating professional black American cakewalkers, who were imitating white minstrel cakewalkers imitating black slaves imitating their masters, who were unable to recognize that they were being mocked. Even if the dancers were not always aware of this parodic shell game, their performance resonated with the oppositions and overlaps between black and white, elite and working-class cultures.

The cakewalk was among the first American mass cultural forms where radically different groups could meet and merge. In the cakewalk, plantation owners and slaves watched one another and laughed, royals mingled with vaudeville stars, and black aspiration shared terrain with white fantasies of black primitivism. Or, rather, their steps did; steps tend to be more mobile than their steppers. For while the cakewalk integrated cultures, much of its power depended on the idea that those cultures were distinct.

The cakewalk had emerged at the nadir of American race relations. In the 1890s, when it rose to prominence, whites' racial anxiety was consuming the nation. It fueled debates in the halls of "Redeemed" legislatures and sparked race riots in Wilmington (1898), New Orleans, and New York (both 1900). It resulted in the lynching of more than 110 black Americans, on average, each year, and in *Plessy v. Ferguson* (1896), the Supreme Court decision establishing the doctrine of "separate but equal."[21] It infused the circling movements of black cakewalkers, the image of America abroad, and the wheeling turns of "Jim Crow," the minstrel character whose name now referred to the new segregation at home.

For all its pep, the cakewalk is haunted by white brutality. That's why Charles Chesnutt, in his 1901 novel *The Marrow of Tradition*, has the white villain Tom Delamere steal his black servant Sandy's clothes, black up, and perform a cakewalk for an audience of visiting Yankees. Later in the novel, Tom puts on the clothes and blacks up again, but this time to rob his aunt, a crime that leads to her death. In both scenarios, a white man steals a black man's identity, redefines it, and uses it against him. Tom does not just parody Sandy; he makes him look like a criminal. Chesnutt sets his attack on Tom's performances against the growing viciousness of white society working to disenfranchise freed blacks. The novel closes with a riot.[22]

Yet the cakewalk is also haunted by the ingenuity of African Americans, including the antebellum slaves, who—in time they stole and satires their masters missed—mocked their oppressors. Their history fueled Chesnutt's righteous anger in *The Marrow of Tradition,* led Williams and Walker to challenge Vanderbilt, and went on parade every time a French artist, British royal, or American reveler launched into the dance's steps. Its undertones might seem to make it a counterintuitive candidate for the country's first national dance—something that should, presumably, make Americans feel good about America. But the cakewalk gets at deeper truths, and deeper patterns, all the way down to the country's great unfinished business of slavery.

Even though few social dancers at the turn of the twentieth century may have been thinking about human chattel on the dance floor, the cakewalk's tangled histories give it an unconscious power. In the puffed-up chest of the imagined dandy, the circular path of society on parade, layers of admiration and satire pile on top of one another like sediments from geological eras. The cakewalk's past may have been buried, but it could always come back to life.

That's what happened in a ghost story that ran in the *Washington Post* in 1907. It went like this: In 1862, when the Confederates at Fort Donelson surrendered to General Grant's Union troops, black Union soldiers were detailed to occupy the nearby town of Dickson, Tennessee. Many were "old men who had been enticed away from good homes where hardships were unknown," former slaves who now encountered "the worst of serfdom." Large numbers of the men died from smallpox, and were "buried hel-ter skelter, never over three feet deep in the earth, and in rude pine coffins furnished by the Federal government." The largest makeshift cemetery was "a low, marshy ground where the union depot now stands." In this burial ground, the Old South—depicted as kindlier to its black population than the victorious North—butted up against the new.[23]

Once a year, in the middle of the night, a great light would fall over the marsh. "Hideous and grinning skeletons of more than a score of human beings" would rise up and "take their po-sitions as in the old-time country dance practiced during the civil war." Two skeletons off to the side served as "bone clappers." The other ghosts moved with "elasticity and apparent delight," with "protruding knee caps, crooked thigh bones, glaring shoulder blades, and V-shaped shins."[24]

Those bone clappers? They come straight from blackface min-strel shows, whose endmen played bones and tambourines. And that dance, making even rigid bones move in impossibly fluid ways? According to the headline in the *Post*, the ghosts were per-forming "A Cakewalk."[25]

The story, about the haunting of a Tennessee town by the ra-cial and regional clashes that came to a head during the Civil War, is itself haunted—haunted by popular conceptions of black performance, which are tied inextricably to those national trau-mas. And it's haunted by the layered parodies of the cakewalk it-self, which would have had those slaves-turned-soldiers mocking their former masters and dancing out their temporary liberation in a performance the entire country would claim as its own.

\* \* \*

In 1947, the ballet choreographer Lew Christensen created *Blackface,* based on nineteenth-century minstrel shows, for Ballet Society, the company that would later become New York City Ballet. *Blackface* premiered on the same bill as *The Seasons,* a Merce Cunningham, John Cage, and Isamu Noguchi collaboration. In one version of history, it is clear who came out on top of this clash of old and new: Cunningham dominated the postmodern dance scene until his death in 2009, while *Blackface* was a critical bomb. Christensen, disturbed by the discrimination he had witnessed while serving in the army during World War II, envisioned the dance as a plea for racial justice, and the cast included two African American guest stars, Betty Nichols and Talley Beatty—a rare occurrence in the predominately white world of ballet. At one moment, a minstrel tried, and failed, to wipe the paint off another minstrel's face, which Christensen might have hoped would show the dangerous solidification of stereotypes. But while the critic John Martin praised *Blackface*'s "thin line of comment on racial intolerance," he found it "pretty pointless and long-drawn-out." Critics Walter Terry, Louis Horst, and Anatole Chujoy agreed, and Christensen's ballet never made it to another season.[26]

Four years later, though, New York City Ballet recycled *Blackface*'s sets and costumes for a new piece, this one a more affectionate picture of blackface minstrelsy: Ruthanna Boris's *Cakewalk. Cakewalk* later became a staple in the Joffrey Ballet's repertoire, performed throughout the 1970s and 1980s, though not with literal blackface. It begins with a grand cakewalk promenade, the whole cast prancing onstage and taking their seats in two long, semicircular rows. A series of set pieces follows. A dainty girl, addicted to sadness, droops comically through her performance. The interlocutor takes a solo with taut little jumps and precise footwork, then collapses into his chair. "Hortense, Queen of the Swamp Ladies" enthralls Harolde, an effeminate young poet, who chases her about the stage in a spoof of *Giselle*. There are also endmen, a fiery female soloist who dances until she collapses, and a magician, Louis the Illusionist. *Cakewalk* made minstrelsy look like a series of colorblind vaudeville sketches; in fact, the critic Doris Hering praised it for helping the ballet dancers "drop their elegance and restraint and romp like vaude-villians." Louis the Illusionist conjures Venus, the Three Graces, and a horse, but the ballet's most magical feat may have been making the complicated performances of race, the dark and pa-rodic heart of the cakewalk, disappear altogether.[27]

But it is never truly gone. Rather, it is buried beneath new steps or new choreography. Someone tells a different story, or doesn't tell a story at all, or builds a railroad station on top of the quagmire and corpses that are the story. And at some point, the unruly past bursts forth in a blaze of light, and ghosts dance out of their graves.

# 2 BILL ROBINSON'S DREAM

In 1918, at a vaudeville show at New York's Palace Theatre, a middle-aged black man from Richmond, Virginia, tapped down the stairs on the side of the stage to greet a few friends and altered the course of American dance history. Or maybe it happened in an earlier year, or at a different theater. Maybe there weren't any friends in the audience, and the dance had been choreographed well in advance. Maybe it was inspired by—or even stolen from—other, earlier performers who danced on flights of stairs, such as Hal Leach, the Whitney Brothers, and "King Rastus" Brown, all of whom have faded from cultural memory. The details are hazy, but this much is clear: Bill "Bojangles" Robinson had begun his career dancing on the street for pennies, and nearly four decades later this new routine, the stair dance, helped make him the most respected tap dancer in the world.[1]

Bill Robinson elevated tap, both figuratively and literally. Tap had sprung to national prominence on the nineteenth-century minstrel stage, where it was known as buck dancing. To the casual observer, early tappers could seem more spastic than skillful. Their steps, a hybrid of Irish and African moves, became associated with ugly depictions of flat-footed, shuffling "darkies," a stereotype whose weight black performers subsequently had to bear. But Robinson sloughed those images off, dancing up on his toes, speedy and swinging. He knew how to joke around, but he was dignified and nattily dressed, a successful, citified man. He was not just the equal of white tap dancers—he was their undisputed better. His taps were clear and sharp: the tiniest movements of his feet emitted clean, loud sounds. Even practiced tappers were unable to distinguish between his left foot and his right: the two were perfectly balanced. Robinson had a sense of drama, too, making easy steps look hard or hard steps look joyously easy as the occasion merited. He inspired a generation of dancers on both sides of the color line and helped audiences and critics alike recognize tap dance as a modern, American art form—a recognition not just that black Americans could embody national identity but also that American identity was itself part black.[2]

Robinson demonstrated these feats in performance after performance, but none was as popular, or as recognizably his own, as that single routine he rolled out in the late teens: the stair dance. Over the course of his career, he must have performed it well over a thousand times. It reportedly made him the highest-paid "single" (solo performer) in vaudeville, a phenomenon that, in turn, helped him land both leading roles in Broadway shows and costarring roles in some of the most lucrative Hollywood musicals of the 1930s.[3]

In the movies, Robinson taps on stairs incorporated into elaborate sets: a Civil War–era stoop, the staircase of a southern plantation manor, the base of a Mardi Gras throne. But the staircase that he used while becoming the face of American tap in vaudeville during the teens and twenties was relatively stripped down: two sets of stairs connected back-to-back to form a stile. Robinson would travel from theater to theater with this prop. He didn't need a backdrop. He didn't need a full band to accompany him. He didn't even need a costume, aside from one of the tailored suits he liked to wear in his everyday life. He just needed wooden split-soled shoes, nerve, and what may have been the best sense of rhythm in American dance.

No footage from Robinson's vaudeville performances exists, but a scene in the 1932 "race film" *Harlem Is Heaven* comes close. Robinson taps his way onstage from the wings, accompanied by a spare piano rendition of Stephen Foster's "Old Folks at Home" (also known as "Swanee River"). Foster wrote it for the Christy Minstrels in 1851, from the perspective of a black man who tells his fellow "darkies" that his "heart grows weary" with "longing for de old plantation." By 1932 the tune had become an American standard, and though it was still associated with blacks, Robinson shows no signs of longing for slavery. Those nostalgic strains are chased off by Robinson's feet, which sound out a competing anthem of grace, urbanity, and power.

In a three-piece suit with boutonniere and bowler, Robinson taps toward his stile—five steps on each side—and kicks at it a few times, making lower, deeper sounds than he can get from hammering the floor, using it as part set, part drum set. He pauses but keeps his feet moving. After a few more kicks and taps, he steps back, gives his hat a gentlemanly tug, and hops onto the first stair, then the second, before pattering back to earth. He swings one leg to the level of the fourth step, then brings it clattering down. Ballerinas lift their legs hip high as a matter of course. When Robinson does it, it's breathtaking.

Bill Robinson, ca. 1928 (Photograph by Vandamm Studio © Billy Rose Theatre Division, The New York Public Library for the Performing Arts)

Instead of going straight up the stairs, Robinson milks the drama of hesitation, ascent, and descent. He taps up and down, up and down. By the time he reaches the top, you half expect something enormous to happen, as when, on a mountain summit, a new landscape stretches out, large and free. But nothing changes, and Robinson heads down as easily as he came up. This is where the stair dance becomes symbolically rich. Robinson can tap all he wants, but he never really goes anywhere. The routine offers motion for the sake of motion, movement set within a frame. It's the drama of rhythm against constraints. Like a ragtime pianist syncopating an even march or a jazz soloist bringing a melody to the edges of recognition, Robinson shapes the standard into the new by pushing at it from inside. He pits the architecture of everyday life against itself and turns it into a world where he can excel.

At the end of the dance, Robinson prances offstage, kicking his knees high in front of him, in a variation on the cakewalk. But Robinson does something new. He bends his knees, throwing the whole picture askew, and instead of circling around a chalk line, he rushes off. It's almost as if he's leaving the past behind.

For the first few decades of his career, leaving the past was just what Bill Robinson seemed to be doing. He epitomized what black leaders like Alain Locke called the New Negro, a member of a generation of African Americans intent on raising collective consciousness and improving the lot of all black Americans. Robinson was heralded as an artistic genius, a leader of his race, and a harbinger of America's gradual move toward integration and equality. But by the mid-1930s, he had begun to seem part of the same past he had been trying to jettison. In the integrated Hollywood films that followed *Harlem Is Heaven*, Robinson was confined to the roles of servant, butler, and slave. Some members of the black press criticized him for playing an Uncle Tom, kowtowing to whites instead of fighting them. Shirley Temple, his most famous partner, was seen as Little Eva, the angelic white child.

Today, Robinson's movies with Temple have eclipsed his early career. In the 1995 Broadway chronicle of tap history, *Bring in 'da Noise, Bring in 'da Funk,* Baakari Wilder portrayed him as "Uncle Huck-a-Buck," dancing with a giant blond Shirley Temple doll that was operated, like a puppet, by Savion Glover. "Who de hell cares if I acts de fool / When I takes a swim in my swimming pool?" Uncle Huck-a-Buck sang.[4] Robinson, in this performance, was a cynic and a sellout, helping hide the real talent and power of black men. But here's something to keep in mind: when those movies came out, audiences knew that Robinson was an acclaimed dancer with a career that spanned both stage and screen. That awareness could lead to some dissonant moments, as when, in *In Old Kentucky,* Will Rogers, whose character employs Robinson as a stable hand and houseboy, asks a visitor, "Do you like good dancing? Well, I've got a boy here that's absolutely the best in the world." The irony is that Robinson was.

One of *In Old Kentucky*'s subplots has Will Rogers learning to tap from Robinson, something Shirley Temple does, too. They weren't the only ones. Throughout the twenties and thirties, Robinson inspired scads of imitators who hoped to pick up on his innovations. He came to stand not just for tap dance but for black American movement, and for what was American about American dance. In the wake of his success, performers who wanted to mark themselves as American dancers did so, largely, with tap.

Compared to the tap stars who came after him—the Nicholas Brothers, Fred Astaire, "Honi" Coles and "Cholly" Atkins, Gene Kelly, Gregory Hines, Savion Glover—Robinson's dancing can look contained. His successors lean their upper bodies off-center, sweep their arms through space, and travel across the floor at high speeds. Robinson keeps his torso erect. His shoulders are almost always in line with his hips, and his arms stay close to his body. When he travels, his path across the floor is relatively slow—instead of moving laterally, he concentrates his energy into the quick up and down of his feet.

If his successors assert their freedom in expansive surroundings, Robinson is king of a smaller country. In a way, the smallness intensifies the drama: he excels within containment. Think of a poet who clings to form and makes it look easy, so that instead of being controlled by meter and rhyme, the words seem to simultaneously fit into a structure and bend that structure to the poet's will.

The delicate dance of freedom and constraint, vertical and horizontal motion, typifies Robinson's career, and illuminates the problem of being a black entertainer under Jim Crow. Robinson figured out how to succeed within, and push against, the social and political confinement he faced. He riffed on received forms—physical objects, melodies, stereotypical roles—and made them new. But vestiges of the old racial order remained. They continued to drive his steps and shape his persona, and they were passed on to the generations of dancers who looked to him for inspiration.

Bill Robinson started dancing in his hometown of Richmond in the 1880s. Richmond, the former Confederate capital, was not an easy place for blacks. When Reconstruction ended in 1877, the federal troops who had been protecting black citizens pulled out of the South, and lynch law ruled supreme. Robinson decided to get out. By 1900, he had made his way to New York.

Legend has it that Robinson went to the big city itching to prove himself as a dancer. That meant heading to a performance of Charles T. Dazey's *In Old Kentucky,* which had been playing to packed houses off and on for seven years. It featured a love triangle with an innocent mountain girl, a moonshiner, and a debonair gentleman, as well as supporting roles for an endearing old Colonel and a faithful Negro. The story climaxed with a stirring horse race in Lexington. But *In Old Kentucky*'s real attraction was its "pickaninny band," a group of black juvenile musicians—all under 5'4", according to an advertisement for new recruits—who played with syncopated pep. Audiences went wild for the musicians, stopping the show with cheers and demands for encores.[5]

Not only the music was lively. *In Old Kentucky* was full of motion. During one scene, reported the *New York Times,* "two little darkies" on the sidelines played a mysterious game that the *Times* saw fit to explain at length to its befuddled readers—craps—while at center stage, to the strains of the pickaninny band, buck and soft-shoe dancers showed off their own rhythmic virtuosity.[6]

Buck dancing is more staid than most of the tap performed nowadays. Like Appalachian cloggers, buck dancers tend to keep their upper bodies, and even their thighs, relatively still; the action comes from the knees and below, as the dancers beat out rhythms in regular time. At least, that's how buck dancing started: by the end of the nineteenth century, dancers had begun to syncopate their rhythms and loosen their legs. In *The Pickaninnies,* a twenty-five-second Edison film from 1894, three black men—members of *The Passing Show,* one of *In Old Kentucky*'s rival productions—do an upbeat, athletic buck dance. One man drops onto his back and raises himself into a shoulder stand, his feet sticking up high in the air, then flips over backward, before moving casually back into his percussive steps. He scoots off to the side, making room for another dancer to play harmonica while splaying his legs out in loose wing steps. The dances in *In Old Kentucky* were probably similarly pounding and virtuosic. At some point producers realized they could make the show even more exciting by opening it up to audience participation. Once a week, the buck dancing scene in act 2 became a contest between new entrants and the show's cast.[7]

And that's where Bill Robinson enters the picture, sometime in or around 1900, beating *In Old Kentucky*'s star dancer Harry Swinton, and making a reputation for himself in the world of New York entertainment. No firsthand accounts of the Robinson-Swinton showdown are extant, but we know that spirits at these contests ran high. At a 1904 performance, the judges picked a winner with whom audiences were so unhappy that they began to hurl vegetables at the stage. The curtain was held for a half-hour to restore order. It's tempting to imagine that Robinson's defeat of Swinton inspired the same volume of excitement, and even more tempting to see it as heroic triumph over a crass commercial picture of southern life, with our hero the Great Artist showing the pickaninny band a thing or two. But the fact is that Robinson had left Richmond playing a pickaninny himself, in the 1892 touring production of *The South Before the War.*[8]

*The South Before the War* was one of the first successful plantation shows—"plant shows" in showbiz parlance—elaborate productions that portrayed antebellum slavery as a happy, pastoral life with plenty of time for singing, dancing, and horsing around. This had been a common fiction in blackface minstrel productions for decades, but *The South Before the War* differed in one important respect. Aside from two white stars in blackface, almost all the performers were black, including buck dancers, cakewalkers, multiple vocal quartets, and the pickaninny band. What's more, the show helped bring the rhythms of ragtime to the masses. That gave it a modern edge, even as advertisements noted that its "genuine colored people" would shuffle "their enormous feet on sanded floors," performing "comical acts of niggerdom."[9]

Robinson probably picked up some steps from the show's leading buck dancers and cakewalkers, and he may have also gleaned some lessons in comic timing and playing to a crowd. But whatever Robinson took from *The South Before the War,* the show was a way for him to get out of the South by pretending that it was a wonderful place to be.

This was the paradox of being a black entertainer when Bill Robinson came of age: performers had to traffic in stereotypes and nostalgia, at least in part, in order to escape them. In the 1890s, a generation after the Civil War, whites on both sides of the Mason-Dixon Line found common cause in squelching blacks' freedom. The promises of Reconstruction had been broken, lynchings were on the rise, and the most popular musical compositions, providing the backing to untold numbers of cakewalks, were "coon songs," whose lyrics portrayed black Americans as sensuous beings with enormous appetites, quick to dance, fight with razors, and steal chickens—in short, people wholly unfit for citizenship.[10]

Yet the rhythms of coon songs came from black ragtime musicians' parodic take on white compositions: at the piano, one hand rags, or syncopates, on the other, turning an even $\frac{2}{4}$ or $\frac{4}{4}$ march (hello, John Philip Sousa) into something that swings (enter Scott Joplin).[11] Like the cakewalk, ragtime music itself was partly a form of mockery. Even while singing the lyrics of coon songs, bringing white stereotypes of blackness to life, black artists like Bill Robinson, with the understanding of black audiences, found ways to separate themselves from the mask. They said yes, but they also said no.

The critic W. T. Lhamon calls this dynamic "fire hydrant theory": fire hydrants are used to put out fires, he notes, only one percent of the time, while the other 99 percent dogs use them for their private communications. Comparing black entertainers to pissing pets may not seem terribly complimentary, but the putdown is part of Lhamon's point. Black artists were shoved into demeaning roles that they found ways to subvert, and audiences in the know picked up on the subversion. No one did this more successfully than Bert Williams, Lhamon's favorite fire-hydrant artist. Williams, who had helped popularize the cakewalk, was a crossover pop star. When Bill Robinson was coming of age, Williams was the black entertainer to emulate.[12]

Bert Williams and his partner George Walker worked their way up from seedy clubs in San Francisco's Barbary Coast to the national black vaudeville circuit. In 1897, when they added a cakewalk to their routine, good reviews turned to raves. Soon they were mounting full-length, all-black musical spectaculars for both black and white audiences, and touring on both sides of the Atlantic. Williams played the shuffling darky of old-time minstrelsy to Walker's elegant, modern dandy, but his career out-lasted his partner's. After Walker became too ill to perform—he died in 1911—Williams integrated Florenz Ziegfeld's *Follies*, recorded dozens of wax cylinders of songs and comic monologues, and performed in films that included the short *Natural Born Gambler* (1916) and an unfinished 1913 feature. Williams was be-loved by audiences and revered by critics as the cleverest "low comedian on our stage today," "one of the greatest comedians America has ever bred," and the flat-out "world's greatest living comedian." He won this acclaim not just for his comedy but for his pathos, playing down-and-out characters who inspired sym-pathy mixed with laughter.[13]

The comedian W. C. Fields called Williams "the funniest man I ever saw, and the saddest man I ever knew," and the theater critic Percy Hammond went farther: "Every time I see Mr. Bert Williams . . . I wonder if he is not the patient repository of a se-cret sadness. In the midst of his decorous and explicit capers in the Follies I think that sorrow concealed, 'like an oven stopped,' must burn his heart to cinders." Was that sorrow part of Wil-liams's performance, the skill of a man who had every reason to feel triumphant about his success and his art? Or was it a pro-found emotional reality? It's easy to speculate, impossible to know. Williams had reasons to feel lonely: he was a Bahamian immigrant in exile and a black man in a racist nation. During the August 1900 New York race riots, angry white mobs beat up his partner George Walker and their friend, the actor and dancer Ernest Hogan. Though Williams's dramatic talent was acknowl-edged by white and black audiences alike, he always performed in blackface.[14]

George Walker did not, and neither did the other members of their company, an idiosyncrasy that helped throw Williams's mask into relief. There was no mistaking it for anything but artifice. For Williams, this was useful: "It was not until I was able to see myself as another person that my sense of humor developed," he explained. If that sounds close to the way W. E. B. Du Bois describes double consciousness, the "sense of always looking at one's self through the eyes of others," it's because it is. When Williams blacked up, he made double consciousness visible, smearing white stereotypes about blackness onto his body. He accepted those stereotypes because he had to in order to work. But to use Lhamon's analogy, he also turned them into fire hydrants and did his business.[15]

Take "Nobody," Williams's most famous song, a litany of instances in which he's been left to fend for himself. The chorus concludes with defiant inertia: "Until I get something from somebody, sometime / I'll never do nothing for nobody, no time." He might as well be flipping the country the bird. Or "Borrow from Me," in which Williams's character, asked to play a "bleedhound" in a production of *Uncle Tom's Cabin*, responds with a series of impossible demands: "Bring me the czar of Russia, just have him come on over here, and blacken up and play Uncle Tom's part." Othello, Williams continues, can play the slave-hunter Marks, and the Statue of Liberty take Little Eva's part. It's an incredible set of propositions, subjecting foreign royalty, a Shakespearean hero, and a symbol of American inclusion to the indignity of appearing in a Tom show. If those symbols consent—an impossibility that Williams milks for all its satiric power—then sure, he'll consent to playing a dog, and though he doesn't say it, because everyone knows the plot of *Uncle Tom's Cabin,* and everyone knows what bloodhounds do, he'll hunt down runaway slaves, and keep his fellow African Americans from running to freedom.[16]

Bill Robinson admired Bert Williams and tried to emulate him. The first written records we have of Robinson the entertainer—after he had left his anonymous stints with the plant show and made enough of a splash in vaudeville to get his name in the papers—is as half of a comic duo patterned after Bert Williams and George Walker. George Cooper played straight man to Bill Robinson's clown, and audiences picked up on the resemblances right away. "Two colored comedians, Cooper and Robinson, are the big hit of the bill," reported a Seattle paper in 1909. "They occupy twenty minutes or so with a Williams and Walker 'stunt' which is a perpetual roar." Cooper and Robinson were one of a handful of black acts to make it onto the otherwise white Keith-Albee and Orpheum circuits, but it is difficult to re-create their skits. Newspapers printed their touring dates—everywhere from Duluth to London—but gave no detailed accounts of their performances.[17]

There are clues that suggest that early in his career Robinson, like Bert Williams, was mocking racial and ethnic stereotypes. In one sketch, the straitlaced Cooper fretted about what one reviewer called Robinson's "ungentlemanly behavior at a social function." Robinson's defense had audiences howling with "heart-aching laughter," perhaps from the pleasure of his acting-out. There are hints of rebellion, too, in an act that black vaudeville veteran Tom Fletcher recalled years after the fact. In the first decade of the twentieth century, when it was common for white vaudevillians to imitate not just black Americans but hosts of immigrant groups as well, Cooper and Robinson "made up like it had been customary to do in impersonating Jews and put on a heavy burlesque of the supposedly Jewish accent" to sing the song "Yoi Yoi Yoi Yoi, Mary Ann." Given Robinson's "shrewdness in meeting and overcoming the problem of racial and religious prejudice," Fletcher wrote, folks suspected that Cooper and Robinson's Jewface was a satirical provocation, meant to protest the ugliness of the "racially obnoxious" acts that were so pervasive. If white actors could change races, Cooper and Robinson seemed to ask, why shouldn't blacks have the same freedom?[18]

Robinson and Cooper clowned around, but as one reviewer put it, they "appreciate[d] the difference between comedy and buffoonery" and always erred on the side of good taste—that is, they found ways to distance themselves from the mask. They never wore literal blackface. Robinson, wrote one critic, joked "without the slightest strain or overdoing himself. You laugh at him, heartily, but not because he does contortion acts with his lips or has any slap-stick methods to offer, but because of the naturalness of his humor." Other black acts would benefit by taking a lesson from the pair "in the point of cleanness, originality, cleverness and up-to-dateness." Cooper and Robinson were modern men posing as minstrels.[19]

Reviews tended to focus on the duo's comedy, though their acts typically included both buck and soft-shoe dancing. Robinson's "fantastic footwork" was later praised for "approaching perfection," but it apparently did not merit much attention until the late teens, when Robinson left Cooper to perform on his own. Perhaps Robinson's dancing had improved over the years, or perhaps, without a comic foil to fill out dialogue, he had more time to show it off. Perhaps he decided that dancing would help him separate himself from his old partner, rather than appearing to be half of an incomplete team. Or perhaps he realized that dance could do for him what comedy did for Bert Williams, allowing him to seem to fit a stereotype even as he pushed against it. Whatever the case, Robinson's solo act took off.[20]

When Bert Williams died in 1922, Bill Robinson's dancing was ready to fill the void. He was making such a splash, speculated the *Los Angeles Times,* that he had "a good chance ending up as another Bert Williams." The *Chicago Defender* later reported that Robinson "pantomimes the Negro in a comic vein that is often as deft and subtle as were the characterizations of the late Bert Williams."[21]

Neither of these comparisons refers to his dancing. Bert Williams was a great mover, but not a great dancer. He thrived on small, subtle gestures and kept his limbs close to his body, playing up his character's clumsiness and fear. Recall that it was George and Aida Overton Walker who performed the refined, elegant cakewalks; Williams's version was comical.[22] Robinson may have equaled Williams in fame and rivaled his mastery of jokes and pantomimes, but he soon became a very different sort of star: grace and command were central to his dancing, and they helped him reach the top of the pack. A decade after Williams began singing "Nobody," Robinson was clearly somebody. He controlled his own body and instructed his educated feet. Audiences appreciated his comedy, but they clamored for the drama of his dancing. Monologues and vocal oddities were mere buildup for the moment when Robinson would leave language behind, whether to pound the stage or, in a routine that went nowhere and everywhere at once, dance up and down the stairs.

Just imagine it: July 1926. Robinson travels to London, where he has been engaged to perform at the Holborn. He sings a song or two and makes a few jokes. Maybe he does vocal imitations—a mosquito, a banjo, a fly landing first on sugar, then on Limburger cheese. At some point, his feet begin to move at a speed Britain has never before witnessed, tapping out a rhythm more intricate than any jazz drummer's. His toes and his heels are banging the floor so quickly it's hard to tell what's hitting where, yet he acts as if it's the easiest thing in the world, doffing his bowler hat, grinning at his feet and the audience, swinging his arms as carelessly as a man out for a Sunday stroll. The audience at the Holborn goes wild. They applaud and cheer for so long that it stops the show. Minutes pass before the next performer can come onstage. That same week, at another London theater, the Victoria Palace, the blackface comedy duo Jones and Jones tried to win the crowd with thick southern accents, mispronounced words, and general buffoonery. They met with lukewarm reception.[23] Robinson's success seemed to herald a new era in black entertainment.

It had taken some seventy-five years, Robinson told a reporter in 1928, "for the Negro actor to emerge from what is known in the parlance of the theatre as a 'freak attraction' to the real artist that he is considered today." Robinson admitted that there was plenty of progress left to make—black and white performers still did not appear in integrated productions.[24] Yet Robinson's own career had followed the path from "freak attraction" to "artist." Black and white Americans recognized something beyond novelty in Robinson's dancing. They saw an artist who rivaled and even surpassed the best of what more highbrow performers, at home or abroad, had to offer.

Robinson, asserted one critic, was "just about 50 times as 'artistic' as most of the much-talked about European celebrities who bring us terpsichorean Art with a capital 'A.'" Others agreed. "No member of the Ballet Russe could grant the human body more upstanding respect," wrote another critic. Robinson's posture alone merited comparisons to "the singing prose of Hemingway or Faulkner." He could "extract as much drama" from a set of stairs "with his toes as Sarah Bernhardt could out of the tears of Camille," and in three minutes of dancing, he would cram in more artistry than could be found in a five-hour performance of *Mourning Becomes Electra*. One nationally syndicated columnist confessed that he "would rather execute one of [Bill Robinson's] tap dances than paint a Mona Lisa." According to the *New York Times*, "the sole of Bill's shoe is as much an artistic instrument as the fiddle of Paganini."[25]

In 1931 Robinson taught at a summer dance program with Ted Shawn, then the most famous male modern dancer in the country. Robinson was paid twice as much. At the 1939 World's Fair, Robinson starred in *The Hot Mikado*, which played for two seasons, with three performances a day. In contrast, Martha Graham's *A Tribute to Peace*—also on the docket at the World's Fair—was performed once.[26]

It would be easy to write off these successes with the assumption that popular art, by definition, is more popular than highbrow art, were it not that the highbrow artists were watching and celebrating Robinson themselves. The Italian conductor Arturo

Toscanini, visiting New York in 1938, rushed to the Cotton Club to watch Robinson in action and loved what he saw. George Balanchine and Lincoln Kirstein recruited Robinson for a 1942 Russian War Relief Benefit concert that featured the stars of ballet and modern dance. Years earlier, Robinson told an interviewer in 1945, he and Vaslav Nijinsky, star of Diaghilev's Ballets Russes, had admired each other's work in Paris. Robinson recalled that "when the Russians came to Los Angeles many of the Paris performers were still in the company, and they came around to see me at one of my performances. Nijinsky: there was a genius."[27]

The comparison of Bill Robinson with highbrow artists served purposes beyond the rhetorical. For the leaders of the Harlem Renaissance, art was a sign of their people's advancement: if blacks could produce fine art, white Americans would begin to understand that blacks had the same emotions and abilities as their oppressors, and that they deserved not just respect but political equality. Bill Robinson's art was a weapon in their fight, and Robinson himself became a soldier for the cause.

In the early years of his success, Robinson was praised for uplifting the race and fighting whites' prejudice, sometimes for simply winning whites over. When Jack George, a white comedian who performed in blackface, became too ill to perform at a San Francisco vaudeville theater, Robinson—then a headliner—took George's place as the opening act. This was a voluntary demotion: audiences tended to walk into the theater and talk through the first number. In addition, Robinson made it a condition that George receive his full salary; Robinson took no money. Whether or not George's blackface act changed after this, his attitude did. "I was born in the South," he said, "and I must confess to my shame that I had all the lack of respect for the Negro as a unit that the southerners have. I say 'had' for Bill Robinson has unconsciously taught me a lesson." That same year, in 1922, at a performance below the Mason-Dixon Line, three middle-aged white women hissed loudly during Robinson's act. He ignored them at first, but after the ushers had escorted the ladies out of the house, *Variety* reported, Robinson told the audience that "in thirty years in the show business such a thing had never happened to him before, and that he had been taught that, should it ever happen, to ignore it. He did, and won his house by the neat way he turned the tide." Robinson may have "ignored" the hissing when it happened, but he was making sure that everybody knew he was doing so.[28]

A few years later, Robinson fought insults more directly. When the chorus girls for *Blackbirds of 1928* took the stage at New York's Liberty Theater one September evening, they faced an audience that included fifty white drunk southern men. The men tried their best to fluster the performers, clapping and cheering at inappropriate times. One tottered to his feet, waved a ten-dollar bill, and hollered, "Get hot there, Colored gals. This is for the first one that meets me after the show. Don't kill yourselves in the rush." The audience murmured in shock, but no one confronted the men. Then Robinson came on, signaling to the band to keep playing despite the ruckus. Instead of proceeding with his act, he kept up a slow tap, like a metronome. "What you men have done tonight is a disgrace to your race," he told the drunkards, then pointed out the unfairness of their relative positions: "If I stepped down the street, entered the New Amsterdam Theater, and waved a bill before a chorus girl, I'd be mobbed." The tapping continued. "I consider you—and you—and you—the low-est men I have ever played before." The audience did not mob the drunkards, but they did cheer, for a full five minutes. The men sheepishly left the theater.[29] The story of Robinson's speech was picked up by newspapers across the country. It seemed to be a sign that blacks were no longer mere entertainers, subject to the whims of white audiences. Robinson did not simply deserve respect. He demanded it.

He earned it, too, becoming the most successful black performer in vaudeville. He owned a Duesenberg limousine worth sixteen thousand dollars. He wore a diamond-studded watch. He dined with politicians, movie stars, and foreign diplomats. He was elected mayor of Harlem. It was an honorary position, but a telling one: to much of America, Robinson seemed to stand for Harlem itself. When he went on tour, he was an unofficial cultural ambassador from the center of black success.[30]

In one show, *Bojangles Revels,* he danced up and down the stairs with what one paper called "a dozen brownskin beauties."[31] Perhaps the routine was a precursor to the "Bill Robinson Stomp," which Robinson performed three years later in *Harlem Is Heaven.* There are no stairs in the latter, but a dozen chorus girls in glittering caps and short skirts accompany him. He sings about earlier crazes, the Charleston and the Black Bottom, which the chorus girls obligingly perform behind him, splaying their legs out below the knees with the floppiness of jazz baby ragdolls. But as Robinson explains, there's a new dance on the scene, one he'll guide them through. "You take two steps and you turn around," he sings, and the girls demonstrate. "You run right up and you run right down," he continues, and they prance in place. The orders continue for a few more lines, then stop: "Follow me, you really can't lose. Sprinkle pepper in your shoes, and dance the way you choose." The "Bill Robinson Stomp" may have a few guidelines, but according to the lyrics it ends up being about freedom—albeit an odd sort of freedom, licensed by Robinson. The girls never do their own thing, however: they continue to dance together, their feet hot from all that imaginary pepper, Mary Janes hammering the stage in unison. They're leggy soldiers to Robinson's happy-go-lucky general.

The "Bill Robinson Stomp" did not have the most innovative choreography, but it was fun. What's more, it was a far cry from the pickaninny chorus in *The South Before the War*. Robinson is no slave or rural rube; he is an urban sophisticate, calling the shots. Still, he and his chorus girls dance in front of a painted backdrop of a white-columned Greek Revival mansion whose porch gives onto rolling pastures. It looks an awful lot like an antebellum plantation. The vestiges of the Old South may be disconnected from the action at center stage, but the past still looms up in the background.

At the close of *Harlem Is Heaven*, Robinson is reunited with his mother, who has come up from Richmond to see her boy make good. This never happened in Robinson's own life—he didn't even know his own mother. In *Harlem Is Heaven*, "Mammy" reminds audiences that Robinson has fulfilled the promise of the Great Migration, when over a million southern blacks moved north to find better jobs and escape the threat of racial violence.[32] Like so many, Robinson headed to Harlem, which became the capital of black American culture. It was, asserted the film's prologue, a "super-symphony" of "roaring subways, rumbling streetcars, rankling milk-wagons and the rat-a-tat of machine guns," a place where "intellectuals mingle with illiterates" to create "the most interesting city of modern times."

Robinson arrived in Harlem with the first wave of black migrants and proclaimed that he'd never look back. "The fact of the matter is," Robinson told a reporter in 1929, "that the North has been pretty good to the colored folks migrating here from the South, and that most of them have little or no reason to regret the move from the sleepy, sluggish confines of their birthplace to the more wide-awake, progressive and prosperous cities. This is particularly true of the colored entertainer, whose earning capacity increases the farther he gets from Dixie. My idea of real loneliness would be to find myself separated from New York City."[33]

Six years later, Robinson was in Hollywood, playing a former slave who is happily employed at his old master's house. In *The Little Colonel* (1935), Robinson is no longer accompanied by a bevy of brown-skinned beauties. Now, he dances with a white toddler, Shirley Temple.

Whereas the "Bill Robinson Stomp" moved the plantation into the background, *The Little Colonel* brought it to the fore. Robinson plays a butler to Temple's sweet young mistress in a post–Civil War South filled with palatial homes, jovial black servants, picturesque baptisms accompanied by gospel singing, and beautiful white ladies in hoop skirts. Only one blot sullies this picturesque dreamland. Shirley's curmudgeonly grandfather refuses to speak to his daughter because she eloped with a Yankee, whose last name, in case viewers need any further hints about regional bitterness, is Sherman. The daughter and her family have come back to the old neighborhood, but her father won't acknowledge her existence. Temple's job is to bring the clan together by endearing herself to her grandfather, symbolically unifying North and South, old and new. Robinson's friendship helps her do this. The *New York Times* called *The Little Colonel* a piece of "magnolia whimsy," but when you think about Robinson's character—a former slave, still loyal to a master who longs for the days of slavery—those blossoms give off a rotten stench.[34]

*The Little Colonel*'s most famous scene shows Bill Robinson doing what he was known for: dancing up and down the stairs. But this time, he's got company. "See Shirley Dance with Bill Robinson in His Original Stair Dance," read the newspaper ads.[35] Whatever the "Original Stair Dance" might have been when Robinson rolled it out at the Palace over a decade earlier, this isn't it. It takes place not on a simple stile but on the gleaming, curved staircase of the grandfather's plantation. Temple's character, who doesn't want to go to bed, leans sulkily against the balusters, and Robinson's butler must coax her into good behavior with a dance.

Robinson begins the stair dance on his own, and his moves are similar to those in *Harlem Is Heaven:* after a series of small, clear taps, he goes up one step, swings a leg to the fourth, and sends it clattering down, knocking each step loudly along the way. After pattering on the floor a bit more, he dances up the stairs backward. There's no instrumentation, only Robinson's syncopated feet and a melody he buzzes out through pursed lips like a kazoo, but they are music enough, catchy and complex. Soon he is bounding up the stairs two steps at a time, in movements that seem enormous and free, a sign that while he has been using the ground, he isn't bound to it.

In moments like these, when Robinson dances—not when he holds Temple's hand a few minutes later and does an easier series of steps for her to follow, but when he really and truly dances—he briefly transcends film narrative to become the biggest, most breathtaking thing on screen. In a movie about regional reconciliation after the Civil War—a reconciliation that, historians have made clear, happened because white northerners and white southerners essentially colluded to disenfranchise blacks—Robinson seems like the sign of a better future. The movie gives us one version of American history, but Robinson proposes something radically different: a world where black men can harness the energies of tap for play and power, triumphing over their surroundings. Watching him dance in *The Little Colonel* is like stumbling across an Andrew Marvell poem wedged between the pages of a cheap romance.

It is hard to blame Shirley Temple for wanting to get in on the action. Indeed, by the time *The Little Colonel* rolled into production in 1935, a host of performers, both amateur and professional, had been imitating Robinson for years, trying to make his seemingly effortless steps their own. Tap dance, and the stair dance in particular, had taken hold of the nation.

In 1927, Lottie Atherton's act at the Palace—the fanciest theater on vaudeville—closed with what *Billboard* described as "a tap routine up and down a series of steps a la Bill Robinson." Two years later, *Billboard* called a number in Stop-Look-Listen's vaudeville act "stair taps a la Bill Robinson." The Five Hot Shots, a black quintet from Harlem, closed their act, too, with "a take-off on Bill Robinson's stair dance," and over at the Pantages in San Francisco, a member of the Vic Honey Trio rolled out "Bill Robinson's stair dance for a burst of applause." The 1929 musical *Bomboola* included a scene for men and women performing "on steps arranged across the stage" in what the *Wall Street Journal* described as "an elaborate development of Bill Robinson's stair dance." At the Orpheum Theater in Los Angeles, a dancer known to posterity only as "Frank, a colored lad," tried to re-create Robinson's routines. In theaters from Seattle to New York, the black vaudeville team of Harris and Radcliffe brought in Radcliffe's little brother to perform the stair dance. Radcliffe the younger got good reviews, but when two different hucksters tried to do the stair dance at the Palace in New York the following year, the *New York Times* reported that they only "succeed[ed] in making Mr. Robinson seem even better." "Sunshine Sammy" Morrison toured the nation for at least two years with a rendition of Robinson's stair dance, and in the 1931 production of *Rhapsody in Black,* Blue McAlister did his version on a set of drums. A young black dancer performing for a graduating class of nurses in Harlem was called a "small edition of Bill Robinson," and the Texas dancer Virginia Self did a "miniature stair dance." Helena Justa's imitation of Robinson's stair dance was good enough to land her an appearance at New York's Hippodrome in 1930 and, three years later, a tour with her own revue. And at the 1930 national convention of dancing masters, the *New York Times* reported, "an elderly soul with glasses was imitating Bill Robinson on the marble stairs" of the hotel. (At the convention the following year, Robinson himself showed up to perform for the attendees.) Even animated animals in a 1930 cartoon were recognized, by *Bill-board*, as doing a "stair dance a la Bill Robinson on a giraffe."[36]

Robinson did not always appreciate these imitations. In the unwritten laws of the Hoofers Club—the Harlem backroom where he and fellow tappers gathered for camaraderie and competition—"stealing steps" was de rigueur, more or less written into tap dance's one-upmanship. In a tap challenge, one dancer would throw another dancer's step back with a new spin. Stealing routines, though, was another matter. As scholars Jane and Marshall Stearns put it, " 'Thou Shalt Not Steal One Another's Steps—Exactly' was the unwritten law. You could imitate anybody inside the club, and it was taken as a compliment. But you must not do so professionally, that is in public and for pay." Glaring violations of that law prompted Robinson to turn vigilante. Fellow tapper Charles "Honi" Coles recalled that when Robinson spotted some of his imitators at the Lafayette Theater, "He walked right down the aisle and stopped a dance team in the middle of their performance. 'That's my dance,' he shouted. 'You don't have any right to perform it.' " On another occasion, Eddie Rector replaced Robinson in the European tour of Lew Leslie's musical revue *Blackbirds,* re-creating the stair dance abroad. Robinson sent Leslie two furious telegrams, considered suing, and took out a full-page ad in *Variety* explaining that Leslie and Rector were stealing his routine. (There's no record of whether Robinson felt vindicated when Rector went to jail in 1934 for illegal possession of a gun, but by then, the two hoofers may have made up. A 1932 newspaper article describes a stair dance–stealing performer with a strong resemblance to Rector asking Robinson for help paying his sister's funeral expenses, and notes that Robinson, a model of benevolence, obliged.) When the novelty string virtu-oso Roy Smeck played Robinson's stair dance on the banjo on the Rudy Vallee Show, after Robinson forbade him to do so, Robinson threatened, again, to sue. Robinson even tried unsuccessfully to patent the dance. The vaudeville and Broadway star Fred Stone, at least, seemed to know the rules: he once sent Robinson a check for fifteen hundred dollars, "in part payment," read the accom-panying note, "for the stair dance I stole from you."[37]

In the 1938 Cotton Club Parade, Robinson marched down Broadway leading fifty chorus girls who wore rubber masks of his face.[38] The thinking behind this bizarre stunt may have been that fifty-one Bill Robinsons were better than one, but it was also a reminder of the huge number of imitators he inspired, and of the pervasiveness of his image: it appeared in cabarets and advertise-ments, on film screens, and even grafted onto the faces of other people. For while some tried to imitate Robinson's moves, others donned their own Bill Robinson masks in greasepaint and burnt cork. They weren't just copying Robinson's routine, his debo-nair style, or his astounding steps. They were after his race, too.

Thirty-five years after Bill Robinson made his New York debut in the buck-dancing showdown of *In Old Kentucky,* he appeared in a film of the same name. The plot departed substantially from Dazey's original, but Robinson still got a chance to show off his moves—this time as Will Rogers's butler, cook, and stable boy. His character's name is Wash, presumably because that's what he does, dancing joyfully as he cleans up the kitchen. He also taps while making biscuits and setting the table, plunking the silver-ware down in a percussion that compliments his feet. Perhaps he is so bored that he needs to dance: riffing on the rhythms of work and teasing them into art lets him exercise a talent that servitude constrains.

The plot of *In Old Kentucky*, however, suggests no such critique. Robinson's character seems happy and contented, and when the Rogers character asks him for lessons, he tries to oblige. Rogers stumbles through the simplest steps, unable to make his feet obey. All that changes, however, when he dons the blackface mask. Rogers's enemies, who want to beat him in a horse race, have had him thrown in jail, and when Robinson visits him—carrying, conveniently, some cork and a match—Rogers blacks up, and

Bill Robinson teaches Will Rogers to dance in *In Old Kentucky*, 1935 (Courtesy Photofest)

master and servant switch places. It's a strange situation: the servant, standing in for the master, is imprisoned; the master, feigning servitude, goes free.

But he is not completely free. One of the cops, who has heard about Robinson's dancing abilities, orders the blackfaced Rogers to perform. "You'll either dance or I'll put you in a cell." The scene has a tutelary edge. Rogers learns about black oppression as well as black dancing. Yet while the film raises this interpretive possibility, the scene's thrust is comical. Suddenly, Rogers knows how to dance, thanks to his identification with blackness. Even the characters' names emphasize Rogers's new skill: whereas Robinson plays "Wash," Rogers is "Steven Tapley."[39]

Rogers's imitation of Robinson was no anomaly. When the film came out, it was common for white dancers essaying tap and jazz to imagine they were black. The dynamic was an open secret, established during the days of the cakewalk craze. In a 1927 editorial in the *Mercury*, H. L. Mencken wrote that "no dance invented by white men has been danced at any genuinely high-toned shindig in America since the far-off days of the Wilson Administration; the debutantes and their mothers now revolve their hips to coon steps and coon steps only." When the *Chicago Defender* ran a photograph from *The Littlest Rebel* of Bill Robinson and Shirley Temple trucking—a swing move that involves shaking one finger in the air—the headline was "Shirley Goes Harlem." If this looks like a typo, with the "to" missing, it isn't: Shirley is "going Harlem" the way she might "go native." In other words, she is trying to become black. Anne Schley Duggan's popular 1932 manual *Tap Dance*, even included a photograph of two white dancers in blackface, captioned "Dancers should feel characteristic rhythmic movements of the American negro." Tapping like a black person, the thinking went, meant loosening up the gait, gaining a sense of rhythm, power, and syncopation—a set of associations that reveals both admiration for black artistry and condescension toward black "primitivism."[40]

Tap dance may have seemed the sole provenance of black men like Bill Robinson, its greatest practitioner, but it had decidedly motley origins. Tap synthesized Irish and African dance steps, with influences from the French, British, and Scottish. Dance historians trace it back as far as seventeenth-century Caribbean plantations, where the upright jigs of Irish indentured servants met the percussive, polyrhythmic dances of African slaves. A hundred years later, the steps had become so muddled that slaves in the American South pounding out music with their feet were said to be doing "jigs." In the nineteenth-century North, black freedmen and Irish laborers watched each other dance in marketplaces and streets, and white men under the burnt cork mask—many of them Irish—presented "authentic" black dances at minstrel shows. The minstrel show's origins were muddled too. Minstrel bands included Irish bones and tambourines alongside African American banjos; minstrel jokes combined black folklore with tall tales from the frontier; minstrel dances yoked together Irish and African, Scottish and British steps—sometimes duplicated, sometimes downplayed, sometimes torqued to grotesque extreme. And long before they entered the minstrel mix, the various steps had soaked up influences from yet other sources.[41]

Authenticity, in culture, is always a false god. But to the extent that the minstrel show and the dance form it helped birth, tap, are authentically anything, they are authentically American—born on American soil, products of American cultural clashes, fruits of American admiration for, parody of, and re-imaginings of self and others dating as far back as (or even before) America existed. All those tensions underlay the blackface mask, though not everyone recognized it as a mask. They confused the performance of blackness with the real thing, then tried to perform it themselves. Often, the performance was a tap dance.

This is what we see in the movie *Honolulu* (1939) when Eleanor Powell does Robinson's stair dance wearing a man's suit, in blackface. Like Robinson, she keeps her upper body relatively still, letting her feet steal the show. But she lacks Robinson's energy and delight—her steps are expert but constrained. The real surprise is the set: Powell's stairs pop out of the ground like trained prairie dogs, emerging right when she needs them. It's as if she is coaxing them from the ground, or willing them into existence—and in a way that is exactly what she is doing to Robinson. She conjures him up to authenticate her own tap dancing, proving that though she's a white woman, she can do all the steps associated with black masculinity.

One of Powell's most famous dance routines turns appropriation into straightforward narrative: "Fascinatin' Rhythm," from the 1941 film *Lady Be Good.* The scene opens with a remarkable performance by the African American flash act the Berry Brothers. In black top hats and tails, the trio taps with uncontainable energy. They don't confine themselves to percussive footwork: they leap over one another's heads, pitch their canes into the air and catch them mid-spin. Propelled by the music of a full swing band, they are part dancers, part acrobats, part magicians. But when they scoot offstage in understated heel-toe pivots, the music slows and fades. In comes Powell wearing a similar outfit, a top hat and a jumpsuit that looks like a tux, but hers are lighter-colored, with shiny trim.

Powell taps through a maze of moving curtains that slide open to reveal one black musician after another, each in a black suit, each playing a black piano, each smiling and nodding, as if to signal delight with her dancing. This happens six times. When the curtains move for the seventh go-round, Powell dances in front of an all-white band, in all-white suits, on a gleaming, all-white bandstand. In dancing, in costuming, in music, and in sets, white has learned from, then replaced, black.

Powell extends her arms in triumph, rushes to the center of the dance floor, and performs with a crowd of white men banging their canes on the ground like lesser versions of the Berry Brothers. And then—as if now that Powell has proved her ability to dance like a black person, she can focus on dancing like a man—the men form two facing lines and propel Powell down between them. She flops head over toes, toes over head. Supported by the men's soft, enclosing arms, her whole body is erect. Even those wariest of Freud could not miss the sexual undertones.

Powell does not black up in "Fascinatin' Rhythm," but she nonetheless authenticates her moves by associating them with black masculinity. Fred Astaire makes the same association in "Bojangles of Harlem," from the 1936 film *Swing Time*. The number opens with a surreal set of oversized lips, quickly revealed to be oversized shoes connected to oversized legs connected to Astaire, who wears white gloves and blackface. Those legs are carted offstage, leaving Astaire to dance on his own. The scholar Elizabeth Abel interprets this bizarre amputation as a symbolic castration of the supposedly hypersexual black man, though it might be nothing more than an ill-conceived set design. Castration or ineptitude, it was almost worse: an early scenario for the scene, called "Hot Fields," parodied the popular play and Hollywood musical *The Green Pastures*—a white vision of how black folk imagined the Bible—and, according to the scholar John Mueller, "involved thirty-three scenes including heaven, hell, Harlem, and an Emperor Jones Jungle" through which "the Bojangles character journeyed, mostly by climbing up, or falling down, flights of stairs."[42]

In the end, "Bojangles of Harlem" had a single set and no stairs. After the chorus girls remove the enormous legs, Astaire hops off a miniature skyline for a piece that, choreographically speaking, shows little debt to Robinson. Instead, Astaire sticks to his own style, a blending of tap, ballroom, and ballet that called for a fuller use of the body than Robinson's dancing. Mueller speculates that Astaire had the black tapper John Sublett—better known John W. Bubbles—in mind. Bubbles, an undisputed tap giant, dropped his heels closer to the floor than Robinson, and his complex, syncopated rhythms swung beyond the standard eight bars of music. Astaire certainly admired Bubbles: he said as much in a 1961 letter to the jazz historian Marshall Stearns, and according to Bubbles, Astaire once paid him four hundred dollars for a one-hour lesson. (Astaire "couldn't catch the dancing as quick as Ann Miller," who was there too, Bubbles said, "so I taught her so she could teach him to save time for them," a story that, true or not, makes the entire episode seem emasculating.)[43]

Still, it's impossible to know whom Astaire was thinking of while making "Bojangles of Harlem," and he may not have been thinking of anyone in particular. The parts of the dance that are not quintessential Astaire are in line with general conceptions of black dance and blackface minstrelsy, from the angular movements—hips off to one direction and arms raised in the other—to the flashy suit, white gloves, and even the estrangement Astaire seems to experience from his own self when, in the trick finale, his shadows take on a life of their own. But the fact remains that the number was named for Robinson. His star outshone those of other tappers. As the national face of black dance, he was the one dancers had to name-check.

According to Astaire's 1959 autobiography *Steps in Time,* Robinson's first words to him when they met in vaudeville in the 1910s were "Boy, you can dance!" If the interviews both men gave in the thirties and forties are any indication, they admired each other a great deal. Astaire called Robinson "a walking jam session" and "the greatest dancer who ever came to Hollywood." He addressed a photograph of himself—which hung on the wall of Robinson's apartment—to "the greatest dancer the world, you or I have ever seen." Jeni Legon, the first female black tapper to sign with a major movie studio, recalled that when she and Robinson were shooting *Hooray for Love* in 1935, they and Astaire and Rogers would watch one another's rehearsals and swap steps. When interviewers asked Robinson to name his favorite dancers, Astaire was consistently on the shortlist. And after seeing the "Bojangles of Harlem" routine, Robinson called Astaire to thank him.[44]

The International News Service ran a photograph of Robinson, his mouth open, one leg raised as if he could not keep still, on a telephone as he looked excitedly at photographs of Ginger Rogers and Fred Astaire. "'Bojangles' Praises Astaire," the headline read, and the caption explained that Robinson had phoned Astaire in London, where he was vacationing. "You always tell me that I'm No. 1 dancing man," the paper quoted Robinson, "but after seeing you do 'me' you're the head man, sure enough."[45]

Swapping compliments was good publicity, and though the photograph was clearly staged, Robinson's admiration for Astaire may have been sincere. But in the cadence of Robinson's quote—the missing *the* before "No. 1 dancing man" and the final "sure enough"—there are hints of the old minstrel mask. It is Robinson who must voice his gratitude to the white star, and Astaire who has the freedom of shifting identities and leading roles. The familiar stories repeat themselves: love and theft, black innovation and white assimilation. The histories of tap are as jumbled and as vexed as the nation that produced it.

Fred Astaire and Eleanor Powell's blackface routines may have been presented as tributes to Bill Robinson, but they were also ways to demonstrate a mastery of black dance, with Robinson representing that larger whole. In the twenties and thirties, this was a common trope. When white critics endeavored to define what was American about American dance, they often hit on its black roots, and in their eyes Bill Robinson embodied those roots.

A few decades earlier, the black origins of the cakewalk had given some tastemakers cause for alarm. Now, dance world leaders as different as the tango star La Argentina and the modernist pioneer Martha Graham proclaimed that the dance of America, still being formed, would owe a debt to Native American and black dance forms, whose rhythms were native to the land itself. Lincoln Kirstein, the arts impresario who brought George

Balanchine to America and helped found New York City Ballet, agreed, at least in part. "Indian dances somehow did not theatricalize easily," Kirstein wrote, but the "American stage character par excellence was the negro minstrel," a type who "look[ed] forward to tap masters like Fred Astaire, Paul Draper, and greatest of them all, the born blackface Bill Robinson." "Born blackface" is an odd phrase, collapsing performer and mask—but then, Kirstein does this throughout his abbreviated history of black influence on the stage. The white man in blackface slides into an actual man, and Bill Robinson stands in for the whole past.[46]

By the time Kirstein was making his proclamation, Robinson was the most famous black dancer in America. Consider the set designer Robert Edmond Jones's opinion, in a 1930 essay "Spirit of America," that the "typical American dance" had a "strange impetus from the dance of the Negro, from Bill Robinson, which suggests something deeper." Nearly half a century later, in a lecture on the development of an American style of dance, Agnes de Mille went through the history of tap and minstrelsy without using a single proper name until she came to Bill Robinson, whom she cited as the first great tap soloist. Even John Martin, the influential dance critic who was skeptical of the "strange notion" that "in the field of jazz dancing lay the solution of the problem of finding the real American dance," praised Robinson's genius.[47]

The 1943 movie musical *Stormy Weather* enacted a similar conflation, using Robinson's career as a stand-in for the history of black American entertainment. Robinson plays Bill Williamson (a name that links him to Bert Williams), and in the opening scene, a neighborhood kid brings him a copy of the glossy

*Theatre World* magazine. "SPECIAL EDITION," reads the cover. "CELE-BRATING THE MAGNIFICENT CONTRIBUTION OF THE COLORED RACE TO THE ENTERTAINMENT OF THE WORLD DURING THE PAST TWENTY-FIVE YEARS." Beneath these words is a picture of Robinson.

The movie's retrospective begins with a parade that the historian David Levering Lewis has called the start of the Harlem Renaissance, when the all-black 369th regiment returned from World War I victorious and marched north through Manhattan to the strains of James Reese Europe and his "Hellfighters" band. The 369th had fought in the trenches for 191 days straight, longer than any other unit in the Allied Forces, and, as members of the French army, because the United States wouldn't accept them, the entire unit won the Croix de guerre. Robinson plays a drum major, which may account for a common misperception that he himself fought in World War I with the 369th.[48] The film frequently diverges from Robinson's career, inserting Lena Horne as a love interest and skipping over Robinson's Hollywood films altogether. On one hand, this lets Robinson be a star—he never has to show subservience to white masters and mistresses, as he had to do in integrated movies. On the other, it obscures the pervasiveness of his influence, which was not confined to black entertainment. Furthermore, by turning the story of the entire "colored race" into a story of Bill Robinson, the film masks the contributions of many other influential black performers, at home and abroad.

In the early twentieth century, the choreographer Bronislava Nijinska and her brother Vaslav Nijinsky received their first dance lessons from two African American tap dancers, Jackson and Johnson, whom their parents had befriended while working at a

Russian café that hosted variety shows. "They brought a small plank to our home one day," Nijinska wrote, "spread sand on it, and taught me how to tap dance on the plank." Vaslav soon joined in. Perhaps Nijinska had Jackson and Johnson in mind when she choreographed heavy-footed, percussive works like *Les noces* (1923). Whatever the case, in the years to come, as American jazz music and dance became increasingly popular at home and abroad, European ballet choreographers followed suit. Léonide Massine's *Crescendo* (1925) included tap dancing. Nijinska had ballerinas do a cakewalk in her choreography for *Impressions de Music-hall* (1927), and she researched steps for *Le train bleu* (1925) at a nightclub. She even donned blackface to perform *Jazz* (1925). George Balanchine had begun experimenting with jazz in Russia in the twenties, and in 1926, he blacked up too, for a performance of *The Triumph of Neptune* in London. Balanchine played— prepare yourself for some irony—a character named Snowball. Cyril Beaumont wrote that Balanchine's solo was "full of subtly contrasted rhythms, strutting walks, mincing steps and surging backwards bendings of the body, borrowed from the cakewalk."[49]

Back home, American ballet and modern dancers were plumbing similar sources in an effort to define themselves against Europeans. As the dance historian Brenda Dixon Gottschild has made clear, modernists from George Balanchine to Martha Graham adopted African traditions such as dancing in bare feet, improvisation and syncopation, holding the body's weight closer to the earth than in European dance, and centering that weight in the pelvis. What Gottschild does not point out, though, is that modern choreographers often used African American forms as part of a conscious effort to Americanize concert dance. "We didn't want to be European," Ruth Page said about the landmark work she and Bentley Stone choreographed for the WPA Federal Dance Theatre in 1938, *Frankie and Johnny*. Men at the saloon where Frankie went looking for Johnny jigged cartoonishly, Frankie did a Charleston, and—in a coup de grâce that Page said made audiences in Paris boo and hiss at the profanation inflicted upon their native ballet (a story we may want to take with a grain of salt, given all the jazz that European ballets had already featured)—Johnny's pallbearers tap-danced.[50]

By the thirties and forties, tap and jazz dancing were showing up in American ballets frequently—sometimes infusing traditional ballet movements, sometimes imported wholesale. Agnes de Mille used tap dancing in *Rodeo* and *American Suite;* Lew Christensen included an acrobatic hoofer in *Filling Station;* and Balanchine used tap in "Slaughter on Tenth Avenue," a piece he choreographed for the Broadway show *On Your Toes* that eventually made it into the New York City Ballet repertoire.

Balletomanes tend to think of Balanchine as a master of the abstract who merged the high art of aristocratic Europe with American athleticism. What many people overlook, though, is where some of Balanchine's athleticism comes from: not just his general impressions of America but specific dancers, experiences, and feelings. As the dance historian Sally Banes points out, Balanchine was experimenting with black jazz dance before he even set foot on American soil. In Paris, he saw—and reportedly choreographed for—Josephine Baker, the African American dancer and nightclub star. In London, he collaborated with the African American choreographer and dancer Buddy Bradley to stage *Charles B. Cochran's 1931 Revue*. When Balanchine came to the United States in 1933, he worked on both ballet compositions and a host of pieces for the popular stage, including *On Your Toes* (1936), *Ziegfeld Follies* (1936, which featured Josephine Baker and the Nicholas Brothers, who set their own dances), and *Cabin in the Sky* (1940, in collaboration with the great Katherine Dunham). Some of Balanchine's pieces for New York City Ballet and its predecessors, too, made explicit use of jazz dance, including *Night Shadow* (1946), *Bayou* (1952), *Ragtime* (1960), *Clarinade* (1964), and *Who Cares?* (1970).[51]

Jazz dance pervades Balanchine's work in subtler ways, too. Take his masterpiece *Agon,* an abstract, narrative-less study in angles and contrasts. Race must have been on Balanchine's mind: he choreographed it for Diana Adams, who was white, and Arthur Mitchell, who was black. In 1957, when *Agon* debuted, putting an interracial couple onstage was still daring. The title of the piece means "conflict," and according to the critic Alastair Macauley, Balanchine seems to have been "especially interested in the precise juxtaposition of white and black skin tones, just where a hand held a wrist or an ankle." Edwin Denby found the piece, to a score by Stravinsky, a more successful exploration of jazz than Balanchine's later *Modern Jazz: Variants,* which featured the Modern Jazz Quartet.[52]

Arthur Mitchell had studied tap and jazz as well as ballet, and Balanchine sometimes asked him to demonstrate jazz steps for the rest of the company.[53] Working with Mitchell might have reminded Balanchine of his other experiences with black dancers such as the Nicholas Brothers, with whom he worked on Broadway in 1937, as choreographer for *Babes in Arms.* One of their signature moves was an electrifying slide into a split, from which they would lift themselves up, effortlessly and without hands, in the space of two seconds. In *Agon,* Mitchell assisted Adams in what looks like a variation of that step, holding her arms as she slid down to the floor, her legs split, and immediately hoisting her up, quick as the Nicholas Brothers, again and again and again. "Ballet is woman," Balanchine remarked—and here a black man leads a woman through a new kind of step, daring, athletic, and heart-stopping. Jazz blurs into ballet.

For those brief moments in Mitchell and Adam's pas de deux, *Agon* almost seems like a remake of Anton Dolin's *Rhapsody in Blue,* which premiered in Paris in 1928. *Rhapsody in Blue* starred a ballerina as classical music and a male dancer as jazz, competing to see who could best represent the modern era. In Dolin's scenario, jazz won. Ten years later, Balanchine used a similar theme for a Romeo and Juliet ballet in the Hollywood musical *The Goldwyn Follies,* in which differing dance styles threaten to tear the lovers apart. A corps de ballet and chorus line duel, and in the first performance Romeo and Juliet die. But there's a twist: the film stars an Everywoman who lobbies for a happy ending. In the end, the lovers get together with the blessings of their parents, promising a new union of styles.[54]

Balanchine may have been inspired by Fayard and Harold Nicholas at an unconscious level, but in *Stormy Weather,* the Nicholas Brothers pay straightforward tribute to an inspiration of their own: the movie's star, Bill Robinson. At least, that's what the set for "Jumpin' Jive" seems to promise. Robinson's modest stile has been transformed into two massive, gleaming white staircases, as if his legacy towers above all who follow. But it quickly becomes apparent that the Nicholas Brothers are more than capable of filling his shoes. Accompanied by Cab Calloway's orchestra, they are triumphant, soaring atop a grand piano and pausing masterfully before they leap into the bandstand crowded with musicians. Where Robinson laid his own rhythms atop "Old Folks at Home," modernizing the minstrel song he used as accompaniment in *Harlem Is Heaven,* the Nicholas Brothers take over this music. They throw their whole bodies into it, and they wear it, move it, power it.

They bound up the staircase and descend in a series of tricks that come quicker than description: Fayard springs up and lands on a step in a split (Bam!), Harold jumps over Fayard's head and lands, on the next step down, in a split (Bam!), Fayard slides out of the split without using his hands, as if yanked up by some invisible force, jumps over Harold's head and lands on the next step down in a split again (Bam!), Harold slides out of the split without using his hands, jumps over Fayard's head and lands on the next step down in a split once again (Bam!) and all the way down the steps, till both are back up on their toes, running, gleeful, taking their bows.

The Nicholas Brothers honor Robinson, but they also outdo him. They announce themselves as the greatest tappers of their generation with a bravura Robinson cannot rival. Robinson seems dwarfed by their acrobatics, and in one comedic scene he can't even comprehend Cab Calloway's jive. *Stormy Weather* makes Robinson begin to seem like a relic from the past.

By the late thirties, members of the black press had begun to see Bill Robinson in just that way. They accused him of debasing his own race to make white folks laugh. They lamented his dancing up and down the sidewalk, which made it easy for whites to write him off as "a grinning pickaninny dancing on the street corners for pennies." They noted that a black Kentucky principal had turned down Robinson's offer to give schoolchildren a free performance because the principal was "disgusted" by Robinson's "'Uncle Tom' antics." And when Robinson refused the title of "world's greatest tap dancer," telling a radio announcer that the honor belonged to Fred Astaire, one columnist interpreted it as a sign of Robinson's belief that "to be white is to be right."[55]

Such criticism made Robinson furious. According to Honi Coles, when the Harlem paper the *New York Age* accused Robinson of Uncle Tomming, Robinson went into a violent rage. "He called me late that evening saying 'Come on with me.' At the time *The Age* was on 135th Street between 7th and 8th Avenues, and he went down there ready to kill somebody. Luckily, nobody was there except a little frightened man running the presses, so nothing happened."[56]

Robinson's pride must have smarted under the criticism the black press heaped upon him following another piece of news: he was to appear in a big-budget Hollywood movie partnered with a white woman in blackface. Worse still, the stories said, he had chosen this partner—a Fox dancing instructor named Geneva Sawyer—himself. "Has Bojangles lost his faith in the ability of his race?" an angry fan wrote to the African American newspaper the *Plaindealer*. Columnist Porter Roberts replied that it was time to start boycotting Robinson's pictures.[57]

Ultimately, the offending scene was cut, but probably not because of promised boycotts. The film, *Café Metropole* (1937), was to open with Robinson playing himself, performing at a swanky white nightclub. The footage still exists: you can watch Robinson in the first number soloing in a top hat, white tie, and tails, tapping over the spare accompaniment of a full orchestra. The crowd smiles and claps. There's no mistaking him for Shirley Temple's butler here.[58]

But it was the second routine that raised public ire. Robinson, in a newsboy cap turned jauntily to the side with a rakish bandana at his neck, plays a member of the Parisian lowlife. Geneva Sawyer, in a puffy gypsy blouse, a tight, shimmering skirt that shows plenty of leg, and makeup that darkens her skin, is desperate for his attention. She blows smoke in his face, then lies on the ground, waving her arms, sultry and beseeching. After this tactic fails, she tries another, caressing, then biting his leg. Robinson whips out a razor and drags her across the floor by her neck. Suddenly the razor disappears, and the two are stepping happily in unison. More suddenly still, Robinson kicks Sawyer on the rump and sends her flying. Out comes the razor, and Robinson slits his own throat. A second later, he grins and wipes his neck, as if to let viewers know that it has all been fun and games.

The whole performance is a bizarre version of the Apache dance, which the ballroom dancer Maurice Mouvet introduced to America from France in the 1910s. The Apache dramatized a fight between a pimp and his whore, and it often got a lot uglier than Robinson and Sawyer's version. Pimps would twirl whores above their heads or spin them around by a wrist and an ankle. Sawyer and Robinson couldn't do any of those moves, and not just because Robinson probably lacked the upper-body strength. She was white, and he was black.

Dancing with little Shirley Temple, Robinson could not be mistaken for a white girl's love interest. But the situation with Sawyer, a grown white woman, was dicier and probably explains her makeup. It also accounts for the way the routine shifts, almost schizophrenically, from threat to comedy. Still, jokes do not change the fact that Robinson is essentially abusing a white woman on-screen. As a later news story pointed out, the dance was "more than Nordic prejudice could tolerate."[59] Nordic prejudice was not ready to tolerate Robinson's sophistication, either: both the Apache dance and his debonair solo were cut from the final version of *Café Metropole*.

Robinson found himself in difficult position: as the most acclaimed tapper in America, revered by highbrow critics as one of the forces shaping the spirit of American dance, he seemed to symbolize absolute freedom in movement. He could outdo music with the rhythms of his feet, stepping with a frenetic control that inspired a generation of jazz dancers. In solo stage appearances or all-black musicals, he was a master of his form. Yet in integrated Hollywood productions, he was reduced to playing a guest performer in a bit role—as in *Dixiana* (1930) and *Hooray for Love* (1935)—or, if his character appears throughout, as someone else's servant.

The tension between what was possible and what was allowed, between what movie plots tell us and what movement makes us feel, is central to Robinson's career, and to the history of American culture. The difficultly of conforming to expectations on one hand and moving beyond them on the other underlies all performances for popular audiences. In his best work, Robinson danced between the two poles. And that—as much as his cultural ubiquity and his undisputable talent—is why he appears to us as a quintessentially American dancer.

At a time when Jim Crow was the law of the land, Robinson seemed like a citizen of another, dreamed America: a place where a black man could earn the respect of his peers and his audiences, on both sides of the color line. In this more just nation, white baseball players and politicians and even cops respected him; white performers scrambled to learn from him and bragged about doing it; and when white racists provoked him, he could tell them off with impunity. But he was also, always, navigating the real country in a painful present: the movies put him back into a version of the minstrel mask he'd jettisoned onstage. Restaurants refused to serve him. Some of the same folks who learned his steps wore blackface to do them, as if race, not art, were central to the dancing.

Many audiences probably agreed with the white critics who attributed his artistry not to talent or work but "instinct." A 1926 article in *The Nation*, by Mary Austin, was typical. Austin argued that black art, free "from the critical oddments of the long European fumble toward cultural expression," could provide "a point of departure for new adventures" in modern art. Robinson was her case study. "The modern American artist," she wrote—and here she meant the white modern American artist—"would give one of his eyes" to access Robinson's knowledge, which came not from training or intelligence but from his closeness to primitive sources. Robinson's dancing worked to "restore, for his audience, the primal freshness of their own lost rhythmic powers," offering "a clean, short cut to areas of enjoyment long closed to us by the accumulated rubbish of the cultural route."[60]

In *Stormy Weather,* Robinson dances that stereotype to pieces. Chick Bailey, who plays Robinson's boss and his rival for Lena Horne's affections, has made Robinson and a dozen or so other men back him up in an operatic setting of Langston Hughes's poem "Danse Africane." Hughes's incantatory poem, published in *The Weary Blues* (1936), takes "The low beating of the tom-toms / The slow beating of the tom-toms" as both subject and rhythmic form, in a celebration of African American folk expression. Bailey, who is light-skinned and wears a khaki explorer's outfit, in his performance both sanitizes the poem and turns it into an account of darkest Africa. Robinson and his fellow backup performers are made to play the drums shirtless, with vaguely tribal squiggles painted on their chests. They are arrayed around the back of the stage, looking more like sets or specimens than real people.

Robinson restores their humanity. As Bailey croons downstage, Robinson climbs atop his drum and taps out syncopated riffs over the song's predictable, steady beats. Soon he's hopping from drum to drum, making them both percussion and staircase. He's rebelling against primitivism, flouting expectations, and turning what should be a demeaning performance on its head. The audience goes wild, Bailey fires him, and Horne adores him.

Robinson may have been pulling a similar prank a couple of years later when, at a Carnegie Hall program of "African Dances and Modern Rhythms," he tapped to the accompaniment of seven African drums and, reported the *New York Times,* "spoke a spurious African tongue to the delight of the crowd."[61] The festival was intended to show the link between Africa and the African American experience, but—particularly alongside more faithful representations of African performance, like the dancing of Asadata Dafora—Robinson's fake language seems to have mocked the idea of direct cultural inheritance.

"What is Africa to me?" Countee Cullen had asked in his 1925 poem "Heritage," a landmark of the Harlem Renaissance. Cullen's various answers reflected a profound ambivalence: Africa was the mother continent, the birthplace of civilization, and an object of longing. But for most black Americans, it was knowable only from afar, and even then by mediation: "Africa? a book one thumbs / Listlessly, till slumber comes." Besides, black Americans had adopted a great deal of non-African culture, including the Christianity that prompted Cullen to voice an unease with the "Quaint, outlandish heathen gods / Black men fashion out of rods."

Back in 1903, Bert Williams and George Walker's musical *In Dahomey* had explored black Americans' ambivalence toward Africa, telling the story of a syndicate hoping to colonize part of West Africa for black American expatriates. When they get to Africa, the land is not the way they imagined it, and the scheme comes to nothing. Other black musicals had similar themes: *The Star of Zanzibar*, performed by the Southern Smart Set in 1909, told the story of a black American who campaigned for colonization as a solution to American racial unease. When he gets to Africa, however, cannibals mistake him for a king, which is all that saves him from being eaten. These stories were not mere parodies of "primitive" Africa. They were also commentaries on the racial separatism that fueled early colonization efforts: in lieu of finding integration and equality at home, the thinking went, black folks could ship off for somewhere else.[62]

Such histories resonate, on a lower frequency, in Bill Robinson's performance at the 1939 New York City World's Fair Mardi Gras Swing Parade. Robinson led the procession from the Battery up Broadway, sometimes waving from his seat in a convertible and sometimes jumping down to tap-dance in the streets. When the parade reached City Hall, it turned into a full-on party, with local jitterbuggers hopping and twirling to the strains of Glen Gray's and Eddie Duchin's bands. Robinson took a solo, but it was a far cry from swing dance. In an enormous feathered and horned headdress, backed by a three-piece African band with leopard skins about their waists and spears and drums in their arms, he did a performance that—in the brief few seconds that made it to film—is markedly different from his usual style. He keeps his normally erect body low to the ground, shifting his weight quickly from one side to the other. It's an impression of primitive Africa. It is also Robinson's version of the New Orleans Zulu.[63]

Zulu is one of New Orleans's most perplexing institutions: a black social aid and pleasure club whose members, come Mardi Gras, wear feathered headdresses and grass skirts, blacken their faces, and toss painted coconuts to the crowd. In the sixties, progressive activists pressured Zulu to disband, accusing the club of perpetuating racist stereotypes. And at face value, that's a legitimate complaint, until you look at the Zulus' faces. Under that layer of black paint is another layer of bright white, a sign that instead of mocking themselves, the club's members are mocking white versions of primitive blacks. They are also mocking white versions of kingship: King Zulu is an insurgent answer to Rex, the elite white krewe of local power brokers that every year crowns a powerful old man and nubile young woman as their divine rulers.[64]

Zulu developed from a black social club known as the Tramps, which decided to swap their Bert Williams–style tattered outfits to impressions of old Africa after seeing the Smart Set's performance of *The Star of Zanzibar* in 1909. When Bill Robinson put on the Zulu headdress thirty years later, he was claiming a kingship that was simultaneously primitive and sophisticated. He imitated regular folk who were imitating performers like himself, who were, themselves, mocking whites' idea of a direct link from African primitivism to black American art.

Bill Robinson's Zulu dance at the World's Fair stands in marked contrast to his appearance in the 1930 musical *Dixiana*, an antebellum romance that climaxes with the crowning of white Mardi Gras royalty in New Orleans. His character has no relationship to the plot: he appears in the final few minutes. Just in time for Mardi Gras—and just in time for Bill Robinson—the movie switches from black and white to color.

Robinson plays a slave in worn-out clothes and an old straw hat, using a feather duster to tidy up the empty, gaudy thrones of Rex and his queen. He sits wearily on one of them, then grins, as if imagining that he is royal too. He starts tapping almost lackadaisically, keeping up a slow, jaunty rhythm, then tosses the feather duster out of sight and picks up speed. His taps are quick, tight, and clear, and he faces forward, occasionally pulling one arm up to his waist in a joke on dainty, mincing movements. The camera begins panning down, and we see that he is on a giant set of stairs—first five, then six, then twenty appear—ready to do a gargantuan version of his trademark routine. Down he goes, hearing the cheers of a crowd and grinning, imagining they are for him. But a quick cut shows that no, the noise comes from the Mardi Gras parade on its normal route. That shot puts the joke on Robinson, but there's another joke afoot, albeit not as fully formed: if Bill Robinson were doing this performance in public, everyone would indeed be cheering for him.

*Dixiana* brought Robinson to a national film audience, even if the structure of the dance works against his dreams of recognition: he starts at the top of the stairs and ends at the bottom. When Robinson first imagined the stair dance, the movement was reversed. His biographers say that the dance originated spontaneously, when at a performance at the Palace he tapped down the steps on the side of the stage to greet some friends in the audience. But Robinson explained it differently to interviewers: "I dreamed I was getting to be a knight, and I danced up to the throne, got my badge, and danced right down again." In some accounts of the story, he specified that the King and Queen of England would do the knighting.[65]

That is quite an image. At the height of Jim Crow, Robinson imagines dancing out of the country altogether and finding recognition in a new land. The idea belongs in a long line of black American Anglophilia that stretches back a hundred years, when monarchical Britain, which abolished slavery in 1833, seemed like a liberating alternative to the supposedly classless America.[66]

Bill Robinson's dream also speaks to the relationship he then held with official power. In the dream, Robinson is getting a badge, which he can carry around and produce at any moment to prove his status. In real life, Robinson carried a golden badge in a diamond-encrusted case. It was a gift from the police department naming him Special Deputy Sheriff of New York County. Robinson's affection for cops was well documented: when he arrived in a new town on tour, his first stop would be the police station, and his wife often sent the local police chief free tickets to a show. Newspapers presented these gestures as proof of his love of law enforcement, but given that Robinson frequented gambling dens and was an easy target for discrimination and racial harassment, being polite to cops was probably intended for his own safety, too. Robinson never relied on officers of the law to protect him: he also carried around a gold-plated revolver, another gift from the NYPD.[67]

In 1930, Robinson pulled out his gun while chasing a black man who had snatched a white woman's purse. A police officer assumed that Robinson was the criminal and shot him in the arm. Nine years later, when a New York cop booked Robinson for disorderly conduct for looking up at a sign for his own show in Times Square, Robinson was fed up. "Why should I move on? Why don't you chase white people?" the officer claimed Robinson said. "Whether Bill said just that is something we don't know," the Associated Negro Press reported with relish. "What we do know is that BILL SAID SOMETHING FOR ONLY LOCKJAW WOULD CONTRIVE TO SO PREVENT." Whatever transpired, the judge dismissed the charges and set the famous dancer free.[68]

The story highlights the strangeness of Robinson's condition: on the ground, he was just another black man, subject to racial harassment. But eyes trained upward saw an image that was larger than life. This Bill Robinson was big enough to talk back to cops, to stand for black striving and dignity and success, and to dream of a knighthood, imagining a nation that would recognize his genius for what it was—not primitive instinct, but a fully self-conscious art.

There's an odd moment, early in *Dixiana*, where the young white hero tells his father how much his slaves, serenading their master as they labor, love him. "You're always freeing some one of them," the son notes. "That's right," his father replies casually. "As a matter of fact, I think I'll go free a couple of those tenors right now." Nothing comes of this suggestion; it's a throwaway, the result of bad screenwriting that can't cope with America's great sin. Yet at the end of the movie, when the predictable love plot draws to a close, in comes Bill Robinson, cast as a slave, and for a few glorious minutes, while he is dancing, he seems to free himself.

He does it again in *King for a Day*, a 1934, all-black Vitaphone short in which he wins a musical in a game of craps and makes himself the star. The film culminates with the performance of *Green's Black Orchids* at the Abe Lincoln Theater, in Harlem. The performers sit onstage in a semicircle, as in a minstrel show, a few wearing blackface. There's some crooning and some comedy, but when Robinson steps out of the ranks for his solo, the tone changes.

Robinson starts riffing. He performs to a medley of songs— "Swanee River," "Old Black Joe," "There Are Smiles," and "Love's Old Sweet Song"—singing bits and pieces of their lyrics: "There are smiles that make you happy. There are smiles that make you—humph! You rascal you! Hoo!" He's not singing for the audience so much as for himself, to keep track of the music and comment on his own movements. But if this is a conversation with himself, it is meant to be overheard. Robinson points first at one foot, then at the other, to make sure viewers are paying attention.[69]

Robinson's solo in *King for a Day* is a feat of joyous, mischievous bravura. He seems to be daring himself to make the biggest impact with the smallest movements—flicking his ankle, scuffing the ball of his foot on the ground, rolling his eyes up to the folds of his eyelids. He leans his torso back, his hands crossed at his belly, everything still except for one foot clattering away at high speed. He waves his arms in a hula and grins, then turns his body into a human pogo stick, jumping straight and erect with the rhythm. When he leaves the stage, he prances off like an elastic rooster: torso thrust forward, one hand cocked at his hip, the other arm fanning forward and back. He's walking, but not the way people usually walk: every time he plants a foot down, he raises and lowers his heels a few times in an ambulatory stutter. The most basic movement of everyday life becomes cause of laughter, amazement, celebration. Onstage, the minstrel show semicircle remains, but Bill Robinson has tapped his way out.

# 3 FRED ASTAIRE AND GINGER ROGERS PICK THEMSELVES UP

When the characters played by Fred Astaire and Ginger Rogers dance together for the first time in the 1936 movie *Swing Time,* they fall in love, jump a fence, and change the course of their lives. Ginger (her name in the movie is Penny, but she and Astaire have such consistent personas in all their films together that to audiences they are always "Ginger" and "Fred") is employed as an instructor at a dance academy, and Fred—though she does not yet know it—is a professional dancer. He first pesters her out on the street, then has the gall to follow her to work, where a sign hangs outside the studio: "To know how to dance is to know how to control oneself." Inside, another promises: "Our young ladies are sweet-tempered, patient, and understanding." But when Fred signs up for a lesson with Ginger, she's livid.

According to the unwritten rules of Astaire-Rogers films, to know how to dance is to know how to cut loose and flout convention: if you're dissatisfied with the world you have, you can dance your way to a better one. As Fred's dance lesson begins he pretends to be so clumsy that he cannot execute a simple triple hop. When Ginger advises him to save his money and find another hobby, her boss fires her: it's the Depression, and the studio can't afford to give up good business. What comes next is no surprise, but that doesn't take away from the delight of seeing Fred dance to Ginger's rescue. He fires off a series of assertive taps to show the boss how much he's learned and to show Ginger that he knows what he wants and how to get it. Her eyes widen, and they're off, launching into a masterful routine as casually as most people tie their shoelaces. He leads her through the triple hops he'd pretended to have such difficulty with a few moments earlier, moving with such speed that her arms can't even find his hand and shoulder for proper ballroom comportment. Instead they float, half-forgotten, at her sides. But she and Fred quickly come together. They step arm and arm as if out for a sunny weekend stroll. They mince about like parodies of music box ballerinas. They fling their bodies off-center into noisy batteries of taps, unified in their unruliness.

As the number picks up speed for a big finish, they circle around each other inside the low fenced edges of the dance floor, then burst into a jagged explosion of limbs. He hoists her over the fence in a tour jeté, a turning leap with legs flung into a scissoring arabesque; does a tour jeté of his own to join her; then lifts her back inside the fence the same way. Together they dart across the floor with an ecstasy the room can't contain. They rush toward the opposite fence, spring over it together, and step arm and arm out of the room and out of sight. They have all the frisky energy of cowboys heading for open country.

That sense of irrepressible freedom is central to the Astaire-Rogers partnership.

Ginger Rogers and Fred Astaire in *Swing Time,* 1936 (Courtesy Photofest)

In the nine films they made for RKO, from 1933 to 1939 (their last film, *The Barkleys of Broadway,* 1949, was for MGM), they danced anywhere and anyhow they pleased. They danced on concert stages and at nightclubs, on top of tables and over couches, at a country club, on a boat, in a gazebo, wearing roller skates in the park. In his solos, Astaire dances while getting dressed, playing golf, improvising with machinery in the bowels of an ocean liner, and shuffling through sand snatched from an ashtray and scattered across the floor of a hotel hallway. Astaire and Rogers dance to show off their individuality, to riff on received rhythms, to get past disagreements, to solve problems, and to fall in love. They dance with the romance of abandon—bodies in motion, giving way to impulse—and the abandonment that comes from romance, when love makes the outside world matter so little it more or less disappears.

Their movements are not only physical. At the height of the Great Depression, when the national unemployment rate rose to a staggering 25 percent, Astaire's and Rogers's characters displayed an incredible social mobility as well. No matter how much or how little money Fred has—he's a sailor in *Follow the Fleet*, a psychoanalyst in *Carefree*—he outclasses everyone around him. Ginger, arch, brassy, and sometimes downright rude, is always chic, whether she plays a working girl or a socialite. The couple's friends include impresarios, attorneys, and women of leisure, people who charter private planes, have personal valets, go to country clubs, and summer at European resorts. Fred and Ginger are perfectly at home in these elite environments, but, as the movies remind us, they're at home everywhere else, too: hopping trains, gambling, socializing with show people and Europeans.

Fred and Ginger often make fun of the rich folks they mingle with, but they treat foreigners as even more comic. The couple spars with effeminate Italians, effeminate Latins, effeminate Brits, and conniving Russians, foils who throw their own homespun charms into relief. When they finally get together at the end of each movie, their union is more than the resolution of a love plot: it seems to stand in for the elevation of the whole country. The American couple—thanks to the American music and American dance that gets them together—triumphs.

Fred and Ginger's dance steps came from all over: gleaming ballrooms and smoky cabarets, ballet schools and vaudeville stages, Latin America and the African American South. Sometimes their movies lay these influences bare, folding them into the plot. At other times, their dancing ignores lines of race and class. When Jim Crow still held sway, and class conflict was at a new high, Astaire and Rogers seemed to head off for an altogether different territory. That may sound, to use a word commonly applied to Depression-era Hollywood, escapist, but the adjective barely gestures toward the power of the Astaire-Rogers films. Instead of giving the fractious nation a break from itself, these movies were melting pot art, yoking disparate groups together, and promising that conflict could be worked out with the smoothness of a man putting his hand on the small of a woman's back. Depending on the movie, Ginger might be fed up with Fred or convinced he's a crook. She might mistake him for a married man, be married herself, or be courted by a rival suitor. Either of them might be engaged to someone else. Time after time, they dance their way out of these conflicts, in a style heralded the world over as the best in America—and, for that matter, as the most American. When two people dance properly—which is to say, when they break the rules to come up with a new way of moving through the world, when they flout convention and create something better, freer, more rebellious, yet more suffused with love—they achieve, Astaire and Rogers seem to promise, a more perfect union.[1]

In 1934, the *Boston Globe* ran a story about Fred Astaire, a dancer, the headline noted, who was "determined to prove his democracy." In the twenties, Astaire and his older sister, Adele, had been stars of the musical stage, embodying a playful, jazz-age elegance that earned them rave reviews at home and abroad. Adele was the bigger draw, a dazzling flapper who entranced audiences with a combination of natural talent and sheer nerve. Fred partnered her unobtrusively, but behind the scenes, he was obsessive, insisting that they rehearse for hours. He created the bulk of their choreography, and she teased him for being a "Nervous Nellie." When Adele retired to marry a British nobleman (upon first meeting his extended family, she cartwheeled into the dining room), Fred had to carry on without her sprightly energy. He started on Broadway, where, in the 1932 Cole Porter musical *The Gay Divorce*, he proved himself an able lead. Soon thereafter, he headed west to conquer Hollywood.[2]

By 1934, when the *Globe*'s Hollywood correspondent Mayme Peak profiled him, Astaire had found a new partner: Ginger Rogers. They first appeared together in *Flying Down to Rio*, billed just below stars Dolores del Rio and Gene Raymond. Their partnership was successful enough for RKO to give them leading roles in *The Gay Divorcee*, an adaptation of the Broadway show. It was a hit, but fame did not go to Astaire's head. In fact, he seemed downright lackadaisical: when he met Peak for their interview, Astaire wore two sweaters, whose sleeves hung down below his suit jacket. "He reminds me," wrote Peak, "of one of those bean pole lads outgrowing his clothes. He's loose jointed and thin, with big ears. He's homely—no beauty nor sex appeal from any angle. And he's darned glad of it."[3]

Peak had intended to write her piece "from the angle of Pavlowa in Pants"—comparing Astaire to the acclaimed Russian ballerina Anna Pavlova—but Astaire nixed the idea. He was an actor, he told Peak, with lines to deliver and characters to play. Distancing himself from Pavlova was probably a good way to prove his democracy, too. Ballet was considered feminine, fancy, and foreign. Sure, Astaire and his sister had been immensely popular abroad, hobnobbing with British royalty. But when he hosted a dinner for the Prince of Wales, Astaire told Peak, he served corned beef and cabbage.[4]

Growing up in Omaha, the son of an Austrian brewer, Frederic Austerlitz—the name change came later—started dancing at the age of four. The way he tells it in his autobiography *Steps in Time,* he put on pointe shoes as a joke, to mess around while his sister went to ballet class. But within a year, their mother had taken both children to New York for a life in showbiz. For their first big routine, Adele and Fred danced up and down a giant musical wedding cake dressed as bride and groom, before scampering offstage and reappearing as a glass of champagne and a lobster. In another, the brainchild of choreographer Ned Wayburn, they played bored siblings, acting out their parents' tiffs. Fred wore a gray baseball uniform modeled on those of the New York Giants. But ballet had not been pushed entirely to the sidelines. The Astaires' first teacher in New York, Claude Alvienne, was married to a famous "toe dancer," La Neva, and the Astaires saw the Danish ballerina Adeline Genée perform in *The Soul Kiss* twenty-eight times. In photos from another early vaudeville routine, Fred wears pointe shoes again.[5]

Still, the grown-up Astaire was careful to represent his own dancing as distinct from ballet, which he described as a repressive system: "I always resented being told that I couldn't point my toe in." Soon enough, as a *Life* magazine story put it, he shifted his attention from "effete ballet" to "the manly art of tap." Astaire was an excellent tapper, but it would be wrong to say that he abandoned ballet altogether. Instead, he folded it into his own developing style. While rhythm tappers like Bill Robinson hammered out patterns at ground level, Astaire used his entire body with an elevation and fluidity that came straight from ballet. He yoked this together with ballroom, jazz, and tap to forge a style that was both ethereal and earthy, romantic and rebellious.[6]

If tap and jazz helped Astaire tie his elegance to native ground, Ginger Rogers kept him there. Like Astaire, she began her childhood in the American flatlands—not the plains of Nebraska but Missouri and Texas. And like Astaire, she traded her given name—Virginia Katherine McMath—for one that seemed both punchier and less ethnically marked. (In her case, though, less manipulation was required: "Rogers" was her stepfather's last name, and "Ginger" was a childhood nickname that stuck.) In 1925, when Rogers was fourteen, she won a Texas-wide Charleston championship. The prize was a four-week tour across the state. Those four weeks led to four years on the vaudeville circuit, initially with some backup dancers, "The Redheads," and later as a single. In one act, accompanied by Paul Ash and his band, Rogers sat in a rope swing and pumped herself back and forth across the stage. It sounds like a takeoff on Jean Honoré Fragonard's famous rococo painting, except that where that leisurely eighteenth-century miss gives her lover a glimpse up her skirts and sends one shoe flying suggestively off, Rogers, in one performance, flew off herself: the rope broke.[7]

In 1929, Rogers quit touring and headed for Broadway, where she first met Astaire. He choreographed a number for her show *Girl Crazy* and took her out on a date. Four years later, they had each moved west and were co-stars in *Flying Down to Rio*, stealing the show from the leads. RKO paired them up again for *The Gay Divorcee*, and despite Astaire's initial protests that he wanted to make it on his own, rather than as part of a team they danced together for much of the decade. Rogers was Astaire's best partner. She lacked the technical proficiency of Cyd Charisse or Leslie Caron, both of whom danced with Astaire in later films, but she had something they didn't: a down-to-earth brashness. Rogers is cheeky, testy, and seemingly steel-willed. But in Astaire's arms, she turns molten.

Off-screen, there was another key to their success: Hermes Pan. Pan, a soft-spoken Tennessean who became friends with Rogers while dancing in the choruses of a few New York shows, had been hired as the assistant dance director for *Flying Down to Rio*. By the time all three worked together on *The Gay Divorcee*, they had set their working pattern. Astaire and Pan would spend weeks behind closed doors, often for twelve hours a day, with Pan playing Rogers's part. Then, when Rogers was ready to rehearse, Pan would teach her the steps, dancing Astaire's part. Finally, Astaire and Rogers would rehearse and film their scenes together. In postproduction, Pan would dub Rogers's taps.[8]

Pan and Astaire had an enormous amount of creative control, especially over how the dancers were shot, but they never acted as the films' directors. Viewers can catch a glimpse of how their ideas about filming dance butted up against the mainstream in the production of the Continental, the most hyped dance sequence in *The Gay Divorcee*. It comes near the end of the movie, when Fred and Ginger break out of a European hotel room and make a run for the dance floor. They are escaping from a fey Italian whom Ginger's lawyer has hired to act as her lover in the hope that when her boorish husband appears and catches her in a negligée with a concertina-playing Lothario, he'll grant her a divorce. Now that she has fallen in love with Fred, she is more anxious for that divorce than ever. But she also wants to feel his arms around her, and embraces in a hotel room while she's still married to someone else would be improper. So they dupe their jailer by replacing themselves with backlit paper dolls and, all flesh and blood, rush downstairs to join a well-heeled crowd doing the Continental.

The Continental, a modified foxtrot with alternating fast and slow speeds, has, as its lyrics explain, a key defining feature: "You kiss while you're dancing." Fred and Ginger, however, ignore that instruction, though at one point Fred does give her a quick peck on the hand. Instead, they redirect their desire into dance. They do some tour jetés, and at one point Fred claps his hands off to the side while Ginger saunters around him in a playful impression of Spanish flamenco. A second later, they're both tap-dancing, combining continental dance with homegrown American movements.

The other dancers at the hotel move aside to gawk admiringly. But the two are so wrapped up in the pleasure of being together that they don't even notice that they are alone on the dance floor—at least, not until, after the music stops and Fred winds Ginger into his arms, the rest of the dancers begin to cheer.

Surprised and bashful, the pair flee up a wide set of stairs. Instead of making an easy exit, they are nearly plowed over by an oncoming army of couples in outlandish costumes—each girl wears a four puffy fur armbands and resembles something from a Dr. Seuss book—streaming through five revolving doors. The doors signal the beginning of an orderly but dizzying modernism, in which individuals are whirled around and spit out into straight lines. It's the inverse of Fred and Ginger's closing move, when he spins her into his arms for a moment of intimacy. Faced with this impersonal mass, the two scamper fearfully off to the side, and the chorus commences a dreary routine.

It wasn't supposed to be dreary. The original chorus experience had been so romantic, according to one newspaper story, that during three weeks of filming, "seven young couples who were engaged for the musical numbers" got engaged to be married.[9] The movie trailer had promised "half the beauties in Hollywood." Close-ups of grinning chorus girls pressed inside revolving doors like goods in a department-store display case mimicked Busby Berkeley's kaleidoscopic commodifications of bodies in movies like *Gold Diggers of 1933*. But the directors lacked Berkeley's fluid camerawork, and every few seconds would cut to another giant formation, as lines of dancers pivoted around a central point, or one woman after the next dove into her partner's arms. Unlike Fred and Ginger, these couples do kiss while they're dancing. But there's nothing romantic about dozens of kisses at once: this is an assembly-line version of love. The whole scene leaves viewers pining for Astaire and Rogers, who move as individuals, telling their own story with their own steps.

Finally, after seven long minutes of watching dancers who aren't Fred and Ginger, we get to see them again. They dance up and down the stairs, ballroom Bill Robinsons who mix tango and waltz with their taps. But their closing moves are more hectic sport than polite dance: they sprint up the steps two by two and, without a bow or sign of good-bye, flee through a revolving door. The camera lingers long enough to show them on the other side, still running. Modernity has not sapped the spunk from these two.

The Continental sequence could be a fable for the way Fred Astaire helped change movie musicals. He didn't just flee from the mechanized spectacle of the Continental's chorus—he fled from the conventions of Busby Berkeley, bringing a new sense of bodily freedom to Hollywood. "Either the camera will dance, or I will," he said soon after getting to Hollywood, and he already knew which one he'd choose. Unlike Berkeley, Astaire had his dances filmed continuously to showcase his incredible talent. There were no zooms from on high, few cuts, and scant close-ups, which would have cut the dancer into pieces like a poetic blason, effectively dissecting the same body the poet—or cameraman—wants to praise. Many of these cuts interrupt the group sequences in the Continental, but Astaire and Rogers redirect attention onto their entire bodies, flung into action with emotional and narrative power.[10]

These days, critics and fans tend to agree that "Night and Day" is The Gay Divorcee's masterpiece. "Night and Day" certainly has better choreography, with more tenderness and more dramatic tension—it's the dance that makes Ginger fall in love with Fred and that, by extension, makes women long to be Ginger. But "The Continental" shows us a different aspect of the team's appeal: the way they encapsulated audiences' desires to move with individuality, poise, freedom, and pleasure. Modern times got you down? Feel like just another member of the masses? Well, take a cue from these two, the Continental seems to say, because they've figured out how to transcend that machine-age monotony. If you step lightly, you might too.

RKO worked hard to foster that sense of audience identification, encouraging Americans to imitate their screen idols. *The Gay Divorcee*'s dance director, Dave Gould, predicted that the Continental would become "an overnight ballroom sensation among nonprofessional dancers." In the weeks surrounding the movie's release, RKO promoted it as a New Dance Sensation.[11]

The New Dance Sensation was an old Broadway staple. For more than twenty years, showmen had been promising to guide audiences through the latest crazes, in lyrics that typically provided such minimal instruction that the effort to spread particular steps often seemed rather half-hearted. For every Black Bottom—a craze that actually took—there were quite a few Edinboro Wriggles and Boulevard Glides. But RKO seemed to be promoting the Continental more seriously. The studio provided newspapers across the country with a series of eight photographs to demonstrate the basic moves. Some film screenings even featured live Continental demonstrations by local dancers, and instructors, ready to meet the demands of eager pupils, took note.[12]

The Continental was not the only dance sensation RKO hoped Astaire and Rogers would ignite. *Flying Down to Rio* promoted the Carioca, *Top Hat* pushed the Piccolino, and *Carefree* introduced the

Yam. Unlike most of the numbers in Astaire-Rogers movies, these would-be crazes never affect the plot. "Cheek to Cheek" exists because Fred needs to woo Ginger, who mistakenly believes he's an adulterous jerk. "Isn't This a Lovely Day to Be Caught in the Rain" enables Fred to realize that, even though he still has a fiancée back home, it's Ginger he truly loves. But in the named dances, Astaire and Rogers tried to popularize new steps, showing audiences what they, too, might do, or how they, too, might feel, as they reel around together with what the critic Arlene Croce calls a "democratic right to elegance." Some members of the Dancing Masters of America complained to RKO that Astaire and Rogers were performing routines that, though they did help popularize ballroom dancing, were "too elaborate" for "the dancing public" to learn. No matter. Astaire and Rogers were not really selling the dances. They were selling a dream.[13]

They were also conforming to a familiar role: ballroom dance teams at cabaret acts. Cabarets had started to pop up in American cities in the 1910s as entertainments that combined eating, drinking, and dancing. This may not sound like a revolutionary business model today, but when the Folies Bergère cabaret opened in New York in 1911, a reporter from the *New York Times* called it "an experiment," and felt it necessary to explain, at some length, that patrons sat on movable chairs at movable tables. Each table at the Folies Bergère also boasted a red button that diners could press to summon a waiter. Customers joked that they were sending "distress signals": sometimes, you really need a drink.[14]

Some cabarets featured elaborate choreographed floor shows, with chorus girls trotting out from backstage. A resident ballroom team, on the other hand, typically remained visible throughout the evening, sitting at a table like the other customers. At an appointed time, the couple would rise up and take to the floor, fancifying the latest dances with their own skillful flourishes. Even though audiences knew this was a choreographed performance, it gave the illusion of spontaneity. When the team finished, audience members could leave their tables, find space on the floor, and start moving. They might not dance as well as the professionals, but they could participate, and they could add their own improvisations. Now they, too, were performers, entertaining the guests who still lingered at their tables, sipping champagne.[15]

Film footage from the period shows Vernon and Irene Castle, the most famous dancers of their day, following—and, given their massive influence, helping to set—this pattern. They get up from a small table and twirl across a cramped floor. At first none of the guests pays them much mind, but by the time Vernon begins to support Irene in a series of graceful dips, her torso bending rapturously back, heads are turning. The couple pivots to face the same direction, Vernon's arms around Irene, stooping to press his cheek against hers as they bob from side to side, their feet continually moving them across the floor. Like Fred and Ginger, they're both partners and lovers. Soon Vernon faces Irene once more, hoisting her up on his hip as she kicks one leg up at the knee, again and again. When they turn to go back to their seats, the other patrons raise their glasses and applaud, demanding at least a bow. Once that formality is out of the way, the Castles sit down again, just another couple out for a night on the town.

The Castles, a married couple, were emblems of respectability, but cabarets reputedly held illicit appeal. At the turn of the twentieth century, upper- and middle-class social dancers tended

Vernon and Irene Castle, ca. 1914 (Library of Congress)

to twirl through spacious, formal ballrooms, dutifully partnering whoever had signed in the appropriate space on their dance cards. Such changing of partners left little time for romance to develop, although T. A. Faulkner's panicky *From the Ball-room to Hell* (1894) warned against the "rapture of sin in its intensity," when a woman's "body thrills with the amorous contact" on the dance floor. At cabarets, on the other hand, no one bothered with dance cards. If you wanted, you could have the same partner all night, and you could hold each other as closely as you liked. The popular ragtime dances sweeping the nation in the teens allowed for more physical contact than the waltzes and polkas of old.[16]

Ragtime dances had evolved from the cakewalk's high struts to a spate of quick two-steps. While it had at least some origins in the rural South, ragtime was a decidedly urban form, popularized on theatrical stages and spread in public dance halls. Most contemporary observers traced ragtime dances to San Francisco's Barbary Coast, a seedy string of saloons and dance halls that catered to both denizens of the underworld and thrill-seeking slummers. It was common for even distinguished visitors to San Francisco to take guided tours of the Barbary Coast—located more or less in today's Tenderloin—and some clubs reserved seats for curious, tittering tourists.[17]

At the Thalia, one of San Francisco's biggest dance halls, tourists watched from a balcony while the working classes lived it up below. Scantily clad women performed back-bending Salomé dances, asked male customers to buy them drinks (sometimes soliciting other activities in back rooms and brothels), and paired up with customers for ragtime dances so vigorous and salacious even their names were bestial: the turkey trot, the bunny hug, the grizzly bear. Partners clasped each other close and bounced about to ragged rhythms, but some of the steps could be playful. In the turkey trot, dancers kicked up their heels at rapid speed. In the bunny hug, they touched cheeks while keeping their lower bodies apart, sometimes sticking out their rumps as far as they could. In the grizzly bear, they raised their arms like fearsome beasts, then cuddled back up.[18]

Soon, the well-heeled observers at the dance clubs would start doing the same steps on their own turf, for ragtime was traveling east with the ferocity of empire. At least, that's the way some reformers saw it: anyone could be a victim. The urge to dance struck all classes and races, leading them out of their mansions, their apartments, and their crowded tenement ghettos and into the clubs. Doing the same steps together, writes the historian David Nasaw, gave people the sense that "they were part of a larger social whole, a new public of pleasure seekers that cut across all social divisions." Such populist rosiness did not last, nor was it ever entirely rosy: with the exception of a few "black-and-tan" clubs, dance halls were strictly segregated. But the music and the steps spread across lines of class and race, sometimes in ugly parodies. One ragtime dance was called "The Nigger."[19]

The rampant cultural miscegenation and sexual energy had the old folks—and some young folks, for that matter—alarmed. The battle over popular dances reflected a fear that rigid cultural hierarchies of class and race were dissolving. The former president of the medical school at the University of Missouri asserted that one-tenth of the insane population in the country "have lost their minds on account of troubles which may commonly be traced to modern"—which is to say, ragtime—"dances." Dancing seemed particularly dangerous for women, since it could lead them to move with such abandon that they would be taken advantage of, or even start working as prostitutes in dance halls. In the 1935 movie *Top Hat,* Astaire and Rogers celebrated the pleasures of dancing cheek to cheek, but in the early twenties, the stance caused considerable alarm. "Should cheek-to-cheek dancers at a public dance hall be hurled into the street or told to ease the 'strangle-hold' stuff?" asked the *Los Angeles Times* in 1921 story about the Moonlight Dance Hall. A 1922 study by the Hartford Council of Women's Clubs found "our better class, our educated class, our moneyed class" were more likely to dance "cheek to cheek" at private parties than were less lofty individuals in regulated, public spaces. For the American Society of Teachers of Dancing, class was not the issue: every year, as one journalist summarized it, they wishfully decreed "the end of the cheek to cheek, and knee to knee wobbling."[20]

Authorities of all kinds seemed to agree: at the height of the ragtime craze, they cracked down. According to one historian, fifteen female employees were fired from their job at a Philadelphia publishing company "for dancing the turkey trot during the lunch break." Another woman was charged with disturbing the peace for doing the turkey trot on the sidewalk while singing "Everybody's Doing It." She was found not guilty, perhaps because she explained to the jury that the pop hit was so catchy, she couldn't stop herself from singing and dancing. Ragtime, like the jazz music and dance it spawned, was infectious. In his brilliantly satiric novel *Mumbo Jumbo,* Ishmael Reed portrays it as a national epidemic that whites, anxious about cultural miscegenation, try desperately to halt.[21]

Reformers also went after the institutions where ragtime flourished. In 1911, Louis Martin, owner of the eponymous New York City cabaret, was taken to court for giving public entertainment without a license. The policeman who brought charges against Martin refused to tell reporters "what he thought of the performance," but apparently he had seen the ubiquitous turkey trot as well as a fiery French routine titled, appropriately, "la danse des detectives." The judge dropped the charges, but two years later, New York City made a new attempt to put the brakes on the cabaret craze, requiring cabarets to close by 2:00 A.M. Businessmen dodged the authorities by opening "private clubs" that could stay open all night. Indeed, as Nasaw points out, it was impossible, economically or tactically, "to police the dance floors properly. . . . How many inspectors would it have taken to police the 49 dance halls in Kansas City and watch over the shoulders of 16,500 dancers, 80 percent of them under 25 years old, who patronized them weekly? Or to supervise the 12,000 to 13,000 dancers who spent Saturday nights in Milwaukee's dance halls and academies?" In cities like New York and San Francisco, those numbers must have been even more staggering.[22]

The numbers arrayed against them did not stop one band of New York City policemen from launching a sting operation that could have come straight from the movies: the "Tango Cops." According to the *New York Herald Tribune*, this band of terpsichorean toughs originated when the police commissioner chewed out his troops for not managing to bring more charges against those pesky cabarets. "Why did you fail?" he demanded. "The man who had not been struck dumb by the glare of the deputy's eye managed to say, 'It is, it is. . . . Well, none of the girls will dance with us.'" Unless the cops knew the latest steps, they couldn't head out on the dance floor with the whores who, presumably, would eventually proposition them. So the commissioner had the policemen take lessons. They soon cracked open a prostitution ring.[23]

The *Herald Tribune* did not quote any cops who admitted to enjoying their work at the cabaret, but the subtext was clear: even law enforcement was getting sucked into the dance craze. The combination of these two worlds, regulation and pleasure, has had perennial appeal. In 1927, Vitaphone released *The Night Court*, a short soundie about performers brought in on a variety of charges, including "murdering the Black Bottom," the racy, rump-shaking jazz dance. A judge orders them to re-create their routines, and ends up so impressed that instead of sending them to jail, he requests a reservation for the floor show. The association between public dancing and criminality also cropped up in a 1934 ballet choreographed by Ruth Page in Chicago. *Hear Ye, Hear Ye* brought jazz dance into the courtroom, this time to re-enact a murder as various witnesses gave their own versions of what they had seen at a nightclub; they included chorus girls, a dance team, and a black waiter.[24]

Vernon and Irene Castle set out to change the perception that cabarets were havens of sin. They helped sanitize social dancing, publicly rejecting the bunny hug, turkey trot, and other ragtime animal crazes. As their manager Elisabeth Marbury explained in their dance-instruction manual *Modern Dancing*, the pair's style "eliminates all hoppings, all contortions of the body, all flouncing of the elbows, all twisting of the arms, and above everything else, all fantastic dips," in which women, supported by their partners, leaned back into a sensuous arc, displaying their bosoms and no doubt rapturous faces.[25] Never mind that Irene did plenty of fantastic dips herself: in rhetoric, at least, these two were graceful, dignified, and married—a symbol not of lusty energy but of lasting, institutionalized romance.

For a few years, the Castles were everywhere. After making their names as cabaret dancers in Paris, they returned to America, where they performed in Broadway shows, as paid entertainers at high society parties, on vaudeville stages across the country, and in a slew of clubs and cabarets, transforming dance floors into spaces of aspiration. (Their fans weren't restricted to the upper classes: the would-be partners of the New York City Tango Cops demanded "the Castle stuff" too.)[26] The Castles taught America the syncopated Hesitation Waltz, the cleaned-up Latin maxixe, and their own wholesome Castle Walk. The rhythms were ragtime, but their posture was straighter, and the racy names were gone. More important, they showed that dance could be a civilizing force. The name "Castle" itself seemed tailor-made for the kind of dance royalty they had become. But above all, it was their movement that made them seem aristocratic. They invented themselves through dance.

By most accounts, Vernon was the better dancer, but Irene was sprightly and appealing, following her husband with one jaunty shoulder a bit higher than the other—a stance Ginger Rogers picked up a decade and a half later. Irene was also a fashion icon, inspiring thousands of American women to shed their flashy jewels and heavy dresses in favor of simpler, dance-friendly styles, to don headbands and little lace caps, and, most daring, to bob their hair. She and Vernon endorsed a small empire of merchandise, including Castle bands (to keep the wispy bobs in place while dancing), Castle cigars, Castle shoes, and Castle hats. Irene even promoted a Castle corset in the pages of their dance-instruction manual. *Modern Dancing* included a list of "suggestions for correct dancing," chief among them: "Drop the Turkey Trot, the Grizzly Bear, the Bunny Hug, etc. These dances are ugly, ungraceful, and out of fashion." The couple also noted that for "freedom of movement," a man should not grip his partner too tightly: "His arms should encircle her lightly, and he should barely rest his hand against her back, touching her only with his finger-tips and wrist." Dancing, the Castles maintained, need not be illicit. In fact, wrote their manager Elisabeth Marbury, American youth would be better off going to a supervised dance hall like the Castle House than "reading with avidity the latest erotic novel or story" or encountering unnamed horrors in "the darkness of a sensational moving picture show."[27]

Not even the Castles were everything an anti-dance crusader might have hoped for: the Castles lent their name and their presence to both Castles in the Air, a rooftop café open until 2:00 A.M., and the Castle Club, which stayed open until dawn in the basement of the same building. They also opened a basement cabaret in Times Square, the Sans Souci, and frequently appeared at Castles by the Sea, overlooking the Coney Island shore at Luna Park. But their most successful venture was also their most dignified: the Castle House, home to afternoon *thés dansants*. For a few dollars and the approval of whoever was taking admission, customers could mingle with high-society patronesses like Mrs. Stuyvesant Fish, Mrs. W. G. Rockefeller, and Mrs. T. J. Oakley Rhinelander. Between servings of éclairs, lemonade, tea, and cake, guests practiced their steps, getting lessons from the Castles' staff or—if they were lucky—from Vernon and Irene themselves.[28]

The Castles were having it both ways. They based their dances on the same syncopated animal crazes they spoke out against. And they refined their art not just by studying ragtime but also by turning to black artists for help. Vernon improved his sense of rhythm through music lessons from the African American drummer Buddy Gilmore. According to W. C. Handy, the black bandleader James Reese Europe—who took the Castles to Harlem nightspots where they could pick up new dance moves—was the real inventor of Vernon and Irene's famous Castle Walk. Europe's band toured with the couple and had a steady gig at Castle House. (Years later, Irene spoke publicly about the Castles' debt to black dance, when she appeared as part of a massive 1934 Chicago pageant on black history, *O, Sing a New Song,* and presented the dances that—as one black paper put it—she and Vernon "made popular." Bill Robinson was also on the program, doing his stair dance.)[29]

The architecture at the Castle House played up the divide between black and white, with two long staircases, one leading to each realm. Up one set of stairs was the masterful band of James Reese Europe, who, a few years later, accompanied the all-black 369th Regiment to France, helped buoy the spirits of World War I soldiers with music, and became a hero for black America. Up the other set of stairs reigned white pianist Henry Lodge, composer of the turkey trot spin-off "Oh! You Turkey!"[30]

World War I ended Europe's time with the Castles, and Vernon's life: he became a pilot for the Royal Flying Corps, won a

Croix de guerre for his missions on the western front, and died during a training exercise in Texas. Widowed, Irene looked for new ways to keep her career afloat. Could she succeed as a solo performer? She called on one of America's other favorite dancing duos for help: Adele Astaire and her little brother, Fred.[31]

When the Astaires were coming of age, they looked up to the Castles as models of sophistication, watching the couple in their musical *The Sunshine Girl* nine times. Their careers had more in common than dance steps alone. Neither Vernon nor Irene had had a privileged childhood, but they danced their way into a higher social milieu. Fred and Adele followed a similar trajectory, working their way from a vaudeville kiddie act to emblems of sophisticated, carefree movement. They even had a brief stint as cabaret dancers, at the Trocadero nightclub in New York. In a bit of inadvertent symbolism, the Astaires made their Broadway debut—in the 1917 show *Over the Top*—at the very theater that had replaced Castles in the Air. The producer Charles Dillingham, who had hired the Castles for the 1914 hit musical *Watch Your Step*, took the Astaires under his wing. He cast them in a series of operettas, meant to outclass ragtime, and introduced them to an elite crowd offstage as well.[32]

Still, audiences loved the Astaires in part because they looked like they were having fun when they danced. Their standout performance, which tended to stop the show, in the musical *The Love Letter* was the Oompah Trot, in which they scampered around the stage in a circle. Performing in London, they seemed to stand—as Kathleen Riley makes clear in *The Astaires*—for America itself, with its perceived freedom, speed, and jazz rhythms. And as Fred Astaire pointed out to the British press, those rhythms were distinctively black.[33]

After Adele Astaire retired from the stage, Fred Astaire became the closest thing America has to royalty: a Hollywood star. No films survive to document his dancing with his sister, which helps explain why she has been eclipsed in popular memory by Ginger Rogers. But it also seems that Astaire blossomed as a dancer and a choreographer in Hollywood, stepping out from his sister's shadow and coming into his own. A story Fred Astaire fans love to tell concerns the anonymous schmuck who wrote the notorious memo to the producer David O. Selznick after Astaire's first screen test: "Can't act. Slightly bald. Also dances."[34] No one seems to have cared, though: Astaire was quickly cast in leading roles. Teamed with Ginger Rogers, he became part of a duo that not only obscured the work he had done with his sister but also surpassed their early idols, Vernon and Irene Castle.

Like the Castles, Astaire and Rogers brought a new level of sophistication to social dance, making a form of public amusement seem glamorous. RKO linked the two dance teams firmly in the public imagination in 1939, when they cast Astaire and Rogers as leads in *The Story of Vernon and Irene Castle*, the last film the two made for the studio during their glorious run. But the resemblances had been on display since their first appearance together.

Astaire and Rogers performed in a vastly different era from that of the Castles, or even that of Fred and Adele Astaire. In the years after the stock market crashed, the country teetered on the edge of economic collapse. Jazz rhythms still propelled popular dance, but the wild abandon associated, appropriately or not, with the Jazz Age was long gone. The Astaire-Rogers films sought to recapture that earlier, imagined innocence. To dance like Astaire and Rogers did not mean simply to move with elegance and rhythm. It was also to ascend to an entirely different world, part glittering past and part longed-for future—prosperous, secure, and loving.[35]

But as those dancing masters pointed out when they complained about the difficulty of performing the Continental, dancing like Fred Astaire and Ginger Rogers was no easy feat. So perhaps it's no surprise that, RKO's publicity efforts aside, only one of their named dances ever caught on, the Carioca. The Carioca—which the pair "discovers" in *Flying Down to Rio*—is basically a samba with the added gimmick, courtesy of Hermes Pan, that the partners touch foreheads as they dance. Although dancers had long been pressing their heads—and for that matter, their torsos and their legs—together in sultry versions of Latin ballroom dances like the samba and the maxixe, in Pan's rendition, touching foreheads could be as goofily flirtatious as the orange-passing relays teenage summer campers use as an excuse to nuzzle one another in public. At the same time, the dance has the charge of foreign novelty. And unlike the ballroom steps the Castles popularized that often concealed their debt to black and working-class cultures, the Carioca plays up that debt.

Fred and Ginger learn about the Carioca at a cabaret, where they watch a crowd of well-dressed Brazilians touching foreheads on the dance floor. Like a good exhibition ballroom team, the couple rises from their table to perform their own version, complete with American tap breaks. The audience claps enthusiastically, showing their approval of this adaptation. Then the floor show begins: two white singers in evening gowns sing the Carioca from balconies, while a chorus of white couples in trussed-up traditional dress dance it on the floor. They do some sexy hip swivels and embrace closely, but for much of the time they grin, as if the Carioca were the most wholesome dance in the world. Then the camera suddenly pans left, deserting the dancers, and everything changes.

The African American singer Etta Moten saunters out in front of some tropical plants, wearing oversized jewelry and a basket of fruit on her head. Her costume marks her as lower class, and unlike the singers in the balcony, she's down on the ground—as if to emphasize her earthiness. In *Gold Diggers of 1933,* Moten has a cameo as the token black woman in the "Forgotten Man" number, where she served as the emotional conscience of the Depression, belting out lyrics with more feeling than the movie's peppy white stars can muster. Here she fulfills a similar function, playing a native informant showing the audience the heart and soul of the Carioca. After a few verses, the camera cuts to a chorus of black dancers, who combine Latin rhythms and forehead fondles with moves straight from black America: they truck, Charleston, wiggle their heads, and open their eyes so wide one would be forgiven for the uncomfortable feeling that they're a crew of up-tempo Stepin Fetchits. Still, these dancers are talented movers, pulling off harder and more interesting steps than their light-skinned counterparts. They've got more individuality, too: one couple takes a lengthy solo, something that their mechanized white predecessors never had a chance to do.[36]

Black Americans embraced the Carioca, or the " 'tete-a-tete' tango," with enthusiasm and pride. Even though RKO publicity materials called Astaire and Rogers the "King and Queen of 'Carioca,'" the black press focused on Etta Moten, the "Carioca girl," who was feted, at a live performance in 1934, with both a gala reception and an honorary brunch. According to one black newspaper, "Since the showing of 'Flying Down to Rio,' which featured, *so far as we are concerned,* Etta Moten singing the 'Carioca' number, dance halls, private dancing studios, frat parties, cabarets and whatnots have gone daft over the new wiggle that's not a fox trot or polka" (emphasis mine).[37] To paraphrase the old ragtime song, everyone was doing it.

Over two hundred guests showed up for the Carioca Fiesta at the Rose Bud Studio in Harlem, and the Savoy, Harlem's swankiest ballroom, hosted the National Carioca Dance Championships. The Ladies Board of Trustees at a black New York church spiced up their annual fund-raiser with a Carioca performance. Students at the Manassas High School "Holland Festival" in Memphis added the Carioca to a program that also included Spanish, English, and Dutch dances. Baltimore couples danced the Carioca at a costume ball. Carioca contests took place in Pittsburgh and Kansas City. White America caught Carioca fever too. Dance teachers learned the step at conventions and advertised it in their studios. White ballroom teams performed their own renditions at clubs and variety shows. An Atlanta menswear store advertised white tuxedo jackets as the most appropriate garb for dancing the Carioca. And in 1936, the *Boston Globe* published a recipe for a "Carioca Cake" that was so popular it reappeared in 1948 and again in 1954. Not surprisingly, it was chocolate.[38]

Hermes Pan may have come up with the Carioca's most notable gesture, but *Flying Down to Rio* takes pains to present the dance as an Afro-Brazilian creation.[39] After Moten's song and the shimmies and shakes of the black dancers, Fred and Ginger are impressed. "Kinda hot," Fred says. "Let's try a little of that, Babe." So they take the floor a second time.

Like well-to-do slummers at a Barbary Coast or Harlem club—or Eleanor Powell later imitating Bill Robinson—they have found their inspiration. For this rendition of the Carioca, the stage begins to rotate beneath them. They're surrounded by the white chorus, who suddenly seem more like set pieces then people: they barely move. In contrast to their staid trappings, Fred and Ginger are all action and ingenuity, traits that the narrative implies they learned from watching the black dancers. While they never share the screen with them, Fred and Ginger do swipe, and tone down, some of their moves. Like the sanitizing Castles, they reject the shimmy, but they stomp and wiggle more than they did the first time.

After their dance together, the camera cuts back to the black chorus, effectively folding Fred and Ginger into the Afro-Brazilian group. But the scene ends by emphasizing racial difference, not cultural blending. The white chorus crams motionlessly together on the rotating stage. Down below, the black chorus keeps dancing, with seemingly unstoppable energy that's presented spatially as closer to the earth.

The Carioca is the only scene in *Flying Down to Rio* that hints at America's internal racial divisions. The separation in that final shot continues the pattern of Jim Crow segregation that in 1933 was still law. But the film's major conflicts take place between countries, played out in the workings of a love triangle. A blond American bandleader (Gene Raymond) and a sultry Brazilian aristocrat (Dolores del Rio) fall in love, but she is engaged to another Brazilian aristocrat (Raul Roulien). After much frustration, Roulien gives up tradition and lets del Rio make her own decisions. Big surprise: she chooses the American, who hails from a land of brawny strength and freedom.

But America makes it up to Roulien, in a fashion: he benefits from the country's cultural output. Roulien is opening a swanky hotel in Rio, and he hires Raymond, Fred Astaire, Ginger Rogers, and their band in the hope that U.S. entertainers will trump the Brazilian offerings of his rivals. Alas, those rivals are in cahoots with the local government, which prohibits Roulien's hotel from having live entertainment on the premises. So the Americans come up with a daredevil workaround: they tie dozens of dancing girls to the wings of airplanes, which zoom around the hotel in a thrilling, vaguely militant display of cultural might. Americans are happy to learn black Brazilian dance moves, but when the going gets tough, the movie seems to say, white Americans win on their own inventive terms.

*Flying Down to Rio* has a throwaway plot, contrived and stagey. But the movie's predictability should give us pause: of course America wins. America came out ahead whenever it came into conflict with another country in any movie Astaire and Rogers made together. America would win, so the storylines went, because foreigners were elite, weak, corrupt, silly, and stodgy, while Americans were strong, athletic, clever, and free. America would win because Fred Astaire and Ginger Rogers danced better than everyone else. They took inspiration where they found it—from ballroom teams, from black dance, from seedy clubs and hotel lobbies—and they turned it into something the whole country could aspire to.

By the time Astaire and Rogers starred in *Shall We Dance* (1937), their seventh film together, they were such big box office draws that thousands of fans probably responded to the title's suggestion with a resounding yes. Maybe that's why RKO didn't bother with a question mark: of course the most famous dance team in America was going to dance. But the title stops short of indicating how they'll dance, or why: as an American couple, poised against—but taking cues from—their highbrow European rivals. *The Gay Divorcee, Roberta, Top Hat,* and *Swing Time* had all pitted Fred and Ginger against various foreign foils, but in *Shall We Dance,* they're up against foreign dance itself.

The movie begins with a tease: a roomful of dancers, not one of whom is Fred or Ginger. Instead, we're watching a ballet class, chandeliers twinkling above two dozen ladies in white tutus, doing turn after anemic turn. They bang their pointe-shoed toes on the ground, their arms splayed above their shoulders in awkward Vs. Their balletmasters walk back and forth waving their arms in what seems to be a wholly ineffectual gesture, like children pretending to conduct a recorded symphony. Everyone is taking him- or herself too seriously.

The camera follows a uniformed errand boy through the ballroom and out into the hall, where he draws a pencil mustache onto a portrait of the company's owner, Jeffrey Baird, played by the character actor Edward Everett Horton. Horton enters the room and catches the boy in the act, but instead of chewing out the little vandal, he gets chewed out himself. The boy rattles off some French insults to the effect that the mustache is appropriate because Horton resembles a camel, and off he goes. Horton, flustered, hasn't understood a word.

Horton is up to his old tricks, reviving the rich, bumbling man-child he played in *The Gay Divorcee* and *Top Hat*. But now he's bumbling amidst that most elite of European art forms, ballet, and though he's the owner of the company, his employees have no respect for him. After he reminds them that he's the person who pays the bills, they point him begrudgingly toward the room where the company's premier danseur, the great Petrov, is supposed to be practicing his "grand leap." Horton opens a door. Finally, a familiar sight: Fred Astaire, tap-dancing to a jazz record.

Horton is enraged. Petrov, we learn, is a regular American guy who Russified his name to succeed in ballet. This was a fairly common practice in an era when audiences tended to believe that the Russians were the greatest ballet dancers in the world, thanks largely to the sway of the various touring companies with some version of "Ballet Russe" in their title. Sergei Diaghilev's Ballets Russes lasted from 1909 until his death in 1929, and in 1932, René Blum and Colonel Wassily de Basil recruited some of its members for their new company, the Ballets Russes de Monte Carlo. In 1934, de Basil enraged Blum by renaming their troupe the Ballets Russes de Col. W. de Basil, and the two eventually split. Two years later, Blum founded the Ballets de Monte Carlo, ancestor to the Ballet Russe de Monte Carlo, which began in 1938 with the help of impresario Sergei Denham. In the meantime, de Basil continued with his own company, which he billed, in 1939, as the "Original Ballet Russe." In the forties, displaced from

Europe by the war, de Basil's company was touring primarily in South America, while Denham's performed mostly in North America, giving many Americans their first taste of ballet.

One could draw a series of Venn diagrams showing the different dancers and choreographers who appeared at different times with these companies; the dance historian Jack Anderson calls them a "species." But they all toured, and they all traded on their "foreign" glamour. The British dancers Alicia Markova and Anton Dolin, who both danced with Diaghilev's company, began life as Lillian Alice Marks and Sydney Francis Patrick Chippendall Healey-Key. When the Native American ballerina Betty Marie Tall Chief joined Denham's Ballet Russe de Monte Carlo, she was billed as Maria Tallchief. Patricia Meyers and Rosemary Doveson, who joined the de Basil company in Vancouver, became Alexandra Denisova and Natasha Sobinova; Marcel Leplat, who'd grown up in the West, became Marc Platoff. (Several years later, performing for Agnes de Mille, Leplat would adopt a name that sounded even more "American" than his own: Marc Platt.)[40]

Remaking oneself to reject one's homeland may sound pretentious, but *Shall We Dance* doesn't let viewers believe for a minute that Fred Astaire actually wants to be Russian. He's just using his showbiz smarts, the same way that, in *Roberta* (1935), Ginger dupes Parisian audiences into thinking she's a Polish countess turned jazz singer. (Astaire, recognizing her from their shared childhood in the Midwest, introduces himself as the "Marquis de Indiana.") The films' Europeans might be fooled by Ginger's theatrics or Fred's grand leap (which is not, incidentally, a real ballet step), but their audiences had the pleasure of knowing better. Besides, neither funny accents nor classical dancing hides what the plots present as Astaire and Rogers's uniquely American style of movement. In fact, their disguises merely enhance, by contrast, their Americanness. Underneath Fred's ballet, and bubbling forth in spite of Ginger's accent, are brassy, down-to-earth movements that owe more to American popular culture than to European courtly arts.

In *Roberta,* Ginger, still pretending to be a Polish countess, rehearses "I'll Be Hard to Handle," then sits down to flirt with Fred. They reminisce about their days in the American heartland, teasing each other with shtick that could have come straight from the vaudeville stage, where both Astaire and Rogers began their careers. When they dance together, they tap—first to punctuate their jokes, like a comic's "badoom-ching," then to one-up each other, and, finally, to keep things from getting mushy when they wrap their arms around each other and step in romantic unison. Every so often, their eyes meet with the conspiratorial joy of kids getting away with something they shouldn't. When the piece ends, they turn giddily around the floor and collapse onto a pair of chairs. The movie culminates with a grand Parisian fashion show, but it's "I'll Be Hard to Handle," about a couple of American kids who have made good, that audiences remember.

Tap stands for American roots in *Shall We Dance,* too: it's what makes Petrov feel like Pete Peters. But when Horton catches him in the percussive act, he rips the needle off the jazz record and proclaims, "The great Petrov doesn't dance for fun!" Fred is fed up. Bored by the classical orthodoxy, he longs to "combine the technique of ballet with the warmth and passion of this other mood"—jazz dance. He has been sneaking away from ballet rehearsals to practice tap, combining it with ballet steps like the entrechat-trois, a beating step done in the air, as the inner thighs cross and re-cross with the speed of a hummingbird's wings. This fusion charms Horton, but he cuts himself off mid-compliment: "Lovely! Beauti—I forbid that! That's not art!" Horton pushes against his impulses in a slavish attempt to follow Old Europe. Fred, on the other hand, is pining for home—and for a home-grown jazz dancer he hasn't even met. But he has visions of marrying her, so that together they can give birth to this new kind of dance, one that mingles high and low, ballet and tap, white and black styles.

*Shall We Dance* provides a love plot for the dance style everyone already recognized as Astaire's: the union of jazz, tap, ballroom, and ballet. Even though ballet serves as something of a whipping boy in the film, it is also recognized as a source of grace and bravura. But Fred uses tap to seduce Ginger—not just because it's a way of speaking her artistic language, but also because it proves his masculinity. Instead of being a hoity-toity danseur noble, he's a manly American, with assertive, noisy steps to prove it. In fact, he has three tap solos before he and Ginger dance together for the first time: two in his private studio, and a third in the bowels of the ship that carries the characters across the Atlantic. Petrov may be a ballet dancer, but he's got a funny way of showing it.

While a group of dainty ballerinas practice on deck, Fred goes below, where muscular black laborers work and play jazz. Fred sits in with the band for a verse of "Slap That Bass," then does a dynamite tap dance routine that lets him exorcise the lingering effete demons of ballet. He notices that his fingers are too stiff, and quickly loosens them up. Seconds later, his arms drift into first position, a ballet cornerstone, so he flings them to one side with an annoyed shake. There's a staircase to a balcony above, and though Fred heads toward it, he decides to skirt such civilities: he vaults up the machinery and hoists himself over the railing instead. The railing itself is threateningly similar to a barre in a ballet class, and he lands in perfect plié. The music stops, and Fred turns his attention to the machines around him: they provide the regular rhythm against which he makes his own, syncopated taps. He spins into third arabesque, one leg behind him, two arms at different heights out front, but as soon as he gets there he frowns in self-disgust and taps off in the other direction. When he finishes, the black men below cheer and applaud. Perhaps they're happy that he's taken up what the scene implies is authentic, black jazz; perhaps—like the Brazilians in *Flying Down to Rio* who clapped for Fred and Ginger's adaptation of the Carioca—they approve of his cultural cooption. Perhaps, by aligning himself with working-class black men—who, according to stereotype, are sexual powerhouses—Fred becomes manlier than pasty-white ballet princes were ever allowed to be.[41]

The next time Fred and Ginger see each other, they're both walking dogs on deck, and Astaire, having been anointed with black male sexuality, makes a move. Ginger is dismissive at first, but eventually they start spending hours together. Their courtship is similar to the one in the scene that precedes Astaire's "Bojangles of Harlem" routine in *Swing Time*. In that confluence of black masculinity, dance, and sex appeal, Ginger kisses Fred, leaving an enormous lipstick smear. It may have been red in real life, but in a black-and-white film, it's the same color as the makeup he smears across his face moments later for his "tribute" to Bill Robinson. Ginger's affections begin that transition. In the dance routine that follows, Fred, in full blackface, partners a long row of chorus girls at once.[42]

Off-screen, Astaire and Hermes Pan did turn to black sources for inspiration. Touring vaudeville in the 1910s, Fred and Adele Astaire appeared on a few of the same bills as Bill Robinson, who traded compliments, and possibly steps, with Fred. Fred also hung out in the alleys near the theaters, picking up moves from black street performers. In the twenties, Fred and Adele had lessons— and Adele, at least, had some choreographic help—from the black choreographer Buddy Bradley, who worked at a New York studio that specialized in teaching white customers popular black dance moves. ("Oh, Buddy has taught me such marvelous, new, *dirty* steps," Adele told a friend after one of her lessons.) Bradley helped choreograph a number of Broadway shows (for which he was never credited) and eventually moved to England. Today, in America, few people remember his name.[43]

Hermes Pan's first teacher is even less well-known. Growing up in Tennessee, Pan learned rhythm tap, he later recalled, "from a black boy," older than Pan, who worked for his family. The teacher's name was Sam Clark, and as a result of his influence, said Pan, "my rhythms became strictly black." John Franceschina's biography of Pan includes a photo of Clark. Handsome in a trim jacket, vest, tie, and natty derby, Clark looks at the camera with quiet dignity. He is hardly the figure conjured up in the description, in a 1935 newspaper, of "the family's house boy, Sam Clark, who inherited from racial instinct all he knew about terpsichore."[44]

According to Pan, Clark stayed abreast of the latest developments in dance. While Pan's father, Pantelis Panagiotopoulos, a Greek immigrant, was busy running a restaurant in Nashville, Clark taught young Hermes to tap, splay out his knees in the Charleston, and shake his hips in the Black Bottom. Given that Hermes's big sister Vasso was enrolled in formal dance classes, it seems likely that she might have passed on some steps to her little brother too. If so, her contribution was never acknowledged in the many interviews in which, for well over fifty years, Pan would mention his debt to Sam Clark.[45]

Pan also chalked up his sense of rhythm to his black mammy, Aunt Betty, who, one of Pan's friends said, took six-year-old Hermes "home with her one night to her apartment in the black ghetto of Nashville," where "the child was first exposed to what was called 'gut-bucket' jazz and the shuffles and foot-slapping of the local black Americans. His reaction was an exhilaration." By the time Hermes and Vasso's father died in 1923, brother and sister were dance crazy. Their mother sold the family house and restaurant and took them to New York City, to try to break into show business. Sam Clark was at the wheel of the Model T that carried them north. In Manhattan, Pan joined the crowds surging north to the Cotton Club, whose black jazz bands and elaborate floor shows catered exclusively to white audiences. He also went to a number of smaller clubs and speakeasies, both black and white, and in tandem with Vasso worked as a ballroom exhibition dancer in the model of the Castles. After a few stints in the chorus lines of Broadway musicals, the Pans decided it was time to try their luck in California. Clark—perhaps because he realized, as the Bill Robinson movie title had it, that Harlem was Heaven—opted to stay behind.[46]

One cannot help wondering whether Pan was telling the truth about the influences of these early teachers. Certainly, like all performers, he would have learned from dancers, both black and white, whom he watched and imitated. But as he made his acknowledgments, he might have been simultaneously polishing his image as an authentic insider. According to a 1935 newspaper article about Pan's childhood, not only Sam Clark and Aunt Betty but also "the gardener, the handy man, and all the dusky crew kept vocal tom toms beating rhythms." It's as if Pan's childhood was a version of the one Shirley Temple had on-screen with Bill Robinson.[47]

Still, it seems clear that Pan wanted to pay his respects to African American culture. One newspaper summarized Pan's beliefs: "Colored people are America's greatest dancers," and "an unobtrusive study of them in their home environment by one who knows and understands them will be productive of a wealth of ideas for screen presentation." Pan was planning a research trip to Beale Street, the main thoroughfare of black Memphis, as well as to nearby rural areas.[48]

Regardless of what Pan might have picked up on his trip, the choreography he and Astaire did afterward was stylistically the same as their earlier work. But if Pan's trip south bore little artistic fruit, his experiences with black vernacular dancing had narrative importance: they authenticated his creations. The story of Pan's "strictly black" rhythms puts him in a long line of white performers who claimed to have learned their trade from black performers, starting with the minstrel sensation T. D. Rice. According to an 1867 *Atlantic Monthly* article published a few years after Rice's death, he had learned to "Jump Jim Crow" from a lame black stable hand in the late 1820s. True or not, the story was retold again and again, so ubiquitous that it eventually became, as the rock critic Robert Christgau puts it, minstrelsy's "foundation myth." The story works because it confirms what everyone already suspected: white Americans learned from black Americans. But the myth has other meanings, too: in it Rice's performances become legitimate, if rebellious, transgressions. Pan's story falls into this familiar pattern, giving black performers backhanded credit, while presenting himself as an intrepid, cross-racial innovator.[49]

"Slap That Bass," the number in which Astaire sheds ballet for black jazz dance, and "Bojangles of Harlem," where he blacks up, present tap as a black cultural form, thus giving black artists some of their due—strange, uncomfortable, and stereotypical as that credit was. But in most Astaire-Rogers films, race isn't an explicit theme, and tap stands for a more general form of power and freedom, a form that denotes not blackness, but Americanness.

In *Flying Down to Rio,* tap lets Fred and Ginger Americanize the Carioca. In *Roberta,* tap lets Ginger shed her Polish disguise. In *Shall We Dance,* tap lets Fred choose American art over European elitism. And in *Top Hat,* Astaire releases a battery of taps in a stuffy British men's club, flouting their rules with his racket. The scene is an eerie echo of what happened when Dan Emmett formed New York's first minstrel band in the mid-nineteenth century. After Emmett and his band secured a gig at a Bowery theater, they stormed into the reading room of the North American Hotel and, as a local paper put it, continued their "horrible noise."[50]

While *Shall We Dance* shows the audience numerous examples of Astaire's tap prowess, Ginger remains unaware that he is capable of such manly feats until they finally dance together, more than halfway into the movie. She plans to retire from the stage to marry a boring rich guy, so her manager—eager to keep her performing—announces to a crowded nightclub audience that she and the great Petrov have agreed to dance together. It's a lie, but it would be rude for Ginger to deny it.

Fred comes vaulting onto the dance floor to a flurry of classical strings. His ballet moves mainly consist of flinging his arms beseechingly off to one side while his torso leans in the other direction, just ridiculous enough to make him seem serious and European. Ginger stands awkwardly to the side, finally deciding to do what she does best: tap-dance. After she unleashes some healthy clatters, Fred does a few more swooshy steps, lands a pirouette with a defiant stomp, and begins some clattering of his own. Ginger grins with recognition. Now he's moving in a way that she understands, and—just as important—in a way that will allow him to assume his rightful, manly position as her partner. Though they also do a few ballroom steps, tap dominates: even when Fred spins Ginger around, he keeps tapping. When the song ends, they're both sitting on a piano, swinging their legs with the kind of casual pleasure they take at the end of "I'll Be Hard to Handle" in *Roberta*—the other piece where, despite a fake foreign identity, tap lets Americans love each other without pretense. It's a mass cultural form the whole country can share.

The director of *Shall We Dance,* Mark Sandrich, wanted to hire Léonide Massine to choreograph the film's closing ballet, which comes after Fred thinks he's lost Ginger forever. Massine was a logical and experienced choice: he had choreographed for both Diaghilev's Ballets Russes and Colonel de Basil's company. But when Massine's agent told Sandrich he wanted five thousand dollars, Sandrich changed his mind, and gave he job to Harry Losee. Losee was fresh from making ice dances for Sonja Henie, and his work dazzles with empty flash. Harriet Hoctor, the guest ballerina, appears to be more of a circus stuntwoman than an artist. "People thought I was meant to be a dancer when I was a child," Hoctor once explained, "because I could take hair ribbons off with my feet." Her gimmick, painfully overused in this final scene, was that she could flutter around doing bourrées on pointe while bending over backward. Fortunately, Ginger steps into the chorus to replace Hoctor, rescue Fred from this rubbish, and confirm their love. They've managed to find each other despite misunderstandings and the efforts of a conniving foreign ballerina who wants Fred for herself—and, presumably, for European ballet. Instead, *Shall We Dance* implies, ballet will marry jazz. Despite what goes on in the bowels of ocean liners, the result will be both approachable and debonair.[51]

The ballet impresario Lincoln Kirstein, a huge Fred Astaire fan, must have been relieved. Kirstein is most famous for bringing the Russian master George Balanchine to America and helping found New York City Ballet, but he was no Edward Everett Horton, blindly dedicated to the art forms of other nations. In fact, Kirstein railed against the "Great Conspiracy" of "Russianballet," a force he found so monolithic that he strung it into one long compound word. "Can the appropriation and Russification by flattery and pigeon-holing of our best young American dancers proceed?" Kirstein wrote in his manifesto *Blast at Ballet*, published a year after *Shall We Dance* came out. He might as well have told the story of Pete Peters becoming Petrov.[52]

For too many Americans, Kirstein wrote, ballet was synonymous with "Russianballet." The problem was not simply that the various Ballets Russes companies had foreign origins, but also that those origins were royalist: the Parisian courts and the Imperial School of Russia. To hear Kirstein tell it, the fact that France no longer had a king and that Russia had become Communist made little difference. Europe had colonized American stages, and it was time to declare artistic independence. Kirstein wrote that Americans needed dance to provide a "legitimate reflection of a Democracy," showing faith in the "political or economic system [that] has the best bet in America."[53] What would this democratic American dance look like? Turns out, a lot like Fred Astaire and Ginger Rogers.

"American style," Kirstein wrote, "springs or should spring from our own training and environment," which embraces more than classical schooling. "Ours is a style bred also from basketball courts, track and swimming meets and junior proms." American style incorporates recreation, sport, fun—and, crucially for Kirstein, a sense of "direct connection, approaching personal intimacy or its theatrical equivalent," between audience and performer. The American style is "frank, open, fresh and friendly," embodied in the "behavior of movie stars like Ginger Rogers, Carole Lombard, or the late Jean Harlow." The American dancer is not a distant performer but rather, like the vaudevillian Paul

Draper, is simultaneously "artist-guest and host." That description could apply as easily to cabaret dancers, who demonstrate the dances they encourage audiences to try on their own—like Fred and Ginger in *Flying Down to Rio* or *The Gay Divorcee*. Indeed, Kirstein drops Astaire's name a paragraph after Rogers's. "The Russians keep their audience at arms' length. We almost invite ours to dance with us. Anyone of us would like to know Fred Astaire, since we have known other nice, clever, happy but unassuming boys like him."[54]

Maybe so, but none of those unassuming boys danced quite like Fred Astaire. Kirstein may have tried to claim him as typically American, but Balanchine, who recognized that Astaire was exceptional, called him "the most interesting, the most inventive, the most elegant dancer of our times." In fact, Balanchine told Kirstein that he had come to America because, as Deborah Jowitt puts it, "it was the country that had produced Ginger Rogers." In 1935, just after he was hired to work with the Metropolitan Opera, Balanchine was the subject of a *New Yorker* profile that emphasized his interest in all things American. He had recently returned from a coast-to-coast road trip that included a bizarre little performance: "In Arizona, Balanchine knotted a red handkerchief around his head, talked Russian to the Indians, and gave them the idea that he was a brave from a distant tribe." Balanchine, reported the *New Yorker,* is "an open-mouthed admirer of Fred Astaire and Ginger Rogers." Not only that, he "considers tap dancing can be used in a serious ballet, and has vague plans in the back of his head involving Fred Astaire."[55]

For decades before his death in 1983, Balanchine considered creating a three-act ballet to be titled "Birds of America." It would take place in the hazy overlaps of myth and history, with a hero who was part Johnny Appleseed, part John James Audubon, and part Buffalo Bill. In the culminating scene, the hero, having made his way west across the great continent, would marry an Indian princess in front of the Golden Gate Bridge. The wedding guests were to include Jimmy Cagney, Buster Keaton, and two dancers who seemed as archetypal as they were historically real: Fred Astaire and Ginger Rogers.[56]

For a brief period, it seemed possible that Balanchine and Astaire might work together. After all, during his first two decades in America, Balanchine did plenty of work on Broadway and in Hollywood, too. In 1941, *Life* reported that "not long ago Astaire was seriously mentioned for the post of soloist with the Metropolitan Opera ballet." It's hard to know how much credence to give the rumor: perhaps the author was thinking of the scene in *Shall We Dance*, in which the Metropolitan Opera invited the great Petrov to perform. Some years later, Balanchine tried to hire Hermes Pan to make a piece for New York City Ballet. "You represent to me the typical American choreographer," Pan recalled Balanchine telling him. Pan was game, but could not get out of his MGM contract. Missed opportunities aside, New York City Ballet's repertoire does include one piece that was meant for Astaire: Balanchine's *Slaughter on Tenth Avenue*, the jazz ballet from *On Your Toes*.[57]

Richard Rodgers and Lorenz Hart had written *On Your Toes* with Astaire in mind for the lead. The plot concerned an American hoofer, a veteran of vaudeville, who lobbies a Russian ballet company to perform a jazz ballet. Initially, the director refuses, but when his American patron threatens to pull her funding, he agrees, and the result is "Slaughter on Tenth Avenue," with the hoofer as the star.[58]

Pandro Berman, who had produced a number of Astaire and Rogers films, was interested in acquiring *On Your Toes* for RKO, but the studio said no. Rumor had it that the higher-ups could not imagine a film in which Astaire didn't have "the opportunity to appear in a high hat." So instead of going straight to Hollywood, *On Your Toes* opened on Broadway, and Balanchine did the choreography—not for Astaire, but for Ray Bolger, he of the "rubbery legs and resilient knees," as one critic put it. Bolger was a sensation, and reportedly had a personal motive to excel in his role: as a youngster at a Russian ballet studio, he had shown off some of his unique legwork and been banished from the premises.[59]

According to Hollywood scuttlebutt, the success of *On Your Toes* on Broadway prompted RKO to reconsider buying it for Fred Astaire and Ginger Rogers. Instead, they trotted out their own Russian-ballet-meets-American-jazz movie. The original title echoed *On Your Toes:* it was to be called *Watch Your Step* (incidentally, the name of a 1914 show in which the Castles appeared). Ultimately, the studio settled on a new, more inviting title: *Shall We Dance.*[60]

"Slaughter on Tenth Avenue" closes with a feat of incredible bravura. The heroic hoofer stars opposite a Russian ballerina, whose Russian lover is so irrationally jealous of her new dance partner that he hires a gangster to assassinate the hoofer in the closing moments of his performance. Fortunately, the hoofer gets wise to these plans midway through his performance. To save himself, he keeps the closing moments from happening, cueing the orchestra to play the same bars of music again and again, as he frantically comes up with new moves. This buys enough time for the cops to arrive and arrest the bad guys. It's a goofy, joyous ending, in which a little innovation—why not call it American ingenuity?—lets the popular artist come out ahead.

The hero's dance is a variation on an old vaudeville gag that Astaire and Rogers also used. In *Follow the Fleet* (1936), Astaire plays a worldly, gum-smacking sailor who used to be Ginger's partner in a dance team known, we learn from an old promotional photo, for their "High-Class Patter and GENTEEL DANCING." The caption is a dig at the aspirations of small-time dancers: these two wish they were Castles.

While Fred's on leave, he and Ginger plan a benefit show with her sister to restore their father's boat. But Ginger is anxious; when Fred's leave ends, he'll have to return to sea. "Look, let's not worry about it," he tells her. "We oughtta run through that new number." Fred knows that Ginger needs distracting. "All My Eggs in One Basket" is his attempt to cheer her up. He starts to sing about his love, but instead of wooing Ginger romantically, he tries to get her with clever wordplay. At first we can barely see how she reacts: her back is to the camera, emphasizing that she is still waiting to be pulled out of her funk. When he grabs her arm and guides her toward a low stage, her performing instincts kick in, and she starts singing too. They begin to tap, two Popeyes up on deck, their feet in rapid motion while their upper bodies stay still. Fred changes steps, but Ginger, beaming, is still stuck in the old one. She's a broken record.

That gag keeps on for the rest of the number—a comic reworking of Ginger's inability to put off her sadness. Fred claps his hands to shake Ginger out of her groove, but every time he moves on to something new, she repeats her old steps. She's stuck in them, but the melancholy has turned into a joke. Fred runs into her arm, then her whole body. Later, when they do a little ballroom turn, he drops her. They are not even able to bow in unison. It's the silliest dance the two ever do together, and it's delightful.

It's also an exaltation of vaudeville, in which Astaire and Rogers both came of age, and which featured acts as varied as comics and acrobats, trained seals, faux-Russian ballerinas, and fan dancers. In *Follow the Fleet*, as in *Shall We Dance*, Astaire and Rogers align themselves with popular American entertainers. They may have mastered the genteel dancing of the Castles, but they also had the chutzpah of old-fashioned troupers.

The ballet choreographer Lew Christensen came of age in vaudeville, too. Christensen was a star in Lincoln Kirstein's company Ballet Caravan, but he began his career in 1927, touring from one small-town theater to the next. Lew and his brothers Willam and Harold had grown up in Utah, taking dance lessons from their uncle and a visiting Italian instructor, but the pull of what Lincoln Kirstein called "Russification" was too strong to resist. In vaudeville, Lew, Willam, and their two female partners remade themselves as Russian ballet dancers, the "Berkoffs." Even when they later billed themselves as "Christensen Brothers and Company," they performed a Venetian Carnival act, complete with capes, tricornes, and women in long, feathery tutus.[61]

Foreign pretense aside, vaudeville taught the Christensen brothers to be showmen. They performed in three or four shows a day. They combined the classical ballet they had learned as children with stuntman-like leaps. They handled their female partners with the speed and strength of professional acrobats. Those early skills served them well when they left the circuit to study with Balanchine. When Kirstein hired Lew Christensen to choreograph a new piece for Ballet Caravan in 1938, Christensen returned to his showbiz roots.[62]

Christensen's *Filling Station* is a valentine to American popular culture, with sets and costumes straight from the Sunday funny papers: flat, spare, and bright. The ballet's hero, Mac, is a gas station attendant whose steps combine virtuosic classical technique with down-home jigs. He follows his sauts de basque—in which he throws one leg forward from back to front, where it quickly becomes the central axis for a high, jumping turn—with a series of looser, but no less impressive, barrel turns, his legs far apart. Mac also arm wrestles two truck drivers, joins them in acrobatic tumbling, and waits on a delightfully annoying middle-class family whose daughter, a would-be Shirley Temple, taps. Her father, explained Willam, who originated the role, was "a cross between W. C. Fields and Caspar Milquetoast," hero of the comic strip *The Timid Soul*.[63]

About halfway through the piece, a woman in a long evening gown and fur stole comes staggering in, followed by her date in a full tuxedo. They do a besotted pas de deux—Fred and Ginger after too many martinis—and when she finally manages to balance on one leg, he lifts her skirt, squats below her leg, and comes up on the other side. They pass out while standing up, slumping into each other's body in a precarious balance.[64]

Parodies of inept dancing had a long history. Even in the thirties, when vaudeville's heyday had passed, Jane Moore and Billy

Revel—the "royal jesters of the dance"—continued to keep audiences in stitches with their skillfully clumsy partnering. Their skits often used Astaire and Rogers's routines as inspiration. In 1934, hot on the heels of *Flying Down to Rio,* Moore and Revel did an impressively sloppy Carioca. A year later, after the release of *Top Hat,* they rolled out a burlesque Piccolino. "The eye of the lay spectator follows with difficulty the intricacies of most our better ballroom dancers—at best his feeling for them is one of awe," wrote one reviewer. "But in the hilarious stepping and misstepping of Jane Moore and Billy Revel he sees himself, and the 'audience identification,' which showmen hold to be so essential to the success of stage people, is made complete." Bringing the virtuosic down to earth is like denying the divine right of kings. Put another way, slapstick is the great democratizer.[65]

In *Filling Station,* Christensen was not simply burlesquing ballroom pretensions. He was also poking fun at the conventions of ballet, with its stately pas de deux; at the upper classes, with their wealth and privilege; and more generally at overseriousness of any sort. Near the end of the ballet, after a gangster shows up and robs the filling station customers, the stage goes dark, save for a few frenetic flashlight beams. When the lights come back on, the rich woman is slumped across her date's body. The truck drivers help hoist her offstage; she's on her back, arms spread out as if she's been crucified. But just before they enter the wings, she pokes up her head, winks, and waves good-bye. It's a charming little disruption Balanchine had suggested, and it gives the audience the sense of being in cahoots with the performers.[66]

Fred Astaire and Ginger Rogers make viewers believe the same thing, but without the playful undermining of surface, and without the reliance on types. Instead, they present themselves as regular Americans, ridiculing pretension, trouncing foreigners in battles both artistic and romantic, and incorporating popular forms into dances that, for all their everyday charms, seem timeless. For they also exist in a world apart, giving form to audiences' dreams. At any moment, their films promise, a night at a cabaret could become life-changing. Your future lover might whisk you away from the crowds, across a bridge, and into a gleaming white dream of a set where no one will disturb your romance.

Astaire and Rogers are better versions of us—more beautiful, more successful, more graceful, and, even when their worlds threaten to fall apart around them, more pulled together. During the height of the Depression, their poise must have brought audiences comfort. Nowhere is their world more perilous, and more gorgeous, than in the final routine from *Swing Time*, "Never Gonna Dance." After the bravura of "Pick Yourself Up," their opening number at the studio, the two have become a successful ballroom team. But when Fred's fiancée, whom he no longer loves, reenters the picture and watches him perform "Bojangles of Harlem," Ginger is heartbroken. Before Fred can break off his engagement and set things right with Ginger, she vows to marry a Latin bandleader. Things couldn't look much worse for our heroes, and their final number is the best they ever filmed.

Fred begins with a serenade for Ginger, who has already climbed halfway up a dark staircase, leaving him below: "I'll put my shoes on beautiful trees / I'll give my rhythm back to the breeze / My dinner clothes may dine where they please / For all I really want is you." He'll become a ghost of himself, he vows, having abandoned what he loves to move hollowly through the world. But not just yet. He is still wedded to the idea of "la belle, la perfectly swell romance," and Ginger can't help but head back down to him.

They begin by walking together. But already their movements are more than walking: they are reprising their entire relationship. He takes her hand, looks her in the eyes, and gently nudges her into a dance. As in "Pick Yourself Up," Ginger keeps her arms out to the side as Fred steers her by her waist. Steps from their courtship keep recurring, like events funneling through the unconscious, reborn in dream.

When they shift into the angular, solitary poses of "Bojangles of Harlem"—arms out to one side, hips cocked in the other direction—Ginger stops dancing. These were steps that Fred did when his fiancée watched from the audience, and the memory of the other woman now prompts her to walk away. But Fred yanks her back, and they begin dancing in unison, mirroring each other. They don't touch, but they don't need to. Their connection is deeper than such formalities. Fred breaks into a quick tap step followed by a tour jeté, the same turning leap with which he and Ginger threw themselves over the fence in "Pick Yourself Up." As in that opening dance, the step releases them into a freer, fuller expression of their feelings.

At the end of the scene, they meet on top of the steps for what ought to be another triumphant union, Ginger falling into Fred's arms as the music slows. Instead, Fred twirls Ginger faster and faster around, ultimately releasing her. She careens into a solitary tour jeté and runs away, leaving Fred behind.

Even if you already know that within the next nine minutes all will be resolved—the fiancée ditched, the Latin bandleader humiliated, Fred and Ginger reunited—"Never Gonna Dance" can break your heart. Not only their love is threatened; everything they stand for is threatened too. In the world Fred and Ginger create, never dancing means never telling the story of where you come from and who you are, never acting in accordance with your true feelings, never finding your proper place in the world. Never dancing might as well mean giving up on life itself.

But of course they do dance, in films we can watch over and over, films that blur the myriad vernacular styles and present them as triumphantly loving, triumphantly American, triumphantly free. In America, Fred and Ginger tell us, tap meets ballet, black meets white, rebellion meets grace, and everything dissolves and resolves into joyous union. If they can only dance together, everything will work out.

# 4 AGNES DE MILLE'S SQUARE DANCE

On October 7, 1942, a horde of westerners descended on New York City for a rodeo at Madison Square Garden. They wrestled steers, roped calves, and rode bucking broncos. Roy Rogers, the singing cowboy, led a square dance and performed in a sketch with six fetching Texan misses. Near the end of the evening, cowboys paraded through the arena costumed as American heroes: George Washington, Thomas Jefferson, Davy Crockett, Buffalo Bill, and General Custer. According to the *New York Times,* "200 cowboys stormed into the arena and then formed the letter V; the garden darkened as the American flag was unfurled on the high rafters"; the evening closed with a rousing rendition of "The Star-Spangled Banner." Mayor Fiorello La Guardia, sporting a ten-gallon hat, said he'd like to use his new silver spurs on Hitler.[1]

Just over a week later and under a mile away, New Yorkers had a chance to see another kind of rodeo. This one was at the Metropolitan Opera House on 39th Street, performed by the Ballet Russe de Monte Carlo, with an American choreographer who also danced the lead: Agnes de Mille. *Rodeo; or, The Courting at Burnt Ranch* included a square dance of its own, as well as plenty of athletic stunts: the dancers leapt about as if jostled by invisible steeds, one of which threw de Mille tumbling, with slapstick pathos, onto the floor. De Mille cast herself as the Girl, a western tomboy in search of a mate. After mooning over the Head Wrangler, who pays her no mind, she ditches her dungarees, dons a dress, and finds romance with the Champion Roper.

At the October 16 premier, the audience cheered through twenty-two curtain calls. Ballet Russe impresario Sergei Denham called the piece "ham and eggs," a repertory staple that was sure to bring in cash. During the choreographic process, de Mille, out to capture the national character, had referred to it simply as her "American Ballet." When the company went on tour to California the following month, the *San Francisco Chronicle* agreed: *Rodeo* was "as refreshing and American as Mark Twain." John Martin, who wrote about the ballet for the *New York Times,* noted that it didn't "need any waving of flags in the finale to prove its citizenship." *Rodeo* may have lacked the patriotic pomp of the real-life rodeo, but when de Mille took her curtain call on opening night, she received a red-, white-, and blue-beribboned bouquet of corn.[2]

*Rodeo* made Agnes de Mille's career. She had been gunning for a job as dance director for a new musical written by Richard Rodgers and Oscar Hammerstein II, and after they came to see *Rodeo* with their producer, they hired her to create the dances for *Oklahoma!* The show ran on Broadway for five years, and it made de Mille the best-known choreographer in the country. In the wake of its success, John Martin proclaimed a new era: the "de Millenium." By creating a vogue for ballet on Broadway, de Mille helped democratize dance. In works like *Rodeo,* she accomplished something

Agnes de Mille as the Girl in *Rodeo* (Courtesy Photofest, photograph by Maurice Seymour)

similar, bringing popular sensibilities and vernacular dance forms to balletomanes.[3]

Writing and talking about *Rodeo* in the years that followed, de Mille presented herself as a patriotic liberator, bringing American rhythms and values to the art of Old Europe. She was the cowhand breaking their wild mustangs, the Fred Astaire syncopating their grand leaps. She was by no means alone. Lincoln Kirstein had argued for a populist, American concert dance in his manifesto *Blast at Ballet*. Ballet Caravan, the company he started in 1936, was a laboratory for that vision: the repertoire included Lew Christensen's *Filling Station* and *Pocahontas* as well as Eugene Loring's *Billy the Kid* and *Yankee Clipper*. (Kirstein also urged George Balanchine to make a ballet based on *Uncle Tom's Cabin;* e. e. cummings wrote a libretto, but it never came to be.) In 1937, Catherine Littlefield had created *Barn Dance,* about a country girl taking her city beau back home, for her Philadelphia ballet company; the following year, Ruth Page and Bentley Stone used the folk song "Frankie and Johnny" as inspiration for their eponymous dance piece for the Federal Dance Theatre. Modern dancers were turning to native themes as well. Martha Graham based pieces on the poetry of Emily Dickinson and on frontier heroines, and, in *American Document,* explored American history and democracy using some of the conventions of minstrel shows. Helen Tamiris's *How Long Brethren?* was set to African American spirituals, and Sophie Maslow's *Folksay* included poems by Carl Sandburg and live performances by Earl Robinson and Woody Guthrie.[4]

Many of these efforts were part of what the historian Michael Denning calls the Cultural Front, a loose alliance of leftists and Communists intent on changing America through art. By celebrating working-class men and women, artists asserted that the masses—not the elites—should define the nation. But dances about America didn't necessarily signal Popular Front politics:

they were also just plain popular, especially during World War II. Self-consciously American dancing showed up on Broadway, in Hollywood, and on the stages of opera houses, where it seemed contemporary, relevant, and true. As a fictional ballet director explained to a young bunhead in the 1940 movie *Dance, Girl, Dance,* "Your interpretation of a bluebird was lovely. But who do you think cares? Have you never heard of telephones, factories, cafeterias?"[5]

De Mille had joined the effort to Americanize dance in 1928, when, in one of her first solos, *'49,* she played a spirited Gold Rush pioneer. By the time she made *Rodeo,* her commitment to an American idiom was fully formed. The country was at war, and her own beloved had been drafted. When de Mille and the Ballet Russe de Monte Carlo toured the nation by train, they saw carloads of soldiers leaving home. She wanted to help her audiences escape the problems of the present and to remind them of America's history, its beauty, and its strength. So she gave them a dream of the frontier, with wide-open spaces and heroic settlers, cowboys at home on the range and couples domesticating the nation.[6]

She also showed audiences movements that they recognized as their own. De Mille had studied the history of folk dancing, and in the middle of *Rodeo,* Aaron Copland's rousing score gives way to an unaccompanied square dance that might almost be an anthropological specimen. Other steps, though, had little to do with America's rural past, including ragtime hops that came straight from 1910s social dance and wide, arcing leaps inspired by tennis, de Mille's favorite sport. De Mille also drew on modern dance technique picked up from Martha Graham, on the physical comedy of Hollywood movies, and on the ebullient choruses of Broadway shows. In *Rodeo*'s closing scene, the revelers at a Saturday night dance party cavort with the energy of Lindy Hoppers at the Savoy, Harlem's most famous ballroom, and the Roper does a tap solo that charms the Girl into falling for him.

These moments of imitation and adaptation identify *Rodeo* as American ballet at a level that is deeper than plot. De Mille's stylistic mixing could be the result of living in a pluralistic society, an integration of traditions that defines America itself. But the result is more mysterious, and more meaningful, than a mere integration of traditions. For one thing, choreography does not happen organically. De Mille picked steps because they held distinct associations, which her audience picked up on, consciously or not. Square dance stood for tradition and community, while tap dance felt manly, assertive, and fun.

While dance moves spread, performed by all sorts of dancers, the dancers themselves were not always able to move as freely. When de Mille choreographed *Rodeo,* the Ballet Russe de Monte Carlo included no black dancers. Jim Crow was still law. Across the West, supposed land of freedom and open spaces, more than a hundred thousand Japanese Americans were being relocated to internment camps. Onstage, though, *Rodeo* gives us a different picture of the nation, a pastoral romance where settlers link arms and create something beautiful.

You could argue that de Mille was whitewashing the past. Presumably, the Girl and the Roper would settle down on land free for the taking, with no signs that it used to be home to indigenous peoples. While an early scenario for the ballet featured a "homesick elderly Mexican" who sympathizes with the Girl's alienation and urges her to join the party, de Mille wrote him out of the story.[7] *Rodeo* shows a West that has no ethnic minorities at all. Even steps from other sources are incorporated into a white, classical tradition.

Yet de Mille was simultaneously presenting an idealized vision of community, a nation where anyone could dance his or her way to the place he or she ought to be. Performed well, *Rodeo* is funny, tender, and, with its insistence that a group of people can come together to form a greater whole, achingly beautiful. While the rodeo at Madison Square Garden showed America's spectacular powers—its strength, pomp, and military might—the one at the Met focused on modest, homespun grace. Some of that grace was rooted in European classicism, transplanted to native soil, but it also came from vernacular American sources, their histories carried forward in movement.

Agnes de Mille caught the ballet bug when she was young, and to her parents' dismay, she never recovered. At age five, she was enchanted by the ballerina Adeline Genée in New York. When her family moved to southern California four years later, she became even more besotted. She performed for family friends (including the modern dancer Ruth St. Denis). She organized pageants of neighborhood children. She kept a scrapbook with photographs of dancers. When her parents finally allowed her to take two ballet classes a week, she supplemented them with nightly solo practice sessions in her mother's bathroom, pointing her toes on the cold tile and dreaming of becoming the next Anna Pavlova. De Mille's father, a playwright who also created scenarios for Hollywood movies, hoped Agnes would outgrow these childish aspirations, follow in his footsteps, and become a writer. He took his fourteen-year-old aside for a serious talk. "Do you honestly think, my daughter, that dancing has progressed since the time of the Greeks?" "No," she answered. "Do you think you write any better than Euripides?"[8]

It was a characteristic de Mille response: smart, stubborn, and self-assured. De Mille didn't have the typical ballerina's body—her torso was too long, her hips too wide, and her legs too short—but she was strong, and she could jump. She also had a knack for character acting, often playing up her own stocky awkwardness. In 1927, she debuted her first successful solo, *Stage Fright*. It was a backstage drama in which a ballerina—modeled after Degas's famous sculpture, in a stiff tutu with a long ponytail—struggles to keep her tights from sagging in ugly bunches, and continually forgets the steps to the part she is practicing. In the middle of a pirouette, she falls to the ground.[9]

At this early stage in her career, de Mille was already injecting her work with what one of her dancers has described as "non-movement movements," the motions of everyday life. When she began a new piece, de Mille wrote, she would imagine how a character "walks and stands" in "the basic rhythms of his natural gesture." But de Mille had more to draw on than natural life. She was also familiar with the heightened life of silent films, where gestures often must communicate what speech cannot. She spent her adolescence in Hollywood, the niece of the pioneering director Cecil B. DeMille, and her mother sometimes took young Agnes and her sister out of school to watch Uncle Cecil at work.

The family would perch on a hill, eating picnic lunches as enormous crowds churned through the sets of an ancient city or sparred on a battlefield.[10]

De Mille responded viscerally to these scenes, even though she knew they were acted. Witnessing a beating in *Anton the Terrible* made her feel faint, and she sought refuge on an empty sound set. After she saw Joan of Arc burned at the stake, she was too worked up to sleep. From a young age, she knew what it meant to be both audience and performer, and she kept both in mind when she started creating dances. Entertaining her audience mattered to her as much as technique.[11]

Often that meant making herself the butt of a joke. After *Stage Fright,* de Mille reprised the character of an anxious dancer in *Ballet Class.* Now the little statue came to life under the demanding supervision of her teacher who kept steady time offstage, beating a cane on the floor. The exercises were repetitive—échappé after échappé—but they became harder as the class went on, and the little dancer couldn't keep up. In another solo from this period, *'49*—an important predecessor to *Rodeo*—de Mille played an ebullient, calico-clad pioneer who throws off her sunbonnet in the middle of a hoedown. Her character is less awkward, but de Mille is still taking risks, pretending to dance with a crowd that is not there, and flinging a handful of tap steps into what was billed as a ballet performance. All these pieces, wrote John Martin, had "that quality, half laughter and half tears, that distinguishes the finest works of comedy in whatever medium." In another review, he compared de Mille to Charlie Chaplin.[12]

Chaplin's Little Tramp was forever running up against humiliation—hoisting a gun onto his shoulder backward, forced by starvation to eat his shoes, or getting knocked out by a boxer and again, moments later, by a boxing glove that falls off a wall. Small and vulnerable, he reminds us of how fragile our hold on our own bodies can be. Watching the Little Tramp traipse through his films, we know that he might be humiliated at any instant. We fear it even as we wait for it. De Mille's work shares this sensibility. Making Chaplinesque gags work, though, requires virtuosity. The Girl in *Rodeo* must do all the steps the men do, but more clumsily. She throws herself off the balance that as a dancer she has spent years cultivating. She follows the men at the rodeo and, hoping to join them, puffs up her chest; when they look back at her and shake their heads, indicating that she can't join them, she shrinks a few inches. She has the sweet confidence of Chaplin as well as his despair.

De Mille had clearly seen Chaplin's work, but the Girl in *Rodeo* may have had a more direct antecedent. In 1919, the comedian Fay Tincher created the title role in *Rowdy Ann*, a silent film about a spunky western maiden. Ann adopts masculinity with even more bravura than the Girl: she wears a floppy hat, a button-down plaid shirt, and enormous fur chaps. She stands with her legs wide apart, her hands on her hips, and her chest tilted up, as if she's trying to take up as much space in the world as she can. She strides across the screen and swings her arms with an aw-shucks bravura. When her father shirks his duties at the ranch to go out drinking, she gallops into town, lassoes him, and drags him away from the saloon. "Ann helped raise cattle," reads one intertitle, "but her sideline was raising . . . CAIN." Ann wields her pistol like a toy, gleefully shooting off volleys at anyone who offers the slightest annoyance. When an unwanted suitor courts her, she punches him off his horse and into a river. Later, she challenges him to a boxing match and wins.[13]

Like the Girl in *Rodeo*, Rowdy Ann must learn to be a lady. Her parents send her away to college, and her first class is in dancing. A crowd of young maidens, barefoot and in Grecian robes, like followers of Isadora Duncan, hop about in arabesque. Ann shows up late, her face shaded by her hat, boots poking out from under her toga, a holster at her hip. Uneasy with her new, high-falutin' surroundings, she punches her classmates and brandishes her pistol.

Unlike the Girl in *Rodeo*, Ann doesn't care about finding a man for herself. She's more interested in preserving the bonds among women; even when she finally wears a dress, she sits cavalierly on the side of a classmate's armchair, her own arm draped about the shoulders of her female friend. In the final scenes, Ann realizes that a man she had once caught cheating at cards is engaged to one of her classmates, whom the marriage will rip from the idyllic, all-girl world of school. Ann lassoes the villain. Soon the cops arrive and arrest him for some never fully explained wrongdoings, and the fiancée returns to the college, where the women all share a dorm. In the last scene, Ann starts a pillow fight.

There is no direct evidence that Ages de Mille ever saw *Rowdy Ann*, but she easily could have done so. In *Rodeo*'s opening scene, the Girl has the same wide stance, the same exaggerated arm swings and swelling chest as Ann. The Girl is a little less capable, of course—that's where the slapstick comes in—and her romance with the Roper makes her a different kind of heroine from the proto-butch Ann; *Rodeo*, with its don-a-dress, find-a-man love plot, takes place within a heteronormative world. Still, both women are tough, lively loners, conveying their characters in action instead of language.

The Girl's most obvious precedent, though, is a character from de Mille's *American Suite*, a collection of pieces she premiered in London in 1937. After a number of choreographic commissions and a series of her own recitals—which generally earned good reviews but little money—de Mille had moved abroad to study with the Polish-born dancer Marie Rambert. Influenced by Rambert and the choreographer Antony Tudor, a master of psychological portraiture, de Mille continued to refine her narrative sensibilities. She began to explore a topic that must have seemed particularly important to a young American alone in a new country: national identity. She choreographed a series of pieces on such subjects as the Appalachian mountain people, Boston Brahmins, and Midwestern farmers falling victim to the Dust Bowl. Then she combined these dances with older pieces—including '49—to create *American Suite*.[14]

One of the new pieces, *Western Dance*, held the kernel of *Rodeo*. Four female dancers galloped across the stage like a stage-coach team, driven by a fifth from behind. In another piece, *The Rodeo*, women pranced, rolled their heads about, and did the same virtuosic leaping attitude turns de Mille would later set on the male dancers of the Ballet Russe. As in *Rodeo*, de Mille was thrown from her horse, but this time she shook her fist in helpless anger.[15]

De Mille's choreographic notes for *American Suite*, which record the steps she was setting, or thinking of setting, on her dancers, still exist. Choreographic notes can be revealingly idio-syncratic, for while there is a standardized notation for recording dance, Labanotation, few choreographers use it (or even learn it). Until video became widespread, most choreographers, de Mille included, used their own methods of jotting down dance ideas, putting movement into language, and language into movement. De Mille, a talented writer, was unusually descriptive.

According to her notes, *Western Dance* began with a line of girls "running, skipping & galloping" across the stage. Other move-ments suggest the influence of tap dance: "shuffling," "tapping," and "clicking of heels." Broadway chorus lines show up too: the girls who enter first do so in an orderly row that "pivots" in unison. After a "tap break," the "line changes direction," still in unison, save for a girl at the end who "leaps and frisks out of bounds."[16] She had the kind of individualism that might have made Busby Berkeley cringe, and that would have added some wel-come relief to those tedious choruses in *The Gay Divorcee*. She was also a descendant of an established showbiz tradition, the unruly chorine.

In the 1913 all-black revue *Darktown Follies,* Ethel Williams had distinguished herself from her fellow chorus girls by falling out of step and improvising a breakdown. Some of her peers claimed she did so out of necessity, not showmanship, because she was unable to keep up with them, but they may have been jealous. Williams herself chalked it up to her superior talent: she kicked her legs higher than the other girls and could not bear to be tied down to their more sedate steps. Eight years later, in the all-black Broadway sensation *Shuffle Along,* Josephine Baker fol-lowed Williams's lead. Baker clowned around at the end of the chorus line, and her insouciance delighted audiences. Though a chorus girl, she was soon paid like a star, and within a few years she had become an international sensation, charming audiences at home and in Paris, and marrying an Italian count.[17] De Mille seemed to be using a version of such roles in *Western Dance,* making the girl who couldn't fit in a standout performer. There may have been some wish fulfillment involved: the little girl who couldn't keep up in class, who shut herself in the bathroom to practice her steps, was now the star. By the time the story evolved into *Rodeo,* the spunk and drive of America's pioneers would get her through.

Years before de Mille created *Rodeo* for Denham's troupe, Colonel Wassily de Basil's Ballets Russes had tried its own luck with American themes. In 1934, in Philadelphia, the company premiered Léonide Massine's *Union Pacific,* about the construction of the Transcontinental Railroad in the 1860s. In the opening scene, Irish workers laid their sleeping brethren down like railroad tracks and ties, using the sleepers' lax arms as construction tools. (Accounts of the piece make it hard to tell whether this was a comic touch or a dark commentary on the many men who died in the grueling work.) The second scene showed Chinese coolies in stiff competition with the Irishmen, hurrying about their work with little bobs and bows. Later, at a saloon, gamblers and dancing girls mingled with Mexicans and a missionary, and Massine—playing the barman—had a jaunty solo, cakewalking and tap-dancing for his patrons. But when the white proprietress made a pass at a Chinese surveyor, an Irishman intervened, and a huge brawl broke out. Chairs, tables, and bottles went flying.

Seconds later, the scene shifted to the celebratory moment when the final, golden spike was hammered into the railroad track, becoming—in the words of John Ford's 1924 film *The Iron Horse*, "the last link in the girdle of the continent." Everyone gathered around for a commemorative photograph that, after that barroom brawl, seemed like sham togetherness. Massine was uninterested in celebrating the American national character; instead, he trotted out familiar types with distinctive styles of movement. American critics were not pleased.[18]

*Union Pacific* received twenty curtain calls on opening night, but reviewers panned the piece for its un-Americanness. Never mind that the American poet Archibald MacLeish had written *Union Pacific*'s libretto, that the score drew on American folk songs, or that Massine himself cakewalked. John Martin denounced the ballet as "not even remotely" "recognizably native in flavor," for it lacked an American "point of view." According to George Amberg, "The ballet was American enough in theme, locale and names, but nowhere was there a forceful assertion of native feeling, implied in or derived from the subjects."[19]

In 1937, Massine approached the American dancer Marc Platt—then known as Marc Platoff—about choreographing an American ballet of his own. Both men soon left de Basil's company for Denham's Ballet Russe de Monte Carlo, and Platoff got his chance. Initially, he pitched a scenario about Coney Island, planning to research it when the company toured New York. But the amusement parks were closed, so Platt found a new topic with familiar allure: the Old West. *Ghost Town* took place in a deserted Gold Rush settlement still infused by its raucous past, and included a doomed love affair, brawling miners, a polygamous Mormon apostle, and performances by the poet Algernon Swinburne and the soprano Jenny Lind. American history was on parade, but the spirit still didn't seem right. When Martin reviewed the piece in 1939, he noted that Platt had covered the "rip-snorting, sweaty, raucous days" of the Old West with "an aura of daintiness that would almost make one believe that the region of the Comstock Lode was where Cinderella and Prince Charming spent their honeymoon." In other words, it was too effeminate.[20]

But the vogue for Americana dances had taken hold. When the Ballet Russe de Monte Carlo decided to mount a new piece, Sergei Denham turned away from his company's rank and file. He hired a plucky Californian who had been working at Ballet (later American Ballet) Theatre: Agnes de Mille.[21]

Could she bring the Ballet Russe the Americana ballet its repertoire needed? De Mille said yes, stipulating that she be allowed to develop her work without other people meddling. In other words, she would keep her own, native point of view. As she put it in her 1951 memoir, *Dance to the Piper*, "Into their stronghold of tradition enforced by an almost Prussian discipline I entered to break down all their cherished habits, to awake instincts curbed and warped by inflexible techniques, to disturb the balance of power, to question their authorities, authorities which had brought them international success, champagne suppers, and glamour." Like *Rodeo*'s cross-dressing heroine, she styled herself as an upstart and a cowboy. But unlike the Girl, she dominated this rodeo. "For two hours," she wrote, "I rolled on the floor with them, lurched, contorted, jack-knifed, hung suspended and ground my teeth. . . . I broke them to my handling."[22]

That sounds pretty tough, but de Mille made sure to let her readers know that she was nervous as well. Otherwise, her story wouldn't have had the same patriotic, feminist drama or self-deprecating charm. A few weeks before rehearsals commenced, de Mille consulted with her friend Martha Graham about how to gain the Russians' respect. "You be arrogant," Graham said. "You're every bit the artist any one of them is. This they won't know because they don't know art from a split kick, but they will recognize arrogance, and for your sake, for our sakes"—and by "our" Graham may have meant women, Americans, or anyone not affiliated with Russian ballet—"show them what it is like to be on the receiving end."[23]

So de Mille stood her ground. She may have embellished the story of her fiery strength for the purposes of autobiography, but her description does jibe with the memories of dancers who worked with her at other times. She often whacked the stones of her wedding ring against the mirror to get attention. When too many people were practicing on the sidelines of the studio in which she was running rehearsal, she once threatened to break the legs of a pirouetting dancer. De Mille was caustic and funny and demanding, and these qualities come through with delightful force in her memoir. She ridicules the men of the Ballet Russe: they "had been trained to move like wind-blown petals," and when they raised their arms, "up came the delicate wrists and the curled fingers of the eighteenth-century dandy."[24]

Like Fred Astaire's character in *Shall We Dance*, de Mille wanted to inject European ballet with the rhythms of real life and, for that matter, with manliness. "Don't *plier*," de Mille told the male dancers, referring to the fundamental ballet move in which the knees bend out while the shoulders, hips, and toes remain aligned. "Sit your horse." The men learned to stride across the stage with their feet hitting the floor heel first, rather than extending their toes like a precious offering. They learned to push up the brims of their hats brusquely, to crouch low, lean against a fence, and hook their fingers into their belt-loops. "We worked for four hours," de Mille writes, "on a boy kissing a girl at a dance." When the European dancers protested that they weren't doing any dancing, de Mille banished them from the studio and cut them from the cast. Those who remained, she wrote, were "mostly English and American," including the British-American Frederic Franklin, playing the Roper, who won the Girl's heart. Even the casting helped de Mille craft a nationalist fable: the Slavic dancer Casimir Kokich, who played the Head Wrangler, doesn't get the Girl.[25]

De Mille's America made room for individuals: the Girl was feisty and vulnerable, the Roper capable and funny. At the same time, she was intent on advancing a vision of the country as a meaningful community. In the midst of World War II, she wrote, *Rodeo* reminded audiences of the "generation on generation of men leaving and falling and the women remembering. And what was left of any of them but a folk tune and a way of joining hands in a ring?"[26]

Watching *Rodeo,* viewers can see that ring. In the middle of the ballet, Copland's music stops, and the dancers do a square dance, or running set, to silence. Music might have diminished this section, forcing the movement into a particular context: a particular song or a particular place and time. Instead, the dance is iconic, stripped to its essentials. The only sounds are stomping feet, the slaps of hands changing partners, and the cries of a caller who leads the dancers: "A runnin' up the river in Injun style, Ladies in the lead and the Gents plum wild. . . . Ladies to the center and the gents bow under. Away we go and we go like thunder!"[27] The caller sets up the order of movements the dancers whiz through, joining and loosening hands with their neighbors, secure in the knowledge that they are all in it together. The square dance also serves as a reminder that generations pass down movements like memories, or, perhaps, pass down their memories in movement.

But whose memories are being handed down? Square dancing descends from English country dance and French contredanse, seventeenth- and eighteenth-century forms that emphasize the patterns made by groups of bodies rather than specific steps executed by individuals. Couples move across the floor in a kind of human kaleidoscope as imagined from above. Each dancer has a part in creating this impression: the dance depends upon cooperation. French contredanse gave rise to the square dance's clearest ancestor, the quadrille, in which four couples form the sides of a square, switching partners and walking about in new formations before returning to where they began. In square dancing, this is the "promenade home," a victorious close of returning to where one belongs—like circling the bases in baseball, or settling down in one's hometown. It's a fitting finale to a dance that, in *Rodeo,* stands for tradition itself, a ritual in which dancers repeat the steps of early Americans.[28]

For de Mille, the square dance symbolized the best of America, a place where individuals come together to form a collective. Contemporary bodies do the rousing but respectful dances of their ancestors, honoring one another while they honor their history. She had seen her first square dance at a Colorado ranch in 1935 and was so overcome by the desire to join in that she improvised a solitary hoedown on the sidelines. That's one story, anyway; it's also possible that this "improvisation" could have owed something to the breakdown she had choreographed a few years earlier for '49. In another version of the story, a man jumped in from the crowd to partner her, swinging her so far into the air that her body was parallel with the ground. Never mind that the move sounds like an aerial straight from the Lindy Hop, then the biggest thing in jazz: de Mille was sold on square dancing. Judging from the reaction of *Rodeo*'s early audiences, balletgoers were too. After de Mille's dancers began the music-less running set in *Rodeo,* knowing audiences would sometimes clap out a beat to accompany them.[29]

When *Rodeo* premiered, square dances were everywhere, part of a wide-scale interest in folk dance. In New York, anyone who wanted to could go folk dancing at a different venue every night of the week, and although Italian, Greek, and Scottish dance were all options, American square dancing was the most prevalent. Americans with televisions could also watch square dancing there: in 1941, CBS began broadcasting *The Country Dance Society* on Sunday nights. De Mille appeared as a guest, as did the modern dancers Erick Hawkins and Charles Weidman. Part of square dancing's appeal came from its relative simplicity: even novices could learn a few steps and join right in. It spanned the political spectrum as well, with both leftist associations—this was the dancing of working-class Americans, whom Popular Front artists were intent on honoring—and conservative appeal: it was a backlash against jazz rhythms, city life, blacks, and immigrants.[30]

Similar biases had motivated many of America's early folklorists, who often looked for evidence of an unbroken Anglo-Saxon lineage in an effort to discount the importance of America's more recent immigrants. Ballad collectors in Appalachia triumphantly pointed to the persistence of songs that originated in Britain. In the 1910s, the folklorist Cecil Sharp even claimed that he had found authentic English peasants living in the American mountains—a perception he seems to have willed into being by deliberately avoiding the 13 percent of the Appalachian population who were black, as well as mountain-dwellers in clean cabins, who he believed would have succumbed to modern tastes. "Dirt and good music are the usual bedfellows," he wrote, "or cleanliness and ragtime!" Sharp also helped revive English folk dances, turning back to John Playford's 1651 manual *The English Dancing Master* for guidance. In 1911, Sharp and his co-writer (identified as "Jenny Pluck Pears") updated Playford's descriptions for a modern audience. Sometimes they updated the steps as well, making them simpler and more accessible.[31]

Their efforts worked, in part because they had good company. By the 1920s, anxieties about the frenzies of jazz had led the Dancing Masters of America to proclaim—as the *Chicago* Tribune put it—"the death knell of the Charleston," and to promote folk dance as a healthy, wholesome alternative. In the years to come, the professors kept grumbling. Urban clubs, the dancing masters argued, were too crowded for Lindy Hoppers. Citizens ought to return to what one American called "the formal movements, the studied steps, the graceful figures" of the square dance.[32]

That American was Henry Ford. In many ways, Ford was the great modernizer: he invented the assembly line, mechanized labor, collapsed distances with his Model T, and sped up the pace of American life. But Ford wanted to slow things down, too. An anti-Semitic isolationist, he believed that America's roots were—and ought to remain—wholesome, white, and Protestant. He started a museum of historic buildings in Dearborn, Michigan, Greenfield Village, where he also aspired to collect an example of every tool Americans had ever used.[33] Museums might keep the past intact, but dancing, Ford realized, could keep it alive. So he promoted square dancing, explaining that it could bring

> back a time that was less hurried and more neighborly. People lived further apart, but knew each other better. They worked harder, but had more leisurely recreations. They weren't pushed by a mania for speed. There was a community of interest, of work, of pleasure. Farmers, folks who are supposed to be rough and ready people, had an innate gentleness of manner that is rare today. The square dances had much to do with that. A man was taught how to approach a lady for a dance. It was formal, respectful, part and parcel of the environment that was building American tradition. Perhaps progress means speed. I don't think civilization does.[34]

In 1923, Henry Ford hired the dancing master Benjamin Lovett as an instructor and caller for square dance parties. Ford would invite friends and employees to dance, but he was as much an authority figure as he was a gracious host. If his guests weren't up to snuff on the dance floor, he would make them take lessons with Lovett. In 1926, Ford and his wife, Clara, published *Good Morning*, a manual of old-fashioned dances. (Most of it, speculates the historian Eva O'Neal Twork, was written by Lovett.) It became one of the most popular square dance manuals in the nation, and stayed in print for the next two decades.[35]

In *Good Morning*, Ford lamented the "one-on-one quality" of contemporary dances, where a single couple dances alone. Dancing, Ford implied, should not be a chance for couples to cuddle up publicly, with their hips shaking in the Black Bottom, their cheeks rubbing in the bunny hug, their torsos pressed together in the slow drag. Square dancing was ideal, in part, because bodies made minimal contact. According to *Good Morning*, "A gentleman should be able to guide his partner through a dance without embracing her as if he were her lover or her rescuer." Under this guideline, even Vernon and Irene Castle, the reformers of ragtime, were too salacious. The Fords recommended that men and women press handkerchiefs between their palms instead of allowing their hands to touch. When a man had to guide a woman by pressing one hand on her back, he should use another handkerchief to protect her gown. This would keep both parties clean, germ-free, and minimally tempted by the pleasures of the flesh.[36]

Ford launched a successful campaign to make square dancing part of public school physical education, beginning in Dearborn and expanding to Detroit. Eventually, Lovett and his assistants were teaching more than twenty thousand students a week. By 1942, at least 378 cities offered square dance classes, and in

Chicago and New York, it wasn't unusual for some six thousand dancers to show up for square dances in public parks.[37]

Ford's campaign worked, in part, because it took place amid a wider nostalgia for rural culture, springing up as thousands of Americans moved from the country to the city. While "race" records by black artist were becoming popular among white audiences, so were "hillbilly" records, with nasal balladeers and fast-paced string bands. For people who had grown up in the country, hillbilly music sounded like home; for city dwellers, it offered a glimpse into a culture that seemed to be vanishing, if it hadn't vanished already—the old, pastoral America, before the days of recordings, when people made their own music.[38]

Country people were supposed to be closer to the earth, and whether they were driving cattle across the West or farming in the mountains of Virginia, they were seen as the heart of the republic and a link to its roots. In the forties, Americans seemed to take particular delight in this romantic past, sometimes offering loving homage, and sometimes with a spirit that looked closer to slumming. In 1941, seven hundred members of Palm Beach's elite Everglades Club donned gingham dresses and overalls to attend a "Back to the Farm" ball complete with animals from Ringling Brothers' Circus, a North Carolina hillbilly band, and a caller who led guests in square dancing. If that sounds like a crowd, try cramming seven thousand under one roof—that's how many servicemen were expected to attend a square dance in 1941. The organizers stocked ten thousand servings of ice cream, twenty thousand sandwiches, and twenty-four thousand bottles of beer.[39]

Dude ranches shot up in the Adirondacks, the Catskills, the Berkshires, and even on Long Island so that urban Yankees could get a taste of rural fun on weekends. "From now until late in the Fall scarcely an office in Eastern cities will be without at least one bad case of Monday morning muscular pains," reported the *New York Times* in 1941. "The office boy, the red-haired stenographer, the sad-faced accountant . . . even the boss himself—any one of these may be the next victim of the dude-ranch craze." Ranch guests transformed themselves into rugged individuals. They took their meals around chuckwagons. They watched rodeos, went on late-night hayrides, and had sing-alongs in the cowboy tradition—or at least in the tradition of Roy Rogers and Gene Autry. Wearing plaid shirts and bright bandanas, they also attended rollicking barn dances, complete with live bands and square dance callers.[40]

In 1940, a Chicago woman wrote a letter to the editor extolling the rise of square dancing, which she contrasted with the antics of "jitterbugs." The jitterbug, a speedy swing dance that spread from Harlem's Savoy Ballroom—where it was known as the Lindy Hop—to the rest of the nation, calls for bent knees, putting the solar plexus closer to the ground; with this low center of gravity, dancers can more easily twist their hips and leap into flips and turns. But according to this concerned citizen "This jumping, stamping, twisting, and wriggling that goes on to the tunes [?]"—and with that bracketed question mark, she suggested that jazz might not even qualify as music—"may be all right in the depths of the jungle, but it's a trifle weird and a good deal barbaric among supposedly dignified, cultured Americans."[41]

The "jungle," of course, was the purported home of black culture; the writer preferred an America that was bleached white and clothed in calico and gingham. Agnes de Mille, however, refused to choose. She loved square dancing, but in her junior year at UCLA, she wrote and presented a skit about the link between jazz dancing and the jungle. De Mille played the jungle.[42]

The battle that raged over social dance during de Mille's youth concerned more than the effects of particular steps. It was a fight to define the nation, to lay claim to America's soul by means of its movement. The fight extended to concert dance, too. John Martin's *America Dancing* (1936) asserted that black and Native American art was not "our art": "Next we shall be hearing of the fine British rafter carvings of the Maoris, and the fascinating French sculptures of the African." Martin was right that, like Britain and France, America had acted as an imperial power, conquering Native Americans and enslaving Africans. But his implication was that cultures should remain unchanged, that assimilation was wrong, and that nonwhite Americans were not real Americans. American dance, in other words, was white dance.[43]

These assumptions echoed the nativist politics that had become pervasive in the twenties, the decade when the Ku Klux Klan reached its peak in popularity, and when Henry Ford was both promoting square dancing and publishing anti-Semitic articles in the *Dearborn Independent*. In 1921, Congress passed restrictive immigration laws over President Woodrow Wilson's veto; by 1927, only 150,000 immigrants a year—none of them Asian—were allowed to enter the United States. Writers like Lothrop Stoddard and Madison Grant popularized eugenics, counseling white Americans to remain free of foreign influence, no matter what the "sentimentalists" who wanted America to accept the world's poor and downtrodden said. Stoddard lamented the decline of America's good colonial stock, when only the most "racially fit" made the journey to the New World. A recent wave of immigrants was changing the country's genetic makeup, Stoddard argued, and America needed time and isolation to "stabilize her ethnic being." The modern dancer Ted Shawn seems to have agreed with at least some of this argument: in his 1926 manifesto for a native concert dance, *The American Ballet*, Shawn called New York City "the most un-American of any spot in the whole United States" because its "huge foreign population . . . intends to remain foreign."[44]

Jazz, wrote Shawn, was the "doggerel" of current society, rising up from cities in which people darted around so quickly, and in such crowded spaces, that they had no inspiration, and no room, to do anything but wiggle. Shawn congratulated Henry Ford for teaching his employees dances from America's Anglo-Saxon roots, "accompanied by music which has just as vital a rhythm as jazz, but with no smell of decay."[45]

But no amount of paranoia could segregate dance along racial lines. It had been crossing those lines for centuries, and Agnes de Mille kept up the practice. As the choreographic notes for *American Suite* make clear, de Mille set jazz steps—at least some of which she thought of as distinctively black—on a group of white female British dancers. *Gershwin* was to include a "colored jazz entrance." *Daybreak Express*, a piece about a train, would contain shoulder shimmies, which she described as "Jungle & Jitter." *Georgia Cracker* had a drunken white sharecropper performing a "shimmy," "continuous tap pulse," "charleston," and "zulu walk."

Plenty of white dancers tapped and did the Charleston, of course, but the "zulu walk," whether it referred to New Orleans Mardi Gras or Africa, was clearly associated with blackness. In the rural Georgia of de Mille's imagination—and in real-life Georgia, for that matter—dance steps came from all over.[46]

De Mille's mingling of black and white, urban and rural styles is reflective of the way American culture itself had long evolved. Even before the cakewalk became a national craze, slave and master watched each other in the Chesapeake, creating the Virginia Jig. Eighteenth-century slaves modified competitive African ring dances, in which an individual dances in the center of a circle, to include couples—something that was common in European, but not African, dance. Thereafter, though, nearly all African American dances were set for couples. From about 1800 to 1820, white slave owners picked up the steps for the Virginia Jig, as well as another, presumably black-originated dance called the Congo minuet at their own fancy-dress balls.[47]

Even the square dance, that supposedly pure Anglo-Saxon form, was not immune to influence. In the forties, some young square dance enthusiasts modernized calls, swapping the old-fashioned "duck for the oyster" and "Spanish cavalier" for the up-to-date "dive for the subway" and "Honolulu Baby." According to a *Los Angeles Times* story, "When a call like 'squeeze your honey, and swing like thunder' echoes at a high school prom, the result is something more akin to Harlem than Kentucky."[48]

Harlem and Kentucky—or black and white, anyway—mingled again in the late thirties, when a group of white college students visited a black nightclub in Columbia, South Carolina. The students sat up in a balcony, watching a circle of black dancers below, who may have been doing a version of the same African ring dance that helped spawn the Virginia Jig and the chalk-circle variation of the cakewalk. But the shape reminded the white students of a form they knew: square dancing. When they imitated what they had seen later on, they added a caller, who hollered out the steps the group should do in unison. The result—named after the nightclub where they took their inspiration, the Big Apple—was part swing, part country.[49]

This origin story was reprinted all over America, a sign that the Big Apple was different from other jazz dances. As Bosley Crowther wrote in the *New York Times*, "Amazing is the fact that, for all the individuality of 'swing,' this latest creation should hark back over the years and join hands in a Virginia Reel with the amiable spirit of the Nineties. Can it be that a circle has been described—that modern youth is coming down to earth?" Crowther praised the dance's "exuberance and exercise," and a dance instructor at the University of Southern California agreed. The Big Apple, she said, would help dancers learn to socialize.[50]

By late 1937, the Big Apple had become a nationwide craze. In Los Angeles, spectators stormed a Shriners Parade and took over the street to dance the Big Apple. In Brooklyn, six young men allegedly stole fifty cars to finance the cost of going to nightclubs to dance the Big Apple. Some schools banned the dance outright. A thousand students in New Jersey gathered under torchlights to protest their school's ban, and they created a "Campus Bill of Rights" that would permit them to do their favorite dance. But country clubs and debutante balls permitted it, as did President Franklin Roosevelt; the guests at his son's engagement party danced the Big Apple late into the night at the White House.

A few years later, even Winston Churchill learned the Big Apple, thanks to an American ballroom dancer who praised the British Bulldog thus: "Not once did he step on my feet."[51]

Not everyone was happy about the melding of dance traditions they imagined as distinctly black or white. In an exhibition of folk dancing in Central Park in 1942, a hundred dancers performed for an audience of thousands. According to a *New York Times* reporter, "There was a semblance of jitterbugging" in the grand finale, the "Paw Paw Patch." Headlines for the story looked as alarmist as Pete Seeger would when Bob Dylan went electric: "CAMOUFLAGED JIVE INVADES FOLK FETE." The same headline could have been written for Agnes de Mille's *Rodeo*.[52]

After *Rodeo*'s near-silent square dance, the music resumes for a Saturday night dance party at the Ranch House. The Girl, still in her dungarees, sits demurely on a bench, watching the Champion Roper enjoy himself at the party. He does a tap shuffle and prances around in a circle, clicking his heels, "rather," de Mille's choreographic notes say, "like Schnozzle [Jimmy] Durante," which is to say, a gruff goof.[53]

As the Roper stamps his feet and flexes his muscles, other couples whirl around in ragtime steps from the 1910s: the bunny hug and the turkey trot, almost cartoonish in their speedy staccato hops. But the action really gets started once the Girl, who has disappeared, reenters the party in a dress. Everyone freezes, shocked. The Roper walks across over to her, claps his hands, and snaps his fingers. Now the hoedown can begin.

The Roper and the Girl face each other from opposite corners of the stage and begin the patterned movements of a country dance. They meet at the center of the stage, bob their heads, and retreat to their corners. Then they approach each other again, grabbing hands as if to shake a how-d'you-do. (The Roper—in a move that would have made Henry Ford cringe—wipes his hands on his trousers first.) But instead of greeting each other, they keep their hands clasped and spin around in a circle, with a civilized distance between their bodies, leaving room for the Holy Ghost.

Their formality doesn't last for long. The Roper and the Girl tap and stamp their feet, their attraction building. The Girl takes one step, then two, then three, then four toward the Roper, rustling her skirt suggestively. De Mille's choreographic notes call this a way of "saying 'shoo-shoo-shoo,'" flirtatious and jazzy. The Roper takes the bait. Every time the Girl comes closer, he inclines farther toward her, his hands forming fans to play up her heat. Here, at this pivotal moment—when the Girl finds someone worthy of her love, when we begin to see her as a star instead of a misfit, when Copland's score reaches its most rousing notes, and when the dance breaks into an ever freer and more frenzied state—de Mille's choreographic notes indicate that the Roper's steps should be "very negroid in character."[54]

In those four words, we can see de Mille falling into the familiar pattern of white Americans acting out their ideas of blackness, from Jump Jim Crow to "Bojangles of Harlem." When the dancer playing the Roper moves in a "negroid" fashion, he escapes his sense of self and assumes a persona that, according to stereotype, is fun-loving, high-stepping, and given to easy abandon. In de Mille's America, this freedom leads to order: when everyone lets loose, their real feelings emerge. The steps provide a structure for liberation, a way to guide the Roper and the Girl

into the loving partnership that, in the America de Mille imagines, knits the nation together. But this freedom depends on a
sense of racial difference, on the assumption that blacks and
whites feel and move in distinct ways. The Roper's "negroid" steps
may have made up only a small piece of the scene, but de Mille
seems to have been thinking through her work by way of a
stereotype.

Yet de Mille did not share the moral judgment that often went
with that stereotype—the kind that prompted bandleader Paul
Whiteman to write to Emily Post bemoaning the effects of jazz
music on young dancers. "Personally I don't blame the kids," he
wrote. "No one has drilled into them the idea that the dance floor
is not a rodeo arena." Post agreed: at "swing orgies," dancers "behave like people possessed." De Mille embraced both the rodeo
arena and the idea that jazz led to bodily possession. In 1932 she
and her then-dance partner, Warren Leonard, were hired to choreograph a Broadway revue, *Flying Colors*. Ultimately, the higher-
ups let them go and replaced them with Albertina Rasch, but one
of their numbers—for a black women's chorus line—remained
in the final production. "Smokin' Reefer" linked black jazz, drug
use, and voodoo possession.[55]

According to de Mille's choreographic notes, the chorus girls'
"hips shoot forward" again and again. They also do a "deep
shimmy," bang their fists on their chests and the ground, make
the "evil eye," and, at one point, "make horns by placing thumbs
at side of head." Ferocious and seductive, they also fall prey to
something like hypnosis. One woman walks onstage slowly, "in
a semi-trance effect. She leans slightly back," her head supported
by a black attendant, her hands resting on the backs of two

others, who bend forward, their arms hanging. The ensemble of chorus girls stare and are "motionless," according to de Mille's notes, until the song mentions marijuana.[56]

Some of the same steps recurred in a scenario de Mille wrote for a never-produced short film, *Voodoo*, that she hoped would star Duke Ellington. *Voodoo* would take place at a crowded club "in the native section of a town in Cuba or the Barbados." Two vacationing white American couples look on approvingly as Ellington, the distinguished guest from Harlem, plays the piano. When a native girl is surrounded by the crowd and pushed off into a curtained room, screaming in protest, "an enormous black leans over the top of the upright" and tells Ellington to keep playing. The white visitors, alarmed, decide to leave. Now the club is shuttered, dark, and mysterious, and the camera zooms in for a close-up of Ellington's concerned face. "He does not dare really to look up and he does not dare to stop," de Mille writes. Offscreen, the girl screams again, and a cornet takes up her cry. "The instruments of the orchestra join in," de Mille writes, and Ellington shifts from observer to participant: "Ellington amazed and fascinated falls in with the rhythm they have set." That rhythm propels the crowd to "fall to the floor" and "drag themselves up" in sensational movements that recall the chorus girls' steps in *Flying Colors*. "Their hips lurch and contort. Their shoulders hunch. Their fingers stiffen and relax. They breathe heavily but not with exertion. Their skins glisten. Their wooly hair has risen on their heads in electric vitality."[57]

The native girl reemerges from behind the curtain, walking "in a hypnotic trance" that replicates more movements from de

Mille's *Flying Colors* notes: "Her head is supported by a young woman. Her hands rest on the backs of the two others bent over like animals." The woman and the crowd begin to move as one. Their motions are "transmitted" back and forth via "sympathetic rhythm," so that "her body has become the token of their bodily joy." She performs "the meaning and not the fact of lust," a "phallic dance" whose power eventually levitates all the other dancers above her. "They are surrounded, uplifted and floated on air," writes de Mille, but the movement saps the life force from the girl, who crumbles to the floor, dead. Ellington is horrified, but he is also to blame, for his music has helped provide the hypnotic beat. This is *The Rite of Spring* by way of Harlem.[58]

In the thirties, Duke Ellington's band played regular gigs at the Cotton Club, home of "jungle jazz." His brass musicians used mutes to make their instruments growl suggestively while audiences watched rows of leggy chorus girls strut and shake. Lena Horne, who performed in the chorus, recalled that the Cotton Club floor shows had a "primitive, naked quality that was supposed to make a civilized audience lose its inhibitions." In one performance, wrote the jazz historian Marshall Stearns, "a light-skinned and magnificently muscled Negro burst through a papier-mâché jungle onto the dance floor" in "darkest Africa" and, with a bull whip, rescued a "'white' goddess" from the dark-skinned natives who worshiped her. The quotation marks around "white" indicate that the woman, who like all the performers at the Cotton Club was black, was light-skinned. But in an all-black setting, she and the man stood in for the white audiences, who saw a fantasy of their own experience playing out onstage. They, too, were surrounded by blacks they saw as primitives, and as the scene culminated in an "erotic dance" between the aviator and his new love, audiences could imagine their own sexual restrictions loosening.[59]

De Mille returned to the topic of voodoo in 1940 when she choreographed *Obeah*, also known as *Black Ritual*, for Ballet Theatre. She cast sixteen African American women, many of whom lacked not only formal dance training but enough money to stay warm and fed. De Mille gave them bread and soup at rehearsals, she said, to keep them from fainting. According to the program notes, the piece, like *Voodoo*, depicted a ritual human sacrifice "somewhere in the West Indies." But the music was American— or at least, American influenced—a jazz symphony by the French émigré Darius Milhaud.[60]

*Obeah* had only three performances and was never filmed; we don't know much about what it looked like. De Mille made no more pieces that were overtly about voodoo possession. But in a way, the Roper's dance in *Rodeo* is a drama of bodily possession in miniature: when he abandons himself to move in a "negroid" fashion, he becomes virile and free, and the Girl follows his lead. Jazz dance's wild energy meets the orderly lines of the square dance in ballet's own Big Apple, all the pieces settling into a new, American idiom.

The Big Apple itself showed up in de Mille's choreography for *Texas Fourth*, which she set on her own, brief-lived company in 1973. *Texas Fourth* takes place during a small-town Fourth of July parade. Imbued with a kind of manic energy, it begins with a parade, at which crowds of teenagers are doing the Charleston and pecking (a swing step in which dancers crane their necks forward like chickens in a barnyard). Baton twirlers cakewalk with the crowd. Someone flings a tambourine in the air. A man turns backward handsprings across the stage while his friends walks on their hands. Cheerleaders rush in with pom-poms. A girl plays a saxophone on top of a piano. After everyone rejoices at the unfurling of a giant Texas flag, a man unicycles around the stage.[61]

American Ballet Theatre revived *Texas Fourth* in 1976 for the country's bicentennial, but the piece didn't live on after that. It is watered-down de Mille—filled with fun and history, yet straining to achieve the magic of *Rodeo*. Her choreographic notes, though, tell an entrancing story: during an afternoon siesta in the second scene, the audience would watch children "stop moving and stand listless, without motivation. Between them, are seen the figures they think they are, the ideal dream-heroes. The boys wear dungarees and sneakers, but as dreams they are all Gary Cooper and wonderfully turned out. The girls wear short ginghams and bobby socks; in the dream they are lovely and romantic in long dresses."[62]

"Gary Cooper and wonderfully turned out": matinee idols blend with classical ballet in a dream that sounds a lot like Agnes de Mille's own. But in *Texas Fourth*, the dream both did and did not come to fruition: audiences would see the dancers achieve these perfect visions, but the scene would end "with reality— Heat—Listlessness—waiting." Art might offer us dreams, but de Mille knew that we would wake back up to everyday life.[63]

*Rodeo* was de Mille's masterpiece, and it is still in the repertoire of major U.S. dance companies; two other of her pieces, *Fall River Legend* (1948), about Lizzie Borden, and *Three Virgins and a*

*Devil* (1941), are still performed as well. De Mille was setting work on ballet companies until a year before her death in 1993, but she reached her biggest audiences in musical theater, creating the dances for *Carousel, Brigadoon, Paint Your Wagon, Gentlemen Prefer Blondes,* and a host of other Broadway productions. She had begun this sort of work years before *Rodeo,* but her Broadway career took off after *Oklahoma!*

For decades, Broadway shows had followed a formula that the historian Ethan Mordden describes as follows: "start with hot performers, add a hot score and hot choreography, and glue it all together with as much humor as possible." This resulted in pleasing diversions, as well as stellar careers, but it also made for "constructions without foundation, circles without center." By the forties, it was starting to seem rather tired. *Oklahoma!* ushered in a new level of sophistication, in which everything cohered. Instead of stopping the show, musical numbers now moved it along, emerging from and advancing the plot. Instead of offering diversions, dances added psychological depth. De Mille recruited her performers from dance studios, not chorus lines; the dream ballet she choreographed for *Oklahoma!* both showcased their skills and examined the complexity of the leading lady's character. Like the children's scene in *Texas Fourth,* "Laurey Makes Up Her Mind," as the dream ballet came to be called, created a kind of alternate, danced reality.[64]

In "Laurey Makes Up Her Mind," ballet dancers substituted for the actors, dancing out Laurey's love for the noble cowboy Curly and her fear of and fascination with Judd, the rough hired hand. You can watch a version of it in the 1955 film, for which de Mille adapted her Broadway choreography. Laurey drifts asleep in a rocking chair and wakes up inside a dream. She walks toward her dream self, and touches her, as if in a mirror. That dream self—and for what fan of musicals is this not true?—is a dancer. Shirley Jones plays Laurey for most of the film, but dream-Laurey—more supple and graceful—is danced by the ballerina Bambi Lynn.

Ballet dancers move with more technical perfection than most in their audiences can ever hope to achieve. Yet audiences still recognize their own emotions in the dancers' movements. When the Girl in *Rodeo* is bucked off her horse, it makes physical what embarrassment can feel like: something so glaring that our mistakes might as well involve our whole body. When Ginger Rogers turns away from Fred Astaire, and he then grabs her by the hand and winds her into his body, they are showing what it's like to feel floored by the magnitude of love. When Bill Robinson's feet one-up their musical accompaniment, they tap out the delight of getting away with something.

The dream ballet in *Oklahoma!* turns Laurey into her own audience, watching her doppelganger dance the scenes of her unconscious. In the main plot, Laurey has turned down Curly's offer for a ride to a hoedown. Dream-Laurey, on the other hand, rushes through clouds, an enormous grin on her face, and leaps into the arms of dream-Curly. He hoists her into the air and into the loving ecstasy she longs for. Her arms reach forward in the taut lines of third arabesque, and though one leg is folded into Curly's arms, the other stretches behind her, as if pleasure is radiating out through the tips of her fingers and toes.

Laurey's dream has its nightmarish side as well. The dirty postcards with which Judd decorates his cabin come to life. The postcard girls wear the black garters and ruffled skirts of dancers, and possibly whores, in an Old West saloon. They hitch up their skirts, shake their legs, and shimmy. The dance is sexuality gone wrong, flashy and forceful. When the postcard girls throw Laurey into Judd's arms, they're embodying her darkest fears— that her own libidinous urges, and her own curiosity about sex, could link her with the man she despises.

Of course, "Laurey Makes Up Her Mind" was not the first ballet to appear in a Broadway musical. In addition to "Slaughter on Tenth Avenue," Balanchine created a ballet for *Babes in Arms* (1937). Albertina Rasch set a ballet on Fred Astaire and Tilly Losch in *The Band Wagon* (1931) and made another for *Lady in the Dark* (1941). Robert Alton set a ballet in *Pal Joey* (1940). But none of these productions had the influence of *Oklahoma!*, which ran for 2,212 performances after its opening—five years straight. According to one historian's count, in the three and a half years after *Oklahoma!* opened, seventy-two new musicals were produced in New York. Of these, "forty-six included ballet, and twenty-one offered dream ballets."[65]

De Mille's choreographic success, along with her writerly chops, made her an ambassador for American dance. She published a series of snappy and engaging memoirs. She wrote editorials and gave speeches calling for increased government funding for the arts. In 1974, she founded the Agnes de Mille Heritage Dance Theatre at the University of North Carolina School of the Arts, with the goal of celebrating and preserving American dance, and giving it a place to thrive outside the reverse-parochial art world of New York. Two years later, at age seventy, she had a stroke; instead of slowing down, she sped up her writing, publishing a book-length study of Martha Graham (*Martha*, 1991), an essay collection (*Portrait Gallery*, 1990), two more memoirs (*Where the Wings Grow*, 1978, and *Reprieve*, 1981), and *America Dances* (1980), a lively popular history that had first taken form in her lecture-demonstration *Conversations About the Dance*.

The 1977 performance of *Conversations About the Dance* was de Mille's first public appearance after her stroke. Joffrey Ballet dancers and other guests, including the tap legend Honi Coles, provided living illustrations of the dance history she recounted from a chair on the side of the stage at New York's City Center. De Mille's doctors knew that sitting and reading aloud for two hours would challenge her stamina, and they were standing by in case she needed them. But de Mille seemed to draw her energy from the history she recounted, and in a recording of *Conversations*, she sounds as animated as the dancers who take center stage. In *Reprieve*, her memoir about recovering from the stroke, she writes that she found her real support in the audience. "They were with me. They were ahead of me. They intended that I succeed. . . . With that collaboration from the audience I knew I could not show weakness or uncertainty. They expected me to be excellent, and so I obliged them. We did it together." When the program ended, de Mille moved both her arms for the first time in two years. She flung them out to her audience.[66]

That sense of collaboration, of art as something created by and for a community, is central to de Mille's sense of what's American about American dance. In *Conversations About the Dance*, she does not bombard the audience with big names, or present a straightforward survey of notable achievements in the world of concert dance. She includes famous and anonymous, high and low, and black and white dancers. Fanny Elssler, Isadora Duncan, and Martha Graham all make appearances; so do Vernon and Irene Castle, Bill Robinson, and a host of anonymous social dancers, from Renaissance courtesans to Harlem Lindy Hoppers.

Not all the dances are intended to make audiences feel good. As an African dancer performs a traditional dance onstage, bare-chested and low to the ground, de Mille explains, with urgency and woe, "Ten million Africans were brought as slaves to the Americas in the seventeenth and eighteenth centuries. Four million died in passage. Out of this hopeless, lost, demoralized, forlorn group, without future and, what is as sad, without past, came our first native music, our first native dancing, came our first—O Agony—came our first theater." Enter a group of dancers in red, white, and blue Uncle Sam outfits, doing a spirited cakewalk.[67]

This is where *Conversations About the Dance* becomes tricky. The dancers represent a minstrel show, but the defining characteristic of minstrelsy, blackface, is erased. These dancers don't wear blackface. They're black. De Mille probably figured that literal blackface would be too incendiary to show onstage, and she might have been right. Yet as she collapsed blackface with blackness, she unwittingly reproduced a confusion that minstrel show audiences had back when the form began, when performers marketed themselves as "original Negroes," and when some audience members mistook the counterfeit for the real thing. Minstrelsy did not arise organically from African dancers; it was a form of the urban, white North, even if many of the white northerners took cues from black dancers.[68]

De Mille talked explicitly about more palatable forms of cultural blending, including the ways black Americans sped up and synchronized the Irish jig to create tap, or the enormous debt American ballet owes to the modern dancer Martha Graham. But blackface is another matter. It gets us to what Ralph Ellison calls "the deep dark bottom of the melting pot," where "the white man's relish is apt to be the black man's gall." This may not be the stuff of polite conversations, but it's at the deep dark bottom of American dance, too.[69]

Watching *Rodeo*, you don't think of the Roper as a blackface minstrel or a vaudeville comic; he just seems talented and free. The Girl does not resemble a film star or a tennis player; she is charming, spunky, and lovelorn. But as de Mille herself wrote elsewhere, "Every gesture is a portrait" of the people who have performed it before. Her own work gives us portraits of white and black Americans, nativists and progressives, minstrels, cowboys, colonial settlers, and jazz babies, all coming together in one capacious, national idiom.[70]

*Conversations About the Dance* ended with the conviction that movement can knit the country together. In the last few minutes of her lecture, de Mille bemoaned the state of social dancing since the Cold War. "The boys and girls didn't dance with one another," she claims. "They danced in spite of one another. Our discotheques became an exercise in mass loneliness." In these undisciplined dances "there was no sense whatever of mutual participation or trust." As she spoke, a cluster of dancers thrashed about and eventually collapsed to the floor, as if the apocalypse had arrived. But in a bit of stage magic, the dancers stood back up, ran into formation, and did a joyous square dance. "We'll survive with gallantry," de Mille asserted. "Our parents taught us how."[71]

In a way, this was a slipshod ending, the sign of a forced and nostalgic idealism. But in *Rodeo* that same square dance, grounded in a plot but set away from its everyday dramas and gags, is profound. De Mille had an enduring faith that dance could allow people to perform a more perfect and graceful union, whether at a party or on the two sides of a golden proscenium. Right movement, she believed, would lead to right society.

It's a theme that also shows up in *Oklahoma!* Set in 1906, when the forty-sixth state entered the Union, *Oklahoma!* is a pastoral romance. But before the story can reach its happy conclusion— a cowboy and the woman he loves settling down to start a farm—conflict must be resolved between freedom-loving cowboys and fence-loving farmers. They tussle at a fundraising dance, and the town's elders and ladies try to make everyone behave. "The farmer and the cowman should be friends" and "Territory folks should stick together," they sing. The crowd clasps arms for some amiable do-si-dos, but soon a full-on brawl breaks out on the dance floor.

Suddenly, Aunt Ellert, a brassy, outspoken spinster, fires a gun. "Ain't nobody here gonna slug out anything," she hollers. "This here's a party." She brandishes her weapon wildly above her head and orders the crowd to keep singing. They oblige, and when the dancing starts up again, it's lovelier than before. We see a community that has room for both domestication and recklessness, where strong young men partner beautiful young women and everyone behaves. Except we know that the dancers are dancing, in part, to escape a threat. Peace, the scene says, is just one more performance.

Agnes de Mille imagined a nation where physical exuberance was part of everyday life, and where people solved problems with movement. Her audiences responded to that vision and recognized it as their own. But they also recognized the histories behind the movements, which pointed to a country that was larger and more complicated than any choreography could capture. In de Mille's square dance, the present joins arms with pasts it both reveals and obscures, carried forward in sashaying bodies and ground beneath shuffling feet.

# 5 PAUL TAYLOR'S BUGLE BOY

In March 1974, Paul Taylor collapsed onstage in the midst of a furious solo about a minstrel show. He was playing Noah in the New York City premiere of *American Genesis,* a dance that spliced together the Bible with U.S. history. *American Genesis* thrived on narrative echoes. Noah's Ark doubled as a Mississippi showboat, and in other sections of the piece, Taylor played Lucifer and a Puritan elder, each role shading the other with sanctimonious cruelty and rigor.[1]

At the time, Taylor was hooked on uppers and downers, and coping with severe stomach ulcers. He had splintered his ankle, and though he didn't know it at the time, he was suffering from hepatitis. He danced with bloody palms, a bloody ankle, and blood in his mouth. Taylor was a force. He was six feet tall and broad-shouldered, with big eyes and strong, graceful movements. When he performed Noah's solo, his quick, angular arms had all the articulate wrath of Jonathan Edwards. He leapt with the stooped aggression of a vulture, scanning the earth for prey.[2]

Near the end of *American Genesis,* Noah hurls his children to the ground. He wants them to move in a dignified manner—backs erect, steps delicate and small, all motions culminating in prayer—but they prefer to cakewalk, tap-dance, leap about in wheeling turns, and partner one another in a cartoonish, hen-pecking, proto-jitterbug. All these steps have origins in African American culture, and Noah is particularly furious with the character played by Carolyn Adams, the only African American dancer in the bunch. As Noah's sprightly child, Adams hops about so much that she seems barely to land. Noah struggles to catch up with and discipline her. But when the flood begins, he manages to herd all his children onto the Ark by hopping like an angry frog. Then he throws Adams off to drown.

Like Pip in *Moby-Dick*—the little dancer who is abandoned in the ocean when the *Pequod*'s crew decides that hunting whales beats saving black men, and who returns to the ship crazed and wizened—Adams's character shifts from a comic to a tragic figure. What starts out as a cartoonish battle about social mores gains chilling depth. According to *American Genesis*, fighting over dance means fighting about race, and American history is a narrative of disavowal, violence, and hatred.[3]

Taylor takes the nation to task for racism, but not in the way one might expect, by condemning minstrel shows for perpetuating ugly stereotypes. Instead, he uses the minstrel show to reveal and celebrate the black influence on American dance. Noah may appear righteous, but it is the dancers who redeem us. Pip, Melville writes in biblical rhythms, was "bid strike in with angels, and beat his tambourine in glory; called a coward here, hailed a hero there!" At the end of *American Genesis*, Adams's character returns from the dead to lead the whole company to heaven.[4]

The night Taylor collapsed in 1974, no one was saved, unless you count Paul Taylor. He was unable to continue, and the curtain came down early. In the months that followed, Taylor kicked his drug habit, retired from the stage, and choreographed one of the most perfect dances ever made: *Esplanade*. The opening movement of *Esplanade* could be the heaven to which Adams was leading everyone in *American Genesis:* a place of bright light and movement so simple and energetic it seems purified. Taylor has said that he got the idea for the piece after watching a woman run to catch a bus in perfect time with the allegro movement of Bach's Concerto in D Minor for Violin. He decided to combine the actions of everyday life—running, walking, skipping, hopping, falling, getting back up—with the structural complexity and soaring beauty of the baroque.[5]

*Esplanade* is ambitiously modest. Its dancers grin, play leapfrog, and fall into patterns that could have come straight from an old-fashioned manual of country dances. They walk in star formations, hold hands in circles, and fall in and out of facing lines that recall the Virginia Reel. Agnes de Mille frequently used such patterns to conjure a vision of an orderly, happy America, but in *Esplanade,* Taylor seems to have been thinking about the nature of pattern itself. Dancing, he shows us, develops from the everyday, in all its mess and glory.

On one level, *Esplanade* is about the possibility—even nobility—of pedestrian movement. But like *American Genesis* and so much of Taylor's work, it is also about how we come together and fall apart. At various times, the dancers act like schoolyard playmates, lovers, flocks of birds, dancers on an antique frieze, members of a dysfunctional family, and upbeat, supportive friends. About two-thirds of the way through the first movement, the lights dim, and everyone crouches in a circle, reaching for one another's shoulders. Will they connect? They do, but

Michelle Fleet, Robert Kleinendorst, Jamie Rae Walker, and other members of the Paul Taylor Dance Company in *Esplanade*, 2012 (© Paul B. Goode Photography)

in the next movement, they separate again: no one touches at all. In a small group that appears to be a family, a mother is unable, or perhaps unwilling, to recognize her daughter. She ends up alone, in the center of the stage, quaking on her knees. The rest of the cast joins her on all fours, crawling in from the wings to form a bestial tableau. It's an image that recurs in other Taylor pieces: *Scudorama* and *Last Look* even feature piles of limp bodies, like Hieronymus Bosch's paintings of hell.

Paul Taylor has created over 130 dances, and they're remarkably varied: his work can be comic, dark, plotless, narrative, lyrical, in line with or in opposition to the score. Community has been one of his abiding preoccupations. Sometimes the theme is explicit: he has made pieces about families, groups of friends out for the evening, small towns and their rituals, even a dance company in rehearsal. Sometimes a sense of community is present because if a choreographer puts a group of people onstage, they can't help being a group. And sometimes Taylor shows us the whole country reckoning with its past.

Taylor began his career when modern dance's heroic age was still fresh in the popular memory, and he worked closely with its pioneers. His teachers—who included Martha Graham, Louis Horst, Doris Humphrey, and Charles Weidman—asserted that modern dance was uniquely American, and Taylor, though he was usually less polemical about it, agreed. In 2015, he drove the point home by renaming his company "Paul Taylor's American Modern Dance," and in the hands of choreographers like Mark Morris and Twyla Tharp, "American Modern Dance" does look, at least in part, like Paul Taylor.

In the sixties and seventies, Taylor became one of the dance world's leading figures, offering more accessible fare than did his former boss and fellow titan Merce Cunningham. But his popularity rankled some members of the avant-garde. They felt that Taylor tried too hard to entertain, that he was pleasing crowds and chasing money when he ought, like Cunningham and his followers, to be questioning what dance meant and what it could do. At a time when it was de rigueur to make art about art, Taylor frequently made dances with subjects. The line between ballet and modern dance sometimes seemed like a hostile border, but ballet fans began to embrace Taylor's work. The critic Sally Banes lamented that Taylor "cater[ed] to every dance constituency" rather than staking out definitive territory of his own. "While this versatility might be a virtue for a politician," Banes wrote, "it leaves a curious vacuum at the core of a choreographer's style." In the words of his former company member Twyla Tharp, Taylor seemed to be "selling out."[6]

Taylor himself agrees that yes, he wants to reach audiences. That desire is part of his populism and his ambition. It's also one of the reasons he's managed to maintain a company of dancers devoted to performing his works for upward of fifty years, and that he has, as Bill Clinton put it, "defined American dance."[7] But sometimes it seems as though even his fans, not to mention his detractors, are missing the point. His dances can be inviting, beautiful, and generous. But they can also be profoundly cynical, as he takes America and, often, its dancing to task for their failings.

Taylor is unlikely to say any of this himself. He has a "just plain folks" demeanor that belies the rigor of his thinking and the scope of his ambition. When asked to name the character with whom he most identifies, Taylor once picked Homer Simpson, explaining, "He's very stupid, and it doesn't bother him." But when asked to identify his personal hero, Taylor named Walt Whitman: "He knew so much, and he loved everybody."[8] Both these men are American icons, albeit of very different sorts: imaginary and real, comic and serious, contemporary and historic, bumbling and poised. Taylor's work unfolds in the places where their personalities overlap.

In 2011, Paul Taylor appeared on a local public television show in University Park, Pennsylvania. He sat quietly on one side of a large wooden table while the interviewer—her blond hair pulled back in a French twist, the collar of her turquoise suit jacket splayed out across her shoulders—welcomed him, with an awkward formality, "to the conversation." She rattled off a litany of his honors: a MacArthur "genius" grant, three Guggenheim fellowships, a knighthood in France, and now the award that had brought him to Pennsylvania, Penn State's Institute of Arts and Humanities Medal for Distinguished Achievement. "But what interests me most about all that," she continued, "is that when you decided to dance in your twenties, which was considered rather late to begin dancing, you knew that you were going to accomplish great things." Paul Taylor leaned forward, took a wad of chewing gum out of his mouth, and stuck it behind his ear.[9]

The interviewer laughed, but Taylor, completely deadpan, barely cracked a smile. Taylor has been a chain-smoker for years; when he's not smoking, he's chewing gum. Still, it was hard to imagine his gesture as anything but calculated insouciance: authority might recognize him, but he didn't recognize it. He proceeded to tell the interviewer that when he made up his mind to be a dancer, "I had no idea I was going to get awarded something for it." Downplaying his own ambition, he rejected the role of the brooding, calculating genius.[10]

A similar impulse must have fueled Taylor's account of the genesis of what would become one of his most popular pieces, *Company B:* while walking to the studio one day, he found an Andrews Sisters LP on the top of a trashcan and decided to use it for a dance. "You must understand that I'm cheap," he told a *New York Times* reporter. "I do this all the time, and then I use the other side of the record for the next piece." The reporter took him at his word. When Taylor tells this story in the 1998 documentary *Paul Taylor: Dancemaker*, he laughs. As he explained else-where, he is asked so often about how he makes dances that he fabricates "completely different answers each time." The notes he took to prepare for an interview in the mid-1970s get at the question with comic banality. Taylor wrote that he approached choreographing a new piece "Across Spring St., up the elevator, and into the studio nervously."[11]

For a writer of one of the great dance books of the twentieth century—*Private Domain*, a memoir that goes from his birth to the end of his performing career in 1974—Taylor is notoriously cagey. When his editor, Robert Gottlieb, told him that a memoir would require him to show himself to his readers, Taylor recalls, "I went home and made a list of all the things I was not going to reveal." Unlike his former employer Martha Graham, whose *Blood Memory* includes excerpts of letters to her psychoanalyst, or his former dancer Twyla Tharp, whose *Push Comes to Shove* chronicles both her art and the men she's slept with, Taylor keeps his private life pretty private. He wants us to focus on his work.[12]

Some critics make much of his difficult childhood—an absent father, a stint on a farm with surrogate parents who, he discovered with some heartbreak, were being paid to care for him—but Taylor's oeuvre is bigger than personal hardship. At the same time, it's intensely personal, in a way that has to do less with introspection than with observation. Taylor is a watcher. He even entertained fantasies of working for the CIA. But he's no rat. He's a spy in the way that James Agee and Walker Evans were spies, posing as a journalist and a photographer, in *Let Us Now Praise Famous Men*. They are observers and chroniclers of American life, interlopers who remain outsiders.[13]

Taylor holds himself apart. He watches people move, alone and together. He watches communities at work—or, in many cases, failing to work. Then he puts what he observes onstage, so that we can be watchers too. He doesn't force issues by mugging for the crowd. In most of his performances, he kept—and he encourages his dancers to keep—a relatively neutral expression, letting the movement do the talking. His pieces are often funny, and often sad, feelings that come across more through the body than the face. Early in Taylor's career, John Martin called his face "a mask, but one that focuses feeling rather than hiding it, in true theater style."[14] In other words, Taylor's flatness is strategic. Even putting a piece of gum behind the ear could be a piece of choreography.

That interviewer for the Pennsylvania television broadcast was right about one thing: Taylor's career did begin rather late. He grew up in Virginia, then left to attend Syracuse University on an art scholarship. The slow pace of painting bored him, so he opted to get his tuition paid by joining the swim team. Swimming gave him his first real training. It strengthened his muscles, increased his endurance, and prepared him to plunge into performance after waiting around on the side of a pool—or, later, the wings of a stage.[15]

Midway through college, Taylor had an epiphany: he was going to be a dancer. True, he had never seen a concert dance, and his own dance experience was basically limited to jitterbugs and foxtrots at high school hops. He knew. So he checked out library books about modern dance, watched the Ballet Russe when the company came to town, and was drafted by University of Syracuse dancers as a brawny, if untrained, partner. In his first performance, Taylor recalls, he shot Anita Dencks—later a founding member of Merce Cunningham's company—into a thicket of thorns.[16]

But Taylor was a quick study. The following summer, he trained at the American Dance Festival, and Martha Graham, after watching him in class, invited him to join her company. He moved to New York and attended Juilliard—looking, recalled his classmate Carolyn Brown, "more like an Olympic athlete than a dancer." The faculty at Juilliard were hungry to work with this young Adonis, but it was Graham who won out. After giving him a correction in class once, she trumpeted, "Young man, I'm grooming you!"[17]

Graham, by then, was the undisputed high priestess of modern American dance. She began her career with Ruth St. Denis and Ted Shawn in the 1910s, when their company, Denishawn, was the hotbed of modern dance. The Denishawn school was the first in America to offer rigorous dance training in forms other than ballet. But to hear Graham and her peers tell it, there was nothing particularly American about Denishawn. St. Denis had been turning to the East ever since she saw an ad for Egyptian Deities cigarettes at a drugstore in Buffalo and decided to trade in the life of a chorus girl for something more exotic. Soon she was performing solos as mysterious priestesses: Radha, Isis, Ishtar. Her company yoked together spirituality and showmanship, with dances that were—or at least purported to be—from Burma, India, Japan, and ancient Egypt. "After a while," said Doris Humphrey,

Graham's classmate at Denishawn and later one of Taylor's teachers, "it began to seem a little scattered. I felt as if I were dancing as everyone but myself."[18]

Humphrey, along with Graham and Charles Weidman—all Denishawn veterans—would eventually slough off these orientalist trappings to create a new form of modern dance. Together with Hanya Holm, they founded the American Dance Festival, made works on American themes, and generally restored American dance to a more authentic order. Or at least, that's how the story often gets told. The real story is more complex.

Exoticism gave Denishawn's artists cover to move in ways that otherwise might have triggered disapproval. Cloaked in Eastern spirituality, Ruth St. Denis could shake her hips, dive into her own sensuality, and escape charges of vulgarity, all the while liberating the American woman. Graham, who idolized St. Denis, was well aware of this feminist project, and she helped expand it. Women in modern dance—and the leaders of modern dance, particularly in the early decades, were primarily women—took control of their own bodies. They asserted themselves as powerful movers and creators of movement, rather than aesthetic objects. This primacy set modern dance apart from ballet, where, with the occasional exception of figures like Agnes de Mille, the most successful choreographers were men.[19]

What's more, Denishawn's repertoire, which included over three hundred dances, did have its homegrown element, particularly in the work of Ted Shawn. Shawn performed as both Native American chiefs and, in *Around the Hall in Texas,* a sauntering, Stetson-hatted cowboy. He also crafted a solo for Charles Weidman as a tap-dancing, baseball-playing crapshooter, cast Doris

Humphrey as a cakewalking Creole belle in *Pasquinade*, and turned Martha Graham into a black mammy flanked by two pickaninnies in *Juba*. The whole crew toured vaudeville in the same years that Bill Robinson was trekking across the country with his stile. Despite Shawn's complaints about the "doggerel" of jazz music, modern dancers, like the rest of the nation, were drawn to the rhythms of black American dance.[20]

"The obvious themes which first come to mind when one thinks of American art production," Ted Shawn wrote in 1926, "are the Indian and the Negro." Graham made a similar declaration a few years later, but hers has more oomph. "We have two primitive sources," she wrote, "dangerous and hard to handle in the arts, but of intense psychic significance—the Indian and the Negro. That these influence us is certain." So, she went on, do the other members of our "polyglot nation," and so does the landscape itself, "its exciting strange contrasts of barrenness and fertility—its great sweep of distances—its monstrous architecture—and the divine machinery of invention."[21]

Graham's essay, "Seeking an American Art of the Dance," appeared in a 1930 collection titled *Revolt in the Arts*. She herself was revolting against all sorts of forces: "the imperialism of ballet, the sentimentality engulfing the followers of the great Isadora Duncan," and—in what may have been a shot at Denishawn—"the weakling exoticism of a transplanted orientalism." Her plea was both revolutionary and of her time. It was part of the same, large-scale interest in American identity that led Grant Wood to paint murals of American life, that moved Carl Sandburg to write folk poetry, and that prompted Agnes de Mille to bring square dance and tap into ballet. But where de Mille helped open

European dance to American influence, Graham cast her own style as wholly homegrown. Though she gave a few eastern-flavored solo performances shortly after leaving Denishawn, she soon shifted to more modest sets and costumes and developed her own technique.[22]

Graham's dancing was simultaneously pared down and amplified. It seemed to come from deep within: instead of imitating American archetypes, she plumbed their psychic depths. She danced with a low center of gravity and emphasized the importance of a bodily rhythm of contraction and release—as opposed to, say, the external rhythms of music. She used these new movements for a spate of dances on American themes: *Frontier* (1935) showed her as a pioneer woman laying claim to the space around her; *American Document* (1938) reworked the form of the minstrel show to explore U.S. history and the workings of democracy; *Letter to the World* (1940) drew inspiration from the poetry of Emily Dickinson; and *Appalachian Spring* (1944) included a folk wedding, hardy pioneer woman, and a fiery preacher whom Paul Taylor had on the brain when he came up with Noah's solo in *American Genesis* decades later.

By the time Taylor joined Graham's company, in 1955, her subjects had shifted away from Americana. Prompted by her own studies of feminism and psychoanalysis, and her tumultuous relationship with fellow dancer Erick Hawkins, she'd begun making dances incorporating Greek drama and Jungian symbolism. But she remained the highest-profile modern dancer in the country, and when asked who should get credit for pioneering a uniquely American dance, Taylor rattled off Graham's name straightaway. It's modern dance, not ballet, that America can claim as its own. Even Balanchine, Taylor said, doesn't count. His dances came from a "Russian background with, you know, changes in it"—and "the whole bit about Balanchine being so American came from Lincoln [Kirstein]." Why was Kirstein so intent on advancing the idea that Balanchine made American dances? "Well," said Taylor, "it sounds good."[23]

Taylor has railed against ballet, often in wonderfully entertaining fashion. "You can always tell ballet dancers by the length of their poses. The thoughtful type[s] stay there long enough to give the critics time to trade opinions. This eats up a lot of time, but if you listen closely you can pick up some French while you wait, since all ballet steps are imported from Europe and referred to in French, unlike modern steps, which are homegrown American and have yet to be given any names at all." Modern dance, Taylor says, lets people be people, rather than forms in an antiquated system. Ballet dancers move "from the hands and the periphery. It makes the ballet dancer look decorative, like a hollow person."[24]

Taylor comes by his disdain honestly: he was good at ballet, too. At Juilliard, he studied with Margaret Craske and Antony Tudor, and in 1959 he appeared as a guest in the Balanchine half of *Episodes.* (Martha Graham choreographed the other half.) Taylor's solo, contorted and strange, so impressed Balanchine that he had Taylor learn parts in *The Four Temperaments, Apollo,* and Birgit Cullberg's *Medea* and offered him a job with New York City Ballet. Taylor said no.[25]

Taylor did admire Balanchine's rehearsal style: he wasted no time, which was more than could be said about Graham. In the years Taylor worked for Graham, she was often drunk, and prone

Paul Taylor in his *Least Flycatcher,* 1960 (Photograph by Carl Van Vechten, courtesy the Van Vechten Trust)

to lecturing her dancers about high-minded ideas instead of teaching them steps. In the late 1950s, the dancer Glen Tetley recalled, Graham asked him and Taylor to stick around after rehearsal and practice grand pliés. (Genre wars aside, ballet steps were still part of a modern dancer's training.) Their right hands were on the barre so that Graham could see their left sides. "The left side is the heart side," she explained, "and I can only see from the heart side." The head, she went on, "must be lifted almost as if something were elevating your ears and you released the animal brain back here, so that your movement is totally strong and male. There was a period of dance when the woman was put on the pedestal and the male was denigrated to this position of looking up at her all the time. No, I want you to be animal and male." Then—wearing, as she often did, a kimono, for the exoticism of Denishawn still had its appeal—she did an "Oriental bow." Marcia B. Siegel has argued that grandstanding was not uncommon for choreographers in Graham's generation, who convinced dancers to work for them largely through the force of their personalities. Dancers were paid little, if at all, so if a choreographer wanted bodies to work on, she or he needed to inspire admiration and devotion. But Taylor was unimpressed. According to Tetley, he blurted, "What a pile of shit!"[26]

Still, Taylor admired and learned from Graham. It was with Graham that Taylor began to catch the dance world's attention, first as a soloist in her company and later as her rebellious child, branching out to make his own work. And it was from Graham that he learned what it meant to have what he has described as a "devotion to dance—almost religious in a way."[27]

Film footage from Taylor's years with Graham is relatively scarce, but there is a recording of Taylor in a 1957 performance of *Night Journey*, directed by Alexander Hammid. Graham had premiered the piece a decade previously, and here Taylor played Tiresias, the blind seer who tells Graham's Jocasta that her husband, Oedipus, is also her son. Taylor wears a long cape and carries a big stick; before the music begins, he plunges it into the circle of rope that Jocasta—who will later hang herself—holds before her. As the scene continues, Taylor waves the stick through the air and whacks at bits of the Isamu Noguchi set. In a later section, after Jocasta and Oedipus have entwined themselves into a kind of full-body cat's cradle, Taylor travels across the stage by repeatedly thumping the stick on the ground and hopping up behind it, see-sawing as if he's working a handcar down railroad tracks. But when Taylor loses the prop, he gains a new fluidity. His long arms and muscled legs sweep him into a series of arabesques. He crumples to the ground and walks forward on his knees. Even with his lower body stunted and buglike, his arms keep rowing forward. You can sense the old swimming training here, with air providing the resistance that water used to, smoothing and strengthening his movements. The other dancers remain still for dramatic effect while this is going on, which seems perversely practical: why bother giving them something to do when all eyes would have been on Taylor's hulking grace?

By the time Taylor performed *Night Journey*, his own work was already heading in a different direction. As a student at Juilliard, he had begun taking classes on the side with the former Graham dancer Merce Cunningham. Cunningham had been one of Graham's golden boys—singled out, like Taylor, for stardom.

But in 1945, he left her company to focus on his own work. With his partner, the composer John Cage, Cunningham experimented with new procedures for art making. They would compose the music and dance independent of each other, then put them together. Sometimes Cunningham would structure a dance according to chance procedures like throwing the *I Ching* or directing dancers to move according to the positions of dots on imperfectly printed pieces of paper. These experiments did more than generate surprising new choreographic forms and patterns. They helped bring dance away from the ego's organizing consciousness and toward the happenstance of daily life. They also helped Cunningham avoid plot or personal emotions, to focus on the nature of dance itself.

Taylor was intrigued. In the summer of 1953—two years before he started dancing professionally for Graham—he followed Cunningham to Black Mountain College in North Carolina, grew a beard, and became a founding member of Cunningham's company. The college, an experiment in interdisciplinary education, had been host for the previous twenty years to some of the most exciting developments in American art. The year before Taylor arrived, for example, John Cage organized his first "Event." The audience sat in the middle of the room, while around them, in overlapping intervals of time chosen by chance, Charles Olson and M. C. Richards climbed up ladders and read their poetry; Robert Rauschenberg projected slides of his all-white paintings and played Edith Piaf records; Cage read a lecture on Buddhism; Cunningham danced while chased by a dog; and the composer David Tudor played piano. (In an alternative description, Olson and Richards were planted in the audience, Cage read texts from the medieval mystic Meister Eckhardt, Cunningham was accompanied by other dancers, and Tudor poured water in and out of buckets.) Whatever happened that night, the nascent leaders of the avant-garde joined together and instead of laboring to perfect their individual artworks, they experimented with new ways of working and sharing that work.[28]

The performances Taylor participated during his first summer at Black Mountain were less chaotic, but no less historic. For six weeks, Cunningham held classes and rehearsals in the dining hall. He and his students would push the chairs and tables over to the side of the room and dance, even as kitchen staff were preparing food in the background. After eight hours of dancing, they would stumble back to their shared cottage, unable to take hot showers because by that point in the day all the hot water would be used up. It was a period of extraordinary productivity. Cunningham premiered several new works in the company's performance that August, including *Banjo, Septet,* and *Dime a Dance.* His pieces ran the gamut: *Banjo,* set to the southern themes of Louis Moreau Gottschalk, was a piece of Americana—complete with cakewalking struts—that might have made Ruthanna Boris and Agnes de Mille feel at home. *Dime a Dance,* on the other hand, involved thirteen choreographed sections, only seven of which would be used in a given performance: an audience member would pay a dime, pick a card, and determine which section came next. Taylor soon decided that chance procedures weren't for him: why labor over work that would not be performed? Why relinquish control when he could ensure a particular result? He left Cunningham's company the following year, in 1954.[29]

Still, those early experiences with Cunningham were formative ones. Taylor continued to think about the purpose, or point-
lessness, of plot, and about what movement might mean on its
own terms. Those concerns animated his first piece of choreography, *Jack and the Beanstalk,* which premiered in New York in
1954. The piece had both dance and story, but clove the two apart.
Seven dancers performed seven sections of what Taylor, in his
choreographic notes, called "pure dance," with "no relation to the
story line." The story came in pantomime interludes, introduced
by a drumroll and concluded with a sound effect: a "rising whis-
tle," a "cymbal," a "raspberry." But the dancing had pantomime
too, as in the "chicken-egg duet," beginning with a long section
of meaningless sign language. The chicken's loving ministrations
toward her unhatched offspring are continually interrupted: two
people stuff a third person into a bag and drag him away, the ogre
and harp waltz by, ruffians have a fight. Finally, the chicken gives
up, picks up her egg—designed, by Robert Rauschenberg, with
an electric lightbulb—"switches it off, & retreats to corner." The
scene has the repetitive pleasures of a slapstick routine, but it's
also about thwarting plans and flouting sentimentality, about
throwing different elements together and seeing what happens.[30]

Rauschenberg's sets and costumes for *Jack and the Beanstalk*
were designed to be temporary, and some were positively flimsy.
After the show, he and Taylor released the beanstalk—a piece of
string held up by helium balloons—into the New York sky. Taylor, as Jack, wore a cropped mesh top and orange leggings. Dancer
Viola Farber, in drawers, a cropped T-shirt, and a beauty pageant
sash, was—the sash helpfully explained—"MOM." Bits of the story
floated about in a kind of collage.[31]

When *Jack and the Beanstalk* premiered, Taylor was finding his place in a downtown community of young, heady artists, including not just Cunningham and Cage, but also painters Rauschenberg and Jasper Johns, and writers such as Frank O'Hara and Edwin Denby. They would gather in Greenwich Village lofts and bars to share ideas and swap critiques. They often collaborated; they were open to experimentation; and they began to push the limits of how art could look and what it might say. For many artists—Taylor included—this meant turning away from what seemed like the sanctimoniousness of the work that typically earned critical acclaim. Some of the new work was comic or deceptively casual. At a time when mainstream academic poetry centered on the confessions of Robert Lowell or the supposed universalism of Richard Wilbur ("Poems," Wilbur explained, "are not addressed to anybody in particular"), O'Hara dashed off verses during his lunch hour, often framing them as missives to particular friends. And in the same year that Martha Graham debuted her psychological masterpiece *Clytemnestra*, Cunningham, following a suggestion from Rauschenberg, danced with a chair strapped onto his back.[32]

These artists were rejecting more than just the artistic status quo. In the early years of the Cold War, if you believed what you saw on TV, nuclear families in the suburbs were the country's spiritual safeguards. The lives on the screens were a far cry from those of artists in New York City, many of whom were gay, living in walk-up apartments, and aligned with various left wing causes. This was the era of the Red Scare, led by Joseph McCarthy, as well as the Lavender Scare, when President Dwight Eisenhower signed an executive order listing "sexual perversion" as a reason to fire federal employees. According to the historian Charles Kaiser, the feds purged at least 640 gay employees from the payroll (more probably resigned of their own accord), and "the State Department fired more than twice as many homosexuals as it did suspected communists." In New York, life for homosexuals was better, but by no means easy. Undercover cops entrapped gay men and harassed women who seemed inappropriately mannish. Two men were unable dance together in public unless a woman was with them. Yet gay New Yorkers carved out worlds of their own, apart from the mainstream, in bars, at parties, and during weekends in the country. The filmmaker James Ivory recalls seeing Paul Taylor, Frank O'Hara, and other men skinny-dipping in a New Hampshire stream. If it hadn't been so chilly, the scene could have passed for a pastoral idyll.[33]

Taylor has never talked much about his sexuality, and while that reticence may sound like a way of avoiding sexual politics, it's also a quiet form of political resistance. The scholar Rebekah Kowal suggests that in the fifties, when psychology still defined homosexuality as a mental illness, dancers like Taylor and Cunningham rejected psychology altogether. In other words, Taylor was not just turning away from Martha Graham's version of Jung, with, as he once put it, all those "caves and columns." He was also turning away from a world that was trying to define who he was and to make him want to be someone else.[34]

And he was turning *toward* a new creative community: friends who would swap ideas and invent scenarios for making art in an environment of creative ferment. "The arts community was much smaller" then, Taylor explains; "all the painters and writers and poets and designers, everyone would get together" and share ideas. Frank O'Hara's poem "Dances Before the Wall" captures some of that communal energy. "My love is like a strong white foot," O'Hara begins, and carries the analogy on for a stanza. There's a break, then "suddenly everybody gets excited and starts / running around the Henry St. Playhouse"—where James Waring's "Dances Before the Wall" premiered. The rest of the poem could be a Who's Who of fifties dance, with cameos by dancers, designers, and critics: "Midi / Garth goes tearing down the aisle towards Fred / Herko while Sybil Shearer swoons in the balcony / which is like a box when she's in it and Paul / Taylor tells Bob Rauschenberg it's on fire / and Bob Rauschenberg says what's on fire." The poem seems to be a reflection on the nature of community: everyone is relating to someone else. Even Shearer, swooning, is connected to Herko, in that they act at the same time and share the same line, and to O'Hara, in that he's observing them. Or so it goes until Doris Hering, the editor of *Dance Magazine,* shows up, and "Doris Hering says Doris Hering was here." But the end of the poem restores everything to a thoughtful togetherness, in a scene that Paul Taylor told me was pretty routine: "we go to Edwin Denby's and talk quietly all night."[35]

Taylor's dances often have the feel of an O'Hara poem: friendly, inviting, and turned toward the wider world—but also strange, unruly, and experimental. "Dances Before the Wall" has no punctuation, and O'Hara sometimes begins sentences, then changes course midway through, introducing a new thought overlaid on the one that came before. There's a story, but you can't quite follow it. And while you have a sense of speed and play, nothing is as slapdash as a cursory glance might suggest. All these traits show up in a piece Paul Taylor first choreographed in 1956, *3 Epitaphs,* now a mainstay of his company's repertoire.

*3 Epitaphs* seemed designed to upend convention. Taylor had been crafting a piece set to Debussy's impressionist piano music, but the movements were coming out rote and too pretty. When his friend James Waring played him a bizarre new release from Folkways Records, Taylor changed course. The record was *Music from the South, Volume 1: Country Brass Bands,* and it featured the Laneville-Johnson Union Brass Band, made up of six elderly black men. The Laneville-Johnson players keep a thudding, military rhythm, yet they lack martial precision. Their arrangements are loose, almost weary, with the instruments drifting into so many different pitches and meters that they seem to belong to several bands playing at once. The music unravels itself and, threadbare, threatens to fall apart altogether. Taylor was smitten.[36]

Folkways, founded by Moses Asch in 1948, was an immense sonic preservation project. The company documented everyday noises (dogs, office sounds, streetscapes), cut new albums of folksingers (Woody Guthrie, Pete Seeger, Leadbelly), re-released out-of-print commercial 78s, and made field recordings, like the one Taylor heard, available to a wide audience. Before Folkways, folk music had entered the national consciousness somewhat smoothed over: in the orchestrated sorrow songs of the Fisk Jubilee Singers, the wholesome renditions of Carl Sandburg's *American Songbag,* and the operatic voices of Marian Anderson and John Jacob Niles. By the thirties and forties, the Popular Front was using folk music to bolster class consciousness: Paul Robeson sang the "Ballad for Americans," Woody Guthrie chronicled the struggles of Dust Bowl refugees, and the Weavers toured union halls. Folkways continued some of that work, but also helped usher in a brand new sound: scratchy old commercial country and blues 78s from an earlier era, as well as recordings of real live rural folk, away from the coastal metropolises, making music. These releases changed the way Americans thought about their musical heritage. Compared to what had once been classified as folk music, recordings like the one Taylor heard sounded rough, raw, even foreign. They seemed to come from what Greil Marcus has called the "Old, Weird America."[37]

Marcus was writing about another Folkways release—Harry Smith's *Anthology of American Folk Music,* which came out a few years before Taylor choreographed *3 Epitaphs*—but the description still fits. As Marcus explains it, in an era of aggressive Americanism, this music seemed to come from an altogether different country. It showed that, "against every assurance to the contrary, America was itself a mystery." Paul Taylor seems to have heard that mystery in the Laneville-Johnson Union Brass Band. Instead of trying to solve it, he danced his way into it, threw it onstage, and left his audiences to puzzle out its meaning. He also lost his first batch of dancers, who quit when he traded Debussy for the Laneville-Johnson Union Brass Band.[38]

We don't know exactly what *3 Epitaphs* looked like in its first performances in the spring of 1956. Back then, it had four dancers, was titled *Four Epitaphs,* and lasted for about twenty minutes. But in 1960, Taylor revised and retitled it for the Spoleto Festival in Italy, creating the version his company now performs. It has five dancers and lasts just over five minutes, the length of two songs—a sly joke in keeping with the uneven music. The casting is lopsided too: a very tall dancer is paired with a very small one.

Three others form a primordial chorus line, flopping their hips from side to side. The dancers often lope about, dragging one leg behind them. When they jump, they force themselves into the air, then thud back to the ground.[39]

Robert Rauschenberg designed the costumes: full-body black unitards that cover the feet, the hands, the head, and even the face. (Taylor had no input in the design, and told me that this was how he wanted it: "I expected he would do something terrific.") Little round mirrors bulge from the dancers' foreheads suggesting gas masks, or the eyeballs of flies. There are mirrors on their palms, too. Years later, in *Dancemaker*, Taylor characterized the piece as an exploration of the split between "our poor, miserable, apelike primitive selves and that striving to be human and to hold our backs up straight."[40]

The description makes the dance sound serious, but it is funny, too—in the way that seriousness sometimes has to seem funny, so that it doesn't make us cry. The dancers don't look like us, and yet beneath the costumes, we know they are the same. When the small dancer follows the tall one around, she seems part pet and part shunned, love-struck child. The two dancers barely make contact, and their few encounters are brief and awkward: they lean into each other and touch at the shoulders, or he hoists her up by the waist and drops her back down. Sometimes the dancers make circles with their forearms with the speed of the cartoon Road Runner. Are they yearning for a fuller motion they can't achieve? Halfway through, in the pause between songs, one dancer comes out with newfound buoyancy, preening and flexing, only to hunch back over and scamper away as the music picks back up.

One could describe *3 Epitaphs* as an exercise in delicious contrarianism, particularly with regard to Rauschenberg's costumes. One of Taylor's former teachers, Doris Humphrey, used to tell her students that the face was "the most eloquent and familiar part of the body," and when Martha Graham saw the piece, she told Taylor, "Naughty boy, we don't cover up their faces." *3 Epitaphs* may even have been a revision of, if not a direct jab at, Graham. In the thirties she had premiered a solo, *Lamentation,* in which she was outfitted in a leotard and a long tube of fabric. The fabric acted as a new skin: she stretched inside it, pushed against it, and at one point raised it over her head, consumed by grief. Taylor also deals in grief—epitaphs, after all, go on gravestones—but Rauschenberg's costumes make the head covering a permanent condition.[41]

They also banish personal identity: all we can judge the dancers in *3 Epitaphs* on is their movement. The piece thus becomes, on some level, about gesture itself: the unexpected ways the body can be carried, the wondrous and weird capabilities of arms and legs. Many critics have focused on this aspect of the piece, seeing *3 Epitaphs* as a marvelous joke, upending dance traditions.[42]

Yet as various versions of the program notes have made clear over the years, *3 Epitaphs* engages with American history as well. The music was "early New Orleans jazz music," or "an ancestor of jazz," played "at weddings and funerals in the Southern United States." As of 2015, the website of the Paul Taylor's American Modern Dance identified the music only as "early New Orleans jazz." In fact, the Laneville-Johnson Union Brass Band was based in Hale County, Alabama—some 280 miles from New Orleans—and for all we know, its members may have never even set foot in the Crescent City.[43]

The Laneville-Johnson recordings are from the early fifties, when the folklorist Fredric Ramsey traveled through the South on a Guggenheim grant, searching for amateur musicians who had not yet been recorded by his colleagues. Ramsey was hunting for the roots of jazz. He hoped that old folks in out-of-the-way places would be able to transmit the sounds of the late nineteenth century. He lacked the evidence to claim outright that the Laneville-Johnson Union Brass Band was a link to the music of Emancipation, but he hoped—and in his liner notes for Folkways strongly suggested—that it was.[44]

In fact, a number of the songs Ramsey recorded are twentieth-century creations. "Precious Lord, Hold My Hand" and "Wild About My Daddy," the compositions Taylor used for *3 Epitaphs,* are from the twenties and thirties—one is by songwriter Thomas Dorsey, the other by Ma Rainey. (The titles seem to be misremembered versions of "Precious Lord, Take My Hand" and "Farewell Daddy Blues.") So the idea that these men were living in a musical vacuum, untouched by the modern world, is bunk. When Ramsey stopped in New Orleans and played his discordant finds for a leading local brass band, asking if the members recognized the sounds of "the old days," they shook their heads in what the music historian Samuel Charters describes as a "stunned silence." Ramsey pressed them. "I never heard anything like that in my life," one musician responded. Finally, another tactfully offered to "help those boys." If Ramsey would bring them to New Orleans, "we could show them how to play so they'd know how to make a sound on those horns."[45]

The brass band tradition in New Orleans, even in the late nineteenth century, was practiced and professional. The

Laneville-Johnson players, by contrast, were old men living in the country, elderly sharecroppers who stored their instruments in a hog shed and got together for a weekly jam session every Saturday afternoon. In the past they had performed more frequently—in fact, in the past, they had been two distinct bands: the Laneville and Johnson bands. But so many members had died that the survivors had joined forces to become the group Ramsey found. Even then, the band Ramsey recorded was incomplete: it no longer had a trumpeter. This is probably why, Charters explains, it is difficult to pick out a melody in the recordings. The music was not, as Ramsey hoped, a direct ancestor of jazz.[46]

Ramsey's apocryphal history is not Paul Taylor's fault—he was probably just going by the Folkways liner notes, trusting Ramsey—but we might pause to consider what it means to have a dance fueled by someone else's fantasy. Part of the emotional resonance of *3 Epitaphs* comes from the idea that these strange, sad sounds once resonated through city streets as dirges at the start of jazz funerals, and the rollicking second lines that follow. Even though none of the gestures from such scenes—marches, breakdowns, the thumping of parasols—is present in the piece, Taylor seems to want viewers to have them in mind. Why else would he have written the program notes? Just over a decade earlier, folk music had made its way onto dance stages in orchestrated form: Aaron Copland composed the scores for de Mille's *Rodeo* and Graham's *Appalachian Spring*, both of which featured folk motifs. Taylor, on the other hand, found a folk music that sounded wild, old as mud yet utterly avant-garde. If the pieces seemed central to the development of America's only native music, all the better.

Taylor often creates work on American themes, but critics never seem to classify *3 Epitaphs* among those works. This is a mistake. Taylor, following Ramsey, imagined that he was hearing the roots of American music. Onstage, he created a community of people who barely make contact, who may not even know who they themselves are, but who labor, nonetheless, to keep moving. His *3 Epitaphs* belongs to no recognizable time period, unlike Taylor's *Beloved Renegade,* which harkens back to Walt Whitman's nineteenth century, or *Black Tuesday,* which turns to the Great Depression, or *Also Playing,* which pokes loving fun at turn-of-the-century vaudeville. But *3 Epitaphs* lives in its own American past, a murky land where old men gather on a farm and haphazardly blow their horns.

While *3 Epitaphs* hinted at the strangeness of the American past, one of Taylor's next works, *Seven New Dances,* got at the strangeness of the American present. Imagine the scene. October 20, 1957: High on the burnished wood walls of the 92nd Street Y's Kaufmann Concert Hall, directly beneath the ceiling, the names of prophets and visionaries are painted in gold letters: Isaiah. Jefferson. Emerson. Einstein. Spinoza. Some dance fans in the audience might even consider adding Martha Graham's name to that roster. She is a titan in her own right, and without her they might not have heard of Paul Taylor. But when the curtain opens on the first piece, *Epic,* the scene is decidedly understated: it has no set, and Taylor is not dressed like a dancer—he wears a dark, trim suit with a dark, skinny tie. He is standing still, facing the wings. There is no music, unless a recording of a woman on the telephone announcing the time at ten-second intervals counts as music ("at the tone, the time will be 2:54 and ten seconds"). Beep. Taylor pivots to face forward, then steps to the side. "At the tone, the time will be 2:54 and twenty seconds." Beep. Taylor has taken a couple more steps to the side, into a spotlight. "At the tone, the time will be 2:54 and thirty seconds." Taylor places his left foot on his right calf, puts it down, does a quarter pivot—Beep—puts the foot back on the calf, puts it back down, and turns to face the audience again. Similarly choppy movements continue, along with the recording, for the duration of the piece. As Taylor moves through a sequence of everyday postures, the audience realizes that this is all he intends to do: he is not going to sweep into the strong, graceful movements for which he is known. and their disappointment becomes apparent.[47]

In one sense, there was nothing epic about *Epic*. Unlike the heady Greek dramas Taylor had danced with Graham, it had no plot. Its sustained, small movements seemed calculated to provoke. But if Taylor was taking a jab at the leaders of the art world, he was also claiming their ambition for himself. *Epic*, he has written, was meant to be a "Rosetta Stone" of postures, an index of "our oldest language." Taylor dissects these postures, sometimes presenting them piecemeal: at one point, he crosses his legs and slides toward the floor, as if he's going to sit down, but freezes before he gets there. A second later, he's back up, facing the audience. This is a difficult feat of balance. In fact, the whole dance is difficult. With no music, no meter, and no flow between movements, Taylor has to keep everything in his head, rather than his muscles. It is, he wrote later, "like trying to memorize a telephone book."[48]

Ezra Pound defined an epic as a poem that contained history; *Epic*, on the other hand, contains time. The ten-second segments pass by in such rote uniformity that they inevitably call up ideas about regimentation, about how clock time both breaks life into pieces and gives it an order. In his trim suit, executing everyday postures, Taylor looks like a well-mannered businessman who might have walked onstage straight from the streets of Manhattan. Everything is so controlled, and so ordinary, that ordinary control begins to look bizarre.

*Epic,* along with the other six dances on the program that night, was an exercise in found posture. Choreographers had used pedestrian movements in the past, but they tended to integrate them into a classical vocabulary. Taylor was stripping things down, presenting posture as its own kind of dance. As he explained years later, "I thought I had discovered a whole new realm, and it was beautiful, and it would make everybody just look around in the street and say, Gee, isn't this pretty here, you know, all these people doing these wonderful things."[49]

But sometimes people weren't doing anything at all: in *Duet,* another piece on the program that evening, the dancer Toby Glanternik sat on the floor, her legs crossed at the ankle beneath a dark, full-circled dress. Taylor stood behind her, off to the side. They made no eye contact. Neither moved. It was the dance equivalent of John Cage's infamous 4'33", in which a pianist takes the stage but never plays a note. At the same time, even in still poses, Taylor and Glanternik unavoidably suggest some sort of human drama: viewers have to wonder who these people are, and what is between them. Creating these kinds of dances, Taylor says, taught him that "posture and gesture are inseparable." The body is always telling you something, even if it doesn't mean to.[50]

Few in the audience got the message. John Martin walked out partway through. Louis Horst, the music director and modern dance tastemaker who had taught Taylor dance composition at Juilliard, gave the piece a four-inch blank review in *Dance Observer,* his own Cagean experiment, as well as an indication that there was nothing to say because nothing had happened. But as the years went by, *Seven New Dances* became a kind of shorthand for talking about Taylor's early, heroic rebellion. He was a golden boy turning his back on his mentors, saying that he could do what he wanted, how he wanted, and it would matter, saying that the unfettered movement of his fellow citizens, looked at closely, might count as dance.[51]

In the coming decade, avant-garde choreographers in New York would employ many of the same strategies Taylor displayed that night in 1957. Like Taylor, they were schooled in Cunningham's technique. And like Taylor, they took cues from Cage, studying his ideas in a composition class led by the musician Robert Dunn at the Judson Memorial Church. As the dance critic Deborah Jowitt puts it, "The new generation noted the discrepancy between Cagean theory and Cunningham practice: if any noise could figure in a musical composition, why wasn't any human movement a fit ingredient for dance?" In other words, they out-Caged Cunningham. Whereas Cunningham used performers with extensive training and refined technique, the choreographers who came out of the Judson school made work that was often anti-virtuosic. In *Three Satie Spoons* (1961), Yvonne Rainer performed simple gestures like squats and rolls. In *Satisfyin' Lover* (1967), Steve Paxton recruited around thirty untrained performers to walk across a gym floor in their every-day clothes, some of them pausing to sit or stand still.[52]

By the time such experiments were afoot, Paul Taylor was moving toward dancing that looked, to some members of the avant-garde, suspiciously mainstream. In January 1962, the Judsonite Fred Herko attacked Taylor in *The Floating Bear,* a magazine co-edited by the poets LeRoi Jones (later Amiri Baraka) and Diane di Prima. It is unclear which pieces Herko was responding to—perhaps *Junction,* to music by Bach, which Taylor premiered in November 1961—but Herko's appraisal was damning. In the past, he wrote, Taylor "made dances because he loved making them," but now his work had become careerist. "It is hard to watch Paul Taylor working at his job," Herko wrote. "A job is not interesting or beautiful or exciting."[53]

Later that year, Taylor gave the more belligerent members of the modern dance community more reason to respond sharply. *Aureole,* costumed in white and set to Handel, was a runaway hit. The movements had such lyricism that, though the steps were not actually balletic, critics called it a "white ballet." But in its way, this piece was as experimental as anything Taylor had ever done: now, instead of pushing against Graham or Cunningham or any other choreographer, he was pushing against his own past.[54]

Still, those early rebellions kept coming back. Taylor reworked pieces of *Epic* in the 1982 dance *Lost, Found and Lost,* and pedestrian gestures have remained a hallmark of his work. They constituted almost all the steps of *Esplanade,* the first piece Taylor created after his collapse in *American Genesis* and one that continues to earn him new fans. Taylor, no longer dancing, was returning to his roots: straightforward, everyday movements. But instead of pairing them with a straightforward, everyday score, he opted for Bach, giving the piece a sense of nobility. Designer John Rawlings costumed the dancers in peaches and oranges that suggest the beginnings of spring or dawn.[55]

*Esplanade* may have been inspired by a woman running to catch the bus, but no one would mistake Taylor's dancers for people in the street. Their movements are too organized, synchronized with one another's or varied in time with different threads of the Bach, and too beautiful, slipping from pedestrian gestures to more mannered ones. They pump their arms when they run, but they also fling them into elegant V's when they turn and jump. They leap into one another's embrace with the absolute trust of babies who don't yet know what it means to fall. But they do fall: sliding across the stage, sometimes alone, and sometimes in pairs, holding each other lovingly as they tumble. When the curtain opens, they look out at the audience with the frankness of equals, but they're really better, or at least more pronounced, versions of ourselves. We know it as soon as they start to walk.

"Amazingly beautiful, so large and clear": that was how Taylor's friend Edwin Denby, the poet and critic, described the walk of New Yorkers in "Dances, Buildings, and People on the Street." Denby wrote the piece in 1954 to encourage young dancers to pay attention to the "dance of daily life." His descriptions of walking are revealing: "Americans occupy a much larger space than their actual bodies do; I mean, to follow the harmony of their movement or of their lolling you have to include a much larger area in space than they are actually occupying. This annoys many

Europeans; it annoys their instinct of modesty. But it has a beauty of its own, which a few of them appreciate. It has so to speak an intellectual appeal; it has because it refers to an imaginary space, an imaginary volume, not to a real and visible one." Daily motions, in Denby's telling, constitute feats of creative invention.[56]

*Esplanade* seems like the embodiment of Denby's essay. Taylor puts everyday dance onstage. In one sense, he doesn't bother, as Denby does, to signify these movements as particularly American: there are no flags, no folkloric archetypes. Yet Taylor takes pains to distinguish the steps from ballet—which, as he's made clear elsewhere, he thinks of as European. In fact, he might as well be picking a fight with one of Denby's favorite choreographers, George Balanchine.

Balanchine, widely hailed as the father of American ballet, trained in Imperial Russia and worked for Diaghilev's Ballets Russes and the Ballet Russe de Monte Carlo before settling in the United States (he continued to work for the Ballet Russe afterward). In his first few years stateside, he did a good deal of commercial work on Broadway and in Hollywood, but *Serenade*, a ballet he choreographed in 1934, is generally identified as his first American creation. This offers, as the scholar James Steichen has pointed out, a convenient focus: it lets dance fans claim Balanchine for the classical, highbrow tradition, rather than the popular one.[57] The focus makes sense on another level, too: *Serenade* seems to be, at least in part, about the beauties of classical tradition. It begins by showing the transformation of women into ballerinas.

When the curtain rises to the impossibly beautiful opening chords of Tchaikovsky's Serenade for Strings in C, seventeen women in pale blue tulle—a trimmed-down version of nineteenth-century Romantic tutus—stand with their heels together, their toes pointing forward. Their right arms are in the air, palms flexed. Balanchine reportedly got the idea for this opening pose when he walked into the studio and saw a roomful of students with their hands in the air, blocking the light from their faces. The dancers in *Serenade* hold the pose for several seconds, then extend their hands to create straight lines with their arms, sharpening the ordinary movement. They drape their hands onto their faces, across their chests, and into a low oval before opening their feet into first position. Still in unison, they stand on one leg while sliding the other across the ground. This movement, tendu, is one of the first exercises in a ballet class. If you have ever studied ballet, *Serenade* will feel familiar. If you believe in ballet, *Serenade* will remind you why. Its opening seconds glorify technique, training, perseverance, and, as the number of bodies onstage indicates, a tradition that is bigger than any individual.

In *Esplanade,* Paul Taylor picks a fight with that tradition. (The titles even rhyme, so long as you pronounce both with either an American or a French accent.) Like *Serenade, Esplanade* begins with simple, straightforward movements: two rows of dancers, beginning to walk. Yet the pieces embody fundamentally different techniques. Where Balanchine's dancers start by shifting their feet into basic balletic stances—first position, then a tendu into fifth—Taylor's dancers start in third position, then give it up.

At least two everyday accidents influenced Balanchine's choreography for *Serenade:* one dancer showed up late for rehearsal, and he worked it into the piece; another fell, and he kept that, too. Taylor's dancers also fall, again and again, sliding across the ground like ballplayers and getting up even faster. But their falls aren't happy accidents. They are the heart of the work.

In the brown wide-ruled notebook Taylor kept while creating *Esplanade,* he made a long list of postures to consider using, including "bow," "rub or pick feet," "tie shoe," "dry with towel," "rub ache," "walk a dog (or let loose)," "grooming: plait hair, clean nails, smooth clothes, button up, pick nose," "sneeze, cough," "console a cryer," "direct traffic," "twiddle thumbs," "kill (choke)," "jump for joy," "wheelbarrow," "blessing," "pick lint." He also considered dance steps that, though some came from ballet, were simple enough to seem similarly natural: pas de chat, skip, sauté. Not all these movements appear in *Esplanade,* but the list demonstrates the capaciousness of Taylor's thought process. He was not simply listening to the music, waiting for it to tell him something. He was thinking, quite deliberately, about both the surging glories of Whitmanic multitudes and the more pedestrian "things people do."[58]

Taylor's choreographic notes also list "antic hay," a phrase from Christopher Marlowe's *Edward II,* when the king's friend plans an entertainment in which his "men, like satyrs grazing on the lawns, shall with their goat feet dance an antic hay." Taylor seems to have been drawn to the phrase for its peculiar linguistic quality—what he described as the "poetic combo of ordinary words." *Esplanade,* in turn, is a poetic combination of ordinary gestures. Gesture, of course, was Taylor's chief concern— but the notebook indicates that he thought hard about words, too. There are long lists of them, often in alphabetized clusters, as if Taylor were going to the dictionary for inspiration. Some are architectural: "gateway," "window," "threshold," "fountain," "door," "causeway," "colonnade," "concourse," "corbel." Others come from nature: "stream," "cumulus," "cascade," "corolla," "larkspur," "laurel," "lawn." Still others refer to human characteristics: "person," "earthling," "mortal," "league." "Anthology" shows up several times, once with the parenthetical "(rt. word)." "Anthology" may refer to a grouping of elements—such as natural gestures—but at its root, *anthology* means a gathering of flowers.[59]

An esplanade, the word Taylor eventually decided to use as a title, is a long, open space. It is often found beside the sea, where people walk for pleasure, but sometimes it is the median in a road, where it provides a kind of green respite, and sometimes it is the top of a wall surrounding a city, where it enables viewers to look at the unrestricted world beyond. The word comes from the Latin *explanare,* which means both "to spread out or flatten" and "to explain." All these meanings are alive in Taylor's work. His dancers expand the space they move through, and they show us the building blocks of movement, especially walking.

Paul Taylor is a connoisseur of walking. "He can imitate gaits and walks beautifully," former company member Dan Wagoner noted. When Taylor holds auditions for his company, often the first thing he asks prospective dancers to do is walk. "I can eliminate half of them by how they walk," he explains. "They're either too self-assured or not assured enough, or they're just weird." But the focus on walking is not just a way for Taylor to observe and judge potential dancers—it is also important because walking, like every other dance step, matters. Taylor wants his dancers to move like real people, not figures in a music box. It's no wonder that the film version of *Esplanade* for PBS's *Dance in America* series opened with close-ups of each dancer's face and gave his or her name below.[60]

Onstage, Taylor wrote, "we see an individual, and we see what that individual is. All this exact training and stylization cannot abstract a body into a nonentity. A person is going to be revealed." That statement comes from a piece for *Dance Magazine* called "Down with Choreography," and when Taylor declared "Up with dancers; down with choreography," he was not simply offering a mock manifesto. It was that, too, but Taylor clearly enjoys the genres' convention even as he mocks them. "These eight dancers are not exactly like tubes of paint with which to cover the canvas of space. Not exactly. They have character and personality, which they ASSERT. They have individualized traits, and just when you think you know how to handle them they CHANGE. Not like canvas that stays stretched once and for all. They sometimes get fat or discouraged or both. They acquire feelings of inadequacy. They have birthdays." Farther on, he explains that dance should be "a vehicle, not necessarily for one star, but for everybody. You try to find aspects in individual dancers that can be exploited. That is what people are for—to be used. They like it." One can almost see the sly smile behind the words, yet Taylor's more serious point holds. He may be president of his own artistic republic—even, as he has said elsewhere, a dictator—but he wants to govern benevolently. So while his dancers are members of a collective, they are also individuals—people in a society, ever on the move.[61]

While the relationship between a dance company and a political body was analogous in "Down with Choreography,"

Taylor had made the correlation more directly a year earlier, with a piece about the performance of national history. *From Sea to Shining Sea* begins with a cast of performers milling about in their bathrobes before launching into a mixture of vaudevillian antics and tableaux vivants of American history. He titled one section of the piece "Us," a pun on U.S.[62]

One could also say that *From Sea to Shining Sea* began with Taylor's anxiety about the state of his own, artistic nation: a dancer who had been with him for four years, Renée Kimball, had resigned with a nasty note; Twyla Tharp, back from a six-month leave of absence after telling a reporter that Taylor's art was "totally commercial," would soon leave for good. Taylor began rehearsals with a series of violent pantomimes, unsure of what they would become. When his costume designer, John Rawlings, suggested clothing everyone in red, white, and blue, Taylor agreed. The piece would be about a discordant America.[63]

Or one could say that *From Sea to Shining Sea* began in a more general sense of postmodern malaise, when, after the unity of World War II—the spirit that helped de Mille make *Rodeo*—the nation had begun to question the myths it once took as sacred, to see that popular culture had become as powerful as myth, and to decide that it was time to tear the myths down.

In 1953, Larry Rivers, who was part of the same downtown New York scene as Paul Taylor, painted *Washington Crossing the Delaware*. In Emanuel Leutze's 1851 painting of the same name, Washington stands in a small boat so full of soldiers it couldn't possibly have floated, leading Revolutionary America into a sunnier future. In Rivers's version, the canvas is dark and smudged, with scattered, disconnected figures—soldiers, civilians, horses, hills, and a dim sun. Washington stands in the center, his left leg in a tall leather boot, his right fading into white. Rivers made history dissolve. His painting was partly rebellious, partly reactionary. At a time when abstract expressionists were the darlings of the art world, Rivers went for figuration. And not only that: he chose one of the most traditional subjects available.

Rivers called the painting a "mixture of grand art and absurdity," a phrase that also applies to Taylor's *From Sea to Shining Sea*.[64] Taylor's Washington emerges from a gaggle of weary performers, standing on a boat made of other people's bodies, backed by a few rowers. But the tableau vivant falls apart after about fifteen seconds, when the boat revolts, making Washington stumble. Everyone stands up and shuffles around, waiting to try out another scene.

*From Sea to Shining Sea*, like Rivers's painting, takes on the stock symbols of American history, then shows that they don't hold water. Taylor premiered the piece to Charles Ives's "Three Places in New England," but royalty difficulties mandated a switch. So he commissioned John Herbert McDowell to compose a score and used it for a new, longer version of the piece. (Clive Barnes wrote that this new version was "sharpened to the point where it now draws almost as much blood as laughs.") McDowell's score is tonal, layered, and atmospheric. Bits of familiar songs float in and out, like pieces of a dream.[65]

"Send me the wretched refuse of your teeming shore," Taylor titled the first section, and the quotation recalls not just Emma Lazarus's words on the pedestal of the Statue of Liberty but also garbage bobbing in the Hudson. Taylor has put the viewers in Trotsky's ash heap of history, and in T. S. Eliot's Waste Land, with its "heap of broken images." Superman kills a flapper. Lady Liberty is consumed by her rocky base, which turns out to be a businessman, with whom she runs off. In his memoir, Taylor described the dance as "old Miss America's wrinkles, patriotism past its prime," noting that "some might call it social satire. Others might be content to call it funny business." But *From Sea to Shining Sea* is too damning to leave Americans smiling for long. Sure, there's comedy. An Indian does a goofy pantomime that involves multiple "How"s, a Boy Scout salute, hunting signs, fishing, and a curvaceous woman. But then the Pilgrims kill him and trample his body. After they leave the stage, Plymouth Rock—played by Lady Liberty covered in gray gauze—consumes his corpse like an ectoplasmic blob, as if erasing not just his claim to the land, but his entire presence in history.[66]

*From Sea to Shining Sea* is an indictment of American hypocrisy, as well as an exploration of how symbols work and what they threaten to hide. That may be why, at one point, a man with a broom sweeps the stage. It's certainly why Taylor focuses so much on the nature of performance. In the last two sections, "Us" and "Living Pictures," dancers cycle through the clichés of both showbiz and American history; the implication is that the two aren't far apart. There are inept chorus girls, half-hearted cancans, and mediocre tap dances. A woman does a back bend, then struggles to sit in the arms of two men who swing her, slowly, as if on a wobbly trapeze. A man stands on his head with a tiny American flag strung between his ankles, dangling just above his crotch. Meanwhile, upstage, someone seems to be dying, covered in red-and-white stripes as if in a shroud. Even this seemingly hidden history turns out to be fake: the would-be corpse jumps up and scampers off.[67]

The performers get at more particular narratives, too: in what almost seems like a direct jab at *Rodeo,* a dancer suits up like a cowboy and dances with his honey. Betsy Ross sews Old Glory. Lady Liberty, as the Virgin Mary, cradles a crucified Jesus surrounded by a cluster of performers with trembling jazz hands: the Pietà on Broadway. A few seconds later, the dancer who played Jesus goes down on one knee like the blackfaced Al Jolson belting out "Mammy." A man solicits a whore. And throughout the last third of the piece, a blasé Marlon Brando—initially played by Taylor, in a leather jacket, boots, and tilted cap—sulks along the sidelines, unimpressed by the troupers' efforts.

The costume came from Brando's role in *The Wild One,* where, as a member of the Black Rebel Motorcycle Gang, his character was—in the words of Pauline Kael—"antisocial because he knew society was crap" and "a hero to the youth because he was strong enough not take the crap." Brando played an instinctive rebel, a naysayer for the sake of nay-saying ("What are you rebelling against?" "Whad'ya got?"). He is the closest thing to a hero that *Sea* has. Taylor seems to have enjoyed emulating Brando's brute physicality: the slow saunter, shoulders tilted, arms crossed. At the end of the performance, he tosses Lady Liberty's crown on the ground. Yet this gesture—a sign that society is crap and he's fed up—doesn't fix anything. The country's damned, and there's no indication that Brando, or anyone else, can redeem it.[68]

*From Sea to Shining Sea* premiered at the end of March in 1965, one of the bloodiest and most galvanizing months of the Civil

Rights movement. Much of the action was focused in Selma, Alabama, where African Americans had been trying for several years to exercise the voting rights accorded to them by law. They had support from the Student Nonviolent Coordinating Committee, and from the Southern Christian Leadership Conference of Martin Luther King, Jr., but these were not enough. Activists lost their jobs. They were legislated against. They were arrested. They were beaten. And when, on March 7, some six hundred protesters began marching from Selma to the state capital of Montgomery, a crowd of angry white men—many of them newly deputized by the racist county sheriff—attacked them. Seventeen marchers were hospitalized. Larger marches followed. A white Unitarian minister came down from Boston to join the cause and was beaten to death by the Ku Klux Klan.

The KKK does not appear in the 1965 version of *From Sea to Shining Sea*, but when Taylor expanded the piece with the new score by McDowell, he gave it what, in vaudeville, would have been a starring position: next to closing. Just before Brando shows up to toss Lady Liberty's crown at her, three members of the Klan march onstage, and one stops to stab a passerby. The Klansman takes off his white hat and robe: he's Lady Liberty. It's a shock, but Taylor doesn't let viewers languish in the pleasure of righteous indignation. The murder victim, Taylor is quick to remind them, is just a performer. After the stabbing, he walks off to join his buddies as if nothing has happened.

*From Sea to Shining Sea* may start with the same impulse as Rivers's painting, but it becomes progressively darker. America's shiny myths don't merely fade; they become stale. They are performances that distract from a violent past—and the performers are accessories to the violence. When they try to take a critical look at the past—the KKK, the genocide of Native Americans—they still can't do anything about it. That's what's truly terrifying about *From Sea to Shining Sea*. When Brando chucks Liberty's crown at her feet and wanders off, we get the sense that Taylor is giving up on his own life's work.

When Taylor next returned to American themes, in 1970, he thought he would make "a dance about social injustice." According to preliminary choreographic notes, this new piece, *Big Bertha*, would "compare the pleasure-seeking 'isolationists' with the unfortunate," the "ins & the outs," the *"haves & have-nots."* He considered various scenarios. Perhaps a bum would ask a rich person for money, and the rich person, refusing, would feed the money to a machine that played dance music. "Find ways to show extreme cruelty of dancers who do not care," Taylor jotted down. But he also considered making dancers the underdogs, who "plea for $ & dance in return."[69]

Taylor had more ideas. Perhaps the "ins" were after "automatic pleasure." Their dancing could reflect the fact that they were "unable to engage anymore." Perhaps they had "tough skin—from overindulgence." And then Taylor landed on a scenario that stuck. "The ins are the present," he wrote. *Big Bertha's* theme would be "the disregard of the past." The piece began to take shape: the "ghosts of the past" would wreak their revenge.[70]

History haunts *Big Bertha*, controlling the dancers' very bodies. The curtain goes up on an antique, buxom automaton perched on a pedestal stage—the kind you might see at an early-twentieth-century fairground, or, these days, in a museum exhibit. Three bodies litter the scene. But the spotlight is on Bertha, who creakily draws a sword from her mouth. By the time she's finished, the corpses have vanished. A wholesome-looking 1950s family—mother, father, and daughter—traipse up to the machine. The father drops a coin into Bertha's hand, and she creakily swallows, burps, and waves her baton. Out comes the chirpy music of a mechanical band, and the family begins to dance.[71]

At first, their motions seem benign, even bland. But when the daughter takes a solo, she repeatedly flings up her poodle skirt, flashing her undies, and ushering in a sense of unease. Is this gesture innocent? Sexual? Her parents smile with approval. They do a quick duet to "My Blue Heaven," and Bertha taps the father with her baton. He stumbles, freezes, and begins to dance in unison with Bertha—a simple box-step with which the mother, then the daughter join in. It's hard to say who is in control. Bertha is orchestrating the father's steps, but it's he who, mid-dip, lets his wife crumple to the ground as the music stutters off. Then he runs back to Bertha, puts a coin in her hand, and gives her pedestal a kick to keep the music going.

Against a chipper rendition of "Take Me out to the Ballgame," the father saunters toward his daughter, thrusting his pelvis and wiggling his tongue. Then he slaps his wife in the face. His limbs propelled by a force not his own, he flops and stutters toward his daughter, yanks her from her chair, and carts her away. When the mother tries to chase them, Bertha freezes her with a point of the baton, and she heads back to her chair, gnawing on her fingernails. Father and daughter keep dancing: they shimmy and thrust; he fondles her thighs; she rides him like a horse; he slides her between his legs; she lies on her back with her thighs splayed apart while he pushes up between them in an erect headstand. Then the pair head behind Bertha's stage for unwatchable horrors. Now the mother—who has fed Bertha a coin of her own— does a desperate striptease. By the time her husband and daughter return, their clothes torn and bloodstained, both women are limp and defeated. The entire family crumples to the ground, and a cannon goes off behind them. But the dance isn't finished. Bertha totters over and coaxes the father up to dance with her. She picks up a discarded poodle skirt and drapes it on him like a cape, depravity turned to glory. By the time the curtain falls, the father and Bertha are both up on her stage.

Audiences are routinely shocked by *Big Bertha*—who expects to be confronted by incestuous rape when they head out for an evening of dance?—and Taylor has joked that it is "always nice to see such a happy, pleasant little family go down the drain." But his approach is quite serious. If *Big Bertha* is about the demise of a family, it takes the long view favored by psychotherapists: as Bertha wreaks her will on the father, he unleashes his own demons on his family, cycles of abuse carrying forward with almost mechanistic precision. It's no coincidence that the program identifies the family only as Mr. B., Mrs. B., and Miss B. Originally, Taylor called them the Banks family. But instead of focusing on their money, he cut the identification down to an abbreviation— which leaves open the possibility that Big Bertha, a Ms. B, is their ancestor.[72]

Bertha is their ancestor in a more general way, too. She represents the past itself. The B. family try to engage with her at the level of nostalgia, but find that the past is filled with horrors that continue to influence them. If America is a family, it does violence to itself, the strong terrorizing the weak. Indeed, the piece codes these horrors as distinctively American. Bertha's stage is topped with a bald eagle, festooned with red sashes and white stars on a blue field. She wears a blue and red cap, blue cape, gold bodysuit, and heeled, knee-high boots: a buxom, militant Uncle Sam. When she swallows that sword, it's as if the whole country is ritually impaling itself.

"Big Bertha" was the nickname of a German cannon in World War I, and when the piece premiered, America was in the thick of the Vietnam War. The critic Anna Kisselgoff has suggested that *Big Bertha* is a "sardonic commentary on patriotic homilies in the immediate aftermath of the My Lai massacre," when U.S. soldiers murdered as many as five hundred South Vietnamese civilians.[73] In other words, a nation made up of seemingly happy families, carnivals, baseball, and dancing is also a war machine. Things that are supposed to proceed according to clear and orderly plans—robots, battle strategies, the spread of democracy—go horribly wrong. When Bertha points her baton, she more or less conscripts the family into a demise that's partly of their making. Just as mother and father keep feeding Bertha coins, citizens vote leaders into office, and stand by as disaster happens.

In Taylor's Americana pieces, the violence of history tarnishes the dancers' polished performances. But corrosion and construction can join forces, nowhere more movingly than in *Company B.* Taylor choreographed the dance for the Houston Ballet in 1991, and companies across the country—including Taylor's own—have been reviving it ever sense. The Andrews Sisters' peppy harmonies set the scene, and while brainstorming for titles,

Taylor even considered using their first names: "Patti, Maxine, & Laverne [*sic*]." Perhaps this was because their careers stood for much of what the piece explores: art that provides an escape from the hardships it simultaneously reckons with.[74]

During World War II, the Andrews Sisters were everywhere, rallying the country to cheerful unity. They were known as the Sweethearts of the Armed Forces Radio Services, their voices broadcast on both sides of the Atlantic. They raised money for war bonds, appeared at servicemen's clubs in the United States, and donned uniforms to travel with the United Service Organizations (USO) and entertain troops abroad. Writing about those experiences years later, Maxene Andrews recalled singing "Don't Sit Under the Apple Tree" for a departing ship, "looking up at all those young men leaning over the ships' rails, waving and yelling and screaming" and wondering how many would return home alive.[75]

Still, she and her sisters kept singing, and so did other entertainers, their voices joining with audiences' as soldiers shipped off to fight. In the midst of war, song and dance took on a new urgency: they represented the freedom Americans felt they were fighting for, even as they provided a respite from that fight. One GI, stationed in Europe, told the USO that he'd "hitchhiked almost two hundred miles" to see their touring production of *Oklahoma!* According to Maxene Andrews, when sixteen thousand GIs watched a performance by Dinah Shore and Spike Jones and his City Slickers in France, "five merchant marines jumped ship and swam to shore" to join the audience.[76]

In the Andrews Sisters' songs, Taylor heard the world that music helped buoy listeners against. When they sing "Everybody has a mania / to do the polka from Pennsylvania" in *Company B,* Taylor's dancers interpret the words literally. They polka with a strange showiness, hopping a little too frantically and kicking their legs up as high as they'll go. Halfway through the song, the meaning becomes clear. Upstage, silhouetted dancers move in a slow-motion line. They shoot. They are shot. Then they enter the light and join in the dance downstage. But instead of vanishing, the war ends up closer to home: when the song ends, three dancers fall down dead.[77]

"Spasms of effort to be cheerful," Taylor wrote in his choreographic notes for *Company B.* A suave hepcat who combs his hair, straightens his collar, and leaps with incredible verve also twitches with posttraumatic stress disorder, and falls as if ducking his own memories of fire. At another point, seven women surround a be-spectacled man, three even leaping onto his body at one time, their legs wrapped around his torso. He shakes them off and wipes his brow. It's funny: with men so scarce, even this goober has become a hot commodity. But there is also a sense of the overwhelming burden of supporting the women of America. Manliness comes off as an excessive performance. The dancer keeps parading back and forth, leaping, snapping his fingers, jumping and flexing his biceps. The women's desire seems equally extreme: they shake their hips in desperate, uniform seduction.

By 1942, the servicemen's clubs where the Andrews Sisters performed were benefiting from a new initiative: the "Dance for Defense" campaign. Private dance studios, in concert with the Office of Civilian Defense, trained young single women to serve as volunteer dance partners for American military men. Volunteers were instructed to dance with any man who asked them;

James Samson and other members of the Paul Taylor Dance Company in
*Company B*, 2012 (© Paul B. Goode Photography)

as the sociologist Maxine Leeds Craig puts it, their job was to
"restore men for war by performing cheerful and chaste subor-
dination." In a way, the men were performing too: these women
were not their sweethearts, and were not there to seduce them.
In fact, the women were instructed not to accept requests for
dates. Instead, servicemen and volunteer dance partners were to
act like lovers only for the length of a song.[78]

*Company B* involves a similar kind of performance: men and
women go through the motions of heterosexual love with a sense
of obligation. They owe it to their country to be as macho or as
feminine as they can. As Taylor makes clear, that model is restrictive. During a melancholy solo to "I Can Dream, Can't I," a
woman succumbs to a spastic fit that rivals the mad scene from

*Giselle* for heartbreak: she's pushed around, turning at off-center angles, feet flexed—then she recovers, curving her arms and resuming her lyrical swoops and turns. She's not the only one hoping to hold on to a dream. Upstage, two silhouetted soldiers face each other with a tenderness that suggests illicit love, then march off in slow unison. During World War II, estimates the historian Allan Bérubé, between 650,000 and "as many as 1.6 million male soldiers were homosexual." But homosexuals were kicked out of the armed forces, and officials called for conformity. Taylor shows all this in a few simple gestures: the heartbroken woman, the closeted soldiers, a stageful of people endeavoring to keep up pretenses.[79]

*Company B*'s most surprising heartbreak, though, comes in a virtuosic solo: "The Boogie Woogie Bugle Boy." According to the lyrics, the bugle boy—a trumpeter from Chicago who's been drafted into the army—restores fun to order, and makes "the company jump when he plays reveille." With no other dancers onstage with him, his commitment to the cause is even starker. It's as if he's collected everybody's energy and packed it into his own taut muscles, so revved up that he can't stand still, and must keep bounding across the stage, snapping his fingers, tooting his imaginary horn. When the song comes to a close, he salutes and marches bouncily off toward the wings. Then he's struck by an invisible bullet, and dies. Usually, the end of such a virtuosic solo would call for applause, but for those who watch *Company B* with attention, it's hard to feel like clapping.[80]

Much of the dancing in *Company B* is signature Taylor—the powerful shoulders, the curved arms, the sporty leaps—but there are also shadows of the Lindy Hop, the dance that originated at

Harlem's Savoy Ballroom in the 1930s and by the 1940s had spread across the country and around the world. The Lindy was smooth, fast, and flowing, danced from a low crouch that gave dancers' fundamental steps bounce and made it easy for them to swing out into larger, virtuosic motions. The story goes that when white dancers, who were unused to moving with a low center of gravity, tried the Lindy for themselves, they looked so awkward that blacks called them "jitterbugs." The name stuck. But as the Lindy's popularity spread, observers celebrated it as a new national folk dance, proof of the American melting pot at work. When the country entered World War II, the Lindy began to seem like a sign of American grace, modernity, and strength.[81]

That was how the Andrews Sisters made it seem, too, despite the arguments of jazz alarmists that the jitterbug reflected a profound social malaise, and was physically dangerous to boot. A man doing the jitterbug with his wife in their apartment, went one newspaper story, "slipped on a rug and dove out the window." And in 1944, a Los Angeles court awarded around eight thousand dollars in damages to a hostess at the Hollywood Canteen who'd been injured when dancing the jitterbug with a "jive-maddened marine." According to Judge Henry M. Willis, the dance "constitutes a real danger for one not skilled in its gyrations."[82] But when the Andrews Sisters appeared in the movie *The Hollywood Canteen* that same year, they mounted an argument, in song, that the only real risks of the jitterbug were fatigue and blisters.

According to the lyrics for "Corns of My Country," volunteer hostesses have partnered so many men that their feet are killing them. Yet a real fervor, induced by both patriotism and jazz, drives them on: "When we think we can't go on, we find we can't get enough." At one point, the jazz backing gives way to strings and a fluttery flute, and Patty Andrews bourrées backward, mocking a mincing ballerina. "I used to be aesthetic, they say, oh yes, I was, really I was. I loved the drama, art, and the ballet," she sings. Her sisters chime in: "But the Theatre Guild came over and said forget about Pavlova, learn to cut a rug." All three then proclaim themselves jitterbugs, clap their hands, and shake their hips in joyful unison. This is dance as a counter to both high art and deep malaise.

When the Andrews Sisters sang "Corns for My Country," they didn't need to say that "corns" could slip into "corny," or that light-heartedness could take people's minds off their pain. They didn't need to say that the soldiers for whom they wore down their feet might be injured far more grievously, or killed, in battle. Their audience knew it, and so, some forty years later, did Paul Taylor. After the New York premier of *Company B,* he took the stage with Maxene Andrews—then seventy-three years old—for a brief, jitterbug encore.[83]

Writing about Ginger Rogers, Pauline Kael once praised "the happy, wide streak of commonness in a person of so much talent. Maybe it's her greatest asset that she always seems to have a wad of gum in her mouth."[84] The same description could almost apply to Paul Taylor, with his happy, wide movements, his talent, his populist sensibilities, the chewing gum handy for the times he can't smoke a cigarette. Yet in Taylor's work, commonness is never entirely familiar. Instead, he makes everyday movement—the encyclopedia of gestures in *Seven New Dances,* the confident walks and runs in *Esplanade*—uncommon. The same goes for national life. The stories Americans think they know take on darker hues. In *American Genesis,* a white father tries to drown his black daughter. In *From Sea to Shining Sea,* the performers' enactments of myths and legends are as stale as whoopee cushions, and just as quick to deflate. In *Big Bertha,* the ghostly past destroys an ordinary family. And in *Company B,* nostalgia gives way to loss.

*Company B* opens and closes with the same song, "Bei Mir Bist Du Schön." Sholom Secunda and Jacob Jacobs wrote it back in 1932, and it became a hit in New York's thriving Yiddish musical theater. When Sammy Cahn heard two black performers belt it out to an appreciative crowd at the Apollo a few years later, he realized the song could have enormous crossover appeal. He and Saul Chaplin translated it into English, keeping the titular phrase intact, and persuaded three sisters from Minnesota, gentiles with parents who had immigrated from Greece and Norway, to record it. By 1938, it had become the Andrews Sisters' first hit.[85]

That sounds like a happy, only-in-America, minority-to-mainstream melting pot story. But 1938 was also the year of Kristallnacht, when the Nazis destroyed Jewish stores, torched a thousand synagogues, murdered nearly a hundred Jews, and sent thirty thousand others to concentration camps. It is the event that many historians cite as the start of the Holocaust. Whether or not they were aware of the unfolding genocide, Americans were dancing to Yiddish lyrics, and the country was on the brink of war.

Recalling the creation of *Rodeo* during World War II, Agnes de Mille wrote that she "thought of the men leaving, leaving everywhere—generation on generation of men leaving and falling and the women remembering. And what was left of any of them but a folk tune and a way of joining hands in a ring?" In *Company B*, Paul Taylor seems to be asking what good joining hands in a ring could do. When the curtain goes up to the strains of "Bei Mir Bist Du Shön," the dancers mill around in sepias and grays, like old photographs coming alive. Soon, they form a circle, their arms around one another's shoulders in what Taylor described, in his choreographic notes, as a "reference to Jewish folk line dance." A few moments in, the ring breaks apart. The dancers line up, then pair off. One man is left lying behind, dead.[86]

When the song plays again, at the end of *Company B*, the dancers come tumbling onstage like fallout from an explosion. Though they resume some upbeat, snappy dancing, it doesn't last for long. There's a blaze of light, and they move into slow motion, a few melting to the ground. Patrick Corbin, who danced with Taylor's company when Taylor choreographed the original piece, has said that he always thinks of this section as the beginning of the nuclear age. The atom bomb has been dropped, not just on enemy soldiers, but on civilians, too. America's stature as a global power seems secure, but so does the fear of a coming apocalypse. The dancers spin out from the center of the stage, and walk toward the wings alone. Then the Bugle Boy snaps his fingers, and the lights go out.

# 6 MICHAEL JACKSON'S MOONWALK

Just over a week after Neil Armstrong and Buzz Aldrin first set foot on the moon on July 20, 1969, the *Los Angeles Times* reported on a possible new dance craze: the moonwalk. Mrs. Lillian Lu Pau, a dance teacher in Houston, hoped to introduce a resolution at the annual Dancing Masters of America convention the following month suggesting a new dance to commemorate America's achievement. She had not yet decided on a name. The newspaper suggested "moonwalk," but Mrs. Lu Pau was considering "lunar lope."

Then again, why settle for a simple social dance? Maybe the moonwalk could help Americanize ballet, too. "Aside from 'West Side Story,' and a few others," Mrs. Lu Pau said, "we don't have very much American ballet." Maybe "something to do with the moonwalk exploration" would "give us a step in the right direction."[1]

What Mrs. Lu Pau didn't know was that what would become the moonwalk had already existed for decades, though nobody called it that. To black dancers in California, it was the backslide. To tappers, it was a skate. To the French mime Marcel Marceau, it was "walking against the wind." None of these incarnations looked much like the lunar lope of Armstrong and Aldrin, who at one-sixth their normal weights bounced across the moon's powdery surface, describing their actions for a rapt, earthbound audience nearly a quarter of a million miles away. "The rocks are rather slippery," Aldrin said, so "you have to be rather careful to keep track of where your center of mass is." He tried a "kangaroo hop" (did he know this had been the name of a ragtime dance?), but found it simpler to put one foot in front of the other. President Richard Nixon called the astronauts from the White House. "Because of what you have done," he told them, "the heavens have become part of man's world."[2]

In the space-age fever that followed *Apollo 11*, dance floors across the world hosted their own moonwalks. The Lem, a novelty dance at a hotel in Nice, involved jumping on one foot six times "in cosmonaut position" as the arms moved "slowly to give the idea of weightlessness," reported U.S. papers. Viennese revelers were doing their own moonwalk in 1970; the *New York Times* described it as a "a slow dance inspired by the hesitant steps of the astronauts." Down in Jamaica, a band called the Mighty Vikings—who advertised, in the *Kingston Gleaner,* that they had introduced the boogaloo, the horse, and the reggae to the island—promised to roll out both " 'THE POPCORN' / America's Newest Dance Craze" and " 'THE MOONWALK' / Jamaica's Newest Dance Thing." The following year, Willie Dickson and the Playboys brought their "Reggae and Moonwalk tunes from Jamaica" up to Montreal. Perhaps this moonwalk was the same one that showed up on the West Coast in 1980, when New Wave club dancers described their form of skanking—the torso tilted forward, the arms splayed out to the side—as "the moonwalk."[3]

By May 16, 1983, when Michael Jackson debuted his moonwalk on the television special *Motown 25: Yesterday, Today, and Forever*, these earlier stabs at dancing in zero gravity seem to have been forgotten, and the heady excitement of *Apollo 11* was a long time in the past. The latest journeys to the moon had happened on a space shuttle, originally called—how's this for the glamour of new frontiers?—a "space truck." President Ronald Reagan had recently proposed the Strategic Defensive Initiative, a massive shield that would protect the country from enemy missiles. It was an outlandish idea, popularly derided as Star Wars, after the George Lucas movies, but it made explicit what had always been part of the space race: militarization to ensure world domination. In an odd way, Michael Jackson was tapping into that same spirit, as his album *Thriller* climbed to the top of the charts and stayed there. Jackson was not content to make a good record or explore new artistic frontiers. He wanted to make the biggest record the world had ever seen. He wanted to be impervious to attack. And he did so, in part, with a moonwalk of his own.[4]

Visually, Jackson's moonwalk had more in common with Lucas's *Star Wars* than with Reagan's. It seemed to be the product of special effects—something an ordinary human body shouldn't be able to do. When Jackson had hired Geron "Casper" Candidate to teach it to him, noted Candidate, he had even checked the bottoms of Candidate's shoes, suspecting that the dancer must be wearing wheels. As the years went on, Jackson integrated the moonwalk into a public persona that emphasized his own exceptional otherworldliness. This was a man who—he told interviewers in the early eighties—did not know how to have friends. He identified with E.T. and the Elephant Man, installed life-size

Michael Jackson performing "Billie Jean" at *Motown 25* (Courtesy Photofest)

figures from *Star Wars* at his Neverland ranch, and had his biological face remade by cosmetic surgery. In the video for "Billie Jean," Jackson has the Midas-like ability to illuminate whatever he touches and a superhero's power to disappear. In the movie *Captain EO*—which George Lucas produced—Jackson leads a crew of aliens and robots. In *Moonwalker,* he turns into a car, a robot, and a spaceship.[5]

Technologically advanced as Jackson's moonwalk seems, it's straightforward human locomotion. That's part of its power: a mere man should not be able to do it, but he can. In this it resembles another dance Michael Jackson helped popularize: the robot. Imitating technology, then besting it, the virtuoso dancer makes the human body seem like a better machine than any machine a human body might build.

Jackson rose to stardom in the age of the television, a medium he helped popularize and transform. He was both a talent and a feat of marketing, a man who in some ways became a product, his likeness plastered onto T-shirts and toy radios and duplicated in flexible, dressable dolls. But he was also, at his most powerful, a man with a body, and viewers could watch him in action. He developed a personal iconography—the glittery socks, the fedora, the single glove—and a roster of signature moves: the moonwalk and robot as well as the tight spin, the high kick, and the perch on the tips of his toes. That last one even shows up in the logo he used for the 1988 film *Moonwalker* and at the foot of each page of his autobiography, *Moonwalk:* pointed feet in black loafers and white socks, lines shooting out from the legs like rays from a neon light.[6]

Jackson was not the first dancer to do any of these steps. He picked them up by watching James Brown and Jackie Wilson and Motown singing groups, by taking lessons from the black dancers on the television show *Soul Train* who brought West Coast funk styles to the masses, and by taking cues from stars like Fred Astaire and Bob Fosse. Just as *Thriller* mixed musical styles—rock guitars, R&B crooning, disco dancing beats—his dancing came from multiple sources. In the end, though, Jackson made the moves, like the sounds, his own. His quick freezes, for example, might have originated with Bob Fosse, the showbiz choreographer Jackson idolized. Or they might have come from Don Campbell, the Los Angeles dancer who pioneered the fundamental hip-hop technique of locking. But Jackson so absorbed their styles that it is impossible to determine who originated them: now they belong to Michael Jackson.

Jackson would know that a song was good when it made him want to dance, and his fans felt the same way. They practiced his moves in front of their bedroom mirrors, out on the streets with their friends, or in front of their televisions, watching VHS tapes that promised lessons in the latest dance trends, Jackson's included. In 1984, an eighth-grader in the town of Itasca, Illinois, blacked up, drenched her hair with styling gel, performed a Michael Jackson song, and won "most original" in the school talent show. She was not the only such original. Thirty to forty Jackson look-alikes roamed the streets of Chicago that year, some of them happily signing autographs as if they were the man himself. Up in Winnipeg, 175 competitors entered a Jackson dance-alike contest, and 13,000 people gathered at a public park to watch the finalists moonwalk it out. Eighteen-year-old Larry T.

Ellis, a Jackson imitator based in Pittsburgh—Ellis preferred the term "illusionist"—brought his fifteen-minute Jackson tribute to high school auditoriums, football halftime shows, and hotel bars across the country, sometimes borrowing a limo from his uncle's funeral home for extra panache. Ellis had never met his idol, but his comments to a reporter implied a mystical connection: "I've always met him in my dreams. I dance with him every night in my dreams."[7]

The stories kept coming. Kids in New Jersey were suspended for wearing single white gloves to school, then staged protests to protect their First Amendment right to look like Michael Jackson. Indian Americans practiced Jackson's moves outside a Hindu temple in Malibu. Preschoolers moonwalked in the District of Columbia, and when a local morning show held a dance contest, contestants could enter in the category "Michael Jackson, Junior Division." In Dallas, a six-and-a-half-foot-tall man started dancing at the grocery store and was so immersed in his performance that he moonwalked into a woman's shopping basket. She screamed.[8]

No one had seen such a fever before. The Castles, the Astaires, Elvis, the Beatles—Michael Jackson was bigger. What's more, he was a black man in a culture that remained largely segregated. Jackson had begun his career playing for black audiences, but he managed to sing and dance his away into cultural ubiquity, the closest thing to a promised land American offers its pop stars. A fifty-one-year-old buying *Thriller* at a Chicago record store in 1984 explained his purchase: "I guess what I like about Michael Jackson is his beat. And that when he dances he defies God's physical laws." The man owned only one other record: Simon and

Garfunkel's *Bridge over Troubled Water*. Like the gospel heroes of yore, Michael Jackson had crossed over.[9]

Michael Jackson started life in the segregated steel town of Gary, Indiana, living in a two-bedroom house with ten other family members. Michael's father, Joe Jackson, moonlighted as a musician, and he groomed his children for the stage—though "grooming" is a mild word for the physical and emotional abuse he combined with rehearsals. Michael, Joe's primary victim, was also the family's biggest talent. By age seven, he was fronting the band, the Jackson 5. Some of the group's earliest work can be seen in the grainy, black-and-white footage of their 1968 Motown audition. While his brothers play in the background, stepping from side to side, little Michael sings James Brown's "I've Got the Feeling." He doesn't just sing: he takes on James Brown's whole being, with a conviction and physicality that belies his mere ten years. At one point he pivots into a tight turn, slides into a split, and springs back up. But for most of the song, the action is in his lower body: he scoots backward and side to side on slippery feet, and knocks his knees together in a mashed potato. This is the "wing" part of the nineteenth-century buck-and-wing, by way of the Charleston, carried forth by minstrel men to Macon, Georgia, where it was funkified by the Godfather of Soul, and mimicked by a little boy from the Midwest.[10]

Michael Jackson idolized James Brown. "No spotlight could keep up with him when he skidded across the stage—you had to *flood* it! I wanted to be that good," Jackson recalled. He studied Brown's moves both on television and up close, off to the side of stages they shared on the chitlin' circuit, the network of black clubs and theaters where rock 'n' roll and soul music were born. Years before the Jackson 5 signed with Motown, they were gaining a reputation on the circuit, gigging on weekends, vacations, and school nights, catching some sleep on the long drives back to Gary. In those early years, the Jackson 5 covered a lot of ground—Phoenix, Philadelphia, Chicago, Bloomington, and New York—and they developed a good reputation among black fans, including Sam Moore and Gladys Knight. But James Brown was already a titan on the circuit, and had found crossover success with white fans, too.[11]

Brown toured the country, picking up dances as he went. As R. J. Smith puts it in his masterful biography *The One*, Brown was the "Johnny Appleseed of dance." He'd watch his audience's moves, refine them, and perform them himself, carrying the mashed potato and the Watusi across state lines, planting steps in city after city. "Mix 'em all together," recalled his band member J. C. Davis, "and now we're doing some of everybody's dance together"—turning regional moves into national ones.[12]

Brown and his band worked it. They were phenomenal musicians, and showmen too. When they met their would-be manager Clint Bradley one Saturday morning in Macon, Bradley asked them to sing a spiritual. They sang "Looking for My Mother," and according to Preston Lauterbach's account in *The Chitlin' Circuit*, they acted it out, "singing and peering under tables around the bar, looking for their mother, already adept at the kind of theatrics that would make the James Brown show unlike any other showbiz attraction in the coming years." Jackson and his brothers would pull similar stunts in their early days of performance, acting out the words to their songs. When they covered Joe Tex's "Skinny Legs and All," Jackson remembered, he would "crawl under the tables, and pull up the ladies' skirts to look under." It was a bizarre combination of innocence and sexuality, and the crowds loved it. When Jackson stood back up to resume dancing, people threw money at his feet.[13]

Young Michael Jackson learned to play up his precocity. Once the Jackson 5 had signed at Motown, he put on a fedora and pretended to dump Diana Ross as part of a TV sketch. He sang about schoolyard romance with the emotional range of a grown man who'd known real heartbreak. He danced with the ease of an old showman—snapping his fingers, neck loose, hips busy—but there was no mistaking his skinny little body for anything but a boy's. Brown, on the other hand, was a man.

At the height of his fame, Brown embodied a defiant form of black masculinity, black power, and black pride. After James Meredith—the Civil Rights leader who had integrated the University of Mississippi and then called for the March Against Fear to register black voters—was shot by white supremacists in 1966 (he survived), Brown performed for the crowds of protesters, weeping as he sang "Please, Please, Please." Two years later, he cut "Say It Loud, I'm Black and I'm Proud." He had a private jet. He endorsed politicians, who courted his approval. And he inspired a generation to move with a power that was equal parts spiritual and carnal.[14]

That power suffuses the cape act, a standard of Brown's show, which he rolled out for a national audience in 1964 on *The T.A.M.I. Show*. He joined a lineup that included the Rolling Stones, the Beach Boys, Chuck Berry, and Marvin Gaye, then blew them all away. When Brown sang "Please, Please, Please," the teenage audience, to put it bluntly, lost their shit. It's worth watching his entire performance, but here's the most important thing to know: the spirit enters James Brown, and, as the Pentecostals say, he falls out.

Partway through the song, Brown is so consumed by energy that he stops singing, drops his head, and stamps his feet. One of the Flames, his back-up singers, comes forward and drapes a floor-length cape over Brown's shoulders. Brown shakes the cape off, returns to his song, and falls to his knees, pulling the mike down with him. Back comes a Flame, and on goes the cape. It's the type of scene you'd see at a Pentecostal church: a member of the congregation feels the Holy Ghost, shakes all over or bobs up and down at the waist, and others gather around, to keep the person safe from the jutting corners of pews. Sometimes a believer enters a trance down on the ground and is covered with a sheet. Brown's cape functions like the protective sheet, but as Smith points out, it also makes him a leader: capes were part of the uniform of Holiness preachers, and Brown channeled their spirits, if not their God. Watch the cape act closely, and you'll see that it's choreographed: when Brown falls down, overcome, he's still keeping time, leading the band with his own convulsions. Here's Smith's take: "Call it shamanism or showbiz, whatever you name it, this is some powerful secular magic."[15]

Shamanism and showbiz. On stage from the start of elementary school, Michael Jackson must have learned that he needed them both—and not just for his audience. He needed them for himself, too. Performance, Jackson later said so frequently that it began to seem hackneyed, was a form of "escape." It was a way for life to seem bigger and more meaningful than its everyday incarnation, and a way for Jackson to feel loved and accepted. Jackson's art emerged from what was clearly a prodigious natural talent: at age four, his performances were so advanced that his precocity frightened his mother. But it also came from hard work, and from his daddy's fists and belt thrashings. And it came from study: Jackson learned to mimic other performers, adapting their moves to his own art. Jackson never stopped working. If he was going to outshine them all—his family, his peers, the country that told him boys of his color would not amount to much—he needed his music, and his dancing, to be perfect.

For Berry Gordy, Jr., the founder of Motown Records, success on the chitlin' circuit hardly counted as success. Gordy was a businessman. To get rich selling records, his artists, as the label's slogan put it, needed to become "the sound of young America," which is to say, mainstream America—white as well as black. Gordy's stars performed at white supper clubs and appeared on national television. They played music that typically avoided overt political statements, sounded good on car radios, and had a beat so steady and pounding that—as one joke had it—even white folks could dance to it.[16]

Motown's appeal was both sonic and physical. In 1964, Gordy hired Maxine Powell, founder of a finishing and modeling school in Detroit, to run Artist Development, a wing of the company devoted to helping entertainers with their physical carriage. Powell taught Marvin Gaye to stand up straight and open his eyes when he sang. She got Diana Ross to exchange her long false eyelashes for shorter ones, and told the Supremes, the Vandellas, and other female singers to tuck in, rather than stick out, their buttocks. The Jackson brothers had some of this training too, though not from Powell: they worked with Suzanne de Passe—later the president of Motown Productions and a successful producer—whom Gordy made their manager. De Passe quizzed them on sample interview questions, gave them advice about manners, and honed their image to seem simultaneously childish and hip, with colorful costumes and Afros. But while their hair signaled that they weren't conforming to white standards of beauty, the Jacksons were supposed to stay away from talk about politics. When an interviewer asked them about Black Power, Michael Jackson wrote in *Moonwalker,* a Motown rep—one was always present when the press came around—interrupted to explain that the Jacksons "didn't think about that because" they were "a commercial product." Later, the brothers "winked and gave the power salute." These products knew how to joke, even—however quietly—to rebel. Generally, though, they followed the label's lead.[17]

De Passe convinced the Jacksons to ditch what Nelson George, in his history of Motown, calls "the James Brownisms." After all, Brown was the musical face of Black Power. His show was rough, sweaty, sexualized, and effortful—descriptions that did not apply to a typical Motown act. Even when Brown's backup dancers were in unison, they seemed on the verge of flying apart, as if all the collective energy on stage might combust. Motown artists, on the other hand, held it together. Singers stood in a line, did an occasional grapevine, leg kick, or Charleston, and stepped in time with the backing music even as their voices sounded out dominant melodies. It was a style the Jacksons would learn too, and it came to them largely because of the work of a single man: Cholly Atkins.[18]

Atkins, a tremendous tapper, helped carry Depression-era movements into the days of Afros and Black Power. He started performing in the thirties as a singing waiter, then as one half of the Rhythm Pals—a duo whose act included a version of Bill Robinson's stair dance. (Unlike many of Robinson's imitators, the Rhythm Pals performed it with Uncle Bo's blessing.) Within a few years, Atkins had begun choreographing chorus lines, appearing in black Hollywood choruses, and dubbing taps for white chorus dancers. He also choreographed for Eleanor Powell, toured with big bands, including Cab Calloway's, and partnered with Honi Coles in one of the most celebrated "class acts" in the history of tap. Class acts, in marked contrast to their minstrel predecessors, were bringing tap to new heights of refinement, and Coles and Atkins set the standard. Coles, erect and precise, tapped with a speed and complexity that dazzled even his most talented peers. Atkins, readier to focus on the movement of his whole body— an awareness that came, at least in part, from watching dancers trained in ballet—brought a loose lyricism to the duo. They liked to close their show with a gorgeous, slow soft-shoe, with minimal accompaniment. Without their dancing, it seemed as though the music would dissolve altogether.[19]

But by the middle of the century, tap dance was losing its cachet. In part, the change came about because of changes to jazz music itself: as the dance historian Jacqui Malone explains in *Steppin' on the Blues*, jazz musicians and dancers used to feed off each other. Their symbiosis was both artistic and financial: they traded rhythms and toured together. The rise of bebop changed all that. Bop arrangements were often too tight to make room for tap solos, and they were hard to dance to socially. Besides, with the 1944 "cabaret tax"—30 percent, later lowered to 20 percent, for any club with a dance floor—jazz began to move into smaller clubs that had no room for dancing. Finally, tap suffered from an image problem: in the burgeoning Civil Rights era, tap seemed uncomfortably close to minstrelsy. Even though class acts like Coles and Atkins defied the minstrel's demeaning image, performing in handsome suits and refusing to play the clown, they found it increasingly hard to get gigs.[20]

There was another reason for tap's wane: Agnes de Mille—or, more precisely, *Oklahoma!* The success of *Oklahoma!* created such excitement about ballet that Broadway demanded more, and correspondingly less tap. But the change did not represent simply a turn to the highbrow. In the past, specialty numbers were thrown into musicals because they could be: a comic might make a cameo, a tapper might dance in one scene and never show up again. These opportunities no longer fit into the more coherent, serious "musical plays," as the precedent-setting shows of Rodgers and Hammerstein were known. Now, dancing served the plot, expressing psychological nuances that script and song could not convey on their own.[21]

Tap did not disappear; de Mille even worked with Coles and Atkins in one of her next musicals, *Gentlemen Prefer Blondes*. (They created their own number, but as the official choreographer she got the credit.) Cholly Atkins had other brushes with ballet, too: he shared a studio with the former Ballet Russe de Monte Carlo dancer Karel Shook, who, like the black New York City Ballet star

Arthur Mitchell, urged his students to take tap to improve their timing.[22]

Nevertheless, by the late fifties, Cholly Atkins needed another way to ply his trade and pay his bills. He found it in the nation's newest dance music: doo-wop, rock 'n' roll, and the crossover hits coming out of the Motor City. The singers had plenty of talent, but many didn't know how to move. They needed to craft stage shows at which to perform their hit records, both live and televised. Atkins taught them how. He adapted steps he'd used with chorus lines twenty years earlier: Charlestons, shimmies, tight turns, and simple, tap-derived slides and glides. He helped singers keep time with their feet, even as their voices wandered into other tempos. And he helped them bring drama to specific songs: in "Get Ready," Atkins had the Temptations strut in place, pantomime a game of hide-and-seek, stretch out their arms to emphasize the reach of long-held notes, and pivot and freeze, one after the next, in a jazzy canon.[23]

Cholly Atkins had been doing freelance choreography for vocal acts in New York for several years when Berry Gordy lured him to Detroit, in 1965, with a full-time job at Artist Development. When the Jackson 5 signed with Motown four years later, Artist Development was dissolving, and the brothers never worked with Atkins directly; they did their own choreography. But they watched Atkins rehearse other artists, and they modeled their act on the ones he had created. In fact, Atkins told Jacqui Malone, the Temptations came to him complaining that the Jacksons had stolen their routines. In footage of the Jackson 5 from this era, the influence is apparent: in a 1971 performance of "I Want You Back"—wearing heeled loafers, bright blue and gray superhero tops, and enormous bell bottoms—they do stac-cato Charlestons, sideways glides, and open their arms wide, fol-lowing the reach of their voices.[24]

Singers weren't the only ones dancing; their fans were too. "The Corporation"—a group of songwriters whom Gordy cred-ited as a single anonymous mass, so that the individual members would not get too much acclaim for their work—was, after all, writing dance music. Singers danced to embody the music for their audiences, and to suggest that audiences, too, could get moving. Given how simple many of those moves were, audiences could easily imagine doing them. The steps Atkins set on his Motown acts were alluring, even inspiring, but by no means virtuosic.[25]

In Cholly Atkins's work, you can trace steps that started out on the streets, made their way up the professional ladder to vaudeville and cabarets, showed up in rock 'n' roll TV shows, and—as teenagers practiced what they saw on screen—filtered back down to a new generation of social dancers. To be fair, many of these steps had never left, and it would be a mistake to credit a single man with their continuation and dissemination. The Jacksons, already showbiz vets by the time they signed with Mo-town, would have seen the steps in plenty of places they per-formed. But Atkins's career demonstrates the resilience of the past, as old forms are put to new uses. Steps that seemed threat-ening in the thirties now seemed, in the tamer versions per-formed by Motown musicians, safe, acceptable, and respectable.[26]

Another pathway by which dance steps passed through the generations was via the black producer Joe "Ziggy" Johnson. Johnson (who also ran a Detroit theater school, emceed at the

Flame Show Bar and the 20 Grand, and wrote a regular column for the *Chicago Defender*—the man was a force) schooled the singer Jackie Wilson in tap-based techniques that the young Michael Jackson, in the wings of chitlin' circuit theaters, committed to memory. Johnson taught Wilson to do splits, throw the mike around, and toss off single, double, and, eventually, triple spins. At school, Jackson writes, he would stand in front of the bathroom mirror, trying to duplicate Wilson's moves.[27]

Watch Jackie Wilson in performance, and you can see why. One second he's standing on the landing of a set on Dick Clark's *American Bandstand* in a trim suit and tie, looking like a man at a cocktail party, and the next he's flying over four steps, landing in front of them on his knees, legs splayed out to each side. He claps his hands, pulls his heels together, and slides back upright. When Bill Robinson is faced with a set of stairs, he plays them, turning architecture into instrument. When the Nicholas Brothers pay homage to Robinson in *Stormy Weather,* jumping down a giant set of steps in split after split, there are hints of the effort it takes: their coattails go flying, their hair comes loose and flops in their eyes. But Jackie Wilson bypasses the stairs altogether. He drops onto the floor and doesn't even seem to make a thump. He appears to be part cat instead of man.[28]

Some of Wilson's movement quality came from boxing, the sport in which he'd tried to make a career before turning to song. (He also fought Berry Gordy, another former boxer, who wrote some of Wilson's hits before founding Motown.) Ziggy Johnson helped Wilson use this background in his dancing: he centers his weight in his hips, but stays light, taut, and bouncy, so that even when he does nothing but walk backward, or hunch over and swing his arms, he could spring into action at any moment. And he does. In another performance—this one on the TV show *Shindig*, in 1965—Wilson flings off his suit jacket and hops on one foot for a full fourteen seconds, the other foot tapping the floor or swinging from side to side as if he's dancing a jig. Then he drops into his trademark rubbery kneel, pops back up, and launches into a spin.[29]

Michael Jackson didn't bounce up from his knees as speedily, but he did learn to drop down onto them, as he does in the opening to the movie *Moonwalker*, when his performance of "Man in the Mirror" is spliced together with scenes of white girls in the audience fainting from excitement. Wilson worked his fans into a similar fever pitch. According to one of his former band members, at a 1960 show in Florence, Alabama, Wilson "would go into these gyrations, he'd do spins and flips" and "these little white girls" in the audience "would scream, then they would stop real sudden because everyone was looking at them." White girls were not supposed to lust after black men, but sometimes they did anyway.[30]

From Jackie Wilson, Michael Jackson learned to be smooth. From James Brown, he learned to be rough, to show off his heroic work and sweaty individualism. From Cholly Atkins, he learned to be inviting, to fall in line with his brothers and inspire fans to do the same. Audiences saw the Jackson 5—like the record label that signed them—as one big happy family, working, singing, and dancing together. But over the years, the image disintegrated. The Jacksons wanted more artistic and financial independence than Gordy was giving them, so they left Motown in 1975. In 1979, Michael Jackson fired his father, who had been his manager, and released *Off the Wall* on his own. Over the next few years, he continued to record and tour with his brothers, but by the time *Thriller* dropped in 1982, it had become obvious that at least some of Michael's family were trying to use his momentum to further their own careers. When the Jackson 5 reunited for *Motown 25* the following spring, Michael seemed to be shedding his brothers like so much ballast. His solo performance that night—full of furious freezes and the smooth, interstellar moonwalk—launched him into a new universe of pop superstardom. When he landed, he was at the center of American culture.

When the Jackson brothers took the stage on *Motown 25*—Jackie, Marlon, Tito, Jermaine, and Michael, with Randy joining midway through the set—their appearance was jarring. First, they had they grown up, which made the montage the audience had just seen of their early career seem more distant than it really was. But additionally, while his brothers bounded onstage with casual grins, Michael came out with his whole body taut with coiled fury. There's a close-up of his face as the music starts: he glances behind him, as if avoiding what's about to happen, or what already has happened. Then he bites his lip, and gets on with the show.

The brothers walk up to a row of microphones, turn their bodies to the side, bend their knees and pulse their hips. Technically, they're in unison, but Michael—who choreographed the routine—barely inhabits the move. His heels tap up and down, restlessly adding extra beats, making his entire body vibrate. When the group launches into a rendition of "I Want You Back," it's hard to believe that Michael means it: he's speeding into a future of his own making. While it was always clear, in the

Jackson 5, that Michael was the real star, they were never as open about it as they are in the brothers' pose at the end of the song, held for several seconds of applause, as if to give everyone a chance to see the perspectival framing: Michael is in the center, one arm victoriously shooting up to the heavens while all the other lines—his brothers' outstretched hands, the necks of Tito's guitar and Jermaine's bass—point toward him, like the vanishing point of a Renaissance painting.

By this time, Jackson was in the process of becoming an international superstar: *Thriller* had climbed to the top of the charts, and Jackson told Gordy he would do the anniversary show only if he could perform his hit single "Billie Jean."[31] So when his brothers left the stage, Michael stayed. "Those were good songs," he said. "I like those songs a lot. But especially, I like"—and here, after strolling back and forth, sometimes looking at the crowd and sometimes down at the stage, he returned to the microphone stand, faced forward, and deepened his voice a bit—"the new songs," launching into "Billie Jean."

But the song did not make pop history that night. The dancing did. If you aren't among the 47 million who watched the show in May 1983, or the 80 million and counting who have seen the performance on YouTube since Jackson's death, go watch it. Jackson grabs a fedora and starts his performance in a variation of the routine he did with his brothers: behind the mike, facing the side of the stage, knees bent. But now he keeps one sequined, white-gloved hand on his groin, the other stretched behind him, index and pinky finger taut. He's concave, contracted—almost like a Martha Graham dancer—and instead of threatening to explode, he explodes. One leg shoots up and hangs in the air a

moment longer than you think it will. He rushes through a series of freezes, mimes combing his hair, sticks the invisible comb
in his back pocket, and takes the mike. The next four minutes
are tense with controlled rage: karate kicks, icy Charlestons, slippery feet, snarled lips and spins. And then comes the moonwalk, which Jackson debuted that night after at least three years
of practice. He hitches up his cropped pants to reveal more of his
glittery white socks and pushes backward across the stage for just
long enough to show everyone what he can do. In a blink, he spins
around and crouches on his pointed toes, a pose that's simultaneously defensive and threatening, fragile and precise.

The moonwalk is a beautiful illusion. Look at the feet, and
you'll see one thing; look at the whole body, you'll see another.
Its success hangs on how Jackson manipulates his weight: first
he has it all on the ball of one foot, slowly lowering his heel while
sliding the other foot backward; then he shifts his weight onto
the ball of that other foot and repeats. Done well, the moonwalk
is otherworldly, staging a break from the laws of friction, space,
even time.

What Jackson turned into his signature step and made appear
almost divine started out as a novelty. The moonwalk originated
in the same mongrel mix as tap dance, on nineteenth-century
minstrel stages—specifically, perhaps, as an offshoot of the
Virginia Essence. The Essence was a slow shuffle that could at-
tain considerable grace. The ragtime composer Arthur Marshall
explained that an Essence dancer "sometimes looked as if he was
being towed around on ice skates." The dancer "moves forward

without appearing to move his feet at all, by manipulating his toes and heels rapidly, so that his body is propelled without changing the position of his legs." In the early years, a good Essence defied logic while getting laughs. Billy Kersands, the most famous Essence dancer, reportedly kept Queen Victoria in stitches.[32]

Kersands, a two-hundred-pound black man who performed in blackface, was also famous for taking off a dozen vests while dancing, and for stuffing a cup and saucer or several billiard balls into his mouth. He was acting out a role carved out by white men in blackface—the ridiculous darky, with oversized lips—and he appeared to perform that role faithfully. But in the Essence, he may have been beating the white men at their own game. His feet looked like they were doing one thing, even as they did another. Not everything was what it seemed.[33]

We cannot judge how closely Kersands's Essence might have resembled the moonwalk, but by the 1920s, at the latest, African American dancers were performing the same step Michael Jackson would later make famous. Footage exists of Johnny Hudgins doing it as part of an eccentric routine in 1927, in a British Pathé short titled *Feet—Fun—and Fancy*. Hudgins, a vaudeville star who, like Billy Kersands and Bert Williams, wore the blackface mask, performed as a Williams-style tramp, in enormous shoes, an oversized jacket, cropped pants, white socks, and white gloves. As they did for Michael Jackson, the cropped pants and bright socks call attention to the dynamism of Hudgins's feet. Jackson probably was not thinking of this outfit when he dressed for *Motown 25*, yet the resemblance is one of those historical accidents that can't help but seem meaningful. Decades after Hudgins's performance, Michael Jackson imbues something once played for laughs with otherworldly grace.[34]

As black entertainers began to shed the blackface mask, and as tap reached new heights of respectability, so did the moonwalk. Hepcat Cab Calloway did it in a gleaming tux in *The Big Broadcast of 1932*. Bill Bailey—who once apprenticed himself to Bill Robinson (and, according to legend, had been scolded by him for trying to swipe his stair dance, though Bailey maintained this never happened)—used it to close his acts in the forties. Bailey's contemporary Cholly Atkins knew how to do it too. But Michael Jackson didn't learn it from Cholly Atkins or from anyone at Motown. He saw it on TV.[35]

In October 1979, the dance group Eclipse performed on *Soul Train* to one of Michael Jackson's singles from *Off the Wall*, "Working Day and Night." The dancers—Casper Candidate, Jeffrey Daniel, and Derrick "Cooley" Jaxson—started their performance by moonwalking, though they called the step backsliding. They seemed casual, almost blasé, each pretending to read a newspaper. Then Don Newton—loping comically across the stage in a suit and tie—snatched their props away, and the dancing picked up. The Eclipse dancers moved like robots, waved their arms with the fluidity of underwater seaweed, threw in some rubbery camel walks, isolated the movements in their arms, their wrists, and their shoulders, and then moonwalked offstage in a smooth, orderly row.[36]

When *Soul Train* host Don Cornelius interviewed Jeffrey Daniel before the act, Daniel—a former *Soul Train* regular who had found disco stardom as part of the group Shalamar—talked about Eclipse's influences. "The name of the dance is the boogaloo, which was originated by a group called the Electric Boogaloos, from Long Beach." Daniel also explained: "It's a popping style."[37]

The origins of the boogaloo—initially a solo soul dance that involved side-to-side pulses and arm swings—are unclear. The word might, as the *Oxford English Dictionary* hazards, be an alteration of *boogie* or *boogie-woogie* in the manner of *hullabaloo.* Amiri Baraka maintains that it spread through black communities after the Deacons for Self-Defense, a black liberation group based in Bogalusa, Louisiana, stood up to the KKK. Bogalusa, which Baraka spells "Boogaloosa," became *boogaloo,* and early boogaloo records resound with a sense of defiance and freedom. Baraka may be wrong about the origins, however. The word showed up as early as 1939, in a letter to the editor of *Time* magazine from a white correspondent, who repeated a joke attributed to "Boogaloo," "a happy-go-lucky Negro" who seems to have had a dark sense of humor: explaining why he would be willing to fight the Germans in World War II, Boogaloo says, "Ise rather be a slave to my folks than to the Germans." But Baraka's story has a purpose: it links the dance not to ignorance or willful servitude but to black roots, black power, and black pride.[38]

The boogaloo dance might have started out in Chicago, where singers Tom and Jerrio, who cut the first boogaloo record in 1965, say they learned it from a group of teenagers at a record store hop hosted by the legendary DJ Herb Kent ("the Cool Gent"). It might, as those teens claimed, have come to them from Spanish Harlem. (If it didn't, it got there soon: by 1966, a new generation of Latin musicians had merged R&B and doo-wop with Cuban and Puerto Rican music, igniting a Latin Boogaloo craze.) This much is clear: in the ever-shifting climate of solo sixties rock 'n' roll

dance crazes—the frug, the jerk, the Madison, the mashed potato, the pony, the popeye, and the twist—boogaloo's seeds were
scattered across the country by touring musicians, James Brown
chief among them. Amateur dancers grafted on their own, regional variations in parks, at hops and socials, and on the teen
dance shows where youngsters bopped for both local and national
audiences.[39]

By the time the five members of the Electric Boogaloos were
strutting their stuff in southern California in the late seventies—
stuff that included the not-yet-called-a-moonwalk move that
Jeffrey Daniel and his buddies would soon re-create on *Soul
Train*—the stuff was a long way from sixties boogaloo. Anyone
watching *American Bandstand* in the late sixties could, with a little
practice, have learned to boogaloo. Electric boogaloo, on the other
hand, took more work and more skill. It was part of a series of
major developments that had taken place in California dancing:
the beginning of funk styles.

Funk styles form one half of the hip-hop family line, b-boying
the other. In the Bronx, DJ Kool Herc, Afrika Bambaataa, and
Grandmaster Flash turned musical breaks into the main events
of their sets, inspiring throngs of dancers to party. (When asked
which records got the crowd moving the most, all three of these
foundational DJs answered, in unison, "James Brown, 'Give It Up,
Turn It Loose.'" Brown is everywhere.) But over in San Francisco,
Oakland, Fresno, and Los Angeles, young dancers were developing a different battery of moves: not the uprocking fundamental
to breaking or the downrocking added later, with floorwork that
included power moves like shoulderspins, buttspins, windmills
and flares, but robotic isolations and freezes.[40]

Dancers had frozen before. Earl "Snakehips" Tucker's sets at the Cotton Club in the 1920s were full of stops and starts, as were William Pittman and Teresita Pérez's mambo performances at the Palladium Ballroom in the fifties. But this was something new. Popping, locking, ticking, roboting, waacking: these moves of stasis and release were not accents but fundamental to funk styles. They began as poses worked out in front of bedroom mirrors, in high school gyms, at playgrounds and dance clubs. After they'd been perfected, they went parading down the *Soul Train* line, making their way from a California studio to the living rooms and dance floors of the nation. Michael Jackson was watching.[41]

Dance steps had always traveled. Passed from the stage to the audience and back again, they spread from city to city, even across the ocean, as dancers met and mingled, imitated and learned from one another. Film had helped speed up this process, and by 1957, when *Dick Clark's American Bandstand* went national, so had television. Clark's was the biggest in a spate of teen dance shows in the fifties and sixties, many of them local: *Dewey Phillips's Pop Shop* in Memphis, *Seventeen* in Iowa, *Phil McClean's Cleveland Bandstand, Jim Gallant's Connecticut Bandstand, David Hull's Chicago Bandstand*—the list goes on. Some shows featured flesh-and-blood musicians, others had DJs spinning hits. Dancers often appeared as couples, but the new steps didn't require the partnering skills of the square dance or Lindy Hop or ballroom. These dances were done by individuals in a crowd.

Dance shows offered teenage audiences guidance about how to dress, how to act, and how to move. The hosts were typically calm, older, vaguely parental presences, but there was still an element of rebellion. Rock 'n' roll dances, like rock 'n' roll music, had black roots, and—as with jazz dance a generation before—everyone knew it. While some shows, including *American Bandstand*, allowed black teens on air, black and white dancers weren't supposed to dance too close to one another. After the black doo-wop star Frankie Lymon danced with a white girl on Alan Freed's *Big Beat* in 1957, the show was canceled.[42]

*Soul Train* was something new. There had been all-black dance shows before—*Teenarama*, which aired in Washington, D.C., from 1963 to 1970, and *The Mitch Thomas Show*, which aired in Philadelphia from 1955 to 1958 and had debuted a lot of the moves picked up by dancers on *American Bandstand*. But in 1971, *Soul Train*, which had started out as local programming in Chicago, began broadcasting from Los Angeles, bringing black dance, black power, and black pride to TV sets across the country. The show was sponsored by Johnson Products, a black cosmetics company. In one commercial, the escaped slave and abolitionist Frederick Douglass tells a young black man that he is "quite familiar with the natural," which is "worn as an outward expression of pride and dignity," but the young man's Afro is a mess. He must always, Douglass admonishes, use his Afro Sheen.[43]

Granted, this was business capitalizing on political sentiment. But it was also a sign that political sentiment was widespread enough to monetize. On *Soul Train*, politics and pop got down together. Jesse Jackson held court alongside black musical stars: Al Green, James Brown, Joe Tex, Gladys Knight, the Jackson 5. Every week the *Soul Train* scramble board highlighted the achievements of famous black Americans, and every week the *Soul Train* line highlighted the achievements of young black dancers.

*Soul Train*'s dancers held the show together, revolutionizing American popular dance in the process. If the twist—as the rock historian Nik Cohn put it—was an excuse for teenyboppers "to stand up in public and promote their ass," the *Soul Train* dancers promoted much more than that; they trumpeted their own individual power. They picked outfits that would help them stand out from the crowd: applejack hats, knickers and striped socks, hot pants, neon bell bottoms. But it was their moves that had audiences tuning in, as they debuted the dances of funk styles, fluid one moment, sharply angled the next.[44]

The histories of street dance can be contested, but consensus exists about at least one of the pioneers of funk styles: Don Campbell, the inventor of locking. Campbell came of age in Watts, the black Los Angeles neighborhood that had been torn apart by riots in 1965. As a teenager, he was an introvert who spent hours in his room drawing. When he started studying art at Trade Tech College in downtown Los Angeles, he tried to learn dance moves from his friends. Ever shy, he kept freezing up. So he decided to make dance out of his own stillness, tightening his body parts and slotting them into place.[45]

Endearing as that story is, it ignores Campbell's considerable talent: the man knew how to move. He could leap off a stage, land on splayed-out knees, and bounce back up. Soon he was trouncing the competition in contests at local clubs like Maverick's Flat and the Climax. When the crowd parted to make way for him and a couple of friends in action one night, Damita Jo Freeman, a black ballet-trained dancer, was watching. Only men were on the floor, but Freeman came up and started throwing Campbell's

ʿmoves back at him, like a tapper in a challenge. A month later, Freeman and Campbell were back at the club dancing in a contest together and blowing away their competitors. Pam Brown, charged with rounding up dancers for *Soul Train*, was impressed. She invited the pair to audition for the show at the Denker Park Rec Center, and in December 1971, Don Campbell and Damita Jo Freeman began locking for a national audience.[46]

Up in Fresno, "Boogaloo" Sam Solomon and his buddies were studying Campbell's moves on TV and adding innovations of their own. When Solomon moved to Long Beach, he recruited new dancers for his group, the Electric Boogaloos: his brother Tim Solomon (Popin Pete) and a fluctuating cast that included their cousin James Higgins (Skeeter Rabbit) and Cedric Williams (Creep'n Sid). Unlike Campbell, the Electric Boogaloos didn't just freeze momentarily. They tensed their bodies so quickly that each pause seemed like a pop into place, which spawned another foundational funk style, popping. Popping turns the body into a kind of percussive instrument, mimicking the pounding rhythms of the funk music it was danced to. Electric boogaloo—for soon the group's name was emblematic of a whole new dance—combined those momentary jerks with a fluidity that could be both gorgeous and contorted: one move took inspiration from the springy release of a Slinky toy; another, from a one-legged man.[47]

The rolling moves in electric boogaloo might have come to Fresno from the Bay Area, or they might have developed in tandem with the northern California moves. Whatever the case, Oakland dancers, too, were enhancing sixties boogaloo with innovations of their own, making it both choppier and more fluid. This new, funk style boogaloo involved considerable isolation: limbs seemed to move on their own, independent of the rest of the body. But as the body got cut up, it also swerved into new wholes, through rubbery moves and off-kilter angles. By the late seventies, boogaloo dancers across the Golden State were not simply grooving and freezing. They were imitating the staccato precision of robots along with the loopiness of Saturday morning cartoons and science fiction movies, where flickery drawings and Claymation beasts contorted themselves into strange new stances. Their performances embodied a kind of found art, akin to Paul Taylor's experiments in *Seven New Dances* and, later, *Esplanade*. Where Taylor was looking on the streets to pedestrian gesture, these dancers were turning to television, to the strange sights of postmodern popular culture. Yes, they were also watching one another on amateur dance shows. But the influences that Jerry "The Worm" Rentie, a pioneer of Oakland boogaloo, names in the hip-hop historian Thomas Guzman-Sanchez's *Underground Dance Masters* are telling: Boris Karloff's *Frankenstein* movies, Walt Disney's Goofy, the short-lived cartoon series *Mighty Heroes* and *Mighty Mightor*, and Dynamation creator Ray Harryhausen's stop-motion special effects in *20 Million Miles to Earth, Jason and the Argonauts,* and *The Seventh Voyage of Sinbad*.[48]

Robots and cartoons: both, in different ways, erase the human body. One signals the end of Fordism, with human jobs on the assembly line taken over by precise and predictable machines. The other signals Saturday morning fluff, kooky and entertaining. These are the two poles of funk styles—sinister and fun, political and pop.

Consider the robot. On one hand, it reflects the promise of a better tomorrow: orderly, precise, controlled. This is a future to which kids could escape through movement. But what these dancers were escaping from imbues their dance with darker overtones. The robot sprang into popularity at a time when traditional manufacturing jobs—the kind that had lured thousands of black Americans from the South to the West Coast and urban North in the first half of the twentieth century—were harder to come by. The white-collar work that was replacing manufacturing was especially difficult for impoverished black Americans to obtain: it required a college degree, which was expensive. For ghetto-dwellers—and ghettos, in the decades after urban renewal, were becoming increasingly isolated, contained, and abandoned—the odds against escape were overwhelming. Robots stood a better chance.

Robot dancers riffed on that history, embodying a technological future and then besting it. If these young, mostly black dancers understood, as the scholar Tricia Rose has said, "that they were labor for capitalism, that they had very little value as people in this society," dancing was a way to fight back, to assert the value of their own talented bodies. Like the tap dancers a generation before them, they were taking on the signs and sounds of a machine age, then one-upping the machines. The dancing was diverting, but it had an edge.[49]

Was Michael Jackson thinking about any of this in 1973 when he danced like a robot on *Soul Train* and helped vault the dance into national popularity? Or when, over the course of 1973–74, he performed the robot more than a dozen times on national television, including three times on *The Tonight Show* alone, and the Lord only knows how many times in concert? He has left no record of his intentions, but the result is plain. While Jackson did not invent the robot, he helped spread it worldwide.[50]

The Jackson 5 would begin performances of their hit "Dancing Machine" by stepping in unison, in the familiar, Motown house style that Cholly Atkins had derived from his work with chorus lines. Chorus lines had themselves been feats of mechanical precision: rows of uniform dancers moving in synch. (A 1926 cartoon even showed the popular chorines the Tiller Girls being churned out on a conveyer belt.) So when the Jackson 5 arrive at the song's break, and Michael Jackson spins into his robot, the effect is oddly individualistic: he's a virtuoso, set apart from his brothers. A faraway look in his eyes, he slides his feet across the floor, then stiffens and jerks his arms, slotting them into place. When his body relaxes back into human form, he grins and heads back behind the microphone, snapping his fingers in time with his brothers.[51]

Michael Jackson almost certainly learned the robot from watching *Soul Train*. It was the signature move of Charles "Robot" Washington, one of the L.A. show's original dancers. Don Campbell did it, and so did Damita Jo Freeman. In fact, watch Freeman's robot onstage with James Brown, first broadcast in February 1973, and you'll start to believe that she's the dancing machine the Jackson 5 sang about. *Soul Train* impresario Don Cornelius didn't like his dancers to mingle with the guest artists, but when Brown invited Freeman onstage, up she went. In knee-high go-go boots and hot pants, she drew on a decade of ballet training, kicking her leg into a jaunty développé and holding it aloft, pivoting around it with masterful, funky stammers.

She switched from fluid hip shakes to animatronic wobbles, with some of Bruce Lee's tiger claw hands thrown in for good measure: fingers taut, ready to fight. Brown, usually a star dancer himself, hung back behind the microphone, watching. But he did keep singing: "I've got soul, and I'm super bad." When Freeman finished her dance, she threw up one fist in a Black Power salute. Down on the floor, the other dancers responded in kind.[52]

"Super bad," "full of color," "self-contained"—the Jackson 5's dancing machine, like Damita Jo Freeman, was an independent black woman who didn't need a partner. "At the drop of a coin she comes alive," Michael sang, as if he was thinking of the dimestops that characterize the robot dance. The lyric also recalls a much older kind of dancing machine—the kind that Paul Taylor showcased in *Big Bertha*, the same year Freeman did the robot with Brown. In Taylor's America, drop a coin in the machine, and the engine of history destroys you. Not so for the Jacksons or Freeman. Their robot isn't part of the fearsome past. It's a "space-age design" for a better, more pleasurable era, a time when the human body seems to defy the very structures it moves within, bending them to its will. "Put your nine to five up on the shelf and just enjoy yourself," Jackson sang a few years later on *Off the Wall,* implying that disco was a kind of release valve for the pressure of the workaday world. The robot had that going for it too, but it was also—at least as danced by Damita Jo Freeman— more like dance as direct engagement.

"Seems to me that the institutions that function in this country are clearly racist, and that they're built upon racism. And the question, then, is how can black people inside of this country move?" These were Stokely Carmichael's words in October 1966, in a speech that would come to define the Black Power movement. "We are tired [of] waiting; every time black people move in this country, they're forced to defend their position before they move."[53] He was not only arguing that segregation restricted blacks' mobility; he was talking about having the freedom to act without apologies, without offering justifications or seeking whites' approval. When Freeman threw her Black Power salute on *Soul Train*, she was linking the freedom to move her body with the freedom to move through her country on her own terms.

Watching *Soul Train*, Michael Jackson must have been as thrilled as the rest of the country to see these brash new movements of black youth. He and his brothers invited the show's dancers back to their home in Encino for dance parties. Jackson would later tap into the spirit behind funk styles, along with its moves. When he saw Eclipse perform their moonwalk (that is, the Electric Boogaloos' backslide) in 1979, he immediately wanted to add it to his repertoire. Jackson had his manager call Eclipse dancer Casper Candidate, who gave Michael two lessons for a thousand dollars, though he later said he'd have "done it for free." Still, he admitted, "Sometimes I feel bad about the fact that I've never been given credit for teaching Michael that step. It would be nice to hear him acknowledge it. But hey, that's showbiz, you know?" Jeffrey Daniel coached Jackson in the step, too, as did Freeman, who left had *Soul Train* for a career as a professional dancer and choreographer. She did the backslide in a show she put together for Cher. Jackson saw the show and asked her about the step. Freeman explained that she had picked it up from a PBS broadcast of the French mime Marcel Marceau's "Walking Against the Wind" sketch. Jackson was already a fan of Marceau; now, Freeman said, he started studying the master more closely.[54]

But when interviewers asked Michael Jackson about how he learned to moonwalk, he gave them a different origin story. He said that he picked it up from "these black children in the ghettos," who "have the most phenomenal rhythm of anybody on the Earth." He claimed to have watched them in action as he was chauffeured around Harlem—doing just what, he doesn't say. "Just riding through Harlem, I remember in the early, you know, late 70's and early 80's, . . . I would see these kids doing these, uh sliding backwards kinda like an illusion dancing." He took "a mental movie of it," went home, and started practicing.[55]

Jackson was not simply hiding his sources. He was emphasizing that he didn't need teaching: he could pick anything up on his own. He was also presenting himself as a conduit of black folk culture, New York's in particular. It was a bid for authenticity, an attempt to tap into the street culture of America's most famous black neighborhood. Perhaps it's no coincidence that he made these claims at a time when hip-hop, which did come out of New York streets, was threatening to outshine his own work.

But those developments were impossible to predict in 1983, when Jackson, at the peak of his powers, rolled out the moonwalk on *Motown 25*. No matter where he learned it, he owned the step from then on. He christened it, too. Maybe the name came from a simple misunderstanding: to the practitioners of funk styles in California, the moonwalk was a different step, with the torso tilted to the side and what Thomas Guzman-Sanchez describes as "floating in a leaning circular motion."[56] But perhaps

Jackson chose the name deliberately. For him it might have been the logical name for a step he'd spent years perfecting, a step that, as he explained to interviewers, defied gravity. Jackson was not just taking the moonwalk from other dancers; he was taking it from Neil Armstrong, from the biggest televised event in the history of the world, and he was so convincing that when you hear the word *moonwalk* today, you're more likely to think of a lithe dancer sliding backward in sequins and a black fedora than an astronaut loping about.

That night, dancing for the largest audience in his life, Michael Jackson was smooth and strong and furious. He didn't raise his fist, and he didn't advance a political message. The gist of "Billie Jean" is a wrongful accusation of paternity, a fate that befalls the famous. But when on *Motown 25*, Michael Jackson's fury is bigger than the song's narrative, bigger than his desire to make his own career apart from his family, bigger than paranoia, than fear, than manipulation. Jackson's fury is as big as his ambitions, and as big as the history that fuels its motions, from the minstrel stage to the blighted neighborhoods of California to the hopes of a generation of young people trying to figure out how black people in America can move.

The morning after *Motown 25*, Fred Astaire called Jackson. "You're a hell of a mover. Man, you really put them on their asses last night," Astaire told the young singer. "You're an angry dancer. I'm the same way." Astaire had watched Jackson's performance twice already—once when it aired, and again on video, the next morning, when he showed it to Hermes Pan. Later, Jackson showed Astaire and Pan how to moonwalk.[57]

Jackson was in the middle of breakfast when he got Astaire's call, and the excitement made him feel too ill to finish eating. "It was the greatest compliment I had ever received in my life," he gushed, "and the only one I had ever wanted to believe."[58] Jackson dedicated his autobiography, *Moonwalk*, to Astaire. In his music videos, he would combine the moves he picked up on the chitlin' circuit, at Motown, and from *Soul Train* with the dream world of Hollywood musicals. Fred Astaire, Bob Fosse, Gene Kelly, and Jerome Robbins are the ghosts whom Jackson's dancing makes flesh.

Homage to Hollywood musicals infuses more music videos than Jackson's. A list, compiled mostly by the dance historian Larry Billman, gives an indication of their ubiquity in the 1980s: Madonna's "Material Girl" (1984) harkens back to Marilyn Monroe's performance of "Diamonds Are a Girl's Best Friend," choreographed by Jack Cole, in *Gentleman Prefer Blondes* (1953). Paula Abdul's "Opposites Attract" (1988) was inspired by Gene Kelly's dance sequence with Jerry, the cartoon mouse, in *Anchors Aweigh* (1945), and her "Cold-Hearted" (1989) revives Bob Fosse's sexy airline number "Take Off with Us" from *All That Jazz* (1979). When Lionel Richie, in "Dancing on the Ceiling" (1986) duplicated Fred Astaire's gravity-defying dance tricks (if not Astaire's steps) from *Royal Wedding* (1951), he called on that film's director, Stanley Donen, to supervise. Janet Jackson turned to the veteran choreographer Michael Kidd—of *Seven Brides for Seven Brothers* and *Guys and Dolls* fame—for both "When I Think of You" (1986) and "Alright" (1989). "Alright" even had cameos by Cab Calloway, Cyd Charisse, and tap dancing dynamos the Nicholas Brothers.[59]

These videos overtly proclaimed the dynamic behind the genre: music videos, as the choreographer Michael Peters told a reporter in 1984, represented "a resurgence of the movie musical that this generation can relate to."[60] In the thirties, movie musicals had more or less consumed vaudeville, turning its short acts into narrative features. Fifty years later, music videos were gobbling up musicals, then spitting them back out as short acts. When Michael Jackson brought in Broadway veterans, Hollywood directors, and professional actors and dancers for his videos—which he insisted on identifying as short *films,* often with credit sequences to prove it—he put music videos at the top of the food chain.

Jackson's own tastes made this move a natural one. He had been studying movie musicals for years, and sometimes seemed to be trying to live in their world. In 1978, he confided to an interviewer that he'd only recently learned that Gerald Ford had become president in 1974. Jackson preferred cartoons to the news. But even more formative were the films of Fred Astaire, Gene Kelly, and Sammy Davis, Jr. "I can watch these guys all day, twenty-four hours a day," he said. "That's what I love most." A year later, when he turned twenty-one, he defined "a real man" by offering four telling examples: Walt Disney, Charlie Chaplin, Fred Astaire, and Bill Robinson.[61]

Jackson practiced emulating these figures in his family's short-lived variety show, *The Jacksons,* which aired from 1976 to 1977. In the first episode, Michael and his siblings performed "Steppin' Out with My Baby," a song Astaire made famous in *Easter Parade* (1948), in which he played—how's this for symmetry?—a variety show performer. The Jacksons' rendition drew on imagery from Astaire's days at RKO: the boys wore top hats and tailed tuxedoes (though theirs were white, with bell-bottoms), the girls long, feathered gowns reminiscent of the one Ginger Rogers wore in "Cheek to Cheek."[62]

In another routine, the family donned billowy plaid zoot suits for a rendition of the 1938 swing hit "Flat Foot Floogie with a Floy, Floy." Their moves are versions of the Lindy Hop, but Michael is the only one who comes close to re-creating its early flamboyance: at one point, he puts on a big red hat, slides into a split, and springs back up. He knew some tap, too, and performed a number with the Nicholas Brothers. In another sketch, Janet—in a blond wig—played Mae West to Randy's Cab Calloway. A few episodes later, she wore another wig, acting as Shirley Temple to Randy's Bill Robinson. Their performance culminated with a dance up and down two sets of stairs. *The Jacksons* put showbiz history on parade, with the young black family cast as its heirs.

As Nelson George has pointed out, the show was designed to help the Jacksons cross over and reach a mainstream—which is to say, largely white—audience. It featured about three times as many white guest stars as black ones.[63] When the show did acknowledge race, it was as part of a carefully managed joke. In the first episode, for example, Michael announced, "We're the Jacksons. All of you who are expecting the Osmonds, do not adjust the color on your sets." In one skit, Randy wore a blond wig to spoof John Denver, and in another, he played Johnny Cash, with Janet as June Carter. In thick southern accents, brother and sister sang about "going to the Jacksons." ("I've seen the town," Randy explains, "that's why I'm going to the show.") They are not explicitly referring to southern racism, but they come close.

In another routine, the Jacksons imitate the Lockers, the dance group Don Campbell helped form, complete with bright yellow knickers, striped socks, and applejack hats. While they jump in and out of splits, slotting their arms into place, Dom DeLuise—the pudgy, white guest—minces about in towering platform loafers, failing to keep up. "Nothing to it, you just shake shake shake / What the heck I know it ain't Swan Lake," he sings. The Jacksons may be ripping off Don Campbell, but they are the ones imbued with authenticity here: the white guy wants to move, but only the black guys can.

Michael Jackson didn't like the show, and with good reason: the Jacksons had little time to rehearse, and the corny jokes took away from the mystique he wanted to build up. Besides, Jackson was getting tired of being, as his father once described him, "the golden watch that makes everything tick" for the rest of the family.[64] He wanted to branch out and pursue his own vision. If anyone had doubts about his ability to do this, *Off the Wall*, his 1979 solo record, laid them all to rest.

*Off the Wall* was a disco masterpiece. Like the Jackson 5's best Motown work, it was dance music, designed to get people moving, and it came out just as disco dancing reached a new peak in popularity. Disco was so ubiquitous that it became hip to hate it. In 1979 a group of rock DJs in Detroit organized the Disco Ducks Klan, and made plans to wear white sheets to a rock club that had gone disco. They never went, but another DJ, Steve Dahl, started a half-hour riot at Chicago's Comiskey Park when he encouraged disco haters to gather for a massive explosion of disco LPs.[65]

The opposition to disco had many motivations: detractors said that it was slick, commercial, and apolitical. But the overtones of machismo and white supremacy in the stories of the disco backlash suggest a different cause. To many onlookers, disco music—and disco dancing—seemed both black and effeminate. Disco's roots are in gay New York, at parties and clubs where men found that they could finally move with freedom. Dance floors had long been policed: it was illegal for two men to dance without a woman present. If owners of gay bars refused to pay off the cops—sometimes, even when they did—their customers could be subjected to raids and arrests. During a raid at Greenwich Village's Stonewall Inn, on June 27, 1969, however, something unexpected happened: the patrons fought back. The police took refuge behind the bar as the queers, fed up with the harassment, mounted a counterattack, with supporters from the neighborhood swarming in to help. The riot that ensued marked what many historians consider the beginning of the gay liberation movement.[66]

The patrons might not have taken their stand had Stonewall not allowed dancing. According to the historian Alice Echols, Stonewall was "the only gay bar in New York City that as a matter of course permitted dancing between men," and on its two dance floors, gay men acted on their desires with revolutionary frankness. Instead of looking longingly across the room, or picking up on signs that a man was open for cruising, customers could saunter onto the dance floor and get into a groove. They were not simply acknowledging their sexuality—they were flaunting it. Movement on the floor developed in tandem with the growing social movement. As the campaign for gay rights escalated, so did the number of gay dance clubs.[67]

Discotheques had existed since at least the 1950s: by definition, they were dance clubs that played records, rather than employing live bands. The term "disco" was not applied to a form of music until 1973, however, when the critic Vince Aletti called the genre that reigned at these clubs "discotheque rock." In its early years, disco had liberatory power—not just for gay men, but for women, African Americans, Italian Americans, Latino Americans, and anyone else who wanted to get caught up in glittering lights, and, as the genre solidified, in smooth vocals, synth sounds, and pounding beats.

By the sixties and seventies, white male rockers had largely abandoned social dancing. If they did move to music, they usually preferred free-style whirls and thrashes to the formality of choreographed steps. But social dancing endured in black and Latin communities, and many white women longed for a return to romantic partner dancing. Disco appealed to all these groups. Yet the music also called for a new kind of dancing. As the critic Jeff Dyer points out, disco music is open, repetitive, and diffuse, a marked departure from both the closed, tidy lyrics of traditional pop songs and the insistent drive of rock. "Rock's eroticism is thrusting, grinding" and "phallic," Dyer writes, making for a dance that mixes "awkwardness and thrust." Disco, on the other hand, engages "the whole of the body . . . for both sexes," allowing lithe and varied dancing.[68]

In 1977, the runaway success of the movie *Saturday Night Fever* helped turn disco dancing into a full-on national phenomenon. From 1975 to 1978, the number of discos in America doubled to between fifteen and twenty thousand. Pretty much anyone who wasn't a white guy committed to the perceived power and purity of rock or a conservative frightened by the sexually suggestive songs and moves (think of Donna Summer's orgasms in "Love to Love You") signed on.[69]

Michael Jackson had been cutting music for discos before he was old enough to attend one: the Jackson 5's disco single "Dancing Machine" hit the top ten in 1974, and the robot Jackson performed to it was imitated in dance clubs across the country. By 1977, when Jackson moved to New York to play the scarecrow in the musical *The Wiz*, an African American retelling of *The Wizard of Oz*, disco was no longer the provenance of minorities: it had gone mainstream.

Away from his family—only sister La Toya was with him in New York—Jackson relished his new independence, and was a regular at Manhattan's exclusive Studio 54. In an interview with Jane Pauley and Studio 54 founder Steve Rubell, Jackson said he loved the place because it promised "escapism." This was Jackson's ultimate praise, applied to any cultural product that lifted observers out of their lives, however temporarily, and took them someplace new. The club was filled with famous people—Liza Minnelli, Bianca Jagger, Truman Capote, Andy Warhol, Woody Allen—but in the interview, Jackson focused on what it meant to dance for fun. "You're just being free then," he said of his time on the celebrity-studded floor. "You dance with whoever you want to, you just go wild." This was the promise of disco: unabashed freedom and propulsive joy, slick and mechanical as the soundtrack might be—and it was the spirit of Jackson's music videos for *Off the Wall*.[70]

In these videos, Jackson drops some of the same moves he had perfected in childhood—tight spins, pelvic pulses, mashed-potato feet—but with a new level of relaxation. He's a young man enjoying his talents and his fame, with nothing to disturb his glittery escape. He dances against changing backgrounds of flashing lights and swirling colors: a concert stage, filtered through the club. In "Don't Stop 'til You Get Enough," he wears a bell-bottomed tuxedo, grinning as he sings. In "Rock with You," he holds the microphone, elated, the sequins on his shirt and pants turning him into a human disco ball.

The best disco floors were packed with sweaty crowds, getting down together. Jackson's videos, in contrast, dramatize the power of a singular body, the space it can create and the pleasures it can feel. Jackson is his own company. In "Don't Stop 'til You Get Enough," he's even joined by two more Michael Jacksons. The gimmick may be a splashy camera trick, but it suggests a sense of personal enlargement, psychedelic pleasures, and the multiplying power of spectacle. Jackson could be an Andy Warhol silkscreen set into motion.

The same year *Off the Wall* was released, Jackson wrote a manifesto for himself: "I want a whole new character, a whole new look," he wrote. "I should be a tottally [*sic*] different person. People should never think of me as the kid who sang 'ABC,' [or] 'I Want You Back.' I should be a new, incredible actor/singer/dancer that will shock the world. I will do no interviews. I will be magic. I will be a perfectionist, a researcher, a trainer, a masterer. I will be better than every great actor roped into one." These are the words of a man fueled by drive and dissatisfaction, scrambling for control and looking for release. With *Thriller*, he found it. Michael Jackson was no longer dancing alone. He had—as the promoter Don King said in the lead-up to the Jacksons' 1984 *Victory* tour—"every race, color, and creed" behind him. Jackson, King proclaimed, with a bombast that the moonwalk helped make believable, had "transcended all earthly bounds."[71]

He did it with a trio of videos that dramatize the power of his dancing. In the first, "Billie Jean," his body lights up everything it touches, Midas-like. Or maybe it's disco-like: when the pavement glows under Jackson's feet, it's as if he's improvising his own version of that iconic light-up floor in *Saturday Night Fever*. His other trick is more furtive: he can disappear. Thank goodness, since a menacing, paparazzi-like private eye keeps pursing him. In "Beat It," Jackson's dancing stops violence and cleans up the streets. In "Thriller," his moves organize the undead into a shared groove, imbuing brittle bodies with grace.

Shortly after the videos came out, they became part of two larger, intertwined stories. One was about the importance of MTV, which helped make Jackson yet more famous. The other was about the importance of Michael Jackson, who helped the struggling channel survive. The television music channel MTV had debuted in March 1981, with opening footage inviting comparisons to space-age pioneers: the space shuttle *Columbia*'s countdown, then the launch of *Apollo 11*, and then Neil Armstrong climbing out of the landing module for the first moonwalk. But until Jackson's *Thriller* videos turned his bestselling album into the best-selling album of all time, MTV's reign was in no way secure. The cable channel had started as a way to reach teenage consumers and was financed by advertisements between music videos that were themselves advertisements. It was a new kind of business model, and some staff members worried that it would fail.[72]

In the early years, MTV played almost exclusively videos by white acts because, said its executives, it was a rock music channel. Never mind that black musicians had essentially invented rock 'n' roll, or that MTV was also playing R&B—a supposedly black genre—by white artists. The music industry had a long history of segregating sound according to genre, from the days of race records on. Whether consciously or not, MTV followed suit. But according to popular lore and a host of sources, when MTV refused to air Michael Jackson's "Billie Jean" video, Walter Yetnikoff, then president of CBS Records (which owned Epic records, Jackson's label), took action. Unless they played "Billie Jean," threatened Yetnikoff, he would pull all of CBS's videos, a sizable proportion of MTV's programming. MTV caved in. (MTV executive Bob Pittman denies this story, and says the producers decided to air "Billie Jean" the moment they saw it.)[73]

Jackson's videos set a new standard for excellence and expense. "Billie Jean," which entered the rotation in March 1983, cost between $50,000 and $75,000 to make—at least double the industry standard. "Beat It," which followed a few weeks later, cost $150,000. "Thriller," which premiered in December, cost at least half a million dollars, and it became the channel's lifeblood. "Thriller" coursed through the nation's cathode-ray tubes hourly, with video DJs (VJs) giving regular updates about how long viewers would have to wait before getting their next fix. As John Sykes, another founding executive at MTV, put it, "Michael Jackson was the reason MTV went from big to huge. He put us at the center of the culture."[74]

Jackson deserves the credit for integrating MTV, but as the rock critic Dave Marsh has pointed out, few videos by other black artists followed. After "Thriller," says Marsh, "10 percent of the clips the channel aired were by black artists. (Those clips were shown infrequently and often in the dead of night, of course)." Rather than blazing a trail, Jackson was an exception, and not just because his videos were of higher quality than the norm. A black teen idol, Jackson navigated the line between shake-what-your-mama-gave-you rhythms and Peter Pan innocence, with music that appealed to all manner of tastes. Jackson's ambitions were clear: he wanted, he said, to be "the biggest star in show business." That meant crafting a record designed, like the Motown hits of the sixties, to cross over.[75]

These factors make it hard to believe that Michael Jackson would have seriously considered the scenario that Steve Baron, who directed "Billie Jean," proposed for the "Beat It" video: Jackson would captain a slave ship with white men as his chattel. The ultimate revenge for the forced enslavement of his people and, perhaps, for having been barred from MTV, the video would have been terrible publicity for Jackson. Whatever went on in those early negotiations, Baron did not get the job. The commercial director Bob Giraldi ended up directing "Beat It," and instead of relying on CBS to pony up the cash, Jackson, intent on success, financed the video himself. This guaranteed him a large measure of creative control. He talked through the scenario with Giraldi, and he sat with the choreographer Michael Peters as they auditioned backup dancers together.[76]

Michael Peters was a wiry African American dancer, who, recalls his friend and colleague Vincent Paterson, "could move with the speed of light." Peters had trained at the Bernice Johnson Cultural Center in Queens (where, for a while, Cholly Atkins taught tap), and had attended the New York High School of the Performing Arts (the school featured in the movie and television series *Fame*). In the late 1960s he performed in the companies of both Talley Beatty and Alvin Ailey, pioneering black choreographers who fused ballet, modern, and jazz dance with movements from everyday black life at churches and rent parties. A decade and a half later, Ailey told an interviewer that Peters was "a terrific dancer, quick, fast, kind of explosive," with the personality to match: "volatile, strong-willed, and restless." He lasted just six months with the company, then left. "Already," said Ailey, "he had that spark of creativity."[77]

By the early 1970s, Peters had joined his friend, the African American dancer and choreographer Lester Wilson, in Los Angeles. Out west, away from the center of concert dance, Peters honed his style and put it to work. (He continued to perform in concerts, however: when Wilson put on his "magical mystery odyssey through Black music and the Black entity from Africa to tomorrow," as he described his *$600 and a Mule,* Peters played both Cab Calloway and the prison activist and Black Panther George Jackson. The *Los Angeles Times* called his pas de deux with Michele Simmons, who played Angela Davis, "a remarkably tender oasis of love in welcome contrast to the frantic pace" of the rest of the production.) New York may have been the center of American highbrow dance, but Los Angeles was the capital of showbiz, the manufacturer of mass-cultural dreams. Los Angeles was where movies were made, television shows shot, stage revues assembled, and commercials cut. It was a world where Michael

Peters thrived, becoming—as "some people" proclaimed in a 1984 profile in *People* magazine—"the Balanchine of MTV." Peters turned what the *New York Times* had praised in 1970 as his "no-nonsense sock-it-to-them mode of presenting movement" into powerful, punchy choreography.[78]

This was dancing that could sell, even compressed into the short form of a music video. Part of its success came from Peters's technique: he yoked what he saw as the freedom of street dancing to the discipline of rehearsal. But it also owed something to his movement vocabulary: quick kicks of the legs, arms tensed in place, and wormlike undulations from the toes up through the pelvis, torso, and head. Peters choreographed videos for Pat Benatar, Billy Joel, Lionel Richie, and Diana Ross, among others, and he found acclaim on Broadway, sharing a Tony with Michael Bennett for *Dreamgirls* in 1982. But the dances in "Beat It" and "Thriller" remain his most visible and enduring legacy. No wonder: Peters had the good fortune to be working for Michael Jackson, who saw the merits of hiring talented dancers and giving them sufficient rehearsal time. And the dancing was embedded in the most expensive music videos yet produced, starring a singer and dancer at the peak of his powers.[79]

"Beat It" harkens back to the musical that had made Peters want to be a dancer himself: *West Side Story*. The opening shots of "Beat It," which show gangs gathering for a rumble, conjure up Jerome Robbins's staging: young men walking through the streets of Manhattan, snapping their fingers in slow, menacing unison, springing into jumps with their arms outstretched and floating on one leg, pushing their arms out as if treading water. They even tell people, several times, to "beat it." (Peters took the snaps directly from Robbins, but a few years later, choreographers Greg Brugge and Jeffrey Daniel would work with Jackson to incorporate Robbins's dance movements in the video for "Bad.") Where the musical chronicles the rivalry of the white Jets and Puerto Rican Sharks, Jackson's video only flirts with such clear-cut differences. One gang leader, played by Peters, is black; the other, played by Vincent Paterson, is white. Yet their rank and file come in all different shades. And where *West Side Story* ends with a death, "Beat It" banishes violence altogether. The leaders pull out their switchblades to duke it out, but when Jackson shows up, they can't help falling into line behind him, his dancing is so powerful. Soon everyone is spinning, pulsing backward, and flinging his arms into the air behind the ferocious, terpsichorean peacemaker.[80]

It was an appealing piece of movie magic, if a bit outlandish. Maybe that's why Jackson decided he needed to include actual gang members for verisimilitude. His production team recruited members of the Crips and Bloods, with men from the LAPD standing by in case of problems. In his memoirs, Jackson—who claimed they had not needed the cops' help—praises the gang members. They were "humble, sweet, and kind," "polite, quiet, supportive," and grateful for the chance "to be seen and respected" on television. But according to Bob Giraldi, some of them became bored during a break and started to fight. The police threatened to shut down the shoot and send everyone home. Giraldi had another idea. The final dance sequence was not slated for shooting until the next day, but with the kind of logic that fuels backstage musicals, the director decided to unleash the power of dance. He convinced the LAPD to allow him one final take.[81]

As Jackson, Peters, Paterson, and the rest of the dancers started their routine, the gang members' mouths dropped open in astonishment. They "watched their brothers, most of them gay, dance in a way they never could," Giraldi says. "It was the most glorious moment of my directing life." Jackson didn't write about this moment, and Paterson told me that he did not recall any fighting on set. But the story has had legs, perhaps because it confirms the message of the video itself: that singing and dancing can change the world. Michael Peters seems to have believed it, even if his comments didn't back up Giraldi's story. Doing the video, Peters told a reporter, gave gang members "a sense of purpose to see their lives legitimized that way, a sense of self," and "many of them came to believe there's another way, a better way, a way out of the street."[82]

If that sounds a little too idealistic—that the temporary sight of a world-famous pop star and some professional dancers would inspire gang members to carve out a new and more peaceful existence—the founding fathers of hip-hop had themselves dreamt a similar dream. When DJ Kool Herc picked up on tensions in the crowds at his Bronx parties, he'd call people out: rival crews could get down together, but he wasn't going to give them a place to fight. Afrika Bambaataa went even farther, founding the group Zulu Nation, in part, to bring about peace through partying.[83] Yet where the DJs were responding to the needs of their audiences, switching records and extending breaks to change the mood and rev up the energy of the dancers, Michael Jackson's vision in "Beat It" and a few years later in "Bad" relied on hours of rehearsals, with trained dancers falling into lockstep behind him. Still, once "Thriller" came out, it was hard not to believe that the whole country, like backup dancers in a music video, was following Jackson's lead.

If "Beat It" harkened back to Hollywood musicals, "Thriller" more or less became one. It was a whopping fourteen minutes long, and because Jackson and director John Landis wanted to make it eligible for an Oscar it had a theatrical premier as well as a televised one. Both a valentine to and spoof of horror films, it traffics in the conventions laid out in George Romero's 1968 *Night of the Living Dead.* But where Romero's film has a sense of political menace, "Thriller" goes for camp.

*Night of the Living Dead* ends with the murder of its black protagonist, Ben. He survives a zombie attack but is no match for a crowd of white men trained to kill anyone in their path. When they catch sight of him, a militiaman shoots Ben between the eyes; then his body is thrown on a pile of the dead undead and set on fire. Romero's camera lingers at the murder scene, showing Ben's body and his looming oppressors in grainy, black-and-white photographs that could have come from a newspaper. Viewers of the movie would inevitably have been reminded of the real-life horror playing out across the country in the 1960s, as white cops and vigilantes brutalized Civil Rights protestors.[84]

The zombies in "Thriller" share visual similarities with Romero's, but little else. For one thing, they know how to dance. Initially, they lurch out of the cemetery and trundle up from the sewers and through the streets, surrounding Jackson and his date. But when Jackson turns into a zombie himself—his eyes wide, his skin cold and green—the zombies line up behind him and begin twitching into a groove. Their moves are tentative at first: shoulder shakes, arms stretching out and swiping the air. Within moments, though, pelvises are pulsing, and the zombies are traipsing from side to side, flinging their arms up high, and dropping to the ground to allow MJ some solo moves of his own: quick spins, balances on his toes. For a few seconds, a satellite group of zombies pops and locks: electric boogaloo ghouls.

Nelson George has called the dancing in "Thriller" "Michael Jackson's most perfect pop product," and "product" is the right word.[85] Jackson is a dynamite mover, but many of these steps are exportable: viewers could take them away, try them on, and make them individual. In the heyday of breakdancing, viewers might not have been able to spin on their heads, master the moonwalk, or even lock their muscles into a convincing robot. But they could hunch their shoulders and let them fall, or swing their arms from side to side like a boogying corpse.

On February 7, 1984, CBS held a party at the American Museum of Natural History in New York to honor Michael Jackson, and to announce that *Thriller* had become the best-selling album of all time: it had sold 25 million copies. (As of 2013, the numbers were up to 66 million.) "For the first time in my entire career," Jackson announced, "I feel like I've accomplished something because I'm in the *Guinness Book of World Records.*" He wore what was quickly becoming one of his new uniforms: the glittery white glove, the gleaming jacket that—depending on whom you asked—was part soldier, part dictator, part doorman. He was Marcus Garvey without the message. The crowd was so large, speculated a reporter for the *Washington Post,* that the rest of the guests were probably "less concerned about what to wear than about getting trampled to death."[86]

Outside there was a little more breathing room. When Michael Peters left the party, he said, "there were all these kids doing the moves from 'Beat It' and 'Thriller' right there on the steps of the Museum of Natural History."[87] You could write them off as aspiring clones, replicating the moves of their idol, but it is hard not to imagine that they'd be insulted at such a conclusion. Up on the steps of the museum, overlooking Central Park West, they threw their own bodies into motion, and they must have liked how it felt.

In the early eighties, hip-hop dance—both the funk styles showcased on *Soul Train* and the b-boying that had taken off in New York—was gaining wider attention. B-boys were learning Electric Boogaloo (they called it electric boogie). Some of the same *Soul Train* dancers who had started out working for nothing but esteem and a boxed chicken lunch on the set were finding ways to make dance pay the bills. Damita Jo Freeman became a choreographer and backup dancer to pop stars. Don Campbell and the Lockers, under the management of Toni Basil, performed on a spate of television variety shows, opened for both Frank Sinatra and Funkadelic, and cut an ad for Schlitz malt liquor. Basil, a former ballet student, had been choreographing since the sixties, including work on the *T.A.M.I.* show and for the Monkees, and she kept at it after the Lockers went their separate ways. She reinvented herself as a pop star for her hit single "Mickey," with a video that drew on her high school cheerleading chops. She also composed the dances for a host of music videos, including the Talking Heads' "Crosseyed and Painless," which featured members of the group Electric Boogaloo.[88]

Funk styles were showing up on MTV, and MTV artists were mingling with the worlds of highbrow dance. Gary Chryst, one of the leading male dancers at the Joffrey Ballet, moonlighted in music videos.[89] David Byrne, the lead singer of the Talking Heads, collaborated with the former Paul Taylor Dance Company member Twyla Tharp on an evening-length work for Broadway, *The Catherine Wheel.*

Tharp, a superstar of postmodern choreography, was no stranger to the world of pop culture. In 1973, she hired members of United Graffiti Artists, a short-lived union of "taggers," to take the stage during performances of her crossover ballet/modern *Deuce Coupe.* Downstage members of Tharp's company joined forces with the classically trained dancers of the Joffrey, their own idioms blurring with sixties rock dances like the swim, the frug, and the boogaloo. Upstage the guys from UGA wielded cans of spray paint and created a fresh set every night. *Deuce Coupe* was a runaway success—an edgy synthesis of pop, highbrow, and avant-garde art. But it was set to music by the Beach Boys. Graffiti may have been hip-hop's visual art, rolling across New York on subway trains for all to admire, but hip-hop's sounds—and dances—took longer to spread.[90]

When the dance critic Sally Banes wrote about breakdancing in 1981 in the *Village Voice,* her piece promoted the first downtown appearance of the Rock Steady Crew, b-boys who—under the leadership of Richard Colón, better known as Crazy Legs—had kept breaking alive even as it faded from widespread popularity. Rock Steady had regular gigs at a series of clubs in Greenwich Village; performed a short but wildly influential cameo in the 1983 movie *Flashdance;* and toured in the United States and abroad.[91]

Breaking, as it was popularized in the eighties, usually took place in a ring, with two crews facing each other for battle. A dancer would enter the ring alone and upright with a few steps to keep the beat, then launch into a short dance—maybe ten seconds, maybe a minute—before freezing into a quick pose and stepping back to the sidelines. His dancing (while there were some female b-boys, most were men) might include power moves like the windmill, legs up in a V as the torso rolled on the floor, the whole body spinning. He might twirl on his head, or leap from his feet to his hands again and again, or swipe one leg beneath the other like a corkscrewing Russian peasant. This was dance as acrobatics and as provocation: showy, aggressive, sometimes physically baffling. Watch footage of Crazy Legs spinning on his hands and his head and his back and his arms, and you'll wonder whether his whole body is covered in calluses.[92]

By 1984, breakdancing was everywhere. According to a poll that year, more than half of American teens had either breakdanced or hoped to learn how.[93] Kids were signing up for breakdancing lessons at suburban dance studios, spreading out makeshift cardboard floors for cushioning in subdivision cul-de-sacs and junior high school gyms. What had begun with inner-city black and Puerto Rican youth became a craze among all colors and classes, and moved from popular to professional art. Breakers took the stage at the 1984 *Kennedy Center Honors*, and again at President Reagan's Inaugural Gala in 1985. Not much hip-hop music was played on MTV in the channel's early years, but hip-hop dance was pervasive. A couple of young black breakers joined some jazzy car mechanics in Billy Joel's "Uptown Girl" (choreographed by Michael Peters). In Cherelle's "I Didn't Mean to Turn You On," King Kong windmilled and tutted—an angular arm movement inspired by the figures on Egyptian friezes. In Don Felder's "Bad Girls" rich white folks climbed out of their limo to join some black dancers on the streets of Los Angeles.

Movies continued the trend. Independent filmmakers had showcased hip-hop dancers in *Wild Style* and *Style Wars;* now Hollywood rolled out not only *Flashdance,* but also *Beat Street, Body Rock, Breakin',* and *Breakin' 2: Electric Boogaloo.* Even *Footloose,* set in a lily-white town in Oklahoma, featured a popper at the prom. These movies may have given the public a sanitized view of hip-hop culture, but they showed professional dancers, with authentic moves—and those moves kept spreading. Adolfo "Shabba Doo" Quinones, who went from dancing on *Soul Train* and with the Lockers to starring in the *Breakin'* movies, said that on weekends kids would show up in front of his new house, ghetto blasters in hand, and start dancing. Generally, he was so happy with his success that he would head out in his socks to join them. But if they moved onto his front yard, he might feel a little grumpy ("Every time they do footwork," he told a reporter for the *Los Angeles Times,* "you see big chunks of your lawn flying in the air"), and would have to remind himself that their enthusiasm was the reason he had been able to buy a house in the first place.[94]

The highbrow dance world was taking note. In 1984, Gerald Arpino, resident choreographer at the Joffrey, called breakdancing and music video choreography ("I tend to link the two") "one of the great breakthroughs in American culture." Breakdancing, said Arpino, was "affecting the classical field as folk art always has, beginning in the streets and working its way up. Already, I've been commissioned by the city of San Antonio to choreograph a piece employing break dance." That same year, San Francisco Ballet surprised attendees at their opening-night gala with a performance by forty-six local breakers, fourteen of whom were given scholarships to a ten-week class combining breaking and ballet. If they did well, the company announced, more scholarships could follow. "It's a promising way to find talented boys and also promote the image of ballet as athletic," said the company's public relations director. Cleveland Ballet had a similar idea: in 1985, its piece *US* featured ten breakers, three of whom became members of the company the following season. "We do ballet backwards," explained Lorenzo "Mister Headspin" Fitzgerald. "We do pirouettes on our elbows, head and back."[95]

It seemed like yet another version of a story that had been around since the days of the cakewalk, with vernacular dance as Cinderella, soon to join the royal family by uniting with ballet. By the 1980s, Cinderella was macho, fresh, and usually black, while Prince Charming tended to be white, and could seem pretty old and effeminate. "The way they move is so earthy. They have that gut street look," Cleveland Ballet's artistic director Dennis Nahat, said of his company's black breakdancers. "They do it without thinking."[96] Nahat probably meant this as a compliment, but the old charge of "primitivism" is still there. In the most hopeful version of the story—the one that American ballet companies, Hollywood scriptwriters, and dancers have loved to tell, and American audiences have often wanted to believe—marriages of highbrow and popular dance spawn a new art form, ready to encompass the country's multitudes. It's *Shall We Dance* all over again.

In the eighties dance movies, characters divided by race and class find unity on the dance floor, a neutral arena that sanctions both rebellious love and the imitation and assimilation that fuels the American vernacular. The heroes and heroines of these movies actively absorb dance styles from all over. They flout the establishment, then are accepted by it, thanks to their new, genre-hopping, indigenous movements.

*Saturday Night Fever* provided an inkling of this plot: Tony's (John Travolta) dance partner, Stephanie (Karen Lynn Gorney), has highbrow aspirations: she practices ballet. But although their climactic duet to "More Than a Woman" is supposed to couple her grace with his machismo, Travolta is a far more lyrical dancer than Gorney. Her shoulders keep tensing up, and our eyes are drawn to Travolta instead. The dance-as-melting-pot plot really took off with *Flashdance* in 1983, starring Jennifer Beals as a would-be ballerina who works days as a welder and nights as an exotic dancer. Thanks to the moves she picks up at the club—and from watching the cameo by Rock Steady dancers out on the street—she lands a spot at an elite Pittsburgh conservatory. Rock Steady president Crazy Legs wasn't just the dancer's inspiration: he was also, thanks to a lot of makeup, the actress's body double. Beals's other double, Marine Jahan, did most of the dancing. In the movies, everyone learns all the steps, but in real life, things can be a little more challenging.[97]

The next year, in *Breakin'*, a formally trained jazz dancer joined forces with two b-boys. An evil jazz choreographer wants to crush their success, but they prove that cultural fusion can trump the seeming purity of both breaking and highbrow art: they eclipse rival crews, then sneak into—and win—a contest that makes them stars in a fancy L.A. production billed as "Street Jazz." In *Breakin' 2: Electric Boogaloo,* a trained dancer gives up an opportunity to dance in Paris so she can collaborate with her friends from the street.

The stories have kept coming. In *Center Stage* (2000), American Ballet Theatre principal Ethan Stiefel cements his role as a renegade by choreographing a rock ballet. In *Save the Last Dance* (2001), a white ballerina gets an injection of soul, confidence, and hip-hop from her black boyfriend. In *Step Up* (2006), a break-dancing vandal falls in love with a ballerina, and in *Step Up Revolution* (2012), a modern dancer joins forces with an Occupy-style street crew to stop her rich, developer daddy from destroying their neighborhood. Lest the revolution seem dangerously anti-capitalist, the movie ends with the crew landing an advertising deal with Nike.[98]

Michael Jackson hoped to star in a dance movie, too: in 1984, he agreed to be in a new film produced by David Geffen. Hollywood scuttlebutt identified it as *Streetdandy,* by *Flashdance* screenwriter Tom Hedley. According to Hedley, *Streetdandy* followed "a pop Charlie Chaplin" out on the streets, where he was "literally finding his voice, both as a man and an artist."[99] The movie was never made, but by then, Jackson had become the most famous dancer in America, and his videos—"Billie Jean," "Beat It," and "Thriller," in particular—played a major role in blurring dance styles that were themselves already blurry.

Jackson deified Astaire, but in many ways, his artistic sensibilities were closer to Bob Fosse's. Like Jackson, Fosse had grown up in the spotlight. As one-half of the Riff Brothers, a juvenile tap duo modeled on the Nicholas Brothers, Fosse got his start playing Chicago amateur nights, Elks lodges, USO shows, and—perhaps the most formative venue, in terms of how it shaped both his thinking and his movements—burlesque clubs. By day, young Fosse was a golden boy. A good Methodist and diligent student, he charmed high school teachers and high school girls alike. At night, he descended into a darker world, playing clubs with broken toilets, floors so filthy that he and his partner changed into their tuxes standing on pieces of cardboard, and girls for whom dancing meant a little bump and grind between the shedding of chemise and garter. When they found out that the tappers were underage, some of the girls decided to provide them with an education. Entranced, harassed, and terrified of having their cover blown, the Riff Brothers submitted. So at age sixteen, Fosse was having bare breasts shoved in his face, and getting surprise hand jobs moments before he had to go onstage. Even without the embarrassment of erections or semen on his pants, he was likely to be heckled: the audience didn't care about a couple of tap-dancing teen boys. They'd come for flesh, not finesse.[100]

Burlesque was a long way from Fred Astaire, whom Bob Fosse, like Michael Jackson, worshiped. As a twelve-year-old, waiting to compete in a talent show that followed a screening of *Swing Time,* Fosse had watched from the wings and after taking off his tap shoes to muffle the sound tried to imitate his idol's steps. Astaire showed him a world of utter grace, where dance was sophisticated, smooth, and full of romance. But Fosse's own experiences indicated that dance didn't always work like that. It could partake of shame, sex, and shine. As a tapper, he learned to close his act with a big finish, milking his audience for applause. In burlesque, he saw dancers who suggested big finishes of another kind. In 1954, when he landed his first big gig choreographing some of the dances for *The Pajama Game,* he began to draw on those influences for his showstopper, "Steam Heat."[101]

"Steam Heat" conjured up the charm of old-fashioned novelty dances, with knocked knees, tossed hats, and quick, mechanical movements to accompany the sound of clanging, hissing radiators. A decade earlier, *Oklahoma!* had made ballet training seem mandatory for Broadway dancers. Now, stuttering forward with one hand on their bellies, the other stretched rakishly out, Fosse's dancers were bringing jazz back to Broadway.

Over the coming decades, Fosse would become an institution, his style so ubiquitous and widely imitated that today it can seem like a cliché. Fosse had studied Astaire, Jack Cole, Paul Draper, Gene Kelly, and Jerome Robbins—the great song-and-dance men of his time. But his own movement vocabulary was flashier and more suggestive. Fosse favored slinky, catlike steps, the body curled, the shoulders rolled exaggeratedly forward. He punctuated dances with snaps, freezes, and slides. His female dancers didn't simply lift their legs—they tended to shoot them up as high as they would go. This was jazz dance, but it lacked the buoyancy of swing dancers at the Savoy, pushing against the floor, bouncy and loose, or the aristocratic shading of Fred Astaire and Ginger Rogers clearing the floor at a cabaret for taps and tender partnership. Fosse's jazz was a study in angularity—the elbows pulled back, the pelvis thrust forward, the toes turned in. While it was sultry and fluid, it was also sharp, even mechanical. "He puts dances together," said Agnes de Mille, "with the precision of a watchmaker."[102]

Fosse's work was showbiz in style and often in substance too: there were plots about cabaret performers, vaudevillians, a stand-up comedian, and—in the autobiographical tour de force *All That Jazz*—a director and choreographer looking back on his life as an artist, husband, boyfriend, father, and philanderer. Sex fascinated Fosse, especially when it involved payment: the taxi dancers in *Sweet Charity* arch their backs and straddle a railing to entice would-be customers; Broadway dancers playing an airplane crew in *All That Jazz* bare their breasts and buttocks; one of the cast members in that routine has slept her way to a part. In such company, all performing artists start to look a little dirty. They are paid to please.

Michael Jackson must have been drawn to all these qualities: the shimmering, slinky steps and show-must-go-on razzmatazz, along with the vague sense that, by putting your body onstage, and living your life in public, you were both looking for love and whoring yourself out. His own upbringing, like Fosse's, was split between the sacred and the profane. Jackson was a devout Jehovah's Witness. He was beaten by his father and ordered by his older brothers to feign sleep in shared hotel rooms while they had sex with groupies on tour. Motown executives taught him to perform both onstage and off, so that even fielding questions was an act. He had performed for so long that, as he told interviewers in the early eighties, he was no longer sure what to do with himself when he was offstage. So he turned even deeper into the only world he knew. His personal life became a theater he directed and choreographed, with mannequins and puppets and amusement park rides. Hiding out at Neverland, he could also be an audience, watching movies in his home theater or taking in the scenery from his Ferris wheel. Discussing friendship with the reporter Gerri Hershey in 1983, he explained that he knew "people in show business," not civilians. He and Liza Minnelli were close, for example, but it was show business closeness: they swapped and admired performances.[103]

Jackson also admired Fosse's outfits: bowler hat, stovepipe pants cut short to show off the movements of white-socked feet, white gloves, various forms of tuxedo jackets (dark, sequined, boxy, or close to the body, or, on women, cropped and paired with fishnets and garters). When Jackson described both his single white glove and the sequined black jacket he wore on *Motown 25* as "so show business," he might as well have said "so Fosse." His moves that night mixed electric boogaloo with Fosse—especially the "Snake in the Grass" routine from *The Little Prince,* where Fosse slithers and freezes across a desolate landscape, seducing a young boy to the sting of death.[104]

Michael Jackson may have loved *Peter Pan,* but on *Motown 25,* the boy had grown up. The lyrics to "Billie Jean" are about the perils of a life onstage, vulnerable to false attacks by crazed fans. The dancing tells a story of sexual menace and physical attack: the pulsing pelvis, the legs and arms shooting into place. With his cocked hat, undulating arms, and single foot, pointed and held for a moment's admiration, Jackson was also telling the story of Bob Fosse.

Jackson asked Fosse to direct the video for "Thriller," but he turned down the job. (Fosse admired Jackson's dancing but told a friend that Jackson was "just too weird.") A few years later, he tried again: would Fosse direct "Smooth Criminal"? Fosse again said no. A note Jackson scribbled down while at work on the video shows how big a sway Fosse had over him: Jackson needed to "study the greats and become greater," which meant knowing "every cut, move, music, etc." from "all BOB FOSSE Movie Dances." The note also lists, more particularly, *Flashdance, All That Jazz,* and Fred Astaire's "Girl Hunt" number from *The Bandwagon.* Astaire's influence was enormous, but Fosse's name is the one in all caps.[105]

Vincent Paterson, who played a gang leader in "Beat It" and had worked as Michael Peters's choreographic assistant, choreographed most of "Smooth Criminal." (Colin Chilvers was the director, but Paterson, who both choreographed and storyboarded the bulk of the scene, seems to have been the dominant shaping force on the group movements. Jeffrey Daniel, of *Soul Train* fame, also contributed—including a moment where gangsters bounce forward in a move Daniel said was inspired by a Bugs Bunny cartoon.) "Smooth Criminal" ultimately looked less like Fosse than Fred Astaire—particularly, the "Girl Hunt" mini-drama.[106]

In that number, choreographed by Michael Kidd, Astaire plays a hardboiled private eye, on the hunt for Mr. Big. (Jackson's nemesis in *Moonwalker* has the same name.) After a few scenes partnering a luscious blonde and a menacing brunette—played, like *Swan Lake*'s Odette and Odile, by the same dancing dynamo, Cyd Charisse—Astaire goes to Dem Bones café. It's named for a black spiritual, but its customers are all white, and they cower from the sides as Astaire deftly outdances, outshoots, and outpunches his opponents. When Jackson enters Club 30s in "Smooth Criminal," he wears more or less the same outfit Astaire did—a

Photograph of Michael Jackson and Vincent Paterson in rehearsal for "Smooth Criminal," courtesy of Optimum Productions (Photographer: Sam Emerson)

white suit with a blue shirt and a white fedora—but he finds a motlier crowd. Black, white, and Asian American dancers meld Jeffrey Daniel's hip-hop prowess with Vincent Paterson's sultry choreography.

Paterson notes that he pulled Jackson from his original idea—himself and ten guys in tuxedos—to the more hardboiled scenario. Paterson had studied acting in college, and he brought an actor's sensibility to the job, encouraging each dancer to imagine his or her own backstory. As the rehearsals went on, there were more and more backstories: Jackson kept suggesting that Paterson take on more dancers, until he was working with about fifty.[107] He made good use of them. Men gamble in a corner; a band plays; patrons bang their fists in time with the music and, in a step borrowed from "Girl Hunt," fling their arms in the air as if at a revival. In a few sections, Jackson leads a pack of dancers, most memorably for his trademark farther-than-is-humanly-possible lean. By and large, though, Paterson's choreography has more varied and dynamic movements than the all-together-now group sequences Michael Peters created for "Beat It" and "Thriller." And where those videos featured dancing within a larger scenario, "Smooth Criminal" is all dancing, all the time. Jackson grabs a microphone at one point, but—given that his vocals are prominent whether he is singing or not—it doesn't seem to be to sing. He's just dancing with it, the way Fred Astaire might dance with a coat rack.

Over the years, "Girl Hunt" reappeared in Jackson's work. He borrowed a line from it for the 1991 song "Dangerous" ("She came at me in sections," Astaire says, when Cyd Charisse glides slowly toward him, her arms undulating as if to mimic her body's own curves.). Jackson's live performance of "Dangerous," choreographed by Travis Payne for the 1995 MTV video music awards, mimics the leaping, cartwheeling men in "Girl Hunt" firing cap guns in the subway. (It may also harken back to the moment in *Top Hat* in which Astaire guns down his chorus with his cane, using taps to make the sounds of shots.) In "Dangerous," a crowd of men in suits and fedoras fill the stage—some jumping in from the sides, some lowered on ropes—to the sounds of jazz and gunshots. As Astaire had told Jackson after *Motown 25*, they were angry dancers.

Perhaps it's no surprise that Jackson wanted to claim Astaire, not Fosse, as his biggest influence. Fosse has too much bump-

and-grind in his art, while Astaire oozes class. Besides, Astaire seems to please all manner of people: highbrow and popular, black and white dancers admire him. He's the kind of ubiquitous presence in American culture that Jackson himself aspired to become and, for a period, was. In its final issue for 1984, *People* ran a series of quotes under the title "The Last Word on Michael." The first was from Fred Astaire: "My Lord, he's a wonderful mover." The second, from the actress Sandy Duncan, compared Jackson's musicality to Astaire's, then went farther. "It's like he's got a direct connection to God, because those moves just come from within him and through the music." Isiah Thomas, basketball star for the Detroit Pistons, reached for the same comparison. "When I see him dance and sing, it touches me, like a spirit; it moves me inside, sort of like the Holy Ghost."[108]

*Thriller* put Jackson at the center of a conversation about the nature of popularity itself. Jackson had integrated MTV, dominated the airwaves, and given hope to a struggling record industry. He inspired devotion in fans of all ages, races, and classes. Jerry Falwell and Louis Farrakhan fretted about his seemingly feminine characteristics, but this didn't bother his fans: Jackson could be all things to all people. In the coming years, that massive acceptance began to erode. Jackson lost a number of fans in the wake of 1993 and 2003 allegations that he had sexually molested young boys, but his popularity had started waning much earlier, beginning with the 1984 *Victory* tour. Tickets for the shows were priced so high that Jackson's poorer, often black fans could not afford a seat. Changes in the music industry also affected him: hip-hop became increasingly popular, and more macho, too. At the same time, Jackson, a falsetto, seemed to be getting increasingly androgynous, with longer hair, lighter skin, and a slimmer nose. He had crossed over musically, and now he seemed to be trying to cross over physically, too.[109]

Jackson's changing appearance has inspired a rash of speculation. Maybe he wanted to look as unlike his overbearing father as possible. Maybe the little ski-jump nose he sought was an imitation of the child star Bobby Driscoll, the voice of Disney's animated *Peter Pan*. Maybe he was abandoning his race. Maybe he lightened his skin to match—and conceal—the discolored patches left by the skin disease vitiligo. Maybe the changes were part of his perpetual desire to reinvent himself. There may even be something to the claims, made since Jackson's death, that his continual self-remaking deconstructs our arbitrary categories of race and gender in favor of a postmodern play of surfaces—though that supposition veers a bit too far into wish-fulfillment, given that Jackson continued to identify as black. Whatever his motivation, Jackson's cosmetic changes put him at the center of another national conversation, about his oddities, and about how to conceive of race and gender in general. When Jackson released "Black or White" in 1991, it was almost too easy to turn the title into a joke about Jackson himself.[110]

The video for "Black or White" premiered after an episode of *The Simpsons,* in prime, families-around-the-TV-together time, and even though Jackson no longer had the cultural clout of his *Thriller* days, more viewers were tuned in than had watched the lunar landing back in 1969. Many were shocked by what they saw. Initially, "Black or White" seems to promise post-racial understanding. In the opening section, Macauley Culkin amps up his electric guitar so loudly that his father is blasted into Africa, returning him, as the critic Eric Lott has pointed out, to the origins of black music. But most of the video emphasizes the mutability of cultures. Jackson performs with dancers all over the globe. Culkin lip-synchs a rap. Standing on the Statue of Liberty, Jackson looks across a skyline composed of world capitals, cobbled together like the interior of a Las Vegas casino. In the final section, one face morphs into another, the entire human family blurred together on the same digital screen.[111]

But the afterword plunges Jackson into a different, darker reality. First, director John Landis congratulates one of the actors, as if to remind us that everything has been a performance. Then Michael Jackson turns into a black panther and slinks underground. He has entered the basement of history, and it resembles a set for *Singin' in the Rain.* But Gene Kelly's haunts give way to ghosts of Rodney King. Think we've found a way to transcend race?—Think again, Jackson seems to say. He turns back into a human (who simultaneously growls and screams) and a wind bombards him with trash. His dancing in this afterword is furious and quick. Jackson pounds his feet on the ground with the speed of a step dancer, and does some tap steps, too. He freezes and glides. He grabs his crotch, breaks car windows with his fists, and hurls a garbage can through a window. He also stands in a puff of smoke, caresses his torso, and ends one of his virtuosic spins crumpled in a puddle, tearing off his clothes, a shower of sparks raining down on him.

"Black or White," argues the film critic Carol Clover, works as a critique of *Singin' in the Rain,* and of the Hollywood musical writ large. Too often, musicals kept black voices, and black bodies, out of sight, even as they relied on black artists for content and inspiration.[112] Look at it this way: half a century earlier, Cholly Atkins was dubbing taps for white dancers. Now, Michael Jackson seemed to be stomping on that history. "Black or White" arguably becomes more of a horror film than "Thriller" could ever be. "Black or White" encapsulates the terror of American race relations. In the aboveground world of the video, we perform our unity, and we know that race and nation are arbitrary divisions: if we want, we can all dance together. But underground, in the back alleys or out on the streets, skin color still matters. Black men are still subject to abuse, and they're angry.

Jackson's masturbatory gestures are signs not just of loneliness but also of defiance: You think black men are aggressively sexual?—Well, here you go, Jackson seems to say. Remember how I morphed into a werewolf in "Thriller"? Now I'll turn into the sign of political radicalism. You can take your happy crossover, and shove it.

According to Vincent Paterson, who choreographed the video with Jackson (Paterson did the group sections, and Jackson set most of his own movement), he, Landis, and Jackson had no conversations about political intentions. They were just trying to make "interesting, fun short films" that would be "visually spectacular." Still, says Paterson, those other messages may well have existed "subconsciously," and the fact that critics are finding them now is a compliment. It means that they weren't cutting elaborate commercials for Michael Jackson—they were making art.[113]

Initially, however, most people did not view "Black or White" as art. When families crowded around their TV sets to watch the video's premiere, they were flummoxed, shocked even. This wasn't the Michael Jackson they remembered. The exceptional black dancer, the man who could unify a crowd just by leading them through group choreography, had been replaced by a one-man, sexually suggestive riot. Was it a cry for help? A plea for headlines? In the wake of such criticism, Jackson back-pedaled. He apologized for the misunderstanding. A new, digitally enhanced version of the video was cut, with racist graffiti that made Jackson's violence seem like a clear protest, rather than the result of a vague and generalized rage. When MTV put the video into rotation, the producers cut the final sequence.[114] The industry was not putting skeletons decorously back in the closet; with Jackson's approval, it was sealing the closet like a crypt.

Michael Jackson has always seemed able to imbue the body with a life force that comes from somewhere else. It's at the heart of his youthful mimicry, when, barely out of kindergarten, he could do the mashed potato and shake his hips like James Brown. It's the joke, and the appeal, of the grooving, robotic "Dancing Machine." It's the fun of "Thriller," where the dead rise from their graves and get down. It's the cosmic power of his early eighties stardom, when he gave the backslide that emerged from electric boogaloo a name that placed it outside the realms of terrestrial possibility—the moonwalk—and when hordes of followers imitated him in dress, song, and dance.

After Jackson died, on June 25, 2009, the heady days of his *Thriller*-era popularity seemed to come rushing back, as people took to the streets to mourn. They crowded outside the UCLA hospital where Jackson was pronounced dead and in a kind of ritual resurrection did the "Thriller" dance. In New Orleans, they danced to brass band renditions of Jackson's songs in a huge second line, the jazz funeral rite that sends off the dead with rejoicing. Parisians held a memorial moonwalk in the shadow of the Eiffel Tower. Fans in San Francisco crouched opposite one another to reenact the fight scene from "Beat It." Outside the Apollo Theater in Harlem, the crowd sang "Wanna Be Starting Something," waving their arms in the air, stepping from side to side, and—when they got to the catchy, mamase-mamasa chorus that Jackson swiped from Cameroonian Manu Dibango's disco hit, "Soul Makossa"—clapping their hands and jumping up and down. It was the stuff of Hollywood musicals, and of Jackson's best dreams: people coming together in music and in movement.[115]

It continues, too, in flash mobs that seek to bring the magic of Hollywood musicals and music videos into real life, and then, on YouTube, put them back on video again. You can watch dancers perform "Thriller" in Baku, Azerbaijan; in Cologne, Germany; in Amsterdam, London, and Tulsa, Oklahoma. In 2009, 13,957 dancers did it in Mexico City—setting a new world record—and that same year, say the organizers of "Thrill the World," over 20,000 dancers in different cities did the dance simultaneously. A reality show in England, *Move Like Michael Jackson,* enlisted Jackson's brother Jermaine as a judge. And the latest round of popular dance TV shows—*So You Think You Can Dance* and *Dancing with the Stars*—have paid tribute to the man who is now seen, androgyny and all, as a pioneer of hip-hop dance.

In 2014, the vaults opened up for a new Michael Jackson record: *Xscape,* which cobbled unreleased Jackson recordings with new work by living artists and producers. The video for Justin

Timberlake's collaboration, "Love Never Felt So Good," features clips of Jackson, Timberlake, and fans of all races and ages, singing and dancing. The thing is, even when the fans lip-synch, you don't hear their voices—only Timberlake's, or Jackson's, come through. But when they dance, you get the sense that you're watching their bodies at the same time as you see Jackson's, moonwalking, spinning, freezing, popping, and locking, hurling themselves into snippets of old choreography and embellishing it with their own sensibilities.

It's tempting to imagine a video that was never made, where "Black or White"–style morphing takes on the slipperiness of dance history itself. James Brown slides across the stage and turns into Michael Jackson. Jackson kicks up his leg and becomes Damita Jo Freeman, who takes ballet class with Agnes de Mille. Freeman locks into Don Campbell, who freezes into Bob Fosse, who slinks back into Michael Jackson at *Motown 25*. Jackson cocks his fedora like Fred Astaire, who spins Ginger Rogers out of his arms and tries on the rhythms of Bill Robinson. Robinson's stair dance is reproduced by Cholly Atkins, who changes into Diana Ross and the Supremes, singing and dancing in synch, and then, again, into Michael Jackson, now with his brothers, and now alone, leaving their line to moonwalk through time. He's Jeffrey Daniel, Popin Pete, maybe even Bill Bailey, or, in the 1880s, Billy Kersands, clowning for the queen. Then Kersands transforms into a little white girl in 1984 wearing one sequined glove and dark face paint, or into Bert Williams, mocking the minstrel mask from behind it. Williams does a cakewalk, and becomes one of Agnes de Mille's cowboys, kicking his legs atop of a train, then walks casually down the street while Paul Taylor takes notes. It could keep going, steps slipping from one body to the next, across TV and computer screens, in mirrors and on stages and just below front stoops.

That back and forth is the essence of Jackson's moonwalk. The moonwalk seems to point forward, toward a spectacular future unconfined by space and time and gravity and everything holding us back, both physically and metaphorically. But it also goes backward, to a past of vernacular and professional dancers stretching for decades, and far beyond. Their histories have always been at the heart of Jackson's work—sometimes pounding and sustaining, sometimes dark, pulsing, and furious. Michael Jackson crossed over, but when he danced, he took his earthly fetters with him.

# DANCE FILMS AND VIDEOS

Choreographers of individual works are listed parenthetically. Performances posted on YouTube are identified in the Notes.

*America Dances! 1878–1948: A Collector's Edition of Social Dance on Film.* Dancetime Publications, October 2003. DVD.

*American Genesis* (Paul Taylor). Performed by the Paul Taylor Dance Company, 1973. Digital video. Paul Taylor Dance Archives.

*Aureole* (Paul Taylor). *See* "Three Modern Classics."

*Ballets Russes.* Directed by Daniel Geller and Dayna Goldfine, 2005. Zeitgeist Films, 2006. DVD.

*The Barkleys of Broadway.* Directed by Charles Walters, 1949. MGM. Warner Home Video, 2005. DVD

*Big Bertha* (Paul Taylor). See "Three Modern Classics."

*Breakin'.* Directed by Sam Firstenberg, 1984. MGM.

*Breakin' 2: Electric Boogaloo.* Directed by Sam Firstenberg, 1984. MGM.

*Carefree.* Directed by Mark Sandrich, 1938. RKO. Turner Home Entertainment, 2006. DVD.

*Company B* (Paul Taylor). Performed by the Paul Taylor Dance Company at the David H. Koch Theater, New York, March 5, 2013. Digital video. Paul Taylor Dance Archives.

*Company B* (Paul Taylor). In *The Wreckers' Ball.* Directed by Matthew Diamond, 1996. Performed by the Paul Taylor Dance Company.

*Great Performances: Dance in America*. WNET/Thirteen, New York, 1996. VHS.

*Conversations About the Dance*. Directed by Charles S. Dubin, 1977. Produced by KCET Community Television of Southern California, 1980. DVD. Jerome Robbins Dance Division, New York Public Library for the Performing Arts.

*Dance, Girl, Dance*. Directed by Dorothy Arzner, 1940. RKO. Turner Home Entertainment, 2007. DVD.

*Dimples*. Directed William A. Seiter, 1936. 20th Century Fox, 2006. DVD.

*Dixiana*. Directed by Luther Reed, 1930. AFA Entertainment, 2011. DVD.

*Epic* (Paul Taylor). Performed by Paul Taylor, October 20, 1957. Digital video. Paul Taylor Dance Archives.

*Esplanade* (Paul Taylor). Performed by the Paul Taylor Dance Company at Jacob's Pillow, Lee, Mass., July 15, 1998. Digital video. Paul Taylor Dance Archives.

*Esplanade* (Paul Taylor). Performed by the Paul Taylor Dance Company, 1978. *Great Performances: Dance in America*. Directed by Emile Ardolino. WNET/Thirteen, New York, 1978. VHS. Jerome Robbins Dance Division, New York Public Library for the Performing Arts.

*Feet—Fun—and Fancy*. British Pathé film, released March 26, 1927, 2 mins., 29 secs. At http://www.britishpathe.com/video/feet-fun-and -fancy.

*Filling Station* (Lew Christensen). Performed by New York City Ballet, 1954. VHS. Jerome Robbins Dance Division, New York Public Library for the Performing Arts.

*Flying Down to Rio*. Directed by Thornton Freeland, 1933. RKO. Turner Home Entertainment, 2006. DVD.

*Follow the Fleet*. Directed by Mark Sandrich, 1936. RKO. Turner Home Entertainment, 2006. DVD.

*Frankie and Johnny* (Ruth Page and Bentley Stone). Performed by Page, Stone, and members of the Federal Dance Project at the Blackstone

Theater, Chicago, 1938. Filmstrip. Jerome Robbins Dance Division, New York Public Library for the Performing Arts.

*Frankie and Johnny* (Ruth Page and Bentley Stone). Performed by the Chicago Ballet, 1978. VHS. Jerome Robbins Dance Division, New York Public Library for the Performing Arts.

*From Sea to Shining Sea* (Paul Taylor). Performed by the Paul Taylor Dance Company at Hunter College, New York, 1965. Digital video. Paul Taylor Dance Archives.

*From Sea to Shining Sea* (Paul Taylor). Performed by the Paul Taylor Dance Company for the Repertory Preservation Project, 2006. Digital video. Paul Taylor Dance Archives.

*The Gay Divorcee*. Directed by Mark Sandrich, 1934. RKO. Turner Home Entertainment, 2006. DVD.

*The Goldwyn Follies*. Directed by George Marshall, 1938. United Artists. Fox Home Entertainment, 2008. DVD.

*Harlem Is Heaven*. Directed by Irwin Franklin, 1932. Lincoln Productions.

*Honolulu*. Directed by Edward Buzzell, 1939. MGM. Warner Archive, 2011. DVD.

*In Groove: N.Y. City Hall Host to Jitterbug Bands*. RKO-Pathé, 1939. At http://wpafilmlibrary.com.

*In Old Kentucky*. Directed by George Marshall, 1935. 20th Century Fox, 2009. DVD.

*Jeni Legon: Living in a Great Big Way*. Directed by Grant Greschuk, 1999. National Film Board of Canada. VHS.

*Lady Be Good*. DVD. Directed by Norman Z. McLeod, 1941. MGM. Warner Home Video. 2008. DVD.

*The Little Colonel*. Directed by David Butler, 1935. 20th Century Fox, 2006. DVD.

*The Littlest Rebel*. Directed by David Butler, 1935. 20th Century Fox, 2006. DVD.

*Michael Jackson's This Is It*. Directed by Kenny Ortega, 2009. Columbia Pictures. Sony Pictures, 2010. DVD.

*Michael Jackson's Vision.* Sony Legacy, 2010. DVD.

*Moonwalker.* Directed by Jerry Kramer, Jim Flashfield, 1988. Warner Brothers, 2010. DVD.

*Night Journey* (Martha Graham). Directed by Alexander Hammid, 1961. In *Martha Graham: Dance on Film.* Criterion Collection, 2007. DVD.

*Noah's Minstrels* (Paul Taylor). Performed by the Paul Taylor Dance Company, 1973. Digital video. Paul Taylor Dance Archives.

*Oklahoma!* (Agnes de Mille). Directed by Fred Zinnemann, 1955. 20th Century Fox, 2005. DVD.

*Paul Taylor: Dancemaker.* Directed by Matthew Diamond, 1998. Docurama, 2000. DVD.

*Performance and Inside Look: "Esplanade" by Paul Taylor.* Company E, for City Dance. Online video. At http://www.companye.org/Filmworks /Esplanade/esplanade.title.html.

*Rebecca of Sunnybrook Farm.* Directed by Allen Dwan, 1938. 20th Century Fox, 2005. DVD.

*Roberta.* Directed by William A. Seiter, 1935. RKO. Turner Home Entertainment, 2006. DVD.

*Rodeo* (Agnes de Mille). Performed by Jenny Workman, John Kriza, Kelly Brown and artists of Ballet Theatre, and originally broadcast on *Omnibus,* CBS-TV, December 21, 1952. Film. Jerome Robbins Dance Division, New York Public Library for the Performing Arts.

*Rodeo* (Agnes de Mille). Performed by American Ballet Theatre, 1972. Film. Jerome Robbins Dance Division, New York Public Library for the Performing Arts.

*Rodeo* (Agnes de Mille). Scene 1. Performed by American Ballet Theatre, 1973. In *American Ballet Theatre: A Close-up in Time.* WNET/Thirteen, New York. DVD.

*Rowdy Ann.* Directed by Al E. Christie, 1919. Christie Film Company. In *Slapstick Encyclopedia: Volume 4.* Chatsworth, Calif.: Image Entertainment, 2002. DVD.

*Shall We Dance.* Directed by Mark Sandrich, 1937. RKO. Turner Home Entertainment, 2006. DVD.

*Soul Train: The Hippest Trip in America.* Directed by Amy Goldberg and J. Kevin Swain, 2010. VH1 Rock Docs.

*Stormy Weather.* Directed by Andrew L. Stone, 1943. 20th Century Fox, 2006. DVD.

*The Story of Vernon and Irene Castle.* Directed by H. C. Potter, 1939. RKO. Turner Home Entertainment, 2006. DVD.

*Swing Time.* Directed by George Stevens, 1936. RKO. Turner Home Entertainment, 2006. DVD.

*Texas Fourth* (Agnes de Mille). Performed by the Agnes de Mille Heritage Dance Theatre, 1973. VHS. Jerome Robbins Dance Division, New York Public Library for the Performing Arts.

*3 Epitaphs* (Paul Taylor). *See* "Three Modern Classics."

*3 Epitaphs* (Paul Taylor). Performed by the Paul Taylor Dance Company at the Koch Theater, New York, 2013. Digital video. Paul Taylor Dance Archives.

"Three Modern Classics" [*Aureole, Big Bertha,* and *3 Epitaphs*]. (Paul Taylor). Performed by the Paul Taylor Dance Company at the American Dance Festival in Durham, N.C., 1981. *Great Performances: Dance in America.* Directed by Emile Ardolino. WNET/Thirteen, New York, January 11, 1982. VHS.

*Top Hat.* Directed by Mark Sandrich, 1935. RKO. Turner Home Entertainment, 2006. DVD.

# NOTES

See the List of Dance Films and Videos for complete information on the performances cited here.

## INTRODUCTION

1. Alvin Moses, "Footlights Flickers," *Plaindealer,* June 2, 1939.
2. My thinking on these issues owes a good deal to Ralph Ellison's description of "Adamic wordplay," which attempts, "in the interest of a futuristic dream, to impose unity upon an experience that changes too rapidly for linguistic or political exactitude." Ralph Ellison, "The Little Man at Chehaw Station," *The Collected Essays of Ralph Ellison* (New York: Random House, 1995), 511–12. See also Benedict Anderson, *Imagined Communities: Reflections on the Origin and Spread of Nationalism* (New York: Verso, 1991).
3. Constance Rourke, *American Humor: A Study of the National Character* (1931; repr., New York: New York Review of Books, 2004), 26.
4. While American Studies, as a field, tends to regard Rourke as something of a pioneer, her work has little traction in theater studies. For a good exploration of her scholarly afterlife, see Jennifer Schlueter, "A 'Theatrical Race': American Identity and Popular Performance in the Writings of Constance M. Rourke," *Theatre Journal.* 60, no. 4 (December 2008): 529–43.
5. Anderson, Rourke, and Ellison are central to my thinking on these subjects, but I would be remiss not to mention some of the reams of other fine criticism devoted to performance and identity, both

national and racial, within the past few years. See, for example, Daphne Brooks, *Bodies in Dissent: Spectacular Performances of Race and Freedom, 1850–1910* (Durham, N.C.: Duke University Press, 2006); Jayna Brown, *Babylon Girls: Black Women Performers and the Shaping of the Modern* (Durham, N.C.: Duke University Press, 2008); Shannon Jackson, *Lines of Activity: Performance, Historiography, Hull-House Domesticity* (Ann Arbor: University of Michigan Press, 2000); and Philip J. Deloria, *Playing Indian* (New Haven: Yale University Press, 1998).

6. Ellison, "Going to the Territory," in *Collected Essays,* 611.

7. Ellison, "Little Man at Chehaw Station," 511; Ellison, "Going to the Territory," 612, 608. Ellison may seem to be supporting a doctrine of American essentialism, but as Hortense Spillers has pointed out, he argues that culture is "dynamic, even restless, over and against closed or poised." See Spillers, " 'The Little Man At Chehaw Station' Today," *boundary 2* 30, no. 2 (2003): 15. My thinking diverges from Ellison's regarding the "gesture toward perfection," though; the vernacular can also fight the move from many to one with both individual and collective force.

8. See John Charles Chasteen, "The Prehistory of Samba: Carnival Dancing in Rio de Janeiro, 1840–1917," *Journal of Latin American Studies* 28, no. 1 (February 1986): 29–47; Nancy Goldner, "The Guards of Amager," *Nation,* June 26, 1976, reprinted in *Reading Dance,* ed. Robert Gottlieb, 286–89 (New York: Random House, 2008).

9. Ellison, "Going to the Territory," 595–96.

## 1 THE CAKEWALK, AMERICA'S FIRST NATIONAL DANCE

1. "No American National Dance," *New York Tribune,* December 11, 1884; "The Kirmes: A Scene of Oriental Splendor at the Academy of Music," *The Sun,* December 18, 1884.

2. "A National Dance," *New York Times,* December 21, 1884.

3. "Dances of the Season: American Dancing Masters' New Tributes to Terpsichore," *Washington Post,* November 1, 1896 (quotation); "New Modes of Dancing," *Chicago Daily Tribune,* December 15, 1886;

"Worship Mars and Terpsichore," *Chicago Daily Tribune,* November 27, 1898.

4. *Comedy Cakewalk on Beach,* newsreel, 1903, in *America Dances!* (DVD).

5. "New Dances for Winter," *Chicago Daily Tribune,* September 16, 1900; "Ban on Ragtime Music," *Washington Post,* September 30, 1900.

6. "Dancing Masters Meet: Exhibit as National American Dance Mixture of Two-Step and Cake Walk," *New York Times,* July 24, 1908.

7. *Cakewalk* and *Comedy Cakewalk* are both in *America Dances!* (DVD).

8. "Which Will It Be?" *Boston Daily Globe,* February 25, 1892.

9. "Cakewalk in Europe," *Arizona Republican,* February 23, 1903. According to the *Republican,* the tale came from "a Berlin paper of recent date," and the original author was "angry with the United States for sending the cakewalk to Europe."

10. "Before 'De War,'" *Detroit Free Press,* November 30, 1902; former slave quoted in Marshall Stearns and Jean Stearns, *Jazz Dance: The Story of American Vernacular Dance* (New York: Macmillan, 1968), 22. A white correspondent for the *South Carolina Gazette* seemed to have had a similar reaction to such dances in 1772. After covertly watching a slave dance outside Charleston, he wrote, "The entertainment was opened by the men copying (or *taking off*) the manners of their masters, and the women those of their mistresses, and relating some highly curious anecdotes, to the inexpressible diversion of that company." Quoted in Lawrence W. Levine, *Black Culture and Black Consciousness* (Oxford: Oxford University Press, 1977), 17.

11. "Before 'De War.'"

12. Henry T. Sampson, *Blacks in Blackface: A Source Book on Early Black Musical Shows* (Metuchen, N.J.: Scarecrow, 1980), 356.

13. You can get a sense for Williams's cakewalking skills in a scene from what MoMA, having discovered footage of a never-completed feature-length 1913 film in which he starred, is calling the *Lime Kiln Field Day Project.*

14. Walker, quoted in David Krasner, *Resistance, Parody, and Double Consciousness in African American Theatre, 1895–1910* (New York: St. Martin's, 1997), 88–91.

15. In Saint Louis, for example, white society blacked up to perform a cakewalk "for the sake of sweet charity." The performers walked with what the local paper called "such grace and elasticity" that some observers suggested spirits were guiding them. "Spirits Attended the Cake Walk of the Fifth Avenue Club," *St. Louis Post-Dispatch,* April 17, 1898.

16. The African American Ne Plus Ultra club in Pine Bluff, Arkansas, threw a cakewalk in 1891 that raised $115 toward the $30,000 A.M.E. Church they hoped to build. The most graceful couple won a two-tiered cake (A.J.R., "Great Cakewalk," *Indianapolis Freeman,* May 30, 1891). The following year the Baltimore Elks, a white club, hired six African American couples from the District of Columbia to participate in a cakewalk that attracted some twenty-five hundred spectators. The winning couple chose a gold medal rather than the six-foot diameter cake, festooned with an elk's head, which went to those in second place ("A Six-Foot Cake," *The Sun,* August 3, 1892). The Madison Square Garden cakewalks are also mentioned in "Walking for a Cake: Eleven Couples Competed," *New York Times,* February 7, 1897. For accounts of San Francisco cakewalks, see "Walking for a Cake," *San Francisco Chronicle,* March 26, 1892, and "The Cake Walk: Brought to a Successful Termination," *San Francisco Chronicle,* March 27, 1892. On Williams and Walker's challenge to Vanderbilt, see James Weldon Johnson, *Black Manhattan* (1930; repr., New York: Da Capo, 1991), 105–6. On Gray's possible challenge, see "Challenge to a Cake Walk," *New York Times,* January 13, 1898. On the Hartford competition, see "Last Night's Cakewalk," *Hartford Courant,* February 28, 1894.

17. "Leader of England's Court Set as the Guest of Perry Belmont Enjoys a Real Negro Cakewalk," *St. Louis Post-Dispatch,* December 15, 1901.

18. "Black Dancers in London Salon," *Atlanta Constitution,* May 6, 1906; "Victim of the Cakewalk Craze: King Edward Charmed with the American Performances He Has Seen," *Boston Daily Globe,* January 25, 1903; "Cakewalk Is a London Fad," *Detroit Free Press,* July 5, 1903. See also Daphne Brooks's account of the Williams and Walker Company's command performance in *Bodies in Dissent: Spectacular*

*Performances of Race and Freedom, 1850–1910* (Durham, N.C.: Duke University Press, 2006): 279–80. Brooks quotes George Walker on the royal family, who he says treated the performers like royalty and whom he compares to "little faeries," a comment that—as Brooks puts it—is "sly and signifying," turning "minstrelsy's incessant rendering of black folks as children" back onto its white audience. Brooks also describes the improvised cakewalk of audience members.

19. *Le cake-walk infernal,* 1903, directed by Georges Méliès, available at https://www.youtube.com/watch?v=-s4qP8b2wH4; C.I.B., "America Has Lent France a New Amusement, Which Is Driving Out the Cancan and Danse Du Ventre," *New York Tribune,* March 22, 1903. This performance should not be confused with the French "Apache dance," which rose to prominence in the 1910s. That dance, which dramatizes the violence a pimp inflects on his dependent prostitute, was so named because of its savagery. For more on the popularity of the cakewalk in France, see Matthew F. Jordan, *Le Jazz: Jazz and French Cultural Identity* (Champaign: University of Illinois Press, 2010). Jordon describes a 1903 Pathé film, *Le cake-walk chez les nains,* in which a giant black-faced Uncle Sam turns a pair of miniature French peasants into modern city-dwellers who know how to cakewalk (35).

20. For an excellent account of the uses to which early white Americans adopted Native American identities, see Philip J. Deloria, *Playing Indian* (New Haven: Yale University Press, 1998). These conflations are also part of America's national architecture: the bronze statue atop the U.S. Capitol dome, *Freedom Triumphant in War and Peace* (now known as *The Statue of Freedom*)—a white woman with a Roman helmet—wears a Native American blanket over one shoulder.

21. For the lynching statistics, see National Association for the Advancement of Colored People, *Thirty Years of Lynching in the United States, 1889–1913* (New York: Negro Universities Press, 1969), 29.

22. Charles Chesnutt, *The Marrow of Tradition* (1901; repr., New York: Penguin, 1993). For an analysis of Tom's performance, see

Eric J. Sundquist, *To Wake the Nations: Race in the Making of American Literature* (Cambridge: Belknap Press of Harvard University Press, 1993), 271–93.

23. "Ghosts Do a Cakewalk." *Washington Post,* July 14, 1907.

24. Ibid.

25. Ibid.

26. Nancy Reynolds, *Repertory in Review: Forty Years of New York City Ballet* (New York: Dial, 1977), 81; Debra Hickenlooper Sowell, *The Christensen Brothers: An American Dance Epic* (Amsterdam: Harwood, 1998), 237; John Martin, "Ballet Society Offers Two Premieres," *New York Times,* May 19, 1947.

27. John Martin, "Yet Again: City Center Ballet Ready with More Novelties," *New York Times,* May 13, 1951; Martin, "Ballet Society Offers Two Premieres"; George Balanchine and Francis Mason, *Balanchine's Complete Stories of the Great Ballets,* rev. ed. (Garden City, N.Y.: Doubleday, 1977), 82–85; Hering, quoted in Reynolds, *Repertory in Review,* 121.

## 2 BILL ROBINSON'S DREAM

1. Jim Haskins and N. R. Mitgang, *Mr. Bojangles: The Biography of Bill Robinson* (New York: William Morrow, 1988), 99.

2. For a sense of Robinson's style and technical achievements, see Marshall Stearns and Jean Stearns, *Jazz Dance: The Story of American Vernacular Dance* (New York: Macmillan, 1968), 179–88. Robinson's fellow tappers heap him with praise throughout Rusty E. Frank's *Tap! The Greatest Tap Dance Stars and Their Stories, 1900–1955* (New York: Da Capo, 1990), esp. 66, 72–73, 98, 149, 180, 225, 266.

3. On Robinson's pay, see " 'Bojangles' Here Next Week." *New York Amsterdam News,* August 31, 1927.

4. *Bring in 'da Noise, Bring in 'da Funk,* quoted in John Lahr, "Big and Bad Wolfe," *New Yorker,* December 4, 1995, 120.

5. *In Old Kentucky* did not play consistently at the Grand Opera House for seven years; it opened at the Bijou and traveled from theater to theater around the country. For records of the show's performances and information about its plot, see "Around the Playhouses: 'In Old

Kentucky' Making a Success Again," *San Francisco Chronicle,* January 21, 1896; "In Old Kentucky," *New York Times,* August 29, 1893; "The Playhouses," *Los Angeles Times,* November 13, 1899; "Musical and Theatrical Notes," *Chicago Daily Tribune,* July 22, 1900; "The Bills at the Theaters," *San Francisco Chronicle,* October 19, 1903. Lynn Abbott and Doug Seroff discuss *In Old Kentucky* in *Out of Sight: The Rise of African American Popular Music, 1889–1895* (Oxford: University Press of Mississippi, 2003): 406–9. They also include the reprint of the advertisement for new recruits, from a July 2, 1904, edition of the *Freeman.*

6. "Fascination of 'Craps.' Mysteries of Dice Game Played by Little Negroes in 'In Old Kentucky,'" *New York Times,* December 3, 1893.

7. "Medal for Best Buck Dancing," *Washington Post,* January 24, 1897; "Classified Ad 8—no Title," *San Francisco Chronicle,* November 11, 1897

8. Some of Robinson's peers insist that Swinton let him win, deliberately drawing a low number and performing long before Robinson, so that Robinson would be fresh in the judges' memories. See Stearns and Stearns, *Jazz Dance,* 75–76; Tom Fletcher, *100 Years of the Negro in Show Business: The Tom Fletcher Story* (New York: Burdge, 1954): 290–91. Constance Valis Hill reconstructs *In Old Kentucky* to imagine the scene of Robinson's performance, which she says occurred in March 1900. See *Tap Dancing America: A Cultural History* (Oxford: Oxford University Press, 2010), 20–22. "Angry Gallery Gods Stop a Harlem Show," *New York Times,* March 25, 1904; Haskins and Mitgang, *Mr. Bojangles,* 43–44.

9. Abbott and Seroff, *Out of Sight,* 360–65; Haskins and Mitgang, *Mr. Bojangles,* 43–44; Hill, *Tap Dancing America,* 56–57. Though plant shows faded, pickaninnies did not. They were trotted out as insurance, to provide lively background dancing for a white star who might not attract as much attention alone. See Joe Laurie, Jr., *Vaudeville: From the Honky-tonks to the Palace* (New York: Holt, 1953), 56.

10. For more on the way whites on both sides of the Mason-Dixon Line found common cause in suppressing black freedom after the Civil War, see David W. Blight, *Race and Reunion: The Civil War in American*

*Memory* (Cambridge: Belknap Press of Harvard University Press, 2001), and Leon F. Litwack, *Trouble in Mind: Black Southerners in the Age of Jim Crow* (New York: Knopf, 1998).

11. See Abbott and Seroff, *Ragged but Right: Black Traveling Shows, "Coon" Songs, and the Dark Pathway to Blues and Jazz* (Jackson: University Press of Mississippi, 2007), and *Out of Sight.* Tim Brooks, *Lost Sounds: Blacks and the Birth of the Recording Industry, 1890–1910* (Urbana: University of Illinois Press, 2004), is also a rich resource. Edward Berlin's study of ragtime is still the most thorough discussion of the music itself: *Ragtime: A Musical and Cultural History* (Berkeley: University of California Press, 1980). James Dorman provides thorough readings of coon songs to argue that they managed and perpetuated white racial anxieties. The lyrics made black Americans seem too base and ridiculous to threaten a white-supremacist social order, but they also played into stereotypes that blacks were violent and driven by appetite, not reason. See "Shaping the Popular Image of Post-Reconstruction Blacks: The 'Coon Song' Phenomenon of the Gilded Age," *American Quarterly* 40, no. 4 (December 1988): 450–71.

12. W. T. Lhamon, Jr., "Whittling on Dynamite: The Difference Bert Williams Makes," in *Listen Again: A Momentary History of Pop Music,* ed. Eric Weisbard (Durham, N.C.: Duke University Press, 2007), 7–25. For years, critics have considered Williams a tragic figure, victim of time and stereotyping; for a moving novelistic treatment in this vein, see Caryl Phillips, *Dancing in the Dark* (New York: Knopf, 2005). However, a host of recent scholars have begun to see Williams as a more progressive and powerful force who, as Lhamon argues, subverted stereotypes from within. See Louis Chude-Sokei, *The Last "Darky": Bert Williams, Black-on-Black Minstrelsy, and the African Diaspora* (Durham, N.C.: Duke University Press, 2006); Karen Sotiropoulos, *Staging Race: Black Performers in Turn of the Century America* (Cambridge: Harvard University Press, 2006); Yuval Taylor and Jake Austen, *Darkest America: Black Minstrelsy From Slavery to Hip-Hop* (New York: Norton, 2012), 109–34; Daphne Brooks, *Bodies in Dissent: Spectacular Performances of Race and Freedom, 1850–1910* (Durham, N.C.: Duke University Press, 2006), 207–80. It's worth

pointing out that years before these studies, Donald Bogle portrayed Williams as the transgressive ancestor of comics like Richard Pryor; see his "Black Humor—Full Circle from Slave Quarters to Richard Pryor," *Ebony,* August 1975, 123–26, 128.

13. Hill, *Tap Dancing America,* 34–38; Felicia R. Lee, "Coming Soon, a Century Late: A Black Film Gem," *New York Times,* September 20, 2014. For Williams as the cleverest "low comedian" see " 'Follies of 1910' on New York Roof," *New York Times,* June 21, 1910; for Williams as "one of the greatest comedians America has ever bred," see Amy Leslie, "Bert Williams: World's Greatest Comedian," *Chicago Daily News,* reprinted in *Chicago Defender,* July 25, 1914; Williams was called the "world's greatest comedian" in "Bert Williams: World's Greatest Living Comedian," *Chicago Defender,* December 26, 1914.

14. "Bert Williams: World's Greatest Living Comedian"; Phillips, *Dancing in the Dark.*

15. Williams quoted in Chude-Sokei, *The Last "Darky,"* 25; W. E. B. Du Bois, *The Souls of Black Folk* (Chicago: McClurg, 1903), 3.

16. W. T. Lhamon discusses both these songs in his excellent "Whittling on Dynamite," which implicitly suggests that Williams does, in fact, play a bleedhound—the one who, according to Lhamon's "fire hydrant theory," does his business, having donned a persona that might, in fact, hinder the progress to freedom.

17. Haskins and Mitgang claim that Robinson worked for Williams and Walker (*Mr. Bojangles,* 55), and a decade after Williams's death, Robinson wrote that "it was always a pleasure to work" with Bert Williams: "Bill Robinson Looks Back Half-Century," *Hartford Courant,* January 2, 1935. The two certainly rubbed shoulders in the world of Harlem entertainment: according to Tom Fletcher, Robinson played for the Black Rats, a baseball team of black vaudeville performers, which beat the Williams and Walker Company team; Bert Williams played first base. See Fletcher, *100 Years of the Negro in Show Business,* 293. Williams and Robinson also shared a bill as part of an evening entertainment organized by the Frogs, a black theatrical society that Williams helped found: "Bert Williams to Star a Big Company," *Philadelphia Tribune,* August 2, 1913. For more on

Cooper and Robinson, see Haskins and Mitgang, *Mr. Bojangles,* 55–60; "Vaudeville Houses Offer Good Attractions," *Seattle Daily Times,* July 27, 1909; "At the Orpheum. Gets a Fair Deal," *Duluth News Tribune,* February 16, 1912; "Holiday Crowds Enjoy Keith Bill," *Philadelphia Inquirer,* December 28, 1912.

18. Marshall, "Cooper and Robinson Arouse NP Things at Keith's," *Freeman* (Indianapolis), January 27, 1912; Fletcher, *100 Years of the Negro in Show Business,* 296–97.

19. "At the Orpheum," *Duluth News Tribune,* February 11, 1912; Marshall, "Cooper and Robinson Arouse NP Things At Keith's."

20. Marshall, "Cooper and Robinson Arouse NP Things At Keith's."; "At the Orpheum," February 11, 1912.

21. "Exceptional Film Showing at Hillstreet," *Los Angeles Times,* July 25, 1922; " 'Bojangles' a Knockout," *Chicago Defender,* October 4, 1924.

22. Even though Robinson modeled himself after Williams when performing with Cooper, he admired and learned from George Walker, too. In 1926 he headed up a benefit for Walker's mother that raised $2,075. See "Bill Robinson Writes," *Chicago Defender,* July 3, 1926.

23. "Bill Robinson Hits." *Chicago Defender,* July 31, 1926.

24. "Negro Actor Being Emancipated, Says Bill Robinson," *New York Amsterdam News,* August 15, 1928.

25. " 'Bo' Gets His," *Chicago Defender,* February 16, 1924; Ashton Stevens, "Maybe Bill Robinson Is No Tap Dancer at All—He's So Different Says Evening American Critic," *New Journal and Guide,* March 31, 1934; " 'Bojangles' a Knockout"; William F. McDermott, "Bill Robinson Explains an Art," *Cleveland Plain Dealer,* March 24, 1932; O. O. McIntyre, "New York Day by Day," *New Orleans Times-Picayune,* November 10, 1930; John Martin, *America Dancing: The Background and Personalities of the Modern Dance* (New York: Dodge, 1936), 13; B. R. Crisler, "Film Gossip of the Week: Dr. Bill Robinson, Tapster—A Delegation From Dublin—Miss Allan Returns," *New York Times,* July 5, 1936.

26. "Music: Black for Bach," *Time,* March 23, 1931; St. Clair McKelway, "Bojangles—II," *New Yorker,* October 13, 1934, 30–34; Susan

Manning, *Modern Dance, Negro Dance: Race in Motion* (Minneapolis: University of Minnesota Press, 2004), 115–16; "Bill Robinson Fair's Big Star," *New York Amsterdam News,* September 23, 1939.

27. "Toscanini Likes Cotton Club Jazz," *Afro-American* (Baltimore), February 5, 1938; "Dance Festival at Carnegie Hall for Russian War Relief," February 3, 1942. Press Release in the Bill Robinson Clippings File of the Jerome Robbins Dance Division, New York Public Library for the Performing Arts. E. C. Sherburne, "Bill Robinson Tells Visitor of His Role and Its Setting," *Christian Science Monitor,* May 1, 1945. Robinson's comments regarding "the Russians" are somewhat confusing and hard to verify; he provides no dates for these encounters. It seems likely that Nijinsky would not have been part of the group in Los Angeles, though; he quit dancing after his being diagnosed with schizophrenia in 1919. Depending on the time of this encounter, "the company" on tour in Los Angeles could have been either Colonel de Basil's or Sergei Denham's Ballet Russe de Monte Carlo, both of which included dancers who had appeared with Diaghilev's Ballets Russes. Perhaps Robinson conjured Nijinsky at the end of this memory not to assert that he was there, but in reference to an earlier encounter.

28. "What 'Bo' Did," *Chicago Defender,* December 16, 1922; "Hissers of Colored Act Told to Leave Theatre," *Afro-American* (Baltimore), September 15, 1922.

29. "Bojangles 'Taps' Rebuke as Broadway Fans Applaud," *Afro-American* (Baltimore), September 29, 1928; Mark Hellinger, "Bill Robinson Gets 'Em Told," *Chicago Defender,* September 29, 1928.

30. " 'Bojangles' Here Next Week," *New York Amsterdam News,* August 31, 1927; "Steak Fete Given for Bill Robinson," *New York Amsterdam News,* February 8, 1933; "Bill Robinson Is Mayor of Harlem; Hero of Broadway," *Chicago Defender,* July 6, 1935; "Haiti President Visits Harlem," *Plaindealer,* April 27, 1934; "He's Victim of Jim Crow," *Atlanta Daily World,* June 1, 1942.

31. "At Harlem Theaters," *New York Amsterdam News,* August 14, 1929.

32. The migration figures are for 1915–30, as outlined in Steven Hahn, *A Nation Under Our Feet: Black Political Struggles in the Rural South, from*

*Slavery to the Great Migration* (Cambridge: Belknap Press of Harvard University Press, 2003), 456. See also David Levering Lewis, *When Harlem Was in Vogue* (New York: Oxford University Press, 1981), and Ann Douglas, *Terrible Honesty: Mongrel Manhattan in the 1920s* (New York: Farrar, Straus and Giroux, 1995), 73–74.

33. "Dear Old Dixie," *New York Amsterdam News,* January 30, 1929.

34. Andre Sennwald, "The Screen: Shirley Temple and Lionel Barrymore in 'The Little Colonel,' the New Film at the Music Hall," *New York Times,* March 22, 1935.

35. Advertisement for *The Little Colonel, Aberdeen [South Dakota] Daily News,* March 17, 1935.

36. R.C. "New Turns and Returns: Lottie Atherton." *Billboard,* December 31, 1927, 20; E.E.S., "New Acts: Stop-Look-Listen," *Billboard,* January 5, 1929, 17; S.H., "New Acts: Five Hot Shots," *Billboard,* May 30, 1931, 42; E. J. Wood, "Coast-to-Coast Vaudeville Reviews: Pantages, San Francisco," *Billboard,* March 16, 1929, 18; Stirling Bowen, "With a Harlem Setting," *Wall Street Journal,* July 1, 1929; Muriel Babcock, "Tried and True Acts at Orpheum," *Los Angeles Times,* November 19, 1929; "Fine Array of Talent on Bill at the Palace," *New York Times,* July 8, 1929; "York and King Give Zest to Palace Bill," *New York Times,* May 26, 1930; Palmer Hoyt, "Orpheum and Alder Give Patrons New Programs," *Oregonian,* March 3, 1930; Nelson B. Bell, "Behind the Screens," *Washington Post,* December 24, 1929; Louis R. Lautier, " 'Rhapsody in Black' Is with Us Again; Better," *Chicago Defender,* November 21, 1931; "Thru Gotham and 'Round Harlem," *Afro-American* (Baltimore), May 27, 1933; "Dallas Dancer to Introduce New Stair Dance," *Dallas Morning News,* September 7, 1934; "Girl Uses Steps of Bill Robinson and Attains Real Fame," *Chicago Defender,* May 27, 1933; Charles Siegferth, "Vaudeville Reviews: Hippodrome, New York," *Billboard,* June 7, 1930, 16; "700 Dance Masters Ponder New Steps," *New York Times,* August 19, 1930; "Dancing Teachers Meet," *New York Times,* November 9, 1931; S.H., " 'Foolish Follies' (PATHE)," *Billboard,* May 3, 1930, 25.

37. Stearns and Stearns, *Jazz Dance,* 338, quoted in Anthea Kraut, " 'Stealing Steps' and Signature Moves: Embodied Theories of Dance

as Intellectual Property," *Theatre Journal* 62, no. 2 (May 2010): 181–82; Coles quoted in Mel Watkins, *On the Real Side: Laughing, Lying, and Signifying; The Underground Tradition of African-American Humor That Transformed American Culture, from Slavery to Richard Pryor* (New York: Simon and Schuster, 1994), 233; " 'Bojangles' Furious When Leslie Steals His Stair Dance," *Afro-American* (Baltimore), July 13, 1929; Ralph Matthews, "Looking at the Stars," *Afro-American* (Baltimore), November 19, 1932; "Eddie Rector Faces Prison," *Chicago Defender,* March 10, 1934; "Bill Robinson Opens War on Dance Stealers," *Afro-American,* August 3, 1935; St. Clair McKelway, "Bojangles—I," *New Yorker,* October 6, 1934, 26–28; Stone quoted in Kraut, " 'Stealing Steps,' "183.

38. "Bill Robinson Masks," *Afro-American,* January 1, 1938. Note the similarity to the closing sequence of *Shall We Dance,* in which Fred Astaire dances with a chorus of women wearing Ginger Rogers masks; the Astaire and Rogers film had just come out in 1937.

39. This scene bears a striking resemblance to one that Robinson's childhood friend Lemuel Eggleston cited as the origin of the stair dance. In Eggleston's memory, the two boys were arrested in Richmond. Robinson danced down the steps to distract the cops, and the friends made a quick getaway. See Haskins and Mitgang, *Mr. Bojangles,* 36.

40. Mencken quoted in Watkins, *On the Real Side,* 145; "Shirley Goes Harlem—Learns to Truck," *Chicago Defender,* January 11, 1936; Duggan quoted in Joel Dinerstein, *Swinging the Machine: Modernity, Technology, and African American Culture Between the World Wars* (Amherst: University of Massachusetts Press, 2003), 236.

41. Hill, *Tap Dancing America,* 1–3; Stearns and Stearns, *Jazz Dance,* 36–37; Eric Lott, *Love and Theft: Blackface Minstrelsy and the American Working Class* (Oxford: Oxford University Press, 1995), 91–95. For more on the origin stories and reception of minstrelsy, see W. T. Lhamon, Jr., *Raising Cain: Blackface Performance from Jim Crow to Hip Hop* (Cambridge: Harvard University Press, 1998); Lhamon, *Jump Jim Crow: Lost Plays, Lyrics, and Street Prose of the First Atlantic Popular Culture* (Cambridge: Harvard University Press, 2003); and David R.

Roediger, *The Wages of Whiteness: Race and the Making of the American Working Class* (New York: Verso, 1991): 115–31. For more on the interactions between the Irish Americans and African Americans in nineteenth-century America, see Noel Ignatiev, *How the Irish Became White* (New York: Routledge, 1995). Ignatiev notes that while the two groups were often lumped together in the public imagination, and in real-life geography, Irish Americans worked hard to distance themselves from African Americans, sometimes—as in the case of numerous nineteenth-century race riots—through extreme violence.

42. Elizabeth Abel, "Shadows," *Representations* 84 (November 2003): 166–99; John Mueller, *Astaire Dancing: The Musical Films* (New York: Knopf, 1985), 108–10.

43. Mueller, *Astaire Dancing,* 108–10. Astaire's letter to Marshall Stearns is quoted in Dinerstein, *Swinging the Machine,* 238. Bubbles mentions the tap lesson in Jane Goldberg, "John Bubbles: A Hoofer's Homage," *Village Voice,* December 4, 1978. I'm skeptical about Mueller's claims that Bubbles is the "real" influence on this number, which seems to me to be less about any single black dancer than about a general conception of black dance, with Robinson inserted as the face. Mueller notes that Astaire's costume resembles the one Bubbles had worn as Sportin' Life in *Porgy and Bess* the previous year, a sign of Bubbles's—and *Porgy*'s—influence on the culture writ large. But Robinson also wore a natty suit and bowlers, and Astaire's garish jacket may owe more to stereotypes of black dandies than to a specific person. Mueller also writes that Astaire had little respect for Robinson, but Astaire's autobiography and numerous public comments indicate otherwise. Still, if Mueller is correct, the fact that Astaire felt compelled to say (and perform) otherwise speaks volumes about Robinson's influence.

44. Fred Astaire, *Steps in Time* (New York: Harper, 1959), 49; Fred Astaire, "Rhythm and Humor," *Chicago Daily Tribune,* February 27, 1939; "Bill Robinson Is Mayor of Harlem"; "Bill Robinson Tells of Big Moments," *Afro-American,* June 20, 1931. Legon also said that Astaire either forgot or snubbed her years later, not speaking to her

on the set of *Easter Parade*, in which she played a maid; see Peter Levinson, *Puttin' on the Ritz: Fred Astaire and the Fine Art of Panache* (New York: St. Martin's, 2009): 161–62. Bennie Williams, "Amusements and Sports: 'Bojangles' Thinks About 'Feet' When He Is Dancing," *Negro Star*, April 5, 1935; Crisler, "Film Gossip of the Week"; "'Bojangles' Praises Astaire," *Capital Plaindealer*, September 20, 1936.

45. "'Bojangles' Praises Astaire."

46. La Argentina and Graham quoted in John Martin, "The Dance: An American Art," *New York Times*, April 3, 1932; Lincoln Kirstein, *Dance: A Short History of Classic Theatrical Dancing* (Brooklyn: Dance Horizons, 1942), 341, 344.

47. Jones quoted in John Martin, "The Dance: American Art. The Case for and Against the Development of National Forms—Current Programs," *New York Times*, November 16, 1930; Agnes de Mille, *Conversations About the Dance*, 1977 (DVD); John Martin, "The Dance: When Jazz Becomes Art," *New York Times*, July 14, 1929.

48. Lewis, *When Harlem Was in Vogue*, 3–5; Arthur E. Barbeau and Florette Henri, *The Unknown Soldiers: African-American Troops in World War I* (1974; repr., New York: Da Capo, 1996), 121 According to Lewis, Robinson was the drum major for Europe's band at the parade, but I have been unable to track down a source confirming Robinson's presence. At the very least, however, it is clear that Robinson danced for a crowd of four thousand at a 1923 tribute for black soldiers in World War I; see "French General Lauds 'Hell-Fighters,'" *Afro-American* (Baltimore), August 17, 1923. While numerous online sources assert that Robinson was a rifleman with the 369th, I have seen no primary sources to confirm that claim, nor do his biographers mention it. Given that Robinson told interviewers he was injured in the Spanish American War (a claim his biographers approach dubiously), it seems likely that he would have been vocal about serving in World War I—something he surely would have been proud of, had it happened.

49. Bronislava Nijinska, *Early Memoirs*, trans. Irina Nijinska and Jean Rawlinson (New York: Holt, Rinehart, and Winston, 1981), 25–26;

Constance Valis Hill, "Jazz Modernism," in *Moving Words: Re-Writing Dance,* ed. Gay Morris (London: Routledge, 1996), 227–44; Gerald Goode, ed., *The Book of Ballets, Classic and Modern* (New York: Crown, 1939), 228–29; Sally Banes, "Balanchine and Black Dance," in her *Writing Dancing in the Age of Postmodernism* (Hanover, N.H.: University Press of New England, 1993), 53–69 (Banes quotes Beaumont on page 58). See also Bernard Taper, *Balanchine: A Biography* (Berkeley: University of California Press, 1984), 91. According to Banes, the librettist for *The Triumph of Neptune* modeled Snowball on a lame nineteenth-century flower seller—a figure not just of blackness, but of disability. It makes for an odd echo with one of the popular origin stories for T. D. Rice's "Jim Crow," supposedly based on the movements of a lame black stablehand.

50. Brenda Dixon Gottschild, *Digging the Africanist Presence in American Performance* (Westport, Conn.: Greenwood, 1996): 49; Ruth Page quoted in *Frankie and Johnny,* 1978 (VHS) (with commentary).

51. Deborah Jowitt, *Time and the Dancing Image* (New York: William Morrow, 1988), 255. See also Gottschild, *Digging the Africanist Presence in American Performance,* 73. The specific examples I cite come from Sally Banes's outstanding essay "Balanchine and Black Dance," in *Writing Dancing in the Age of Postmodernism,* 53–69.

52. Alastair Macauley, "50 Years Ago, Modern Was Given a Name: 'Agon,'" *New York Times,* November 25, 2007; Denby quoted in Banes, "Balanchine and Black Dance," 67.

53. Gottschild, D*igging the Africanist Presence in American Performance,* 77.

54. For Dolin's piece, see Goode, *Book of Ballets,* 194. Banes discusses *The Goldwyn Follies* in "Balanchine and Black Dance," 60–61; the ideas about *Agon's* relationship to those stories are my own.

55. "Bill Robinson Selects White Girl as Dancing Partner in New Film," *Capital Plaindealer,* February 21, 1937; "Can Bill Robinson Cut the Fool as Much as He Pleases?" *Afro-American,* September 14, 1935; "Uncle Tom Role Pleased: 'Bo' More Popular Among White Persons," *Afro-American,* December 3, 1949; Porter Roberts, "Praise and Criticism," *Plaindealer,* March 5, 1937; Porter Roberts, "Praise and Criticism," *Plaindealer,* March 19, 1937.

56. Coles quoted in Watkins, *On the Real Side,* 233.

57. "Bill Robinson Selects White Girl as Dancing Partner in New Film"; Porter Roberts, "Praise and Criticism," March 5, 1937, and "Praise and Criticism," March 19, 1937.

58. For the scene, see https://www.youtube.com/watch?v=C_Qz0gnA9rY.

59. "Robinson Not in New Picture," *Plaindealer,* May 14, 1937. For the scene, see https://www.youtube.com/watch?v=lSLuFBiBBhc.

60. Mary Austin, "Buck and Wing and Bill Robinson," *Nation,* April 28, 1926, 476.

61. John Martin, "African Festival at Carnegie Hall," *New York Times,* April 5, 1945. The First Lady, Eleanor Roosevelt, was in the audience, and the program also included more faithful representatives of African performance, such as Asadata Dafora, who presented "Festival at Battalakor," "set in West Africa in the seventeenth century." Robinson's parody probably looked even more parodic next to Dafora's esteemed productions. It may have been the same patter he performed for an audience of soldiers in a 1918 "African act" at the Palace, which also, surely, had an edge: these were men who had fought for a country that denied black men the rights of full citizens. See "Soldiers See Fine New Bill at Palace," *Republic,* July 12, 1918.

62. Daphne Brooks argues that we read the close of *In Dahomey* as structurally defiant, too: the African scene stages a "flamboyant lack of closure," in which people become animals and sets at once. It's a much stranger scene than standard primitivism. See Brooks, *Bodies in Dissent,* 208–9. In another instance of careful management of the blackface mask, *In Dahomey* begins with a Will Marion Cook song, "Swing Along," that, while in dialect, is about black survival. Its lyrics encourage black Americans to "swing along" even when "white fo'ks a-watchin' and seein' what you do / White fo'ks jealous when you'se walkin' two by two." See Krasner, *Resistance, Parody, and Double Consciousness in African American Theatre, 1895–1910* (New York: St. Martin's, 1997), 69, and Sotiropoulos, *Staging Race,* 10. For more on *The Star of Zanzibar,* see Abbott and Seroff, *Ragged but Right,* 112.

63. *In Groove: N.Y. City Hall Host to Jitterbug Bands,* 1939 (RKO-Pathé News), wpafilmlibrary.com, where it is archived as "World's Fair

Parade"; "Jitterbugs Invade Peace of City Hall," *New York Times,* September 23, 1939.

**64.** The Zulu history is fairly well documented; for the official story from the club itself, see "History of the Zulu Social Aid and Pleasure Club," http://www.kreweofzulu.com/history. For a savvy analysis of their masking, see Joe Roach, *Cities of the Dead: Circum-Atlantic Performance* (New York: Columbia University Press, 1996), 18–24.

**65.** According to Edward D. C. Campbell, *Dixiana* was extraordinarily popular, playing to huge crowds across the country, and "was held over in cities such as Washington, Los Angeles, San Francisco, and Philadelphia." Thousands lined up for the premiere in Little Rock, Arkansas, and "demand was so heavy in Memphis that crowds had to be turned away." See *The Celluloid South: Hollywood and the Southern Myth* (Knoxville: University of Tennessee Press, 1981), 98–99. For Bill Robinson's performance at the Palace, see Haskins and Mitgang, *Mr. Bojangles,* 99. Haskins and Mitgang place this spontaneous event in 1918, though it took some six years for Robinson to get a stile and integrate the stair dance into his normal routines. For Robinson's dream of knighthood, see McKelway, "Bojangles—I"; "The Mikado, Himself," *New York Times,* April 9, 1939; Stearns and Stearns, *Jazz Dance,* 188.

**66.** "The Mikado, Himself"; Elisa Tamarkin, *Anglophilia: Deference, Devotion, and Antebellum America* (Chicago: University of Chicago Press, 2008).

**67.** "The Mikado, Himself"; Haskins and Mitgang, *Mr. Bojangles,* 164.

**68.** "Bill Robinson, Chasing Thief, Shot by Mistake; Negro Star Wounded in Arm in Pittsburgh," *New York Times,* October 6, 1930; "Footlights Flickers," *Plaindealer,* June 2, 1939.

**69.** Clip available at https://www.youtube.com/watch?v=NusZgfCQ634.

**3** FRED ASTAIRE AND GINGER ROGERS PICK THEMSELVES UP

**1.** Morris Dickstein's work has shaped my sense of how conflict works in Astaire and Rogers movies; Dickstein argues that screwball comedy appealed to audiences who saw their own world awash in conflict and longed for the feeling of resolution the films provided. Dickstein's writing on Astaire and Rogers themselves is also stellar.

See his *Dancing in the Dark: A Cultural History of the Great Depression* (New York: Norton, 2009).

2. Mayme Peak, "Insisted the Prince of Wales Eat Corned Beef and Cabbage," *Daily Boston Globe,* December 2, 1934; on Adele's cartwheel, see Kathleen Riley, *The Astaires: Fred and Adele* (Oxford: Oxford University Press, 2012), 152. Riley also provides the most thorough history of Fred and Adele's history available.

3. Peak, "Insisted the Prince of Wales Eat Corned Beef."

4. Ibid.

5. Fred Astaire, *Steps in Time* (New York: Harper, 1959), 11–25. Genée inspired the young Agnes de Mille as well. See Agnes de Mille, *Dance to the Piper* (Boston: Little, Brown, 1951), 10. Riley discusses some of the Astaires' early vaudeville performances in *The Astaires,* 26–36; see also Larry Billman, *Fred Astaire: A Bio-Bibliography* (Westport, Conn.: Greenwood, 1997).

6. Lincoln Barnett, "Fred Astaire: He Is the No. 1 Exponent of America's Only Native and Original Dance Form," *Life,* August 25, 1941, 72–85; Marshall Stearns and Jean Stearns, *Jazz Dance: The Story of American Vernacular Dance* (New York: Macmillan, 1968), 220–28.

7. Ginger Rogers, *Ginger: My Story* (New York: Harper Collins, 1991), 50–53; see also Jocelyn Faris, *Ginger Rogers: A Bio-Bibliography* (Westport, Conn.: Greenwood, 1994).

8. For a history of Pan and Astaire's work together, see John Franceschina, *Hermes Pan: The Man Who Danced with Fred Astaire* (Oxford: Oxford University Press, 2012), 52–101. See also "Fred Astaire's Silent Partner," in *25 Years of Celebrity Interviews from Vaudeville to Movies to TV, Reel to Real,* ed. David Fantle and Tom Johnson, 86–92 (Oregon, Wisc.: Badger, 2004).

9. "Vivacious Charms Marks 'Gay Divorcee,'" *Los Angeles Times,* October 16, 1934.

10. Astaire quoted in John Mueller, *Astaire Dancing* (New York: Knopf, 1985), 26. Joel Dinerstein discusses machine-age dancing in his excellent *Swinging the Machine: Modernity, Technology, and African American Culture Between the World Wars* (Amherst: University of Massachusetts Press, 2003).

11. Nelson B. Bell, "Noted Dance Director Forecasts Increased Output of Musicalized Film Plays," *Washington Post,* August 21, 1934.

12. On the New Dance Sensation, see Ethan Mordden, *Anything Goes: A History of American Musical Theatre* (Oxford: Oxford University Press, 2013), 65–66; "'The Continental,' a Kiss Dance—How It Is Done," *Chicago Daily Tribune,* October 28, 1934; "[No headline]," *La Prensa,* November 4, 1934; "Celebrities Attend Preview of 'Gay Divorcée' at Keith," *Daily Boston Globe,* October 12, 1934; "They Are Doing the 'Continental' Up Here," *New York Amsterdam News,* December 19, 1934; "Dancing Teachers See 'Continental' from New Film," *Hartford Courant,* October 15, 1934.

13. Arlene Croce, *The Fred Astaire and Ginger Rogers Book* (New York: Dutton, 1972), 155; Dancing Masters of America quoted in Franceschina, *Hermes Pan,* 56. For a convincing argument that Astaire was the first to create truly integrated musicals, a distinction usually given to Agnes de Mille for *Oklahoma!,* see John Mueller, "Fred Astaire and the Integrated Musical," *Cinema Journal* 24, no. 1 (1984): 28–40.

14. "Folies Bergere Full of Novelties," *New York Times,* April 28, 1911.

15. Julie Malnig, "Apaches, Tangos, and Other Indecencies: Women, Dance, and New York Nightlife of the 1910s," in *Ballroom, Boogie, Shimmy Sham, Shake: A Social and Popular Dance Reader,* ed. Julie Malnig, 72–90 (Urbana: University of Illinois Press, 2009), 79; James Traub, *The Devil's Playground: A Century of Pleasure and Profit in Times Square* (New York: Random House, 2004), 35–41.

16. Thomas Faulkner, *From the Ballroom to Hell* (1894), in *I See America Dancing,* ed. Maureen Needham (Urbana: University of Illinois Press, 2002), 116. For more excerpts from nineteenth-century tracts against dancing, see Elizabeth Aldrich, *From the Ballroom to Hell: Grace and Folly in Nineteenth-Century Dance* (Evanston, Ill.: Northwestern University Press, 1991). On the newly physical dances, see Malnig, "Apaches, Tangos, and Other Indecencies."

17. For a history of ragtime music, see Edward Berlin, *Ragtime: A Musical and Cultural History* (Berkeley: University of California Press, 1980). For the genealogy of ragtime dances, see Stearns and Stearns, *Jazz Dance.*

18. David Nasaw, *Going Out: The Rise and Fall of Public Amusements* (Cambridge: Harvard University Press, 1993); Nadine Graves, " 'Just Like Being at the Zoo': Primitivity and Ragtime Dance," in *Ballroom, Boogie, Shimmy Sham, Shake,* 55–71; Malnig, "Apaches, Tangos, and Other Indecencies"; "Have You Danced the Daring 'Dallas Dip'? Or the 'Bunny Hug' Or the 'Todel-O,' " *San Francisco Chronicle,* July 16, 1911; Herbert Asbury, *The Barbary Coast: An Informal History of the San Francisco Underworld* (New York: Knopf, 1933), 293–96.

19. Nasaw, *Going Out,* 118, 104–19.

20. Former medical school president Dr. S. Grover Burnett quoted in Eve Golden, *Vernon and Irene Castle's Ragtime Revolution* (Lexington: University of Kentucky Press, 2007), 81. "Ban Put on Downtown Dance Hall: Charges Against Moonlight, Place Sustained at Police Board Hearing," *Los Angeles Times,* September 14, 1921; "Dance Evils Laid to the 'Better Class,' " *New York Times,* June 23, 1922; "Cheek to Cheek Waddle to Go; Waltz Returns," *Chicago Daily Tribune,* August 25, 1924.

21. Golden, *Vernon and Irene Castle's Ragtime Revolution,* 81, 79. Ishmael Reed, *Mumbo Jumbo* (New York: Scribner's, 1972).

22. "Says Public Wants the Cabaret Shows: Restaurant Men Contend That They Are Merely Deferring to the Wishes of Patrons," *New York Times,* December 24, 1911; "Court Indorses the Cabaret Show," *New York Times,* February 3, 1912; James Traub, *The Devil's Playground* (New York: Random House, 2004), 37–40; Nasaw, *Going Out,* 110.

23. " 'Tango Cops' Score a Hit; Dance in Cabaret; Then Raid It," *New York Tribune,* March 16, 1915.

24. Page's choreographic notes for *Hear Ye, Hear Ye* are in the Ruth Page Collection, (S)*MGZMD 16, Jerome Robbins Dance Division, New York Public Library for the Performing Arts.

25. Mr. and Mrs. Vernon Castle, *Modern Dancing* (New York: World Syndicate, 1914), 20.

26. " 'Tango Cops' Score a Hit."

27. Mr. and Mrs. Vernon Castle, *Modern Dancing.* The corset is advertised on page 142; the "Castle House Suggestions for Correct Dancing"

appear at the end of the book; and the Elisabeth Marbury quotations are from pages 22–23.

**28.** Irene Castle, *Castles in the Air* (New York: Doubleday, 1958), 137; Golden, *Vernon and Irene Castle's Ragtime Revolution,* 86–94, 114–115, 128; Castle, *Modern Dancing.*

**29.** Stearns and Stearns, *Jazz Dance,* 96–98; Golden, *Vernon and Irene Castle's Ragtime Revolution,* 69–70; "Irene Castle in Negro Epic at World's Fair," *New Journal and Guide,* August 18, 1934; "Expect 75,000 to See Negro Pageant Tonight," *Chicago Daily Tribune,* August 25, 1934; Seymour Korman, "Mighty Pageant of Negro People Seen by Throng," *Chicago Daily Tribune,* August 26, 1934.

**30.** David Levering Lewis, *When Harlem Was in Vogue* (New York: Oxford University Press, 1979), 4; Golden, *Vernon and Irene Castle's Ragtime Revolution,* 86–94.

**31.** Castle, *Castles in the Air,* 188.

**32.** Stearns and Stearns, *Jazz Dance,* 225; Riley, *The Astaires,* 52–53, 59–66.

**33.** On the first Oompah Trot, see Riley, *The Astaires,* 65–66. Explaining the difference between jazz in America and abroad, Fred Astaire said, "You play it far too slowly—it's a dreary business—the tempo is absolutely wrong. Why, man, the 'Blues' is nigger music—full with life and vivacity. Most of the London bands play it like a slow-step dirge" (quoted ibid., 93).

**34.** Arlene Croce, *Fred Astaire and Ginger Rogers Book,* 14. The quotation comes down in a variety of forms; see, e.g., Larry Billman, *Fred Astaire: A Bio-Bibliography,* 13. Debbie Reynolds claims the memo was written by the studio official Burt Grady. Selznick wrote that Astaire's screen test was "wretched," but bargained that "in spite of his enormous ears and bad chin line . . . his charm is so tremendous" that he'd make a success: see Joseph Epstein, *Fred Astaire* (New Haven: Yale University Press, 2008), 19.

**35.** On nostalgia for the Jazz Age, see Croce, *Fred Astaire and Ginger Rogers Book,* 33.

**36.** While Astaire and Hermes Pan tended to work out the routines he appeared in, credit for the group sections of the Carioca went to the dance director Dave Gould, assisted by Pan.

37. "Carioca, Startling New Dance, Is Feature in 'Flying Down to Rio,'" *Atlanta Daily World*, January 25, 1934; "Etta Moten Thrilled Audience in Cincy," *Pittsburgh Courier*, November 24, 1934; "On the Air," *Plaindealer*, April 27, 1934.

38. "200 At Carioca Festival," *New York Amsterdam News*, April 28, 1934; "Championships At Savoy Ballroom," *New York Amsterdam News*, March 31, 1934; "Misstep Exposes Fan Dancer Shocking Ladies at Festival," *New York Amsterdam News*, May 19, 1934; "Memphis, Tenn.," *Plaindealer*, June 1, 1934; "Dance Mood as Recorded by the Magic Eye of the Camera at the Junior Pedagogue Club Costume Ball in Baltimore Last Week," *Afro-American*, January 4, 1936; "At the Apex," *Plaindealer*, April 27, 1934; "Carioca Contest at Labor Lyceum Big Feature of Friday Nite Sport Prom," *Pittsburgh Courier*, June 9, 1934; "Dancing Teachers Meet: Members Demonstrate the Latest Steps at the Hotel Astor," *New York Times*, February 5, 1934; "Series of Plays to Be Produced," *Los Angeles Times*, January 21, 1934; Read Kendall, "Around and About in Hollywood," *Los Angeles Times*, December 7, 1935; "Steppers," *New Journal and Guide*, January 26, 1935; [Display ad—no title], *Atlanta Constitution*, April 21, 1934; "Household Department," *Daily Boston Globe*, September 17, 1936; Carioca Cake," *Daily Boston Globe*, July 23, 1948; "Carioca Cake," *Daily Boston Globe*, January 12, 1954.

39. RKO did drum up some real Brazilian musicians for the occasion: see Edwin Schallert, "Film Sponsors Carioca Dance," *Los Angeles Times*, May 31, 1933.

40. For a timeline of the various companies, see the Vicente García-Márquez's chronology in *The Ballets Russes: Colonel de Basil's Ballets Russes de Monte Carlo, 1932–1952* (New York: Knopf, 1990): xiii–xiv; see also Jack Anderson, *The One and Only: The Ballet Russe De Monte Carlo* (New York: Dance Horizons, 1981).

41. Joel Dinerstein includes an outstanding analysis of this scene in *Swinging the Machine*, 237–46.

42. See Elizabeth Abel, "Shadows," *Representations* 84 (2004): 166–99.

43. Billman, *Fred Astaire: A Bio-Bibliography*, xiii, 5, 45; Adele Astaire quoted in Stearns and Stearns, *Jazz Dance*, 164 (see also pages 160–69).

44. Pan quoted in Rusty E. Frank, *Tap! The Greatest Tap Dance Stars and Their Stories, 1900–1955* (New York: Da Capo, 1990), 77; Franceschina, *Hermes Pan,* 17–22; "Hollywood Dance Director Says Negroes Best Dancers; Comes South for New Ideas," *New Journal and Guide,* July 20, 1935.

45. Franceschina, *Hermes Pan,* 17–22.

46. Ibid., 14, 21–33.

47. Quoted ibid., 18.

48. "Hollywood Dance Director Says Negroes Best Dancers; Comes South for New Ideas," *New Journal and Guide,* July 20, 1935.

49. Robert Christgau, "In Search of Jim Crow: Why Postmodern Minstrelsy Studies Matter," *The Believer,* February 2004, available at http://www.robertchristgau.com/xg/music/minstrel-bel.php. For more on Rice, see W. T. Lhamon, *Jump Jim Crow: Lost Plays, Lyrics, and Street Prose of the First Atlantic Popular Culture* (Cambridge: Harvard University Press, 2003).

50. Dan Emmett, *New York Clipper,* 19 May, 1877, quoted in Eric Lott, *Love and Theft: Blackface Minstrelsy and the American Working Class* (Oxford: Oxford University Press, 1995), 136.

51. Arlene Croce mentions Massine as a possible choreographer in *Fred Astaire and Ginger Rogers Book,* 122; the detail about Massine's fee comes from *American Dancer* 10 (1936): 36; Hoctor is quoted in Hoosick Township Historical Society, "Harriet Hoctor," http://www.hoosickhistory.com/biographies/HarrietHoctor.htm, accessed October 26, 2014.

52. Lincoln Kirstein, *Blast at Ballet: A Corrective for the American Audience* (New York: Marstin Press, 1938), 11, 48.

53. Kirstein, *Blast at Ballet,* 44.

54. Ibid., 44–45

55. Deborah Jowitt, *Time and the Dancing Image* (New York: Morrow, 1988), 255–66; "Met's Maître," *New Yorker,* October 26, 1935, 18–19.

56. Bernard Taper, *Balanchine: A Biography* (1984; repr., Berkeley: University of California Press, 1996), 388; Jennifer Dunning, "A Ballet Epic George Balanchine Never Finished," *New York Times,* July 31, 1983.

57. Barnett, "Fred Astaire"; Svetlana McLee Grody, "Interview with Hermes Pan," in *Conversations with Choreographers,* ed. Svetlana McLee Grody, Lister Grody, and Dorothy Daniels (Portsmouth, N.H.: Heinemann, 1996), 6.

58. Richard Rodgers, "Words Without Music: In Which One of the Authors Details the Origins of 'On Your Toes,'" *New York Times,* June 14, 1936.

59. Ibid. The description of Bolger and anecdote about his youth are from Nelson B. Bell, "1937 Theatrical Season Marches on Apace Without a Dark Week to Date: Three Stars Come to Town in an Amusing Satire on Art of Ballet," *Washington Post,* March 7, 1937.

60. Edwin Schallert, "R.-K.-O. and Other Studios Seeking to Buy 'On Your Toes,'" *Los Angeles Times,* May 12, 1936; Edwin Schallert, "Fred MacMurray Chosen as Gladys Swarthout's Partner," *Los Angeles Times,* May 26, 1936; Sidney Skolsky, "Hollywood: The Gossipel Truth," *Washington Post,* September 1, 1936.

61. Debra Hickenlooper Sowell, *The Christensen Brothers: An American Dance Epic* (Amsterdam: Harwood, 1998), 49–75.

62. Ibid.

63. Willam Christensen quoted ibid., 147–48.

64. Lew Christensen, *Filling Station,* 1954; see also Sowell, *Christensen Brothers,* 145–49.

65. "Dance Team Is Unique in Its Clumsy Method," *Washington Post,* August 18, 1935; "New Films Reviewed," *Daily Boston Globe,* August 4, 1934. Bill Robinson did a "tipsy tap" routine as well; see Tattlin' Twins, "Footlights," *Chicago Defender,* December 6, 1930.

66. Marcia B. Siegel, *The Shapes of Change: Images of American Dance* (Boston: Houghton Mifflin, 1979), 114–17. Siegel, who finds the piece dated, also refers to Astaire, as a contrast to Christensen. She argues that Astaire builds his dances organically around daily life, rather than forcing new idioms into a ballet form.

## 4 AGNES DE MILLE'S SQUARE DANCE

1. "The Mayor Welcomes the Rodeo to New York." *New York Times,* October 8, 1942.

2. Denham quoted in Agnes de Mille, *Dance to the Piper* (Boston: Little, Brown, 1951), 227, "Original Script of RODEO 1942 given to Copland," also titled "American Ballet," Agnes de Mille Correspondence and Writings (S) *MGZMD 100, Jerome Robbins Dance Division, New York Public Library for the Performing Arts (hereafter Agnes de Mille Correspondence); Alfred Frankenstein, "Ballet Opening: 'Rodeo' Is Refreshing and as American as Mark Twain," *San Francisco Chronicle*, November 20, 1942; John Martin, "'Rodeo' Presented by Ballet Russe." *New York Times*, October 17, 1942; bouquet of corn described in de Mille, *Dance to the Piper*, 233. Note that "ham and eggs" was not a phrase restricted to *Rodeo*. Denham and the Ballet Russe dancers used it to refer to other staples of the repertory as well; see, for example, Leslie Norton and Frederic Franklin, *Frederic Franklin: A Biography of a Ballet Star* (Jefferson, N.C.: McFarland, 2007), 124, 137.

3. Max Walk, *Ok! The Story of Oklahoma!* (New York: Grove, 1993), 114–16; Martin, "The Dance: On Broadway. Musical Shows Continue 'Long-Hair' Trend Choreographically," *New York Times*, November 14, 1943. Martin writes that a "certain wag" came up with the term "de Millennium," and agrees that the spate of ballets on Broadway is due to de Mille's influence.

4. On Balanchine's never-made *Uncle Tom's Cabin* ballet, see John Martin, "The Dance: American Ballet in Debut," *New York Times*, November 4, 1934; Bernard Taper, *Balanchine: A Biography* (Berkeley: University of California Press, 1984), 162; and Michael A. Chaney, "E. E. Cummings's *Tom: A Ballet* and Uncle Tom's Doll-Dance of Modernism," *Journal of Modern Literature* 34, no. 2 (2011): 22–44. On Martha Graham's *American Document*, see Susan Manning, "*American Document* and American Minstrelsy," in *Moving Words: Re-Writing Dance*, ed. Gay Morris (London: Routledge, 1996): 183–202. Julia Fowlkes offers an excellent account of the efforts of modern dancers to Americanize concert dance in *Modern Bodies: Dance and American Modernism from Martha Graham to Alvin Ailey* (Chapel Hill: University of North Carolina Press, 2002).

5. Michael Denning, *The Cultural Front* (New York: Verso, 1996); *Dance, Girl, Dance,* 1940 (DVD). See also Ellen Graff's history of leftist thirties dance: *Stepping Left: Dance and Politics in New York City, 1928–1942* (Durham, N.C.: Duke University Press, 1997), and Ethan Mordden's discussions of self-consciously American dance on Broadway—much of it in the wake of de Mille's work on *Oklahoma!*—in *Anything Goes: A History of American Musical Theatre* (Oxford: Oxford University Press, 2013) and *Beautiful Morning: The Broadway Musical in the 1940s* (New York: Oxford University Press, 1999). Lynn Garafola writes about the strong ties between Kirstein and Popular Front politics in "Lincoln Kirstein, Modern Dance, and the Left: The Genesis of an American Ballet," *Dance Research* 23, no. 1 (2005): 18–35.

6. De Mille, *Dance to the Piper,* 204, 226–27.

7. "American Ballet by Agnes de Mille," in Agnes de Mille, 1905– Collection, (S) *MGZMD 37, Jerome Robbins Dance Division, New York Public Library for the Performing Arts (hereafter Agnes de Mille Collection), and also in Agnes de Mille Correspondence. De Mille wasn't the only choreographer who considered using an indigenous character and then changed her mind. Martha Graham originally intended to have an Indian maiden in her now-canonical *Appalachian Spring* but opted instead to let the maiden's "spirit" imbue the work. Jacqueline Shea Murphy discusses Graham's omission, as well as other fascinating issues surrounding modern and Native American dance, in *The People Have Never Stopped Dancing: Native American Modern Dance Histories* (Minneapolis: University of Minnesota Press, 2007).

8. De Mille, *Dance to the Piper,* 39–61 (quote, 61).

9. Easton, *No Intermissions,* 60–64.

10. Denis Nahat discusses the "non-movement movements" in *Agnes de Mille and American Ballet Theatre,* panel with Barbara Barker, Victor Barbee, Gemze de Lappe, Kathleen Moore, Denis Nahat, and Georgina Parkinson, New York Public Library for the Performing Arts, New York, November 14, 1997 (VHS), Jerome Robbins

Dance Division, New York Public Library for the Performing Arts. The de Mille quotations are from her *Dance to the Piper,* 237, 23–24.

11. Diary, 1916, Agnes de Mille Collection.

12. John Martin, *America Dancing: The Background and Personalities of Modern Dance* (New York: Dodge, 1936), 266; Martin quoted in Easton, *No Intermissions,* 63.

13. "Rowdy Ann," 1919 (DVD).

14. Susan Jones, *Literature, Modernism, and Dance* (Oxford: Oxford University Press, 2013), 270–73; Barbara Barker, "Agnes de Mille, Liberated Expatriate, and the *American Suite,* 1938," *Dance Chronicle* 19, no. 2 (1996): 113–50.

15. Easton, *No Intermissions,* 145–50.

16. "Choreographic Notes: *American Suite,*" Agnes de Mille Collection.

17. Marshall Stearns and Jean Stearns, *Jazz Dance: The Story of American Vernacular Dance* (New York: Macmillan, 1968), 29–130, 133–34.

18. Gerald Goode, ed., *The Book of Ballets: Classic and Modern* (New York: Crown, 1939); Vicente García-Márquez, *The Ballets Russes: Colonel de Basil's Ballets Russes de Monte Carlo, 1932–1952* (New York: Knopf, 1990), 101–7.

19. Jones, *Literature, Modernism and Dance,* 189; John Martin, "The Dance: Surrealism and Americana," *New York Times,* November 19, 1939; George Amberg, *Ballet in America: The Emergence of an American Art* (New York: Duell, Sloan and Pearce, 1949), 40.

20. Marc Platt, " 'Ghost Town' Revisited: A Memoir of Producing an American Ballet for the Ballet Russe De Monte Carlo," *Dance Chronicle* 24, no. 2 (2001): 147–92; Martin, "The Dance: Surrealism and Americana."

21. Easton, *No Intermissions,* 186; de Mille, *Dance to the Piper,* 231.

22. De Mille, *Dance to the Piper,* 214, 218.

23. Ibid., 209–10.

24. *Agnes de Mille and American Ballet Theatre,* panel with Barbara Barker; de Mille, *Dance to the Piper,* 210–18.

25. De Mille, *Dance to the Piper,* 218–19.

26. Ibid., 227.

27. "Rodeo *****Running Set," Agnes de Mille Collection.

28. Karen Van Winkle and Genevieve Shiner Keller, "Playford's 'English Dancing Master' (1651) and Country Dancing in America," in *I See America Dancing: Selected Readings, 1685–2000*, ed. Maureen Needham (Urbana: University of Illinois Press, 2002), 61–65; Ralph G. Giordano, *Social Dancing in America, vol. 2: Lindy Hop to Hip Hop, 1901–2000* (Westport, Conn.: Greenwood, 2007), 123.

29. Easton, *No Intermissions*, 149; Barker, "Agnes de Mille, Liberated Expatriate," 138; Claudia Cassidy, "Crowd Enters into Spirit of 'Rodeo' Ballet," *Chicago Daily Tribune*, January 1, 1943.

30. John Martin, "The Dance: New Company. Eugene Loring Heads Dance Players, Inc.—Events of the Week and After," *New York Times*, December 7, 1941; John Martin, "Folk-Dance Boom," *New York Times*, February 23, 1941; John Martin, "Folk Dance Events," *New York Times*, October 12, 1941. For more on CBS's *Country Dance Society* broadcasts, see Brian G. Rose, *Television and the Performing Arts: A Handbook and Reference Guide to American Cultural Programing* (Westport, Conn.: Greenwood, 1986), 23. For a cultural history of folk and contredanse in modern America, see Daniel J. Walkowitz, *City Folk: English Country Dance and the Politics of the Folk in Modern America* (New York: New York University Press, 2010).

31. Benjamin Filene, *Romancing the Folk: Public Memory and American Roots Music* (Chapel Hill: University of North Carolina Press, 2000), 14–27; Sharp is quoted on cleanliness on page 26. See also Van Winkle and Keller, "Playford's 'English Dancing Master' (1651) and Country Dancing in America" and Cecil J. Sharp, *The Country Dance Book Part I. Containing a Description of Eighteen Traditional Dances Collected in Country Villages* (London: Novello, 1909).

32. "Folk Dance Revival Is Aim of Teachers. United Dancing Masters, Formed by Union of Two Associations, Holds Convention Here. Expect Ford as Guest. He May Visit Them Tomorrow, It Is Said—War Is Declared on Charleston," *Chicago Daily Tribune*, August 24, 1926; "Jitterbugs off USO Floors," *New York Times*, August 26, 1942; Rose C. Feld, "Ford Revives the Old Dances. He Explains That, with Time at Last for Recreation, He Has Turned to the Statelier Life and to the

Manners of Another Generation—But He Is Not a Critic of the Modern Dance," *New York Times,* August 16, 1925.

33. Robert Cantwell, *When We Were Good: The Folk Revival* (Cambridge: Harvard University Press, 1996), 31; Eva O'Neal Twork, *Henry Ford and Benjamin B. Lovett: The Dancing Billionaire and the Dancing Master* (Detroit: Harlo, 1982), 50. It's worth noting that while Ford was an anti-Semite, de Mille, who was part Jewish, was not. See Easton, *No Intermissions,* 6.

34. Feld, "Ford Revives the Old Dances."

35. Twork, *Henry Ford and Benjamin B. Lovett,* 56.

36. Ibid., 86, 93.

37. "Ford Teacher Shows Old Square Dances," *New York Times,* October 14, 1940; Beatrice Oppenheim, "Swing Your Partners!" *Los Angeles Times,* December 6, 1942.

38. For a helpful analysis of the continued popularity and cultural place of hillbillies in America, see Anthony Harkins, *Hillbilly: A Cultural History of an American Icon* (Oxford: Oxford University Press, 2003).

39. "'Back to Farm' Theme of Party at Palm Beach," *New York Times,* February 23, 1941; "7,000 Service Men to Dance Tonight," *New York Times,* December 27, 1941.

40. John Markland, "The East Goes West. A Tenderfoot Gets Tough Riding a Dude Range Not Far from City," *New York Times,* May 25, 1941.

41. Mrs. J.K.S., "Voice of the South Side," *Chicago Daily Tribune,* April 14, 1940.

42. De Mille, *Dance to the Piper,* 76.

43. Martin, *America Dancing,* 34. By the 1940s, Martin had become more open-minded, writing that the Lindy Hop, like the square dance, was a national folk dance. See "The Dance: Folk Festival. Second Thoughts on the Recent Event at Madison Square Garden—News Notes," *New York Times,* May 17, 1942.

44. Lothrop Stoddard, *The Rising Tide of Color Against White World-Supremacy* (New York: Scribner's, 1920), 275, 263–66; ; Ted Shawn, *The American Ballet* (New York: Holt, 1926), 8. See also Madison

Grant, *The Passing of the Great Race; or, the Racial Basis of European History.* (New York: Scribner's, 1916).

45. Shawn, *American Ballet,* 46–53.

46. "Choreographic Notes: *American Suite,*" Agnes de Mille Collection.

47. Juretta Jordan Heckscher, "Our National Poetry: The Afro-Chesapeake Inventions of American Dance," in *Ballroom, Boogie, Shimmy Sham, Shake: A Social and Popular Dance Reader,* ed. Julie Malnig, 19–35 (Urbana: University of Illinois Press, 2009).

48. Oppenheim, "Swing Your Partners!"

49. "Southerners Give Up Their Fancy Truckin' for the 'Big Apple,'" *Chicago Daily Tribune,* July 26, 1937.

50. Bosley Crowther, "From the 'Turkey Trot' to the 'Big Apple,'" *New York Times,* November 7, 1937; "Permanency of 'Big Apple' Prophesied by Instructor," *Los Angeles Times,* May 8, 1938.

51. "Dance Stolen from Visitors by Youngsters of City," *Los Angeles Times,* June 7, 1938; "Auto Thefts Laid to 6 Dancing Boys," *New York Times,* February 13, 1938; "'Big Apple' is Banned at Washington and Lee," *Washington Post,* October 10, 1937; "'Big Apple' Leads to Student Protests," *New York Times,* November 10, 1937; Hope Ridings Miller, "White House Rafters Quiver to 'Big Apple,'" *Washington Post,* December 31, 1937; "President's Sons Entertain at White House with Dance," *Los Angeles Times,* December 31, 1937; "Big Apple to Roll into White House," *New York Times,* December 18, 1937. "Churchill Can 'Big Apple,'" *New York Times,* January 5, 1942.

52. "Camouflaged Jive Invades Folk Fete," *New York Times,* June 7, 1942.

53. Choreographic Notes for Rodeo, Agnes de Mille Collection.

54. Ibid.

55. Emily Post, "Do Jitterbugs Need Traffic Rules?" *Los Angeles Times,* June 18, 1939; Easton, *No Intermissions,* 89–90. Easton writes that the dance number, "a sensational treatment of voodoo ritual . . . had no connection with the song lyrics, which were about smoking marijuana," but my sense, from examining de Mille's notes, is that she was deliberately associating these elements, implying that drug use and swing music "possess" the body like a ritual spirit.

56. "Smokin' Reefers Colored Chorus Routine," Agnes de Mille Correspondence.

57. "Voodoo," March 15, 1936, Agnes de Mille Correspondence.

58. Ibid.

59. Lena Horne, *Lena* (New York: Doubleday, 1965), 104, and Marshall Stearns, *The Story of Jazz* (New York: Oxford University Press, 1956), 183, both quoted in A. H. Lawrence, *Duke Ellington and His World* (New York: Routledge, 2001), 116.

60. Easton, *No Intermissions:* 254; John Martin, "De Mille Ballet Seen as Novelty," *New York Times,* January 23, 1940.

61. Choreographic Notes for *Texas Fourth,* Agnes de Mille Correspondence; *Texas Fourth,* 1973 (VHS).

62. Choreographic Notes for *Texas Fourth,* Agnes de Mille Correspondence.

63. Ibid.

64. Ethan Mordden, *Beautiful Morning: The Broadway Musical in the 1940s* (New York: Oxford University Press, 1999), 3–5, 78.

65. On the earlier dream ballets, see Tim Carter, *Oklahoma! The Making of an American Musical* (New Haven: Yale University Press, 2007), 128. The statistics are quoted from Richard Kislan, *Hoofing on Broadway: A History of Show Dancing* (London: Simon and Schuster, 1987), 75.

66. Agnes de Mille, *Reprieve: A Memoir* (New York: Doubleday, 1981), 208–9.

67. Agnes de Mille, *Conversations About the Dance.* For a history of the development of the "long tail'd blue" coat and red and white pants that shifted from the symbolic clothing of a white Yankee to the costumes of white men in blackface, see Constance Rourke, *American Humor: A Study of the National Character* (1931; repr., New York: New York Review of Books, 2004), 70–73.

68. Agnes de Mille, *Conversations About the Dance;* Eric Lott, *Love and Theft: Blackface Minstrelsy and the American Working Class* (Oxford: Oxford University Press, 1995), 20.

69. Ralph Ellison, "Change the Joke and Slip the Yoke," *The Collected Essays of Ralph Ellison* (New York: Random House, 1995), 104.

70. Agnes de Mille, *And Promenade Home* (New York: Atlantic Little Brown, 1956), reprinted in *Leaps in the Dark: Art and the World,* ed. Mindy Aloff (Gainesville: University Press of Florida, 2011), 153.

71. De Mille, *Conversations About the Dance.*

### 5 PAUL TAYLOR'S BUGLE BOY

1. Clive Barnes, "Dance: 'Genesis' and U.S.: America's Beginnings Compared Biblically," *New York Times,* March 16, 1974; Paul Taylor, *Private Domain* (New York: Knopf, 1987), 332–53.

2. Taylor, *Private Domain,* 339–55; "Noah's Minstrels," from *American Genesis,* 1973 (digital video). Descriptions of the dance in this chapter rely on this footage.

3. I am not the only person who thought of *Moby-Dick* in connection with *American Genesis;* in his choreographic notebook for the piece, Taylor wrote "Melville," and underlined it twice; below that, he listed the titles of *Moby-Dick, Bartelby the Scrivener,* and *Billy Budd* (Paul Taylor Dance Archives).

4. Herman Melville, *Moby-Dick* (1851; repr., New York: Modern Library, 2000), 174.

5. Taylor, *Private Domain,* 355, 363; Patrick Corbin in "Episode 2: Bringing It to Life," *Performance and Inside Look: "Esplanade" by Paul Taylor* (online video).

6. Sally Banes, "Paul Taylor Dance Company," *Dance Magazine,* August 1981, reprinted in her *Before, Between, and Beyond: Three Decades of Dance Writing,* ed. Andrea Harris (Madison: University of Wisconsin Press, 2007), 97; Twyla Tharp, *Push Comes to Shove* (New York: Bantam, 1992), 77. On the contrast between Taylor and Cunningham, see Clive Barnes, "The Cold War in Modern-Dance," *New York Times,* July 28, 1968.

7. Clinton quoted in *Paul Taylor: Dancemaker,* 1998 (DVD).

8. Taylor quoted in Edward Lewine, "The Dance Maker's Dwelling," *New York Times,* October 15, 2009. Taylor also has—or had, as of 2010—a postcard of Mount Rushmore, with Homer Simpson's face glued next to the presidents', hanging above his desk. See Robert

Greskovic, "Dance's 'Naughty Boy' at 80," *Wall Street Journal,* August 5, 2010.

9. "Paul Taylor: Dancemaker—Conversations from Penn State." *Conversations at Penn State,* WPSU: November 30, 2011, available at http://www.youtube.com/watch?v=Gs3B-Bzo_HM.

10. Ibid.

11. Nadine Brozan, "Chronicle: From Trash to Ballet." *New York Times,* April 29, 1991; *Paul Taylor: Dancemaker;* Lewine, "Dance Maker's Dwelling"; Paul Taylor, Choreographic Notebooks, Paul Taylor Dance Archives.

12. "Paul Taylor Interview," [199?, n.d.], streaming video file, recorded by the New Jersey Network, Jerome Robbins Dance Division, New York Public Library for the Performing Arts.

13. See, for example, Lewine, "Dance Maker's Dwelling," where Taylor says: "I have always wanted to be a professional spy. I love watching people when they don't know I am looking"; and "Fantasy About Joining the CIA," in Paul Taylor, *Facts and Fancies: Essays Written Mostly for Fun* (New York: Delphinium, 2013), 109–13.

14. John Martin, "Dance: An Artist. Some Belated Notes on Paul Taylor and His Most Recent Concert," *New York Times,* February 26, 1961.

15. The comparison between swimming and performing is Taylor's, not mine: see *Private Domain,* 25.

16. Taylor, *Private Domain,* 26–27. Carolyn Brown, who danced with Taylor at Juilliard and later in Merce Cunningham's company, recalls that Taylor—then nicknamed "Big Pete"—"was brimming with self-confidence in those years and had an absolute conviction that he would succeed." See Brown, *Chance and Circumstance: Twenty Years with Cage and Cunningham* (New York: Random House, 2009), 60.

17. Brown, *Chance and Circumstance,* 61.

18. Referring to Graham as a "high priestess" was fairly common: Carolyn Brown uses the phrase in *Chance and Circumstance,* 61. On St. Denis, see Deborah Jowitt, *Time and the Dancing Image* (New York: Morrow, 1988), 124–47; Jane Sherman, *Denishawn: The Enduring Influence* (Boston: Twayne, 1983). Doris Humphrey, from " 'Doris

Humphrey Speaks to Students': Speech to Students of the Dance Department, Juilliard School of Music, November 7, 1956," in *New Dance: Writings on Modern Dance*, ed. Charles Humphrey Woodford (Hightstown, N.J.: Princeton Book Company, 2008), 65.

19. Jowitt, *Time and the Dancing Image*, 123; see also William Deresiewicz, "The Salome Factor: How the Sexualization of Concert Dance Helped End a Golden Age," *American Scholar* 74, no. 2 (2005): 112–16.

20. Sherman, *Denishawn*. Shawn's use of black dance forms is particularly notable given his own disavowal of jazz music and dance and his assertion, in *The American Ballet*, that "when one sees a white man" perform black dance, "it is disgusting, because the negro mental and emotional conditions cannot be translated into the white man." At the same time, Shawn admits that "we"—which is to say, white Americans—"can study negro dancing with great profit as a source of production, and certain phases of it for the art dance of America" (*The American Ballet* [New York: Holt, 1926], 22).

21. Shawn, *American Ballet*, 15; Martha Graham, "Seeking an American Art of the Dance," in *Revolt in the Arts: A Survey of the Creation, Distribution, and Appreciation of Art in America*, ed. Oliver M. Sayler, 249–55 (New York: Brentano's, 1930), 253–55.

22. Graham, "Seeking an American Art of the Dance," 252.

23. For a thorough account of the transition in Graham's career, see Mark Franko, *Martha Graham in Love and War: The Life in the Work* (New York: Oxford University Press, 2012). Paul Taylor, discussion with the author, January 12, 2014, and quoted in Anna Kisselgoff, "Dance: Paul Taylor, Ballet's Beloved Enemy," *New York Times*, March 4, 2001.

24. "How to Tell Ballet from Modern," in Taylor, *Facts and Fancies*, 101; Taylor quoted in Kisselgoff, "Dance: Paul Taylor."

25. Taylor, *Private Domain*, 88–95. For more on *Episodes*, see Angela Kane, " 'Episodes' (1959): Entente Cordiale?" *Dance Research* 25, no. 1 (2007): 54–72.

26. Agnes de Mille relates the story from Glen Tetley, in *Martha: The Life and Work of Martha Graham* (New York: Random House, 1991):

337–38; Marcia B. Siegel, *The Shapes of Change: Images of American Dance* (Boston: Houghton Mifflin, 1979), 20–21.

27. "Paul Taylor Interview" [199?, n.d.], streaming video.

28. David Vaughan, *Merce Cunningham: Fifty Years* (New York: Aperture, 1997): 65–68; for the years Taylor was there, see pages 72–78.

29. Brown, *Chance and Circumstance*, 62–76; Vaughan, *Merce Cunningham*, 72–78; Taylor, *Private Domain*, 48–41; Jeff Slayton, *The Prickly Rose: A Biography of Viola Farber* (Bloomington, Ind.: Author House, 2006), 33–37. Carolyn Brown points out that *Dime a Dance* wasn't wholly chance-derived. "Be assured," she writes, "that whenever Merce's solo *The Eclectic* came up, he always performed it!" She suggests that Taylor's reasons for quitting the company had as much to do with his ambition as his feelings about Cunningham's choreography: "He was quick to recognize that there wasn't a place in Merce's company in those years for another featured male dancer" (102–13).

30. Carolyn Brown and Viola Farber, who danced in Cunningham's company with Taylor, both write that Taylor began work on *Jack and the Beanstalk* during a Cunningham composition class at Black Mountain in 1953; *Jack's* "Mother-Son duet" was performed on a bill there that summer (Brown, *Chance and Circumstance*, 74, 103; Slayton, *Prickly Rose*, 36–37). When I asked Taylor about this, he denied it, which may point to a desire to distance himself from Cunningham or may be a sign that it's hard to remember something more than fifty years and a hundred compositions ago (Taylor, interview with the author, January 12, 2014); See also Paul Taylor, Choreographic Notebooks.

31. Slayton, *Prickly Rose*, 36–37 (Farber remembers the sash reading "Mother," but Taylor's choreographic notebooks have it as "Mom"); Taylor, *Private Domain*, 54–55; Taylor, Choreographic Notebooks.

32. Wilbur quoted in Marjorie Perloff, "A Step away from Them: Poetry 1956," Lecture Given at the University of Copenhagen, September 1997. Available at http://marjorieperloff.com/stein-duchamp-picasso /poetry-1956.

33. Charles Kaiser, *The Gay Metropolis: The Landmark History of Gay Life in America* (New York: Grove, 2007), 80–84; James Ivory and Robert

Emmet Long, *James Ivory in Conversation: How Merchant Ivory Makes Its Movies* (Berkeley: University of California Press, 2005), 37.

**34.** Rebekah J. Kowal, *How to Do Things with Dance: Performing Change in Postwar America* (Middletown, Conn.: Wesleyan University Press, 2010); Taylor, *Private Domain*, 36.

**35.** Frank O'Hara, "Dances Before the Wall," in *The Collected Poems of Frank O'Hara* (Berkeley: University of California Press, 1995), 344–45; Taylor, interview with the author.

**36.** Taylor, *Private Domain*, 75; Taylor, interview with the author; *Music from the South: Field Recordings Taken in Alabama, Louisiana, and Mississippi Under a Grant from the John Simon Guggenheim Memorial Foundation by Frederic Ramsey, Jr., with Photographs, Notes, and Personnels*, 1955 (Folkways Records FA 26501).

**37.** Robert Cantwell, *When We Were Good: The Folk Revival* (Cambridge: Harvard University Press, 1996), 34–36; Greil Marcus, *Invisible Republic: Bob Dylan's Basement Tapes* (New York: Holt, 1997), 89.

**38.** Marcus, *Invisible Republic*, 96; Taylor, *Private Domain*, 75.

**39.** Taylor, *Private Domain*, 75, 99; Angela Kane, "A Catalogue of Works Choreographed by Paul Taylor," *Dance Research* 14, no. 2 (1996): 7–75, esp. 11–12; *3 Epitaphs*, 2013 (digital video). My description of the dance relies on this footage.

**40.** Paul Taylor, interview with the author; *Paul Taylor: Dancemaker*.

**41.** Humphrey, "Doris Humphrey Speaks to Students," 61; Graham quoted by Taylor in *Paul Taylor: Dancemaker*. Graham describes *Lamentation* in her autobiography, *Blood Memory*: "I wear a long tube of material to indicate the tragedy that obsesses the body, the ability to stretch inside your own skin, to witness and test the perimeters and boundaries of grief" (117).

**42.** Sally Banes, for example, writes, "Part of [*3 Epitaphs'*] delight must also lie in its utter recalcitrance to everything dance has traditionally meant" ("Paul Taylor Dance Company," 100). For more on the way *3 Epitaphs* does away with issues of personal identity, see Kowol, *How to Do Things with Dance*, 161–78.

**43.** Kane, "Catalogue of Works Choreographed by Paul Taylor," 11–12; notes on *3 Epitaphs* can be found at the Paul Taylor's

American Modern Dance website, PTAMD.org (accessed March 3, 2015).

**44.** Frederic Ramsey, Jr., liner notes to *Music from the South.*

**45.** Samuel Charters, *A Language of Song: Journeys in the Musical World of the African Diaspora* (Durham, N.C.: Duke University Press, 2009), 99–100.

**46.** Frederic Ramsey, Jr., *Been Here and Gone* (Athens: University of Georgia Press, 1960), 66–72. Charters, *Language of Song,* 99–100.

**47.** *Epic,* October 20, 1957 (digital video). Taylor describes the piece in "Two Bozos Seen Through a Glass: An Epiphany," in Taylor, *Facts and Fancies,* 66–77, and in *Private Domain,* 76–81.

**48.** Taylor, "Two Bozos Seen Through a Glass," 72, 74.

**49.** "Paul Taylor Interview," [199?, n.d.].

**50.** The comparison to Cage's piece is not my own: Deborah Jowitt makes it in *Time and the Dancing Image,* 312. Taylor appears in "Three Modern Classics," in *Great Performances: Dance in America,* 1982 (VHS).

**51.** Taylor, *Private Domain,* 76–81; Taylor, "Two Bozos Seen Through a Glass," 66–77.

**52.** Jowitt, *Time and the Dancing Image,* 311; Sally Banes, *Democracy's Body: Judson Dance Theater, 1962–1964* (Ann Arbor, Mich.: UMI Research Press, 1983); Nancy Reynolds and Malcolm McCormick, *No Fixed Points: Dance in the Twentieth Century* (New Haven: Yale University Press, 2003), 398–423.

**53.** Herko quoted in Banes, *Democracy's Body,* 55–57.

**54.** Angela Kane suggests that Taylor's work with Balanchine on *Episodes* influenced *Aureole;* see "'Episodes' (1959)," 66.

**55.** *Esplanade,* July 15, 1998 (digital video). I have also relied on the 1978 version of *Esplanade* filmed for *Great Performances: Dance in America.*

**56.** Edwin Denby, "Dancers, Buildings, and People in the Streets," in *Dance Writings and Poetry,* 252–60 (New Haven: Yale University Press, 1998), 256–57.

57. James Steichen, "The Stories of *Serenade:* Nonprofit History and George Balanchine's 'First Ballet in America.'" Paper presented at the Princeton University Center for the Arts and Cultural Policy Studies Working Paper Series, 2012.

58. Paul Taylor, Choreographic Notebooks.

59. Ibid.

60. Wagoner quoted in Wendy Perron, "Taylor Made," *Dance Magazine,* March 2005, 32–35; Taylor quoted in Sarah Kaufman, "A Singular Vision: Nearing 80, Paul Taylor Is as Moving a Dance Figure as Ever," *Washington Post,* July 18, 2010; Paul Taylor, *Esplanade, Dance in America.*

61. Paul Taylor, "Down with Choreography," *Dance Magazine,* reprinted in *The Modern Dance: Seven Statements of Belief,* ed. Selma Jeanne Cohen, 91–102 (Middletown, Conn.: Wesleyan University Press, 1966), 92, 97, 92, 97. Deborah Jowitt has pointed out that watching "the same performers in every work" of Taylor's makes it "easy to believe we're watching the same society of people," in all the shades society can take on ("Old Words, New Tales," *Village Voice,* March 17, 1998).

62. Paul Taylor, *From Sea to Shining Sea,* 1965 (digital video) and 2006 (digital video). The rest of my discussion relies on both these videos.

63. Taylor, *Private Domain,* 223–36; Tharp, *Push Comes to Shove,* 77.

64. Larry Rivers quoted in "Seminal Works: Washington Crossing the Delaware, 1953," Larry Rivers Foundation, http://www .larryriversfoundation.org/seminal_works_washington.html (accessed October 28, 2014).

65. Clive Barnes, "Modern Dance—Fifth Generation," *New York Times,* January 7, 1968.

66. Taylor, *Private Domain,* 222–36; Taylor, Choreographic Notes.

67. Professor Julia Foulkes of the New School talked with me about *From Sea to Shining Sea*—and about Taylor's work in general—on January 30, 2014; I owe much of my thinking about the piece to her insights about Taylor's critique of both theatrical and political performance.

68. Pauline Kael, "Marlon Brando: An American Hero," *Atlantic,* March 1966, available at http://www.theatlantic.com/past/unbound /aandc/movies/movies4.htm.

69. Paul Taylor, Choreographic Notebooks.

70. Ibid.

71. Paul Taylor, *Big Bertha,* 1981, in "Three Modern Classics" (VHS). My description of the dance relies on this footage.

72. Taylor quoted in Gia Kourlas, "Looking Back with Darkness and Insects," *New York Times,* March 9, 2012; early scenario from Taylor, Choreographic Notebooks. Nancy Dalva has suggested that Bertha could represent Martha Graham, in whose pieces Taylor found himself "up to his ears in onstage incest"; see "Letter from Manhattan," The Performance Club, April 12, 2012, at http://theperformanceclub.org /2012/04/letter-from-manhattan/. "Mr. B" might also refer to Balanchine, which would cast his famous assertion that "Ballet is woman" in a rather tawdry light.

73. Anna Kisselgoff, "A Taylor Dancer Choreographs Her Farewell," *New York Times,* April 15, 1989.

74. Taylor, Choreographic Notebooks.

75. Maxene Andrews and Bill Gilbert, *Over Here, Over There: The Andrews Sisters and the USO Stars in World War II* (New York: Zebra Books, Kensington Publishing, 1993), 35.

76. Ibid., 205, 169.

77. *Company B,* March 5, 2013 (digital video).

78. Maxine Leeds Craig, *Sorry I Don't Dance: Why Men Refuse to Move* (New York: Oxford University Press, 2014), 68–70. For more on USO volunteers and sexual politics, see Megan Winchell, *Good Girls, Good Food, Good Fun: The Story of USO Hostesses During World War II* (Chapel Hill: University of North Carolina Press, 2008).

79. Allan Bérubé, *Coming Out Under Fire: The History of Gay Men and Women in World War II* (1990; repr., Chapel Hill: University of North Carolina Press, 2010), 3.

80. I should note that not all the audience members share my feelings; both times I've seen *Company B* performed live—once by the San Francisco Ballet, and once by the Paul Taylor Dance Company—

audience members have clapped right after the Bugle Boy is shot. At the Taylor Company performance, the women sitting behind me also sang or hummed along with nearly every song.

81. Joel Dinerstein, *Swinging the Machine: Modernity, Technology, and African American Culture Between the World Wars* (Amherst: University of Massachusetts Press, 2003), 250–68. Craig offers a wonderful account of the way the jitterbug played into wartime masculinity in her chapter "Dancing in Uniform" in *Sorry I Don't Dance*, 54–72.

82. "Jitterbugging Swings Itself Out," *Washington Post*, November 16, 1940; "Court Rules Jitterbug Is All Word Implies, Jitter for 'Nervous' and Bug for 'Crazy,'" *New York Times*, May 3, 1944.

83. Anna Kisselgoff, "Paul Taylor on Love, War, and Their Subtext," *New York Times*, October 24, 1991.

84. Pauline Kael, "The Current Cinema," *New Yorker*, November 25, 1972, 186.

85. Stephen J. Whitfield, *In Search of American Jewish Culture* (Hanover, N.H.: Brandeis University Press, published by University Press of New England, 1999), 1–3.

86. Agnes de Mille, *Dance to the Piper* (Boston: Little, Brown, 1951), 227; Taylor, Choreographic Notes.

**6** MICHAEL JACKSON'S MOONWALK

1. "Moon 'Rock'? Dance Craze May Start," *Los Angeles Times*, reprinted in *Seattle Daily Times*, July 22, 1969.

2. Ibid.; David Seeley, "Moonwalk Madness Hits Dallas Dancers," *Dallas Morning News*, June 30, 1984; "Man Walks on Another World: Historic Words and Photographs by Neil A. Armstrong, Edwin E. Aldrin, Jr., and Michael Collins," *National Geographic*, December 1969, available at http://ngm.nationalgeographic.com/print/1969/12 /moon-landing/astronauts-text.

3. "Moon 'Rock'? Dance Craze May Start"; Paul Hofmann, "To Waltz and Schmaltz Vienna Is Adding Salz," *New York Times*, January 31, 1970; advertisement, *Kingston Gleaner*, August 16, 1969; "Jamaican Atmosphere at Montreal Exhibition," *Kingston Gleaner*, August 25,

1970; Andrew Epstein, "L.A.'s New-Wave Discos: Dancing to a New Beat," *Los Angeles Times,* September 21, 1980. I'm also grateful to the music scholar Michael Veal, who gave me some background about Jamaican dance and music by e-mail (March 21, 2014).

4. Eliot Rose spurred much of my thinking on Jackson's relationship to the space race in the Reagan era. Teasel-Muir Harmony, a historian of space exploration, provided background on the changing perceptions of the space program by e-mail on March 25, 2014.

5. Details from J. Randy Taraborrelli, *Michael Jackson: The Magic, the Madness, the Whole Story* (New York: Grand Central Publishing, 2010), 243–44. Jackson's shyness has been well documented; see, for example, Gerri Hershey, "Michael Jackson: Life as a Man in the Magical Kingdom," *Rolling Stone,* February 17, 1983, available at http://www.rollingstone.com/music/news/michael-jackson-life-as-a -man-in-the-magical-kingdom-19830217.

6. Jackson's feats of postmodern marketing have been well chronicled; for a good sampling of perspectives, see Seth Silberman, "Presenting Michael Jackson^tm," *Social Semiotics* 17 (2007): 417–40; Anthony DeCurtis, "80's," *Rolling Stone,* November 15, 1990; and Dave Marsh, *Trapped: Michael Jackson and the Crossover Dream* (New York: Bantam, 1985). Marsh's book—unfortunately out of print—merits special mention. It's a wonderful read, and shaped much of how I think about Michael Jackson and fame.

7. "Cassette Offers Breakdancing Lessons," *Greensboro News and Record,* July 29, 1984; Laura Kavesh, "Frenzied Fans Prove the Appeal of a Thriller Knows No Bounds," *Chicago Tribune,* reprinted in *Elyria Chronicle Telegram,* March 19,1984; "Moonwalk Gig Draws a Horde," *Medicine Hat News,* April 17, 1984; Matt Neufeld, "Larry T. Ellis Gives the Illusion of Michael Jackson," *Frederick News Post,* May 11, 1984.

8. Associated Press, "Mimicking Michael: You Can't Beat it," *Annapolis Capital,* March 26, 1984; "3,000 Attend Inauguration of Hindu Temple in Los Angeles." *India-West,* May 18, 1984; Elizabeth Kastor, "Weaned on 'Billie Jean,'" *Washington Post,* May 26, 1984; David Seeley, "Moonwalk Madness Hits Dallas Dancers," *Dallas Morning News,* June 30, 1984.

9. Laura Kavesh, "Frenzied Fans Prove the Appeal of a Thriller Knows No Bounds," *Chicago Tribune*, reprinted in *Elyria Chronicle Telegram*, March 19, 1984. Dave Marsh writes about the gospel overtones of "crossing over" in *Trapped*, 203.

10. Taraborrelli, *Michael Jackson*, 14–23; Marsh, *Trapped*, 14–26. Footage from the Motown audition is available at ever-changing YouTube addresses.

11. Michael Jackson, *Moonwalk* (New York: Random House, 1988), 36–50; Nelson George, *Where Did Our Love Go? The Rise and Fall of the Motown Sound* (Urbana: University of Illinois Press, 1985), 184; Marsh, *Trapped*, 26–38. For a history of the chitlin' circuit— preceding the Jacksons' involvement with it, but in many ways setting the stage for them—see Preston Lauterbach, *The Chitlin' Circuit and the Road to Rock and Roll* (New York: Norton, 2011).

12. R. J. Smith, *The One: The Life and Music of James Brown* (New York: Gotham, 2012), 357–58.

13. Lauterbach, *Chitlin' Circuit*, 247; Jackson, *Moonwalk*, 37.

14. Smith, *The One*, 156.

15. Ibid., 146–50.

16. See George, *Where Did Our Love Go?*; Gerald Early, *One Nation Under a Groove: Motown and American Culture* (Ann Arbor: University of Michigan Press, 1995).

17. Margalit Fox, "Maxine Powell, Motown's Maven of Style, Dies at 98," *New York Times*, October 16, 2013; George, *Where Did Our Love Go?* 88, 185; Jackson, *Moonwalk*, 72–75, 87–88.

18. George, *Where Did Our Love Go?* 185.

19. Marshall Stearns and Jean Stearns, *Jazz Dance: The Story of American Vernacular Dance* (New York: Macmillan, 1968), 305–8; Cholly Atkins and Jacqui Malone, *Class Act: The Jazz Life of Choreographer Cholly Atkins* (New York: Columbia University Press, 2001), 117–22. Jacqui Malone also devotes a chapter to Atkins in her masterful *Steppin' on the Blues: The Visible Rhythms of African American Dance* (Urbana: University of Illinois Press, 1996).

20. Malone, *Steppin' on the Blues*, 110–17.

21. See Malone, *Steppin' on the Blues,* 114–117; Stearns and Stearns, *Jazz Dance,* 168; Ethan Mordden, *Beautiful Morning: The Broadway Musical in the 1940s* (New York: Oxford University Press, 1999).

22. Atkins and Malone, *Class Act,* 103.

23. Ibid., 191–92; The Temptations perform "Get Ready" on YouTube at https://www.youtube.com/watch?v=fqZ-hDJHbQ0.

24. Atkins and Malone, *Class Act,* 151–78; Atkins describes the complaint from the Temptations on page 171. See also George, *Where Did Our Love Go?* 90–92. The Jackson 5 performance is at http://www.youtube.com/watch?v=s3Q80mk7bxE.

25. Jackson, *Moonwalk,* 85; see also George, *Where Did Our Love Go?*

26. Malone discusses the way Atkins's choreography brought old steps to a new generation in *Steppin' on the Blues,* 125.

27. "'Ziggy' Johnson Dies of Heart Attack in Detroit," *Jet,* February 22, 1968, 51; Tony Douglas, *Jackie Wilson: Lonely Teardrops* (New York: Routledge, 2005), 55; Jackson, *Moonwalk,* 48–49. Johnson's *Defender* column, which ran from the early fifties to the mid-sixties, was called "Zig and Zag with Ziggy Johnson" and later, "Zagging with Ziggy." Cholly Atkins also worked with Ziggy Johnson: Johnson produced summer revue shows in Idlewild, Michigan, for which Atkins did vocal choreography (Atkins and Malone, *Class Act,* 147).

28. I saw footage of Wilson on *American Bandstand* at https://www.youtube.com/watch?v=OeLT—_sBXw (October 25, 2014), but it is no longer available.

29. Douglas, *Jackie Wilson,* 55; footage of Wilson on *Shindig* is at http://www.youtube.com/watch?v=1WXZmjUtlJw.

30. *Moonwalker,* 1988 (DVD); Douglas, *Jackie Wilson,* 103–4. Wilson was known as "Mr. Excitement," as well as the "Black Elvis," a nickname it's hard not to bristle at. But in the murky amalgam of styles that makes up American culture, Elvis—who could be called the "White Arthur Crudup" or "White Little Richard," or "White a whole host of other performers"—was a fan of Jackie Wilson's. When Wilson performed in Vegas, said Four Tops singer Levi

Stubbs, Elvis was in the audience "every night" (quoted in Douglas, *Jackie Wilson,* 49).

31.  Jackson, *Moonwalk,* 208.

32.  Brenda Dixon Gottschild, *Digging the Africanist Presence in American Performance* (Westport, Conn.: Greenwood, 1996), 100; Marshall quoted in Stearns and Stearns, *Jazz Dance,* 50–51.

33.  Mel Watkins, *On the Real Side: Laughing, Lying, and Signifying; The Underground Tradition of African-American Humor That Transformed American Culture, from Slavery to Richard Pryor* (New York: Simon and Schuster, 1994), 113; Stearns and Stearns, *Jazz Dance,* 50–51.

34.  *Feet—Fun—and Fancy,* 1927, http://www.britishpathe.com/video/feet -fun-and-fancy. Henry T. Sampson quotes a 1922 review of Johnny Hudgins that calls him the "black Charlie Chaplin" in *Blacks in Blackface: A Source Book on Early Black Musical Shows* (Metuchen, N.J.: Scarecrow, 1980), 286.

35.  Atkins describes Bailey's closings in Atkins and Malone, *Class Act,* 198; he can be seen in various clips on YouTube, including to "Taking a Chance on Love" in *Cabin in the Sky.* Richard Street, of the Temptations, notes that Atkins "was showing [them] how to moonwalk before Michael Jackson was doing it" in Malone, *Steppin' the Blues,* 126.

36.  See Stephen McMillan, "Michael Jackson's First Moonwalk Thirty Years Later," May 24, 2013, at soultrain.com, http://soultrain.com /2013/05/24/michael-jacksons-first-moonwalk-thirty-years-later/; Cooley Jaxson posted a video of the *Soul Train* performance on YouTube, https://www.youtube.com/watch?v=rb4vUxhow_s. See also Taraborrelli, *Michael Jackson,* 243–45.

37.  Cooley Jaxson *Soul Train* performance on YouTube.

38.  Thomas Guzman-Sanchez, *Underground Dance Masters: Final History of a Forgotten Era* (Santa Barbara, Calif.: Praeger, 2012), 6–7; Amiri Baraka, *Digging: The Afro-American Soul of American Classical Music* (Berkeley: University of California Press, 2009), 243; Mary J. Phillips, "Yes Sir, Boss (a Letter in Time Magazine)," reprinted in *Lethbridge Herald,* October 30, 1939.

39. For the Chicago roots of boogaloo, see Robert Pruter, *Chicago Soul* (Urbana: University of Illinois Press, 1992), 204–5. Oliver Wang also offers some early history in "Boogaloo Nights," *Nation,* January 28, 2008, 34–36. For a discussion of Latin Boogaloo, see Juan Flores, *From Bomba to Hip-Hop: Puerto Rican Culture and Latino Identity* (New York: Columbia University Press, 2000), 78–112. For more on boogaloo's West Coast transformations, see Guzman-Sanchez, *Underground Dance Masters,* 5–22.

40. For the interview with Herc, Bam, and Flash, see Nelson George, "Hip-Hop's Founding Fathers Speak the Truth," in *That's the Joint: The Hip-Hop Studies Reader,* ed. Murray Forman and Mark Anthony Neal, 45–55 (New York: Routledge, 2004), 47. For more on the history of hip-hop music, see Jeff Chang's outstanding *Can't Stop Won't Stop: A History of the Hip-Hop Generation* (New York: Picador, 2005). Robert Farris Thompson's discussion of funk styles is also quite useful: "Hip Hop 101," in *Droppin' Science: Critical Essays on Rap Music and Hip Hop Culture,* ed. William Eric Perkins, 211–19 (Philadelphia: Temple University Press, 1996); Guzman-Sanchez, *Underground Dance Masters,* also covers some of these developments.

41. Thompson, "Hip Hop 101," 217. Katrina Hazzard-Donald brings up Snakehips Tucker's freezes in "Dance in Hip Hop Culture," in *Droppin' Science,* 220–33.

42. Julie Malnig, "Let's Go to the Hop: Community Values in Televised Teen Dance Programs of the Fifties and Early Sixties," paper presented at the CORD Conference, March 6, 2005. My thanks to Malnig, who e-mailed me a copy of this talk, which is the version I rely on here. Matthew Delmont's history of *American Bandstand* and racial politics is also informative: *The Nicest Kids in Town: "American Bandstand," Rock 'n' Roll, and the Struggle for Civil Rights in 1950s Philadelphia* (Berkeley: University of California Press, 2012).

43. Delmont, *Nicest Kids in Town,* 5. For the history of *Soul Train,* see Christopher Lehman, *A Critical History of "Soul Train" on Television* (Jefferson, N.C.: McFarland, 2008); Nelson George, *The Hippest Trip in America: "Soul Train" and the Evolution of Culture and Style* (New York: Harper Collins, 2014); and Erica Blount Danois, *Love, Peace,*

and Soul: Behind the Scenes of America's Favorite Dance Show "Soul Train"; Classic Moments (Milwaukee: Backbeat, 2013). The Afro Sheen ad is included in the VH1 documentary (for which George's book is a tie-in) Soul Train: The Hippest Trip in America, 2010, dir. Amy Goldberg and J. Kevin Swain, written by Sean Gottlieb.

44. Nik Cohn, Awopbopaloobop Alopbamboom: The Golden Age of Rock (Boston: Da Capo, 1969), 89.

45. The basics of Campbell's biography are covered in the Soul Train histories by Lehman (Critical History of "Soul Train"), George (Hippest Trip in America), and Danois (Love, Peace, and Soul). For more details, see Jeff Spurrier, "So L.A., A Hoofer's Place in History: Before Popping, Posing, Breaking, Hip-Hop and Even Disco, There Was Locking. And Don Campbell Invented It." Los Angeles Times, July 23, 1995; and Campbell's interview with Stephen McMillan, "Diary of an Ex-Soul Train Dancer: The Creator of Locking, Don Campbell," January 31, 2013, at Soul Train, http://soultrain.com/2013/01/31 /diary-of-an-ex-soul-train-dancer-the-creator-of-locking-don -campbell/.

46. Guzman-Sanchez, Underground Dance Masters, 38; Damita Jo Free-man's interview at the Soul Train website is also a good read: Stephen McMillan, "Diary of an Ex-Soul Train Dancer Presents: The One and Only Damita Jo Freeman," http://soultrain.com/2012/08 /20/diary-of-an-ex-soul-train-dancer-presents-the-one-and-only -damita-jo-freeman-part-1/.

47. Guzman-Sanchez provides a fuller history of the group and its prehistory in Underground Dance Masters, 109–24.

48. Ibid., 18–20. Mimes played a role, too: Charles "Robot" Washington, who did the Mechanical Man on Soul Train in 1971, pointed to the mime Robert Shields's performances at the Los Angeles Wax Museum as inspiration. Shields would later partner Lorene Yarnell and appear on a number of variety shows; their work inspired New York b-boys, too. See Sally Banes, "Breaking," in That's the Joint! 13–20; and Jimmy Magahern, "Robot Wars: A Thriving Arizona Break-Dancing Culture Rediscovers the State's Grandmasters of Boogaloo," Phoenix New Times, January 9, 2003.

49. Mark Dery, "Black to the Future: Interviews with Samuel R. Delany, Greg Tate, and Tricia Rose," in *Flame Wars: The Discourse of Cyberculture*, ed. Mark Dery, 179–222 (Durham, N.C.: Duke University Press, 1995): 212–214. The entire piece is worth reading; in it Dery coins the term "Afrofuturism" to describe artwork that "addresses African-American concerns in the context of twentieth-century technoculture—and, more generally, African-American signification that appropriates images of technoculture and a prosthetically enhanced future" (180).

50. For the number of performances of "Dancing Machine," see Jake Austen, *TV-a-Go-Go: Rock on TV from "American Bandstand" to "American Idol"* (Chicago: Chicago Review Press, 2005), 261; see also Jackson, *Moonwalk,* 111.

51. For the cartoon of the Tiller Girls, see Felicia M. McCarren, *Dancing Machines: Choreographies in the Age of Mechanical Reproduction* (Stanford: Stanford University Press, 2003), 144. Motown boss Berry Gordy took cues from Detroit's auto industry, running his label like a factory; taking up this observation, the scholar Judith Hamera argues that Jackson's robot symbolizes a "longing" for the "vanishing industrial past" in the wake of Detroit's decline. While I disagree with her, it's a helpfully provocative claim. See Judith Hamera, "The Labors of Michael Jackson: Virtuosity, Deindustrialization, and Dancing Work," *PMLA* 127, no. 4 (2012): 751–65.

52. For a description of Freeman's raised fist, see Marcus Reeves, *Somebody Scream! Rap Music's Rise to Prominence in the Aftershock of Black Power* (New York: Faber and Faber, 2008), 6. Freeman's performance can be seen on You Tube: https://www.youtube.com/watch?v=Jk8D7L7EPcg.

53. Stokely Carmichael, "Black Power," October 29, 1966. Available on *Voices of Democracy: The U.S. Oratory Project, at* http://voicesofdemocracy.umd.edu/carmichael-black-power-speech-text/.

54. Casper is quoted in Taraborrelli, *Michael Jackson,* 245; Jeffrey Daniel discusses his contributions in *BAD25,* 2012, directed by Spike Lee, 2012 (DVD; Optimum Productions, 2013); Damita Jo Freeman talks

about Cher and Marcel Marceau in her interview with Stephen McMillan, "Diary of an Ex-Soul Train Dancer Presents."

55. These quotations come from two interviews: one with Jesse Jackson on the *Keep Hope Alive Radio Show,* March 27, 2005; available at http://www.allmichaeljackson.com/interviews/jessejackson.html, and from one with Oprah Winfrey, February 10, 1993, available at http://www.oprah.com/entertainment/Oprah-Reflects-on-Her -Interview-with-Michael-Jackson.

56. Guzman-Sanchez, *Underground Dance Masters,* 120.

57. Astaire quoted in Jackson, *Moonwalk,* 213–15, and Taraborrelli, *Michael Jackson,* 242–43.

58. Jackson, *Moonwalk,* 213–15.

59. Larry Billman, "Music Video as Short Dance Film," in *Envisioning Dance on Film and Video,* ed. Judy Mitoma, Elizabeth Zimmer, and Dale Ann Steiber, 12–20 (New York: Routledge, 2002), 16.

60. Peters quoted in Sid Smith, "Video Dance Steps in a New Direction," *Chicago Tribune,* March 4, 1984.

61. Taraborrelli, *Michael Jackson,* 174, 189.

62. Footage of *The Jacksons* is sometimes available on YouTube.

63. Nelson George, *Thriller: The Musical Life of Michael Jackson* (Cambridge, Mass.: Da Capo, 2010), 48.

64. Joe Jackson quoted in Bob Lucas, "Special Report: The Jacksons 10 Years Later," *Jet,* February 1, 1979, 60.

65. Alice Echols, *Hot Stuff: Disco and the Remaking of American Culture* (New York: Norton, 2010), 205–7.

66. Echols writes about the history of Stonewall as well as the homo-phobic and racist politics that fueled the anti-disco movement; for more on the policing of dance floors, see Charles Kaiser, *The Gay Metropolis: The Landmark History of Gay Life in America* (New York: Grove, 2007), 83–84.

67. Echols, *Hot Stuff,* 44–47.

68. Maxine Leeds Craig, *Sorry I Don't Dance: Why Men Refuse to Move* (New York: Oxford University Press, 2014), 99–104; Craig's book pointed me to Richard Dyer's "On Defense of Disco," Gay Left (London) 8 (1979): 20–23.

69. Echols, *Hot Stuff*, 40, 197–98. For an in-depth look at the underground roots of New York City's dance music scene, see Tim Lawrence, *Love Saves the Day: A History of American Dance Music Culture, 1970–1979* (Durham, N.C.: Duke University Press, 2004).

70. "Michael Jackson Studio 54 Interview," n.d., available at https://www.youtube.com/watch?v=gMDSXveSj0M.

71. "MJ's 'Manifesto,' Penned in 1979," September 8, 2013, *CBS News*, http://www.cbsnews.com/news/mjs-manifesto-penned-in-1979/; Don King quoted in Gary Smith, "Michael!" *People*, August 17, 1984, available at http://www.people.com/people/article/0,,20088528,00.html.

72. Rob Tanenbaum and Craig Marks, *I Want My MTV: The Uncensored Story of the Music Video Revolution* (New York: Dutton, 2011), 165–88.

73. Ibid.

74. Sykes quoted ibid., 179. See also DeCurtis, "80's"; Marsh, *Trapped*, 217–27; Roger Wolmuth, "Rock 'n' Roll 'n' Video: MTV's Music Revolution," *People*, October 17, 1983, available at http://www.people.com/people/archive/article/0,,20086163,00.html; and Faye Zuckerman, "Video Artists Past Screen Test to Home Market," *Billboard*, November 17, 1984.

75. Marsh, *Trapped*, 218; Jackson quoted in Taraborrelli, *Michael Jackson*, 191. For more on the mixture of styles in *Thriller*, see Tamara Roberts, "Michael Jackson's Kingdom: Music, Race, and the Sound of the Mainstream," *Journal of Popular Music Studies* 23, no. 1 (2011): 19–39. Roberts argues that by navigating the tension between "realizing and transcending race through sound"—that is, performing music that both is and isn't racially marked—Jackson virtually invented the sound of contemporary pop (20).

76. Siobahn Baron, John Sykes, Paul Flatery, and Ronald "Buzz" Brindle discuss the never-made slave ship video in Tanenbaum and Marks, *I Want My MTV*, chap. 14. See also Doug Camilli, "Michael Jackson Wanted Video Set on Slave Galley," *Montreal Gazette*, July 2, 1986. Vincent Paterson told me about the "Beat It" auditions in a phone conversation on June 10, 2014.

77. Vincent Paterson, phone conversation with the author, June 10, 2014; Atkins and Malone, *Class Act*, 104; Daniel Chu and Barbara Rowes, "Michael Peters Is the Hot New Choreographer Who Makes Dancers out of Video's Rock Stars," *People*, June 25, 1984, available at http://www.people.com/people/archive/article/0,,20088152,00.html.

78. Wilson quoted in "*$600 and a Mule* Debuts on Coast," *Jet*, September 20, 1973, 48–49; Sylvie Drake, "'Mule' Traces Black History, *Los Angeles Times*, August 28, 1973 (more information on the production is in Richard Mentzer, "New Black Musical Song-Dance Delight," *Santa Ana Orange Country Register*, September 3, 1973); Chu and Rowes, "Michael Peters Is the Hot New Choreographer"; Don McDonagh, "Benjamin Dancers Present 5 Works," *New York Times*, November 10, 1970.

79. Talking with Vincent Paterson helped me refine my thoughts on Peters; Paterson also reports that Jackson put his dancers in "Smooth Criminal" on an SAG (Screen Actors Guild) contract to guarantee them the same union wages actors were paid. Peters's former agent Julie McDonald also helped me think through some questions on dance in music videos; our interview took place on June 16, 2014. More information on Peters's career comes from Jennifer Dunning, "Michael Peters, a Choreographer of 'Dreamgirls,' is Dead at 46," *New York Times*, September 1, 1994.

80. Brugge and Daniels discuss their work on the "Bad" video in *Bad25*. According to an episode of the podcast *Thrillercast* with Popin Pete and Dane XXXX, two members of the Electric Boogaloos, they gave Jackson the idea of updating *West Side Story* for the "Beat It" video before Jackson had hired Bob Giraldi to direct it: *Thrillercast*, September 12, 2008.

81. Jackson, *Moonwalk*, 204. Giraldi has discussed his version of the story on multiple occasions; see his remarks in Tanenbaum and Marks, *I Want My MTV*, 180–81; and "Bob Giraldi Talks About Making 'Beat It,'" "Celebrity Taste Makers," bonus footage, September 28 2013, at http://www.youtube.com/watch?v=-LUVl5JRR6c.

82. Giraldi quoted in Tanenbaum and Marks, *I Want My MTV*, 180–81; Paterson, phone conversation with the author; Peters quoted in Greg Quill, "Choreographer Left Mark on Los Angeles Street Gangs," *Toronto Star*, November 25, 1987.

83. Chang, *Can't Stop Won't Stop*, 80, 101.

84. The film scholar Richard Dyer argues that Romero's zombie trilogy—*Night of the Living Dead, Dawn of the Dead,* and *Day of the Dead*—concerns the horrors of whiteness. The white militamen move through the landscape as reflexively and uniformly as zombies. And, Dyer says, zombies—like white people—value the head and try to separate it from the body: they eat brains. See "White," *Screen* 29, no. 4 (Autumn 1998): 44–64.

85. George, *Thriller*, 109.

86. Elizabeth Bumiller, "Back in Step: 'Thriller,' Throngs and a Letter from Reagan," *Washington Post*, February 8, 1984. *Thriller* is often said to have sold a hundred million copies, but Bill Wyman puts the number at 66 million in a *New Yorker* blog piece, "Did 'Thriller' Really Sell a Hundred Million Copies?" http://www.newyorker.com /culture/culture-desk/did-thriller-really-sell-a-hundred-million -copies, January 4, 2013. Greil Marcus discusses the implications of Jackson's "accomplishment" in what he calls "the Year of Michael Jackson" in *Lipstick Traces: A Secret History of the Twentieth Century* (Cambridge: Harvard University Press: 2009), 91–104.

87. Peters quoted in Smith, "Video Dance Steps in a New Direction."

88. Sally Banes writes about Toni Basil in "Lock Steady" and "Break-ing," both anthologized in her *Writing Dancing in the Age of Postmod-ernism* (Hanover, N.H.: University Press of New England, 1993): 133–36, 143–53.

89. Smith, "Video Dance Steps in a New Direction."

90. Chang, *Can't Stop Won't Stop*, 152. For more on Twyla Tharp, see Marcia B. Siegel's excellent *Howling near Heaven: Twyla Tharp and the Reinvention of Modern Dance* (New York: St. Martin's, 2006). Siegel also writes wonderfully about *Deuce Coupe* in her *The Shapes of Change: Images of American Dance* (Boston: Houghton Mifflin, 1979), 262–70.

91.  Sally Banes, "To the Beat Y'All: Breaking Is Hard to Do," *Village Voice*, April 10, 1981, reprinted in her *Writing Dancing in the Age of Postmodernism*, 121–25; Chang, *Can't Stop Won't Stop*, 137–39, 156–59;

92.  Banes, "To the Beat Y'All" and Michael Holman, *Breaking and the New York City Breakers* (New York: Freundlich, 1984).

93.  Elisa Spungen Bildner, "Breakdancing Fails to Break the Age Barrier," *Newark Star-Ledger*, August 26, 1984.

94.  For a discussion of popular films on hip-hop, see Chang, *Can't Stop Won't Stop*, 192. Shabba-Doo is the charming subject of a profile by David Ferrell in "Shabba-Doo: Break-Dancing's King Started on the Streets; Now Young Fans Imitate His Moves on His Cerritos Lawn," *Los Angeles Times*, July 29, 1984.

95.  Smith, "Video Dance Steps in a New Direction"; "Ballet Gets a Break," *Milwaukee Journal*, March 4, 1984; Wilma Salisbury, "Breakdancers Hit Yellow Brick Road," *Plain Dealer*, March 2, 1986. Sally Sommers gives a useful overview of hip-hop and ballet interacting in "Balletic Breakin'," *Dance Magazine*, January 2012, available at http://www.dancemagazine.com/issues/january-2012 /Balletic-Breakin.

96.  In 1903, the *New York Times* quoted a ballerina in France: "It may not be too hazardous to assume that the long, waving, processionlike action of the cakewalk will influence the composition and scientific conception of our ballet movements and groupings" (C.L.B., "America Has Lent France a New Amusement, Which Is Driving Out the Danse du Ventre," *New York Times*, March 22, 1903). Nahat quoted in Salisbury, "Breakdancers Hit Yellow Brick Road."

97.  Jahan's work as Beals's body double is well documented; see, for example, "At the Movies, *New York Times*, June 10, 1983. For a reference to Colón's work as a body double in *Flashdance*, see Brian Siebert, "Nostalgic Finale, with Latin Touch, for a B-Boy Original," *New York Times*, August 1, 2013.

98.  Joan Acocella discusses many of these movies—and the work that they do—in "Happy Feet: The Pleasures of Teen Dance Movies," *New*

*Yorker,* August 24, 2011 (http://www.newyorker.com/culture
/culture-desk/happy-feet-the-pleasures-of-teen-dance-movies,
accessed October 25, 2014).

99. Michael London, "Geffen Gets Jackson for New Feature," *Los Angeles Times,* November 9, 1984. In the late seventies, Jackson also considered starring in a biopic of Bill Robinson. He didn't take the part: perhaps because he wouldn't have been able to tap nearly as well as the old master, or perhaps because, as Dave Marsh speculates, it would have associated Jackson too closely with a black tradition. See Marsh, *Trapped,* 190; Jacqueline Trescott, "The Jackson Decade: Still Shaking—And Making—Their Booty," *Washington Post,* June 11, 1979.

100. Sam Wasson, *Fosse* (New York: Houghton Mifflin Harcourt, 2013), 22–28; Martin Gottfried, *All His Jazz: The Life and Death of Bob Fosse* (Boston: Da Capo, 1990), 13–28.

101. Gottfried, *All His Jazz,* 17, 28; Wasson, *Fosse,* 22–28, 96–98.

102. De Mille quoted in Moira Hodgson, "When Bob Fosse's Art Imitates Life, It's Just 'All That Jazz': Bob Fosse's 'All That Jazz,'" *New York Times,* December 30, 1979. See also Joan Acocella, "Bob Fosse: Dancing and the Dark," *New Yorker,* December 21 1998, reprinted in *Reading Dance,* ed. Robert Gottlieb (New York: Random House, 2008), 1087–97.

103. Gerri Hershey, "Michael Jackson: Life as a Man in the Magical Kingdom," *Rolling Stone,* February 17, 1983.

104. Jackson, *Moonwalk,* 217, 219. YouTube features quite a few videos mashing up Jackson's *Motown 25* performance with Fosse's to show the resemblance, which is striking.

105. Wasson, *Fosse,* 532–33, 568–69. Jackson's note appears in *Bad25.*

106. Paterson, phone conversation with the author; *Bad25.*

107. Paterson, phone conversation with the author.

108. "The Last Word on Michael," *People,* December 30, 1984, available at http://www.people.com/people/archive/article/0,,20196980,00 .html.

109. Falwell asserted that "the projection of a femaleness by a male performer presents a very bad role model for the millions of children who literally idolize this very talented performer."

Farrakhan agreed: "This Jheri-Kurl, female-acting, sissified-acting expression, it is not wholesome for our young boys nor our young girls"; both are quoted in "Last Word on Michael." For a good analysis of the debacle that was the *Victory* tour, see Marsh, *Trapped*, 230–59. Nick Marino also points out the difference between "rugged" hip-hop street fashion and Jackson's "elaborate outfits," which "seemed like costumes." "Jackson," he writes, "has always been more Sharks and Jets than Bloods and Crips," an accurate summation, and especially pointed given that the "Beat It" video plunged actual Bloods and Crips into a musical dreamworld: "Pop Notes: Hip Hop's Rise, Michael's Demise; How Rap Hastened Michael Jackson's Decline, Long Before the Latest Scandal," *Atlanta Journal Constitution*, November 1, 2003.

110. On Jackson erasing his father's face from his own, see Bill Wyman, "The Pale King: Michael Jackson's Ambiguous Legacy," *New Yorker*, December 24, 2012, 135; for the Bobby Driscoll speculations, see Randall Sullivan, *Untouchable: The Strange Life and Tragic Death of Michael Jackson* (New York: Grove, 2012): 221–22. On Jackson's body deconstructing conceptions of race and gender, see Julian Vigo, "Metaphor of Hybridity: The Body of Michael Jackson," *Journal of Pan African Studies* 3, no. 7 (2010): 29–41.

111. Tanenbaum and Marks, *I Want My MTV*, 478–80. John Landis claims that the video "had more audience than the moon landing." On the controversy in the wake of the video's premiere, see Daniel Cerone, "Michael's Video Takes Beating; 4 Minute Cut Reaction: Negative Response Causes Michael Jackson to Apologize for Video Sequence in Which He Attacks a Car and Simulates Masturbation," *Los Angeles Times*, November 16, 1991; and "Jackson's New Video Causes Controversy," *Weekend All Things Considered*, November 16, 1991. Talking with NPR's Scott Simon, the critic Elvis Mitchell lamented how apolitical "Black or White" seemed, noting that hip-hop artists like "NWA and Ice Cube are talking about things that are fare more vital, and—and they're issues that deal in everyday lives." In the following years, a number of scholars have argued that "Black or White" does engage with vital political issues,

particularly when viewed with the controversial "Panther Dance" included. Eric Lott's analysis is the earliest I have found: "The Aesthetic Ante: Pleasure, Pop Culture, and the Middle Passage," *Callaloo* 17, no. 2 (Spring 1994): 545–55. Carol Clover's "Dancin' in the Rain" followed a year later and, with Lott's essay, has helped shape the way I see the video: "Dancin' in the Rain," *Critical Inquiry* 21, no. 4 (1995): 722–47. See also Elizabeth Chin, "Michael Jackson's Panther Dance: Double Consciousness and the Uncanny Business of Performing While Black," *Journal of Popular Music Studies* 23, no. 1 (March 2011): 58–74.

**112.** Clover, "Dancin' in the Rain."

**113.** Paterson, conversation with the author.

**114.** Elizabeth Chin sees the graffiti as a form of "defacement" of the video's original power, one that protects the audience's "right to feel comfortable" by rendering Jackson's "anger intelligible to audiences who apparently lacked the ability to understand Black rage" ("Michael Jackson's Panther Dance," 71–72). For a contemporary sense that the video offered a "cry for help," see Adrianna Alty, "It Doesn't Matter? Race, Sexuality and a Desperate Million-Dollar Cry for Help," *Gay Community News,* November 30, 1991.

**115.** On the "Thriller" dance in front of the hospital, see Brooks Barnes, Jon Pareles, Brian Stelter, and Ben Sisario, " "Michael Jackson, 50, Is Dead," *New York Times,* June 25, 2009; for the scene in New Orleans, see Keith Marszalek, "Huge Second-Line Honors King of Pop Michael Jackson," *Times-Picayune,* June 28, 2009; for Paris, see Sharon Otterman, "Around the World, Shock and Grief over Jackson," *New York Times,* June 26, 2009; footage of the celebration at the Apollo is at http://www.youtube.com/watch?v=X2TTn_ -3WcA; for the story of "Soul Makossa," see Sean Michaels, "Rihanna and Michael Jackson Sued by African Singer," *Guardian,* February 4, 2009.

# INDEX

Page numbers in *italics* indicate illustrations.

**377**

American Society of Teachers of Dancing, 12, 102

*American Suite* (de Mille), 68, 149–50, 164

Anderson, Jack, 117

Anderson, Marian, 205

Andrews, Maxene, 231, 236

Andrews, Patty, 236

Andrews Sisters: in *The Holiday Canteen*, 235; songs in *Company B*, 230–31, 232, 233–34, 235–36, 237–38; in war effort, 231–32

*Anthology of American Folk Music* (Smith), 206

antic hay, 219

Apache dance, 73–74

Appalachia, folk music of, 158

*Appalachian Spring* (Graham), 194, 210

Armstrong, Neil, lunar walk of, 239, 240, 275

*Around the Hall in Texas* (Shawn), 192

Arpino, Gerald, 296–97

Asch, Moses, 205

Astaire, Adele: as child performer, 90–91; partnership with brother, 89, 90, 108–9; retirement of, 89, 109; in vaudeville, 121

Astaire, Fred: black dance as influence on, 6, 63, 121; in blackface routines, 61–62, 64, 121, 124; "Bojangles of Harlem" routine of, 61–63, 120, 124, 135; on Broadway, 89, 108; as cabaret dancer, 108; as child performer, 90–91; dance style of, 5, 34–35, 62, 91, 119; influence on Fosse, 300, 301; influence on Michael Jackson, 276, 277–78, 304–5; on moonwalk, 275–76, 307; *On Your Toes* offered to, 129–30; partnership with sister, 89, 90, 108–9, 121; and Bill Robinson, 1, 63–64, 72, 121; as tapper, 74, 91, 118–21, 124, 125; in vaudeville, 121, 132. *See also* Astaire-Rogers partnership

Astaire-Rogers partnership: Americanness of, 118; Balanchine's admiration of, 128; blend of dance steps in, 7, 9, 88, 119; in Carioca dance sequence, 110–13; Castles as model for, 108, 109; Continental dance sequence, 93–96; dance settings of, 86–87; dancing style of, 84, 85, 88–89, 134–35; in *Flying Down to Rio*, 89, 92, 110–15, 124; in *Follow the Fleet*, 131–32; in *The Gay Divorcee*, 89, 92, 93–96; glamour/sophistication of, 109–10; melting pot art of, 88; new steps popularized by, 96–97; parodies of, 134; in

Campbell, Don, 244, 267–68, 271, 279, 293
Candidate, Geron "Casper," 241, 262, 273
*Carefree,* 87, 96–97
Carioca, 96, 110–13, 134
Carmichael, Stokely, 273
Caron, Leslie, 92
cartoons, influence on bugaloo, 269
Castle, Vernon and Irene: as ballroom dance team, 98, *99;* black dance as influence on, 107; as cabaret owners, 106–7; dance style of, 105, 106; death of Vernon, 107–8; merchandising by, 105–6; as model for the Astaires, 108, 109; sanitization of social dancing by, 104–5
Castle Club, 106
Castle House, 106–7
Castles in the Air, 106, 108
Castle Walk, 105
*Center Stage,* 299
Chaplin, Charlie, 146–47
Chaplin, Saul, 237
Charisse, Cyd, 92, 276, 304, 306
*Charles B. Cochran's 1931 Revue,* 68
Charleston, 15, 49, 91, 158
Charters, Samuel, 209
"Cheek to Cheek," 97
cheek-to-cheek dancers, 102
Cherelle, 296
Chesnutt, Charles, 24–25

*Chicago Defender,* 44, 58, 256
*Chicago Tribune,* 158
chorus lines, 271
Christensen, Lew, 9; *Blackface,* 27; *Filling Station,* 68, 133–34, 141; *Pocahontas,* 141; in vaudeville, 132–33
Christgau, Robert, 124
Christian, William, 2
Chryst, Gary, 294
Chujoy, Anatole, 27
Churchill, Winston, 167
Civil Rights movement, 225–26
*Clarinade* (Balanchine), 69
Clark, Sam, 121–22
Cleveland Ballet, 297
Clinton, Bill, 187
*Clorindy, or The Origins of the Cakewalk,* 19
Clover, Carol, 309–10
*Clytemnestra* (Graham), 202
Cohn, Nik, 267
Cole, Jack, 276, 301
Coles, Charles "Honi," 34, 55, 72, 177, 252, 253
Colón, Richard "Crazy Legs," 294–95, 298
colonization movement, 77
Columbia dance, 11
*Comedy Cakewalk,* 13, 15–16
*Company B* (Taylor), 5, 188, 230–36, *233,* 237–38
Congo minuet, 165
Continental dance sequence, in *The Gay Divorcee,* 93–96

MTV, 284–86, 295
Mueller, John, 62
*Mumbo Jumbo* (Reed), 102
*Music from the South,* 205

Nahat, Dennis, 297
Nasaw, David, 101, 103
Native American themes, in
    modern dance, 192–93
nativism, and racial bias,
    163–64
*Natural Born Gambler,* 40
"Never Gonna Dance" dance
    sequence in *Swing Time,*
    135–37
New Orleans jazz, 208–9
Newton, Don, 262
*New York Age,* 72
New York City Ballet, 27, 65, 69,
    126, 129, 195
New York City Police Department:
    in cabaret crackdown, 103–4;
    Bill Robinson's relations with,
    80–81
New York City World's Fair (1939),
    46, 78
*New Yorker,* 128
*New York Herald Tribune,* 103–4
New York race riots of 1900, 40
*New York Times,* 10, 35, 52, 54, 76,
    97, 139, 162, 166, 167, 188,
    240, 288
Nicholas Brothers, 34, 69, 70–71,
    256, 276, 278
Nichols, Betty, 27

"Night and Day" dance sequence
    in *The Gay Divorcee,* 95
*Night Court,* 104
*Night Journey* (Graham), 198
*Night of the Living Dead,* 291
*Night Shadow* (Balanchine), 69
Nijinska, Bronislava, 66–67
Nijinsky, Vaslav, 47, 66–67
Niles, John Jacob, 205
"Nobody," 41, 44
Noguchi, Isamu, 27

*O, Sing a New Song,* 107
*Obeah* (de Mille), 172
O'Brien, Margaret, 13
*Off the Wall,* 258, 272, 279, 282
O'Hara, Frank, 202; "Dances
    Before the Wall," 204
*Oklahoma!,* 12–13, 139, 174–76,
    180, 231, 253
"Old Folks at Home" (Foster),
    31, 71
Olson, Charles, 199
*On Your Toes,* 68, 69, 129–31
Oompah Trot, 108
Our Flag dance, 11
*Over the Top,* 108

Page, Ruth, 68, 104, 141
*Pal Joey,* 176
Pan, Hermes, 275; and Astaire-
    Rogers partnership, 92–93,
    112; and Balanchine, 129;
    black dance influence on, 6,
    121–24